Public Health

Public health is the science and art of improving the health and well-being of communities. Public health interventions go beyond individual healthcare to focus on preventing diseases and injuries, promoting healthy behaviors, and addressing sociocultural, economic, and environmental factors that impact health.

While topics of public health, such as maternal health, child health, and epidemiology of infectious and noncommunicable diseases, require familiarity with clinical terms and concepts, the author demystifies medical knowledge to make it accessible to a wider audience. Challenges faced by low-income countries, as well as success stories from developed nations, are included to make the book relevant for global readers.

With a focus on essentials and priority issues, the author employs simple and straightforward language to present situational cases that shed light on global public health challenges and possible interventions. To stimulate analytical thinking and encourage readers to approach the subject with scientific rigor, concepts and facts are substantiated with their background, rationale, or application. Readers should be able to relate learnings with their field experience.

While this book is primarily for public health practitioners, including community health nurses and physicians, social workers, and health managers, it may be a valuable resource for anyone interested in public health and its application in creating healthier societies.

Public Health
A Global Perspective

Hari Singh, MD
Dean, School of Public Health,
SRM Institute of Science and Technology, Chennai, India

Formerly
Director, Institute of Health Management Research, Bengaluru, India
Executive Director, Foundation for Research in Health Systems, India
Country Director, EngenderHealth, India
Director – Clinical Services, Marie Stopes International, India
Global Fund Liaison, USAID, India
Advisor, Danida, India

A PRODUCTIVITY PRESS BOOK

Cover Image Credit: Dr. Anshu Jammoria

First published 2024
by Routledge
605 Third Avenue, New York, NY 10158

and by Routledge
4 Park Square, Milton Park, Abingdon, Oxon, OX14 4RN

Routledge is an imprint of the Taylor & Francis Group, an informa business

ISBN: 978-1-032-64423-3 (hbk)
ISBN: 978-1-032-64422-6 (pbk)
ISBN: 978-1-032-64425-7 (ebk)

DOI: 10.4324/9781032644257

To my wife,

Lt. Col. Rupinder Kaur

Contents

SECTION I Health and Disease

SECTION II Basic Epidemiology

SECTION V *Public Health Nutrition*

SECTION VII Sociocultural Dimensions of Health

SECTION VIII Maternal and Child Health

SECTION IX Health Promotion

SECTION X Other Topics of Public Health

SECTION XI Management of Health Projects

Preface

Being a multidisciplinary field, public health encompasses, in addition to epidemiology and biostatistics, some aspects of medical sciences, sociology, economics, and management. Topics of public health, such as maternal health, child health, and epidemiology of infectious and noncommunicable diseases, require familiarity with clinical terms and concepts. In this book, we have made an effort to demystify medical knowledge to make it accessible to a wider audience.

Every country has unique public health challenges. Predicaments of low-income countries, as well as success stories from developed countries, are included in the book to make it relevant for global readers.

To stimulate analytical thinking and encourage readers to approach the subject with scientific rigor, concepts and facts have been substantiated with their background, rationale, or application. Readers should be able to relate learnings with their field experience. The focus is on essentials and priority issues, and the language is simple and straightforward.

While the book is primarily for public health practitioners, students of public health, medicine, and nursing may also find it useful. The author envisions this book as a valuable resource for anyone interested in the application of public health in creating healthier societies.

Acknowledgments

I am grateful to Ms. Neetu Ralhan for editing the manuscript and making it into an eloquent reading.

My sincere thanks to Dr. Anshu Jammoria for creating the cover and other artwork for the book. Thanks also to Mr. Rupal Singh Randhawa for creating the schematic drawings for the book.

I appreciate my friends for reviewing many chapters of the book and providing valuable suggestions to improve the contents. The contributions of the following colleagues are particularly appreciated:

Dr. Nirmala Murthy, PhD
Founder, Foundation for Research in Health Systems (FRHS), Bengaluru, India

Dr. S D Gupta, MD, PhD (Epidemiology, Johns Hopkins University), FAMS
Adjunct Professor – Epidemiology, Johns Hopkins University School of Public Health
Gates Leadership Fellow

Dr. Ravi Shankar, MD
Medical Director and Maternal-Fetal Medicine Specialist
Cone Health Center for Maternal Fetal Care, Greensboro, NC, USA

Dr. Gladius Jennifer H, PhD
Associate Professor – Biostatistics
School of Public Health, SRM Institute of Science and Technology, Chennai, India

Dr. Ashutosh Mishra, MBBS, MPH, MS (Epidemiology)
Senior Regional Technical Director – Asia
Vitamin Angels

Dr. Neeta Bhatnagar, MBBS, DGO, PGCFP
Senior Technical Advisor, Reproductive Health
Jhpiego, an affiliate of Johns Hopkins University, Washington, DC, USA

Dr. Ravi Anand
Director, Technical and Operations, Dimpa Project
Abt Associates

Dr. Suresh Khanna, MD
Neonatologist, North Shore University Hospital
Northwell Health System, Manhasset, New York

Dr. Rakesh Ghosh, PhD
Senior Epidemiologist and Global Health Specialist
UCFS School of Medicine, University of California, San Francisco

Dr. Balraj Dhiman, MD
Professor Director, Community Medicine
Lady Harding Medical College, New Delhi, India

Dr. Vivek Ranjan, MD
Former Senior Consultant, Gyne-Obstetrics
Delhi Government Hospital, Najafgarh, India

Dr. Benson Thomas M, PhD
Associate Professor – Health Economics
School of Public Health, SRM Institute of Science and Technology, Chennai, India

Dr. Selvamani Y, PhD
Assistant Professor
School of Public Health, SRM Institute of Science and Technology, Chennai, India

Dr. Rakhi Sahi, MBBS, DGO
State Clinical Services Manager, Marie Stopes International

Dr. Chandrashekhar, MD
Former Additional Director General
Indian Council of Medical Research (ICMR), Government of India

Dr. Sudhir Gupta, MD
Former Additional Director General, Non-Communicable Diseases, DGHS
Ministry of Health and Family Welfare, Government of India

Dr. Sunita Singhal, MD
Senior Technical Specialist, EngenderHealth

Dr. Harish Kumar, MD
Senior Technical Advisor, IPE Global, India

Section I

Health and Disease

1 What Is Public Health?

In 1920, Charles-Edward A. Winslow, a public health pioneer and founder of the Yale School of Public Health, defined public health as follows:

> *Public health is the science and art of preventing diseases, promoting health, and prolonging life through organized community efforts.*

In other words, public health aims to improve the health of communities by taking measures to prevent diseases and promote health. It strives to change sociocultural practices that are harmful to people's health by involving and educating community members.

CHARACTERISTICS OF PUBLIC HEALTH

Dealing with Communities Rather than Individuals

When a child has diarrhea, her parents seek treatment from a medical practitioner or a hospital. These facilities treat individual patients. However, unless diarrhea is prevented at the community level, cases will keep occurring. To prevent diarrhea, people should have access to clean drinking water and toilet facilities; they should practice basic hygiene, particularly handwashing; and children should be vaccinated against rotavirus, a common cause of diarrhea. It is the domain of public health that organizes such community-level interventions.

Similarly, while a medical practitioner or hospital's responsibility begins when a sick or injured person comes to them for treatment, public health has a proactive role even when people are not sick. Public health workers reach out to people at community gatherings or through home visits. For example, health workers engage with mothers of young children and encourage them to have their children vaccinated.

Focus on Preventing Diseases, Promoting Health, and Prolonging Life

Disease Prevention

While medical practitioners and hospitals mainly provide curative services, public health focuses on preventing diseases, injuries, and disabilities. Prevention is not only better than cure but also more cost-effective.[1] Earlier, poliomyelitis (polio) was hyperendemic[2] in many countries, causing disability in hundreds of thousands of children every year. Under the polio immunization program, all children up to age five are vaccinated against polio. Consequently, polio has been successfully eliminated from most countries. Once it is eradicated globally, polio vaccination programs will no longer be required, thus saving countries millions of dollars.

Hospitals also provide vaccination services, but they serve only the children who come to them. However, not everyone can visit a hospital. In low-income countries, a large section of the population lacks access to hospitals. This is where the role of public health becomes crucial. Again, the polio vaccination campaign serves as a classic example. To eliminate polio in a country, all eligible children in the country must be vaccinated on the same day. Reaching children living in far-flung or flood-affected areas, or those who may be on the move on the day of vaccination, is a monumental task, and yet the public health system has been doing it effectively for many decades.

DOI: 10.4324/9781032644257-2

Health Promotion

Health promotion is about empowering people to take care of their own health. By creating awareness about common health problems, we can help people make better choices. For example, people can be educated that consuming clean food and water can help prevent diarrhea. They can be encouraged to include green vegetables in their diet to prevent iron-deficiency anemia. They can be educated about the dangers of tobacco use. Thus, health promotion is an integral part of public health. It is discussed in detail in a separate chapter.

Prolonging Life

When people are healthy and protected from diseases and injuries, they will naturally live longer. The chapter "Measuring Mortality" explains the concept of life expectancy in detail.

Treatment of Common Ailments

Since public health's focus is on preventing diseases and promoting health, does this mean that it does not care about the treatment of diseases? Certainly not. The goal of public health is to improve the health of communities, but this goal cannot be met if people are not treated for their existing health problems. Therefore, the treatment of diseases, injuries, and disabilities is given equal importance. However, due to limited resources, public health limits itself to treating common ailments.

When a disease affects many people in a population, it is considered a public health problem. In such situations, the public health system takes over the responsibility to organize diagnosis, treatment, and prevention measures. For example, leishmaniasis is a disease found in some parts of India and its neighboring countries. The public health system in these areas organizes to identify the cases[3] and provide them treatment. Complicated cases are referred to a hospital. In areas where leishmaniasis is not a public health problem, isolated cases can be treated at the local hospital.

An efficient public health system helps avoid overcrowding at hospitals by preventing diseases and by treating common ailments at the local level. Cases beyond the capacity of the public health system are referred to hospitals. In this way, the public health system and hospitals complement each other.

More Efforts in Underprivileged Communities

Are public health services more relevant for rural or remote areas? No, urban areas equally require these services. However, limited resources constrain the public health system to focus on populations with greater healthcare needs and limited access to hospitals. In low-income countries, rural, remote, and tribal populations are often underserved in terms of health services. They need facilities for safe delivery, immunization, and treatment of childhood pneumonia and diarrhea. Young couples need contraceptive services. Accordingly, public health services have greater involvement in these areas.

Urban areas have their own health challenges, such as a high burden of noncommunicable diseases (NCDs) like diabetes and heart disease. Industrial towns in some countries have a high prevalence of tuberculosis (TB). People living in urban slums are often deprived of healthcare services. Lately, there is increasing realization that urban areas also need more public health engagement.

Community Involvement

Why is it important to involve the community? This is because many health problems have a root cause in sociocultural practices. The public health system works with communities to try and change beliefs and practices that adversely affect health. For example, in the early stages of the polio immunization program, some communities opposed vaccination—they believed it was a conspiracy to control their fertility and refused to vaccinate their children. This posed a challenge for healthcare workers. To resolve the impasse, health workers liaised with local religious leaders, took them into confidence, and educated them about the benefits of polio vaccination. Once convinced, these leaders encouraged their respective communities to go for vaccination. Thus, a public health intervention could be implemented effectively by involving the community. Health Communication is a specialized branch of public health that deals with such issues. It is discussed in a separate chapter.

PUBLIC HEALTH VERSUS CLINICAL PRACTICE

To gain a better understanding of public health, we can draw parallels between public health and clinical practice. While clinical practitioners diagnose and treat diseases in individual patients, public health practitioners diagnose health problems in populations and propose appropriate interventions.

When a clinical practitioner sees a patient, her first concern is to diagnose the ailment. Similarly, a public health practitioner tries to understand the health problems affecting a population and assesses their magnitude.

To diagnose the disease, the clinical practitioner takes the patient's history and conducts a physical examination. To understand the health problems of a population, the public health practitioner collects information from key stakeholders and analyzes existing records. For example, she may seek information about the number of teenage pregnancies, the number of breast cancer cases, or the number of people with obesity in a region.

To confirm the diagnosis, the clinical practitioner orders laboratory tests. A public health practitioner may recommend an epidemiological study to identify the root cause(s) of a health problem in a population.

Based on the findings from patient history, physical examination, and laboratory reports, the clinical practitioner prescribes treatment. The public health practitioner develops strategies and designs programs to combat the health problems of the population.

PUBLIC HEALTH SERVICES

Both government agencies and nongovernmental organizations (NGOs) provide public health services. The government system consists of a network of hospitals and health posts, as well as community health workers who reach out to people in their villages and homes.

In the nonprofit sector, various national and international NGOs deal with specific health-related issues or provide healthcare services in underserved areas. For example, some work with commercial sex workers to reduce their risk of HIV/AIDS, some provide family planning services, some train healthcare workers in low-income countries to diagnose and treat pneumonia in children, and some advocate for gender equity. CARE International, PATH, Jhpiego, EngenderHealth, Pathfinder International, and Futures Group are some international NGOs.

PUBLIC HEALTH VERSUS PREVENTIVE AND SOCIAL MEDICINE

The discipline of public health was earlier known as *Preventive and Social Medicine*—a term that aptly highlighted both the importance of disease prevention and the role of social determinants in health. In Western countries, *public health* is the most commonly used term. Their Master of Public Health (MPH) programs are available to both medical and nonmedical graduates.

In some countries, the medical curriculum includes a similar subject, called Community Medicine, which has both clinical and social components. Each component is equally important and complements the other. The MD Community Medicine program is open only to medical graduates as it gets into the technicalities of diagnosing and treating common health problems at the community level.

The terms *public health*, *preventive and social medicine*, and *community medicine* are considered interchangeable by this author. In this book, *public health* is the predominantly used term.

NOTES

1. An intervention is called cost-effective if it yields good results with minimum investment.
2. A disease is considered hyperendemic in an area if it occurs continuously in large numbers in that area.
3. A person having a disease or health problem is referred to as a case.

2 Concept of Primary Health Care

Low-income countries have a limited capacity to provide healthcare services to their people. To address this, the World Health Organization (WHO) mooted the idea of *primary health care* (PHC) at the first International Conference on Primary Health Care, held in Alma-Ata, USSR, in 1978. The proposal was accepted by all member states. According to the concept of PHC, all countries should provide at least the essential healthcare services to their citizens.

What are essential healthcare services? Safe delivery services, immunization, and treatment of childhood diarrhea and pneumonia are some examples. Countries can design their PHC package based on their specific needs and available resources. For instance, low-income countries may limit their PHC services to maternal and child health, while high-income countries may include specialized services like cardiac care in their package. As countries develop, they upgrade and expand the scope of their healthcare services.

Does this mean that people in low-income settings cannot get specialized medical care? They can, if there is a referral system in place linking primary health facilities in underserved areas to higher-level facilities. People in remote areas who need specialized care can be referred to these facilities as needed.

The importance of PHC was reiterated at the Global Conference on Primary Health Care, held in Astana, Kazakhstan, in 2018, where PHC was recognized as the most inclusive, equitable, cost-effective, and efficient approach to enhancing people's physical and mental health and social well-being. Member states reaffirmed their commitment to achieving universal healthcare and meeting Sustainable Development Goals (SDGs) through the implementation of PHC. A revised definition of PHC was presented:

> *Primary Health Care is a whole-of-society approach to health that aims at ensuring the highest possible level of health and well-being and their equitable distribution by focusing on people's needs and as early as possible along the continuum from health promotion and disease prevention to treatment, rehabilitation, and palliative care, and as close as feasible to people's everyday environment.*

PRIMARY HEALTH CARE STRATEGIES

The fundamental premise of PHC is to ensure *equitable distribution* of services, meaning that all citizens, regardless of their paying capacity, should have access to all the services their country can afford to provide. Further, countries are urged to strive for the highest possible level of health and well-being for their citizens. How can this be achieved? The concept of PHC suggests the following strategies.

Addressing Felt Needs

When designing healthcare services, the primary focus should be on people's needs. For example, where child mortality from pneumonia or diarrhea is high, facilities for the prevention and treatment of these diseases should be set up. Vaccines to prevent these diseases are readily available. If maternal mortality is high, emergency obstetric care facilities should be established. Additionally, where possible, services should be provided close to where people live.

DOI: 10.4324/9781032644257-3

Comprehensive Package of Services

Healthcare services should go beyond curative services to include a comprehensive package of health promotion, disease prevention, treatment, rehabilitation, and palliative care.

Multisectoral Policies and Actions

People's health is influenced by many other factors beyond healthcare. Safe water, clean air, and basic sanitation are prerequisites for health, and they fall beyond the purview of health departments. Nutrition is important for maintaining health, but the availability or consumption of nutritious food depends on agricultural production, the public distribution system, and people's buying capacity and dietary habits. Education increases people's understanding of their health and well-being. Social security is helpful in sickness and old age. Therefore, a comprehensive, multisectoral approach is needed to improve the health status of communities.

Greater Community Participation

No public health program can succeed without community participation. If people do not practice basic sanitation, waterborne diseases will increase; if they do not shun tobacco chewing, cases of oral cancer may rise; and if children are not immunized, vaccine-preventable diseases will increase. To increase community participation, the WHO recommends involving community members, civil societies, NGOs, informal providers, community leaders, and other stakeholders in the planning and implementation of healthcare services. This will also increase the utilization of health services. People can be encouraged to get involved in health programs by contributing their labor, funds, or supervision.

Proactive Health Systems

PHC calls for countries to develop health systems that can identify outbreaks and disasters early and to have a sound emergency response mechanism in place to contain such events.

ROLE OF WHO

The WHO supports countries in strengthening their PHC services tailored to their unique contexts and priorities. It promotes the adoption of best practices, success stories, and innovative solutions and encourages partnerships between governments, NGOs, civil societies, donors, development partners, and UN organizations. Envisioning health as a fundamental right of every human being, the WHO recommends that every country allocate an additional 1% of its GDP toward PHC.

3 What Is Health?

The World Health Organization (WHO) in 1946 defined health as follows:

> *Health is a state of complete physical, mental, and social well-being and not merely the absence of disease or infirmity.*

DIMENSIONS OF HEALTH

Three broad dimensions of health, as stated in the WHO's definition, are as follows::

1. Physical
2. Mental
3. Social

Physical Health

Physical health relates to the physical body—proper functioning of limbs, senses, and organs. Some diseases primarily affect physical health. For example, leprosy affects the skin, TB damages lung tissues, and stroke causes paralysis of limbs. A road accident may cause skin lacerations, bone fractures, or tears in internal organs. Cancer can affect any organ of the body.

How do we assess the physical health of a person? In clinical practice, the doctor does this through a medical examination. This involves history-taking, physical examination, and laboratory tests as necessary. In history-taking, the doctor asks if the person is experiencing a problem, such as fever, pain, or cough. In a general physical examination, the doctor observes the person's physical appearance and measures vitals such as pulse rate, blood pressure, and body temperature. In a systemic examination, the doctor checks a particular organ system, such as the digestive, respiratory, or cardiovascular system. She palpates the abdomen to see if the liver or the spleen is enlarged and uses a stethoscope to listen for any abnormalities in respiratory and heart sounds. If required, she advises laboratory tests, for example a blood sugar test or chest X-ray.

Mental Health

Sound mental health is integral to a person's overall health. It is essential for thinking clearly, analyzing information, relating to people, expressing emotions, coping with everyday stresses, and enjoying life. A combination of good mental and physical health enables us to work productively, earn a living, and realize our potential.

Contrary to common belief, mental health disorders are quite common globally. However, most of these conditions can be treated. Effective treatments are available for anxiety disorders, adjustment disorders, eating disorders, and others. Unfortunately, the social stigma associated with mental illness often prevents people from seeking professional help.

In clinical practice, a doctor evaluates a person's mental health by combining detailed history-taking with observation. The doctor begins by observing the patient's behavior—how he enters the doctor's cabin (body language and facial expressions), how he reacts to questioning, and what he says in his responses. Information provided by family members or colleagues is helpful. Occasionally, laboratory tests such as electroencephalogram (EEG), magnetic resonance imaging (MRI), or blood biochemistry (e.g., thyroid function tests) may be needed. In many cases, these tests are done to exclude any physical conditions that could be contributing to the mental health symptoms.

DOI: 10.4324/9781032644257-4

Social Health

Social health refers to a person's ability to maintain good relationships and live harmoniously with others. We need other people to live a wholesome life. We rely on our family members for basic needs like food, shelter, and clothing, and for emotional support. We count on our neighbors for peaceful coexistence. We buy provisions from shopkeepers. We need friends for companionship.

For good social health, we must appreciate that we are members of a society and have certain duties toward others. We must follow sociocultural norms and practices that benefit everyone. Fighting over petty issues with neighbors or colleagues, disposing of garbage improperly, driving or parking carelessly, spitting in public places, or playing loud music are some examples of poor social behavior that impacts the well-being of those around us.

We can get some idea about people's social health by observing them in their living or work environment, such as how they behave and interact with one another.

CRITIQUES OF THE WHO'S DEFINITION OF HEALTH

The WHO's definition of health is far from ideal. First, it may not be right to call health *a state*. Health is dynamic; meaning, it changes constantly. We keep swinging in the broad spectrum of health, feeling well and energetic at times and unfit, lethargic, or low at others.

Second, the term *well-being* is subjective and open to interpretation. Since we cannot measure well-being, we cannot use it to categorize people as *healthy* or *unhealthy*. This limits the practical application of this definition.

Third, while the definition states that health is "not merely the absence of disease or infirmity," the fact remains that epidemiologists are constrained to gauge the health status of populations from the burden of diseases.

Fourth, the three dimensions stated in the definition—physical, mental, and social—do not cover all aspects of health. Health has many more dimensions, as will become clear in the succeeding discussion.

OTHER ASPECTS OF HEALTH

To address poverty and unemployment in India, in 2005, the government introduced a scheme that aimed to provide regular work and minimum daily wages to unemployed youth in rural areas. The work involves manual labor, such as digging ponds or tunnels. However, many eligible people are unable to benefit from the scheme because they do not have the physical strength or stamina for hard labor. For all practical purposes, these people are medically fit and healthy—they do not have a disease, injury, or disability—but their bodies are weak. Thus, mere physical, mental, and social well-being is not enough. People should have the strength and stamina to earn a livelihood. They should have reasonable height as well as the musculature and capacity to do hard labor.

Some professions, such as the armed forces, sports, professional dancing, or paragliding, demand a certain level of physical and mental fitness. Only those who are physically and mentally fit can be successful in these fields. That means, in addition to physical, mental, and social well-being, people should also have the fitness necessary to realize their aspirations.

Recognizing the significance of these aspects, member states at the Thirtieth World Health Assembly in 1977 resolved to strive to achieve a level of health for their citizens that enables them to lead socially and economically productive lives.

Some experts feel that happiness is an important aspect of life that should be included in the definition of health. While there is no denying that happiness is linked to health, our understanding of happiness is still limited. People feel happy under different circumstances; there is a lot of subjectivity. Furthermore, we do not yet know how to measure happiness. This makes it difficult to incorporate happiness into the definition of health.

Some people argue that spiritual health should be the fourth dimension in the WHO's definition of health. What we understand about spirituality is that spiritually healthy people believe in a divine power that governs the universe. These individuals are at peace with themselves and are committed to a righteous path. They are concerned about the welfare of living beings and the environment. They strive to control their ego and greed and seek to understand the meaning and purpose of life. However, these concepts are based on faith and lack scientific evidence. So, again, it is difficult to incorporate spiritual health into the definition of health.

From the foregoing discussion, it is clear that drafting an ideal definition that incorporates all possible dimensions of health is a challenge. However, this limitation has not impacted the field of public health in any way; the discipline continues to thrive.

Currently, the WHO's definition of health is widely accepted and remains in use.

EMERGING ISSUES

With time, new health issues emerge that force us to rethink the meaning of health. Diabetes is one of them. In recent decades, diabetes has become so common that people now see it as a part of their lives rather than a serious disease. By restricting their sugar intake and popping a few pills, they believe they can live a normal life. It is true that many people with diabetes can lead an active and productive life by managing their blood sugar levels, but if a large number of people in a population are diabetic, not every one of them will be able to successfully manage their blood sugar. Uncontrolled diabetes has serious and debilitating consequences. In many countries, diabetes is taking the form of an epidemic, but both the authorities and the public seem to be indifferent to this concern. The same is true for hypertension and obesity.

There are also other concerns. The consumption of tobacco or alcohol is becoming a cultural norm in some communities. We need to acknowledge that these behaviors are dangerous for our health and cannot be a way of life. There are strategies to reduce tobacco and alcohol consumption in communities. The increasing level of environmental pollution is also impacting people's health. The need is to address these challenges before they become unmanageable.

4 Determinants of Health

Why do people differ in their heights? Why are some people muscular and others lean? Why do some people fall sick repeatedly, or die early? What are the factors that influence a person's health?

In general, people's health depends on the characteristics they are born with, the lifestyle they adopt, and the environment they live in—these are the three key determinants of health. In addition, access to healthcare services can also have some influence on people's health.

As Figure 4.1 shows, some of these determinants are modifiable and others are not. For example, we have no control over our genes, age, or biological sex, but we do have control over our lifestyle in terms of what we eat or how much physical activity we get. Naturally, public health has greater interest in the modifiable factors, because there lies the opportunity to make interventions to improve people's health.

MODIFIABLE FACTORS

Nutrition

To a large extent, our health depends on the nutrition we consume. Although nutrition is important at every stage of life, its significance during childhood, adolescence, pregnancy, and lactation is overriding. Childhood malnutrition has been a pressing public health concern in low-income countries. In many countries of sub-Saharan Africa and South Asia, nearly one-third of under-five children are short (stunted) and a fifth are underweight (wasted). This is extremely worrying, as the physical and cognitive[1] effects of childhood nutritional deficiencies are irreversible. Poor nutrition is equitant to poor health.

At the same time, overeating and the increasing consumption of junk food have become major health concerns, particularly among the well-off. This has increased the risk of obesity and NCDs such as diabetes, hypertension, and coronary artery disease.[2]

Hygiene and Sanitation

Prior to the 1850s, infectious diseases like cholera, plague, smallpox, and TB caused high mortality and morbidity in most countries. As scientific knowledge about the causation and prevention of diseases grew, the Western world made drastic improvements in areas such as supply of clean

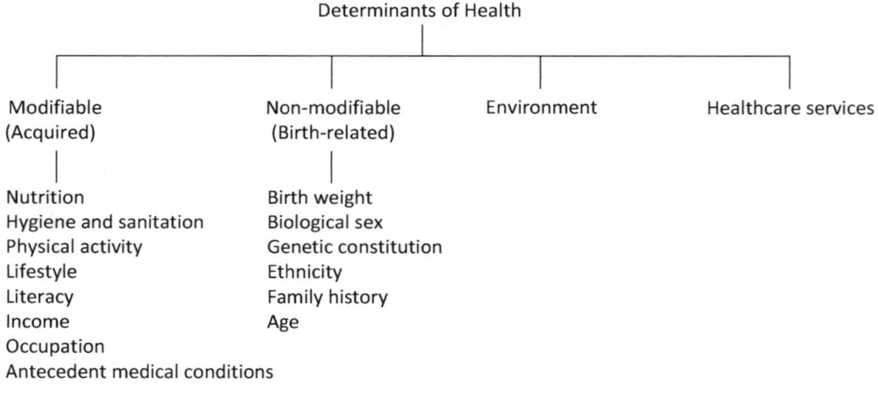

FIGURE 4.1 Determinants of health.

DOI: 10.4324/9781032644257-5

drinking water, housing, drainage, and sanitation. The Industrial Revolution brought economic prosperity, further improving literacy and nutrition in these countries. As a result, many infectious diseases were either controlled or eliminated in the West. However, countries in Asia and Africa did not benefit from these advances. A large number of people in these countries still do not have access to safe drinking water, sanitary latrines, or handwashing facilities. Many prepare or eat food in an unsanitary environment. Low literacy levels further contribute to poor hygiene practices, increasing people's risk of infectious diseases.

Physical Activity

Physical activity is important at every stage of life to maintain good health and prevent NCDs. Despite this, many people in high- and middle-income groups lead a sedentary life and avoid physical exertion. They escape the effort of cleaning their homes and other physical chores as domestic helpers are easily available. In cities, encroached footpaths and other constraints force people to drive even for short distances. Children prefer to stay indoors using mobile phones or other devices. Further, our congested cities offer little open space for children to play. Few schools give attention to physical training or sports activities. The increasing lack of physical activity is the root cause of many NCDs.

Lifestyle

Lifestyle refers to the way we live. Our dietary habits, personal hygiene practices, and physical activity are all part of our lifestyle, but these have been discussed separately due to their vital role in our health. Other aspects of lifestyle that adversely affect our health include:

Substance Abuse

Smoking increases the risk of lung cancer and coronary heart disease. Chewing tobacco is associated with risk of oral cancer. Excessive consumption of alcohol can cause liver cirrhosis, heart disease, stroke, or pancreatitis. It is encouraging that the habit of smoking seems to be declining in cities.

Unsafe Sex

Unprotected sexual intercourse, particularly with more than one partner, increases the risk of sexually transmitted infections (STIs), including HIV/AIDS. Early sexual initiation and having multiple sexual partners are risk factors for cervical cancer.

Others

Unsafe practices such as reckless driving and failing to wear helmet or seat belt increase the risk of injury or death in road accidents.

Literacy

Education has a profound effect on people's health. Low literacy is associated with poor hygiene practices, unhealthy dietary habits, and high fertility rates. High fertility in turn contributes to high maternal and neonatal morbidity[3] and mortality.[4] Children born to illiterate mothers are more likely to be undernourished.

Income

Disease patterns vary by economic status. Maternal and child health issues, infectious diseases, and undernutrition are more common in low-income communities, whereas obesity, diabetes, coronary heart disease, and cancer tend to be more prevalent in middle- and high-income groups.

Occupation

Some occupations expose people to a higher risk of certain diseases. For example, workers employed in coal mines or stone-grinding work are more likely to develop chronic respiratory diseases. Ragpickers can get injuries from sharp objects when collecting or segregating waste. Healthcare workers in hospitals can contract infections from patients.

Conversely, people who do strenuous physical work have a lower risk of obesity and NCDs.

Antecedent Medical Conditions

Some medical conditions predispose people to additional health problems. For example, severely anemic women are at a higher risk of postpartum hemorrhage (excessive bleeding after childbirth). People with hypertension face a higher risk of developing stroke[5] or coronary artery disease. Those with uncontrolled diabetes may develop complications of heart, retina, kidneys, or nerves. Treating the antecedent condition can help prevent these complications.

NON-MODIFIABLE FACTORS

Birth Weight

Preterm birth and low birth weight[6] (LBW) are common problems in low-income countries. These infants are susceptible to infections and face an increased risk of death. If they survive, they grow up into short-statured and physically weak adolescents and adults. This is the reason for the large number of short-statured and physically weak adults in low-income countries.

Biological Sex

People's biological makeup predisposes them to certain health problems. Women face complications of pregnancy and childbirth, as well as the risk of breast cancer or cervical cancer. Men may develop prostate enlargement (hypertrophy) as they age.

Gender differences also play a role. Young boys may be at a higher risk of road accidents or drug addiction due to their greater tendency for risk-taking behavior. Panic disorder is seen to be more common in girls.

Genetic Constitution

Parents pass their genes on to their children, and most people are born with normal genes. Genetic disorders such as thalassemia, sickle cell anemia, Down syndrome, and autism occur when abnormal genes are transferred from parents to their children.

Ethnicity

Some diseases are more common in certain countries or ethnic groups. For example, studies show that Black adults in the United States are at a higher risk of heart diseases than white adults.

Family History

People with a family history of diabetes or heart disease are at a higher risk of developing these conditions. These individuals should be particularly careful to avoid smoking, obesity, and inactivity—that is, the modifiable risk factors.

Age

Age predisposes us to certain illnesses or injuries. Death from pneumonia or diarrhea is more common in younger children. Adolescents and young adults are at a higher risk of being involved in road accidents. Older people are susceptible to heart diseases, diabetes, Alzheimer's disease, Parkinsonism, and falls.

ENVIRONMENTAL FACTORS

Environment plays an important role in the spread of some diseases. During the nineteenth and early twentieth centuries, TB was common in Europe. In fact, London was known as the world's TB capital. Interestingly, Western countries were able to control TB long before its cause or treatment was discovered. Better housing conditions, better nutrition, and improved sanitation led to this achievement. Currently, India, China, and Indonesia have a high burden of TB. Large numbers of migrant laborers suffer from malnutrition and live in overcrowded dwellings in urban slums with no facilities for basic hygiene. Tuberculosis is common in these settings.

The absence of safe drinking water and sanitary latrines increases the risk of water- and food-borne infections such as diarrhea, dysentery, typhoid, hepatitis A, and worm infestation. High air pollution in cities causes chronic respiratory diseases. Vector-borne diseases like malaria, dengue, and chikungunya are more common in places where mosquitoes can breed in stagnant water. Road accidents increase where road conditions are poor. These are all environmental factors that impact health.

ROLE OF HEALTHCARE SERVICES

Access to affordable and quality healthcare can help improve people's health and well-being. High immunization coverage reduces the risk of vaccine-preventable diseases such as poliomyelitis, diphtheria, whooping cough, tetanus, measles, pneumonia, diarrhea, and hepatitis B. In settings where healthcare services can provide regular blood transfusion to thalassemia patients, these patients can lead normal lives. People with head injuries can die if they do not receive prompt surgical intervention. Timely care can prevent fatalities and enable full recovery.

NOTES

1. The term *cognitive* refers to mental functions such as knowing, learning, thinking, and understanding.
2. When coronary arteries (arteries inside the heart that supply blood to heart muscles) become blocked, it is called coronary artery disease. It may lead to heart attack.
3. Morbidity refers to disease or injury.
4. Mortality refers to death due to disease or injury.
5. Stroke is paralysis of limbs caused by rupture or blockage of arteries of the brain.
6. Preterm birth refers to babies who are born before completing normal gestation of 37 weeks. LBW babies are defined as those who weigh 2.5 kilograms or less at birth, regardless of their gestational age.

5 What Are Infectious Diseases?

GERM THEORY OF DISEASE

Prior to the 1850s, people thought diseases were caused by bad air (miasma), evil spirits, bad deeds, or wrath of God. Discovery of microorganisms was a turning point in the history of medicine. In the 1860s, nearly two centuries after the Dutch scientist Antonie van Leeuwenhoek discovered the microscope, a French chemist and biologist named Louis Pasteur spotted living microorganisms in the fermentation process and formulated the *germ theory of fermentation*. On the request of the King of France, Pasteur devised a method to preserve wine by heating. Named *pasteurization* after its inventor, today this method is rarely used for wine preservation, but it is universally used for disinfecting milk. During the same period, the German physician Robert Koch isolated anthrax bacilli from infected sheep and identified the bacteria responsible for TB and cholera. Thus, it became known that diseases were caused by microorganisms or microbes. This is known as the *germ theory of disease*. It was further established that every disease is caused by a specific microbe. Many disease-causing microbes were identified in the ensuing years.

EPIDEMIOLOGICAL TRIAD

More than a hundred years ago, scientists tried to explain the origin of diseases using a model known as the *epidemiological triad*, as shown in Figure 5.1.

In this model, *agent* refers to the disease-causing microbe (pathogen). *Host* is the person affected by the disease. *Environment* includes factors such as air, water, and food. The epidemiological triad proposes that diseases arise from the interaction between agent, host, and environment. In normal conditions, these three elements remain in equilibrium. Any disruption in their balance leads to disease.

At the time the epidemiological triad was developed, our understanding of diseases was limited to infectious diseases. Now that many more types of diseases are known, such as NCDs, nutritional disorders, and degenerative conditions, this model finds limited application. Nevertheless, it is historically significant in providing insight into how our understanding of diseases evolved over time.

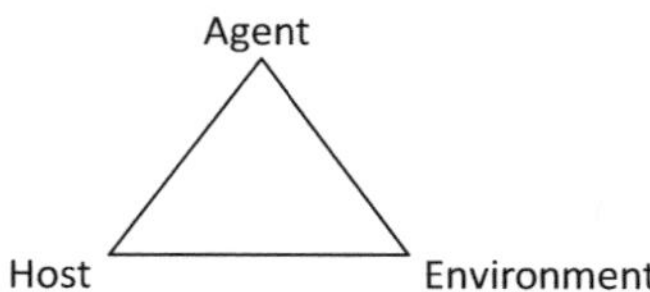

FIGURE 5.1 Epidemiological triad.

DOI: 10.4324/9781032644257-6

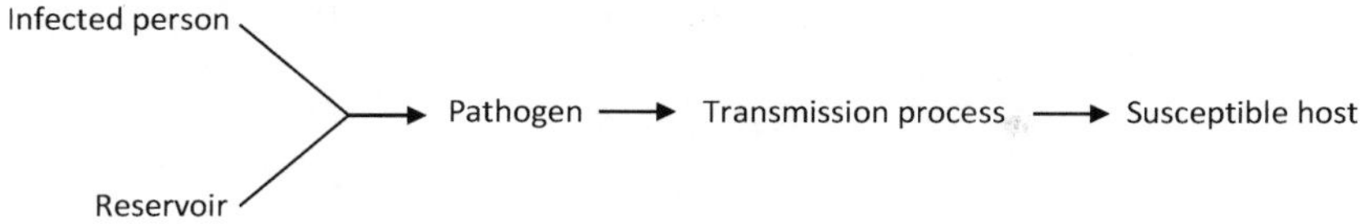

FIGURE 5.2 Chain of infection.

CHAIN OF INFECTION

Figure 5.2 depicts the process of infection.

Pathogens originate from an infected person or from a reservoir. A reservoir is a natural habitat where a microbe normally lives, grows, and multiplies. This habitat can be an animal, a human, or contaminated food, water, or soil.

In human-to-human transmission, pathogens exit the body of the infected person from specific points. For example, some are released from the mouth or nose when coughing, while some pass along with feces. These pathogens then enter the body of a new host through specific points depending on the mode of transmission. Thus, there are six key elements in the chain of infection:

1. Pathogen
2. Infected person
3. Point of exit
4. Transmission process
5. Point of entry
6. Susceptible host

Environment can be considered the seventh element in this chain that can influence some of the other elements.

An infection can be controlled or prevented by breaking the chain of infection. However, the point at which this chain can be broken varies as different diseases have different weak links. Let us briefly discuss the components of the chain of infection.

PATHOGEN

A microorganism that causes disease is called a pathogen. Pathogens can be unicellular or multicellular. Every pathogen is programmed to infect a particular type of host—human or a specific animal. Pathogens that cause disease in animals seldom infect humans, but occasionally they jump from animal to human. The COVID-19 pandemic is a classic example of this shift.

Pathogens are programmed to attack specific tissues or organs of the host body. For example, *Pneumococci* attack lungs and cause pneumonia, while *Salmonella typhi* invades the intestines and gall bladder, causing typhoid.

Types of Pathogens

There are several types of pathogens: Bacteria, viruses, protozoa, fungi, and helminths.

Bacteria: Bacteria are single-celled microorganisms devoid of a nucleus. Their genetic information is stored in a single chromosome of double-stranded DNA. The bacterial cell is enclosed by a cell membrane and a cell wall. Most bacteria can exist independently and can grow in vitro, while others multiply and grow only in host tissues (in vivo).[1] Bacteria grow and multiply by synthesizing their nucleic acids and proteins. Some antibiotics act by interfering in this process.

After Robert Koch discovered *Mycobacterium tuberculosis* and *Vibrio cholerae* in the 1880s, several other bacteria were identified:

Bacterium	Disease
• *Yersinia pestis*	Plague
• *Salmonella typhi*	Typhoid fever
• *Corynebacterium diphtheria*	Diphtheria
• *Shigella dysenteriae*	Dysentery
• *Clostridium tetani*	Tetanus
• *Bordetella pertussis*	Whooping cough

Koch suggested a method to classify bacteria according to their shape. Round bacteria are called cocci. *Streptococci* cause sore throat, *pneumococci* cause pneumonia, and *staphylococci* cause skin infection. Rod-shaped bacteria are called bacilli. *M. tuberculosis* (also known as tubercle bacillus) is a rod-shaped bacterium that causes TB. *Spirochaetes* are spiral-shaped bacteria that cause syphilis.

Viruses: Smallpox was a common killer disease in the early twentieth century. Nearly a century after the British scientist Edward Jenner discovered a method to prevent smallpox by vaccination, the cause of smallpox was still unknown. It was believed that it spread through the fluid in the patient's skin lesions. However, scientists could not isolate the causative pathogen from the fluid. In 1935, an American scientist named Wendell M. Stanley discovered an organism that was much smaller than bacteria. He named it *virus*. Stanley's discovery paved the way for identification of other viruses, including the smallpox virus. It was also realized that smallpox mainly transmitted through cough droplets. Later, causative viruses for poliomyelitis, hepatitis, influenza, measles, mumps, and rabies were identified. This was followed by the discovery of dengue, chikungunya, and Zika viruses. HIV was identified much later, in 1983. Viruses are normally named after the disease they cause.

A virus is not a complete cell; it is a nucleic acid–protein complex. Its genetic material, or genome, is single- or double-stranded DNA or RNA, which is enclosed in a protein coat (capsid). Some viruses have an additional lipid envelope. Interestingly, non-enveloped viruses tend to survive longer in the environment.

Unlike bacteria, viruses can only replicate inside a host cell. They multiply by using the host's cellular mechanisms and materials to synthesize their nucleic acids and proteins. Some viruses can even infect bacteria; they are known as bacteriophages.

Fungi: Pathogenic fungi mostly exist in filamentous form. Most fungi reproduce by producing spores that can survive in extreme conditions. Spores of some fungi disperse in the air and can cause infection when inhaled. Some common fungi and fungal diseases include:

Fungus	Disease
• *Candida*	Vaginal candidiasis
• Ringworm	Ringworm infestation of skin (tinea cruris)
• Onychomycosis (nail fungus)	Nail infection
• *Aspergillus*	Aspergillosis

Protozoa: Protozoa are single-celled organisms larger than bacteria. Protozoa and helminths are parasites. Common protozoan diseases are:

Protozoa	Disease
• *Plasmodium spp.*	Malaria
• *Entamoeba histolytica*	Amoebiasis
• *Leishmania spp.*	Leishmaniasis
• *Trichomonas vaginalis*	Trichomoniasis
• *Giardia lamblia*	Giardiasis

Helminths: They are commonly known as intestinal worms. Adult helminth worms are visible to the naked eye, but their ova (eggs) are microscopic. Most helminths infect the human gastrointestinal tract, although some can infect other organs. Common species include:

- *Ascaris lumbricoides* (roundworm)
- *Ancylostoma duodenale* (hookworm)
- *Trichuris trichiura* (whipworm)
- *Enterobius vermicularis* (pinworm)
- *Taenia solium* (tapeworm)

Antigen

Antigens are specific proteins on the surface of pathogens that trigger an immune response or production of antibodies in the host body. Some pathogens also produce toxins.

Virulence

Virulence refers to the degree to which a pathogen can harm host tissues. In other words, it refers to the severity of disease or the potential fatality the pathogen can cause in a host. For example, common cold is generally mild and self-limiting due to the low virulence of the causative viruses. In contrast, the measles virus has a relatively higher degree of virulence. Measles may begin as an upper respiratory infection, but in some cases it may complicate and cause pneumonia or encephalitis. While many children died from these complications in the past, introduction of the measles vaccine has led to a considerable decline in fatalities.

Different strains of a pathogen can have varying degrees of virulence. For example, some strains of *Hemophilus influenzae*,[2] a bacterium, are less virulent and cause mild ear infection, while others can cause potentially fatal infections such as pneumonia or meningitis.

Rabies is caused by the highly virulent rhabdovirus. When a rabid dog bites a human, pathogens are transmitted through the dog's saliva to the person's wound. Through blood circulation, these pathogens move to the person's brain and start multiplying there. Once infection is established, death is inevitable.

Mutation

RNA viruses constantly undergo mutation, which leads to changes in their genetic codes. Occasionally, they become highly virulent, as seen with the SARS-CoV-2 virus during the second wave of COVID-19 in some countries.

Reservoir

Pathogens need a reservoir where they can live and multiply. Rodents are the natural reservoirs of *Y. pestis*. Dogs are reservoirs of rhabdovirus. Humans are reservoirs of *S. typhi* and the hepatitis A virus. Stool of a human infected with rotavirus is a reservoir for rotavirus.

Host

After pathogens invade host tissues, they start multiplying. This triggers the host's immune system into action and a duel ensues between the pathogens and the host's immune response. If the host's immune system is strong, the pathogens are destroyed and the host remains unaffected. If pathogens survive the immune response, they continue to multiply and get established in host tissues, causing infection. An infection may cause a disease.

Types of Immune System

Innate immune system: The innate immune system provides immediate protection to the host. This system is nonspecific, meaning it is effective against a variety of pathogens. It consists of anatomical barriers and white blood cells.[3] The skin and mucous membranes are the primary anatomical barriers. White blood cells engulf and kill pathogens through a process called phagocytosis. Among all types of white blood cells,[4] neutrophils and monocytes play a particularly important role in phagocytosis. Cilia in the respiratory tract mucosa, which trap and expel microbes out of the airways; salivary amylase; and hydrochloric acid in the stomach are other barriers.

Adaptive or acquired immune system: If pathogens overcome the innate immune system and continue their attack, the acquired immune system gets activated in host body. This immune response is specific to the type of pathogen encountered. It provides two types of protection:

- Cellular
- Humoral (fluid)

Cellular immunity is provided by T lymphocytes, a specific type of white blood cells that directly kill target cells. Humoral immunity is provided by B lymphocytes, which produce antibodies that can recognize and bind the antigens produced by the pathogens. Antibodies, also known as immunoglobulins (Ig), are a type of protein. The five types of immunoglobulins are: IgG, IgA, IgM, IgE, and IgD.

In addition to these immune systems, beneficial microorganisms present in the body, known as normal flora or commensal bacteria, also provide some protection from pathogens. These microorganisms colonize the skin, the intestines, and distal ends of body openings such as the nares, mouth, distal urethra, vagina, and rectum.

The host's immune response is primarily aimed at protecting the host. Fever (hyperthermia), a cardinal response to infection, interferes with replication of microorganisms. However, in some cases, the host's immune response becomes overaggressive and starts causing self-harm. This is a major concern in medical practice.

On repeated exposure to a pathogen, people may acquire partial immunity against that pathogen. Over time, this may reduce the risk of the associated disease or lessen its severity. For example, in low-income settings, people may consume unhygienic food or fail to wash their hands before eating and yet they do not fall sick. This is because they have acquired some immunity. However, foreign travelers who eat the same food may get severe diarrhea. Thus, acquired immunity helps. But remember that it is generally incomplete and we cannot rely on it. After all, diarrhea continues to kill a large number of children in low-income countries.

INFECTION

Infection is a condition in which microorganisms, after invading host tissues, start multiplying and cause a reaction in host body.

It is important to note that infection does not always result in disease. Therefore, ideally speaking, the terms *infection* and *disease* are not interchangeable.

DISEASE

A disease occurs when there is significant damage to host tissues. Symptoms[5] and signs[6] signal the onset of a disease. As we know, diseases are not always caused by infection; there can be many other causes.

DIAGNOSIS

To treat an infectious disease effectively, we must know the causative pathogen. The following laboratory tests are commonly employed to detect or identify pathogens:

Direct Visualization

In some diseases, the pathogen can be visualized in the patient's blood or body fluids by examining the sample under a microscope. For example, malaria parasites can be seen in peripheral blood smear, and tubercle bacilli can be seen in sputum smear.

Culture

In some diseases such as typhoid, even if pathogens are present in the patient's blood, they cannot be visualized unless they are in large numbers. To increase their count, the patient's blood sample is placed on a culture medium under favorable temperature and conditions for a few days. Once the pathogens multiply and grow in number, they can be seen under a microscope.

Nucleic Acid Amplification Test (NAAT)

Every pathogen has a unique DNA or RNA pattern from which it can be identified. However, the amount of genetic material present in a sample of blood or body fluid may not be sufficient for detection. Genetic material can be amplified through a polymerase chain reaction (PCR) in vitro, and then the pathogen can be identified. The reverse transcription-polymerase chain reaction (RT-PCR) test used in SARS-CoV-2 testing is a type of NAAT.

Antigen Detection

In some diseases, antigens produced by pathogens can be detected in the patient's blood sample. Rapid antigen tests are available for malaria, COVID-19, and many other diseases.

Antibody Detection

Antibodies produced by the host body in response to an infection can be detected in blood sample. Presence of antibodies serves as indirect evidence of the infection. Enzyme-linked immunosorbent assay (ELISA) is a type of antibody test for diagnosing HIV.

Nonspecific Markers

Bacterial infections lead to elevated white blood cell count, a condition known as leukocytosis. Leukocytosis is a nonspecific marker of infection, but it provides valuable information as it indicates the severity of infection. Repeated leukocyte counts during the course of treatment can inform whether the infection is subsiding.

NOTES

1. *In vitro* refers to something occurring in an artificial medium outside a living body, while *in vivo* refers to processes occurring inside a living body.
2. Note that *H. influenzae* is different from the influenza virus that causes the flu.
3. White blood cells, along with red blood cells, platelets, and plasma, compose blood.
4. White blood cells are of several types: neutrophils, lymphocytes, eosinophils, basophils, and monocytes.
5. Problems experienced by patients, such as pain, fever, or difficulty in breathing, are called symptoms.
6. Patient problems identified by clinicians are called signs. Hypertension, tachycardia (increased pulse rate), and swelling in liver are examples of signs.

6 What Are Noncommunicable Diseases?

Until a few decades ago, there was a perception that NCDs were predominantly a problem of high-income countries and affluent people, whereas low-income countries mainly struggled with infectious diseases. But now we know that NCDs disproportionately affect people in low- and middle-income countries. Socially and economically disadvantaged people are more susceptible to NCDs and are more likely to die prematurely from these diseases. This is due to their higher risk of exposure to tobacco and alcohol use, poor dietary intake, and poor access to healthcare. Notably, NCDs now account for more premature deaths in some of these countries than infectious diseases.

Cardiovascular diseases (CVDs) are the leading cause of NCD deaths globally. Chronic respiratory diseases, cancers, and diabetes are common. Kidney diseases associated with diabetes also cause significant mortality. These diseases are primarily driven by population aging and rapid and unplanned urbanization. Physical inactivity, unhealthy diet, and use of tobacco and alcohol increase the risk of mortality from NCDs.

MULTIFACTORIAL ETIOLOGY

While we know that every infectious disease is caused by a specific pathogen, etiology of many NCDs is not known. For example, we do not know the definitive causes of diabetes, coronary heart disease, and many types of cancer. What we know are the *risk factors* associated with some of these diseases. A risk factor contributes to the causation of a disease but it is not sufficient to cause the disease. For example, smoking is a potent risk factor for lung cancer, but everyone who smokes does not get cancer. On the other hand, some people get lung cancer without having smoked a cigarette in their life. What we know for sure is that a large proportion of those diagnosed with lung cancer are heavy smokers. From this, we interpret that smoking increases the risk of lung cancer.

It can be assumed that a risk factor causes the disease in conjunction with some other, unknown factors. Additionally, a disease can have multiple risk factors—for example, diabetes is linked to family history, obesity, and physical inactivity.

Certain infectious diseases are also influenced by risk factors. We know that TB is caused by a specific agent, but people who are undernourished or live in overcrowded dwellings face a higher risk of contracting TB. People with HIV also face a higher risk of TB due to their weakened immunity.

CARDIOVASCULAR DISEASES

CVDs involve the heart and blood vessels. They are the most common cause of premature deaths worldwide. In CVD, lipoid-rich materials get deposited in lumen of arteries, reducing blood supply to the affected organ. This process is known as atherosclerosis. Coronary heart disease, a type of CVD, occurs when blood supply to a part of the heart is impaired. Sudden cessation of blood supply to a part of heart muscles can cause ischemic heart disease. The brain is also susceptible to blood vessel disorders. Reduction of blood supply to the brain leads to cerebrovascular disease. It may cause cerebrovascular accident, commonly known as limb paralysis or stroke. The majority of CVD-related deaths are caused by heart attack or stroke.

DOI: 10.4324/9781032644257-7

Why does atherosclerosis occur? The exact cause is not known. What we do know is that people affected by atherosclerosis are more likely to have a history of exposure to one or more of the following risk factors:

- Smoking
- Obesity
- Hypertension
- Hyperglycemia (high blood sugar)
- Hyperlipidemia (elevated blood lipids)

As you can see, these are all modifiable risk factors. Smoking can be avoided. Obesity can be reduced with physical activity and a healthy diet.[1] Hypertension, hyperglycemia, and hyperlipidemia can be diagnosed and treated with medicines. They can be managed by physical activity. Thus, many CVD-related deaths can be prevented in this way.

There are also some non-modifiable risk factors for atherosclerosis. CVD runs in families, increasing the risk for first-degree relatives. Atherosclerosis increases with age, which means middle-aged and older adults are more likely to be affected. Women have a lower risk of CVD in their younger years, but after menopause, they are at equal risk as men. People with non-modifiable risk factors of CVD should be more careful to avoid the modifiable risk factors, which are mostly behavioral.

CHRONIC RESPIRATORY DISEASES

Chronic respiratory diseases are the third most common cause of premature deaths globally (after ischemic heart disease and stroke). The two most common types of chronic respiratory disease are chronic obstructive pulmonary disease (COPD) and asthma, as depicted in Figure 6.1. Prevalence of these diseases has been rising globally, mainly due to factors such as tobacco use, rising air pollution, and population aging.

Chronic Obstructive Pulmonary Disease

COPD generally occurs after 40–50 years of age and progresses slowly. It is characterized by chronic cough with sputum due to a persistent reduction in airflow. In the initial stages, there is breathlessness on exertion, which gradually progresses to breathlessness on rest. COPD can be life-threatening. More than 90% of COPD-related deaths occur in low- and middle-income countries.

Smoking is the primary cause of COPD. Indirect exposure to tobacco smoke also causes harm. Indoor and outdoor pollution, industrial dust, and frequent lower respiratory infections in childhood are other risk factors.

Due to a lack of proper diagnostic facilities, COPD mostly remains underdiagnosed in low-income settings. Spirometry, a test that confirms COPD by measuring airflow obstruction, is often unavailable in lower-level health facilities.

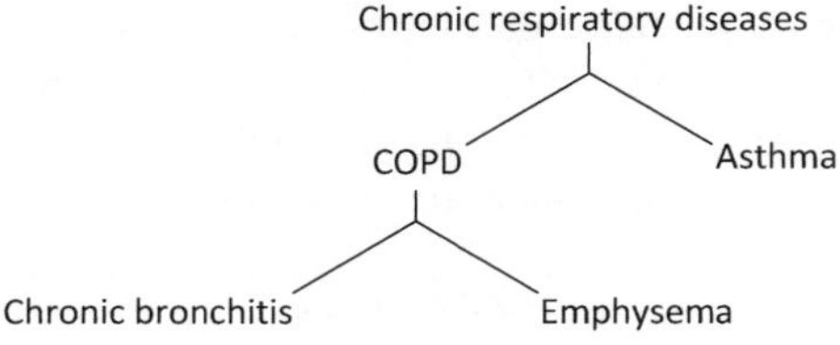

FIGURE 6.1 Types of chronic respiratory diseases.

Avoidance of smoking, or at least early cessation, can prevent COPD. Once COPD is established, treatment can provide temporary relief, but the condition is incurable. Chronic bronchitis and emphysema are the two main forms of COPD.

Asthma

Asthma generally begins in childhood. It is the most common chronic disease in children, although no age group is spared. It is characterized by intermittent shortness of breath and wheeze[2] caused by inflammation and constriction of small airways in lungs. It is important to note that asthma causes intermittent acute attacks, unlike COPD, where symptoms are persistent. A person with asthma can be perfectly fine between episodes.

Factors that trigger acute symptoms of asthma vary from person to person. Dust, smoke, pollen, air pollution, and changes in weather are common triggers. Family history or personal history of allergy is a risk factor. Certain events in early life, such as preterm birth, low birth weight, exposure to tobacco smoke, and repeated respiratory infections, also increase the risk. Urbanization is linked to the increasing occurrence of asthma. All of these are risk factors for asthma.

People with asthma need to protect themselves from triggers that induce symptoms. Avoiding exposure to tobacco smoke can help one manage and even prevent the disease. In most cases, inhaled medications—bronchodilators or steroids—can provide relief from symptoms and help one lead a productive life. Case fatality of asthma is low. The majority of deaths occur in low- and middle-income countries due to lack of treatment.

DIABETES

Diabetes is characterized by high blood sugar levels. It damages nerves and blood vessels, affecting multiple body organs. The WHO estimates that over 8% of the world's adult population has diabetes. The occurrence of diabetes is increasing rapidly in many low-income countries.

There are two types of diabetes. Type 2 diabetes is more common in middle-aged and older adults, though lately it has also been reported in children. Obesity, overeating, and underactivity are principal risk factors for type 2 diabetes. Smoking increases the risk. Genetic predisposition also plays a role, placing first-degree relatives at greater risk. Ethnicity is also a factor; studies show that people of color in the United States and Indians have a greater predisposition to diabetes.

Diabetes is a major risk factor for blindness, heart attack, stroke, and kidney failure. Maintaining normal body weight, regular physical activity, and a healthy diet can prevent or delay the onset of diabetes. Cessation of smoking can be helpful. Effective medicines are available to reduce blood sugar levels.

Type 1 diabetes is caused by insufficient production of insulin in the body and has its onset in childhood. It is relatively less prevalent.

CANCERS

Cancer refers to the rapid and uncontrolled multiplication of cells, leading to the formation of abnormal cells known as tumors. A tumor can occur in any part of the body. Tumors that do not spread to other parts of the body (i.e., tumors that do not metastasize) are called benign tumors, while those that spread to other parts are called malignant tumors, neoplasm, or cancer. Malignant tumors are dangerous.

Cancer is one of the leading causes of death worldwide, with breast cancer being the most common form of cancer. Lung cancer is the second most common, but it claims more lives globally than any other cancer. Cancers of colon, rectum, prostate, and skin are common in high-income countries, whereas stomach cancer is common in low-income countries. Oral cancer is common in India due to the prevalence of tobacco chewing.

Tobacco and alcohol consumption, inactive lifestyle, unhealthy diet, air pollution, and advancing age are risk factors for any type of cancer. Additionally, certain chronic infections increase the risk of some cancers. Human papillomavirus (HPV) infection and HIV infection are risk factors for cervical cancer. Hepatitis B and C infections are associated with liver cancer. *Helicobacter pylori* infection increases the risk of stomach cancer.

Early detection and treatment can prevent many cancer-related deaths or halt progression of the disease. Breast cancer, cervical cancer, colorectal cancer, and oral cancer are notable in this context. In general, risk of cancer can be reduced by adopting preventive measures such as:

- Avoiding tobacco and alcohol
- Maintaining a physically active lifestyle and a healthy body weight
- Eating a nutritious diet rich in vegetables and fruits
- Vaccinating against HPV (for girls and women) and hepatitis B
- Avoiding ultraviolet rays
- Avoiding environmental pollution

Screening can help identify cancer or precancer before a person develops symptoms. Screening is particularly useful in:

- Cervical cancer (by HPV testing)
- Breast cancer (by mammography)
- Oral cancer (by physical examination)

Prevention strategies include raising awareness among the general population about symptoms of common cancers, screening for specific cancers, and improving access to diagnostic and treatment services.

Treatment for cancer includes surgery, radiotherapy, and chemotherapy. Different types of cancer have different treatment protocols. When cure is not possible, palliative care is provided to alleviate suffering and improve quality of life.

Breast Cancer

Breast cancer commonly develops in epithelium of ducts in glandular tissues, where it does not cause any symptoms and has limited scope for spreading. Breast cancer can be treated effectively if diagnosed early. Over time, it invades nearby lymph nodes, and then it spreads rapidly and can be fatal.

High-risk groups for breast cancer include women who are obese, who are physically inactive, who had a late first pregnancy (after age 30), who did not breastfeed, who take hormone replacement therapy, or who consume alcohol regularly. Note that these are all modifiable risk factors. Specifically, prolonged breastfeeding is known to reduce the risk of breast cancer—perhaps nature's way of protecting women against this cancer.

Non-modifiable risk factors for breast cancer include history of breast cancer in first-degree relatives (mother, sister, daughter), advancing age (women older than 50 years are at greater risk), history of early menarche or late menopause (and therefore longer exposure to female sex hormones), or dense breasts (having more connective tissue than fatty tissue). Lastly, women who inherit a harmful variant of the *BRCA1* or *BRCA2*[3] gene have a higher risk of developing breast cancer and ovarian cancer at younger ages.

In its early stages, breast cancer can be identified by mammography. Epidemiological studies have determined that periodic screening of older women by mammography reduces mortality from breast cancer.

Lung Cancer

Cigarette smoking is the biggest risk factor for lung cancer. Exposure to secondhand smoke from others also poses a risk. In some parts of the United States, presence of radon, a radioactive gas, is an additional risk factor for lung cancer. The US Environment Protection Agency recommends testing all homes for presence of radon.

Since lung cancer treatments are not very effective, the best preventive measure is to avoid smoking. Lung cancer screening can be done by a low-dose CT scan, but repeated CT scan itself poses a risk of cancer. People aged 50–80 years with a history of heavy smoking are advised to undergo lung cancer screening, but it should be noted that screening is not a substitute for quitting smoking.

Cervical Cancer

Cervical cancer is the most common cancer in women in low-income countries. Nearly all cases of cervical cancer are caused by HPV infection.[4] People with multiple sexual partners are at a higher risk of contracting HPV infection. Tobacco use is another risk factor as it increases the risk of cancer almost anywhere in the body, including the cervix.

HPV infection is very common, but most cases resolve spontaneously. If the infection persists, it can lead to cancer. HPV vaccination can prevent cervical cancer, making it the only type of cancer with a potential to be eliminated.

Early detection is crucial for successful treatment of cervical cancer. There are two effective tests available for this: HPV test and Pap smear test[5] (cervical cytology). In low-resource settings, visual inspection with acetic acid is a simple and cost-effective option.

Cancer of Colon and Rectum

Colon and rectum cancer is the third most common cancer and the second leading cause of cancer-related deaths worldwide. The highest risk of colon and rectum cancer is observed in Asia, notably in China and Japan. Risk factors include alcohol consumption, smoking, obesity, and HPV infection.

To reduce the risk of this cancer, people are advised to maintain a healthy weight and follow a nutritious diet with plenty of fruits and vegetables. According to some studies, including fish in diet may have a protective effect.

Treatment for colon and rectum cancer is more effective if the disease is diagnosed early. Therefore, screening high-risk individuals can be advantageous. For community screening, a simple method is testing for the presence of blood in stool. There are several methods available for this, and the test can be repeated yearly. Additionally, doctors can identify polyps or cancer in rectum and colon by sigmoidoscopy, colonoscopy, or CT colonography.

Oral Cancer

Oral cancer is the most common cancer among men in India. It includes cancers of the oral cavity, lips, nasopharynx, and pharynx. Tobacco chewing, a common practice in many parts of India, is a definitive risk factor for oral cancer. Other forms of tobacco consumption, such as smoking cigarette or bidi, also increase the risk.

A simple visual examination can identify white patches in oral cavity, which are premalignant lesions known as leukoplakia. This has high significance—if the person stops chewing tobacco at this stage, the lesions can regress. Unfortunately, inspection of oral cavity is often missed out during routine physical examination.

NOTES

1. A healthy diet is low in fat and sugar and includes fresh vegetables.
2. Wheeze is breath with a whistling sound, caused by narrowing of airways.
3. *BRCA1* and *BRCA2* are cancer-suppressor genes.
4. Another infection that causes cancer is hepatitis. It causes liver cancer.
5. Pap smear test stands for Papanicolaou test. This test identifies precancer cells in cervix that might develop into cancer.

7 Classification of Diseases

Healthcare professionals deal with a variety of diseases and health problems. In preceding chapters, we learned about infectious and noncommunicable diseases. There are many more categories of diseases, such as degenerative diseases, hereditary diseases, immune disorders, and metabolic disorders. It is challenging to classify diseases in delineated groups. For example, pneumonia is an infectious disease, but it can also be classified as a respiratory disease. Further, pneumonia can be bacterial or viral or fungal. If some doctors diagnose a condition as pneumonia and others label it as a lower respiratory infection, the data will get distorted. To enable uniformity in diagnoses, the WHO publishes the International Classification of Diseases (ICD), which assigns a unique identification code to all known diseases and health problems and classifies them into groups. Clinical practitioners are expected to follow this system when diagnosing a disease or certifying the cause of death. The ICD enables countries to measure and monitor disease burden in their populations and facilitates international comparisons. The WHO updates the ICD periodically.

Major ICD groups along with examples of common diseases within each group are enumerated below. Note that this list is not exhaustive and is only provided to give readers an idea of the spectrum of diseases.

Group	**Diseases**
Bacterial diseases	pneumonia, tuberculosis, leprosy, typhoid, *E. coli* infection, streptococcal pharyngitis, staphylococcal infection, bacillary dysentery, diphtheria, cholera, plague, trachoma
Viral diseases	rotavirus, norovirus, coronavirus, measles, rubella, influenza, dengue, chikungunya, viral hepatitis, mumps, chickenpox (varicella), herpes zoster, human papillomavirus, Japanese B encephalitis
Fungal infections	aspergillosis, candidiasis, dermatophytosis
Parasitic diseases	malaria, helminthiasis, amoebiasis, filariasis, giardiasis, leishmaniasis, schistosomiasis, helminthic infestations caused by hookworm, roundworm, threadworm, and tapeworm
Pregnancy, childbirth, and puerperium	postpartum hemorrhage, obstructed labor, abortion, ectopic pregnancy
Perinatal period	preterm delivery, birth injuries, infections of fetus or newborn, birth asphyxia
Nutritional disorders	iron-deficiency anemia, stunting in children, wasting in children, iodine deficiency-related thyroid disorder, vitamin A deficiency, obesity
Endocrine diseases	diabetes mellitus, hypothyroidism, thyrotoxicosis
Diseases of circulatory system	hypertension, ischemic heart disease, endocarditis, heart valve disease, heart failure, cardiac arrhythmia, chronic rheumatic heart disease
Diseases of respiratory system	acute nasopharyngitis, tonsillitis, bronchitis, emphysema, chronic obstructive pulmonary disease, asthma, pneumonia
Diseases of digestive system	coeliac disease, intestinal malabsorption enteropathy, appendicitis, hernia, alcoholic liver disease, nonalcoholic fatty liver disease, cholecystitis, acute pancreatitis
Diseases of genital system	endometriosis, infertility, leiomyoma uterus, menstrual bleeding disorders, non-menstrual bleeding disorders, recurrent pregnancy loss, hyperplasia of prostate
Diseases of urinary system	nephrotic syndrome, urolithiasis, kidney failure
Diseases of musculoskeletal system or connective tissues	osteoarthritis, rheumatoid arthritis, gout
Diseases of skin	dermatitis, eczema
Conditions related to sexual health	male erectile dysfunction, female sexual arousal dysfunction
Mental and behavioral disorders	panic disorder, adjustment disorder, depressive disorder, bipolar disorder, obsessive-compulsive disorder, schizophrenia

(Continued)

DOI: 10.4324/9781032644257-8

Group	Diseases
Neoplasms	carcinoma of oral cavity, carcinoma breast, carcinoma cervix uteri
Diseases of eyes	cataract, myopia, hypermetropia, glaucoma, conjunctivitis
Diseases of nervous system	epilepsy, headache disorder, migraine and other types of headaches, cerebrovascular disease, multiple sclerosis
Diseases of blood or blood-forming organs	anemia, coagulation defects, hemorrhagic conditions
Metabolic disorders	hypercholesterolemia, cystic fibrosis
Diseases of immune system	primary or acquired immunodeficiencies, allergic or hypersensitivity conditions
Sleep-wake disorders	insomnia, sleep-related breathing disorders
Others	injuries, burn, poisoning

The focus of public health is on common health problems that affect populations—referred to as public health problems. These problems vary from region to region. Some public health problems that have overwhelming implications are highlighted below.

A large proportion of adolescent girls in low-income countries are anemic. Many girls get married at an early age and become pregnant and deliver. Many women die from complications of pregnancy and delivery. Many babies are born preterm or with low birth weight, and many among them die prematurely. Stunting and wasting as a result of undernutrition are prevalent in children in economically deprived communities. Pneumonia and diarrhea kill many children. Infectious diseases such as TB, malaria, dengue, influenza, and typhoid are common in many countries. Emergence of drug-resistant TB is a big challenge. Diseases like leprosy, filariasis, leishmaniasis, leptospirosis, and Japanese encephalitis are localized in specific areas.

Historically, NCDs like diabetes, hypertension, CVD, and cancer were more prevalent in developed countries, but now they are increasing rapidly in many middle-income and low-income countries. Gender-based violence and discrimination are common. Female genital mutilation is a pernicious social problem in some African countries, as are female feticide and infanticide in South Asian countries. Deaths from road traffic accidents are increasing globally. The rise in mental health disorders is a cause of concern. Recently, developed countries are experiencing a unique problem of declining birth rates and an increasing proportion of aging citizens. Outbreaks of diseases like COVID, SARS, and Ebola have always been a threat everywhere.

Section II

Basic Epidemiology

8 What Is Epidemiology?

Epidemiology began as a branch of public health, but over time it grew phenomenally and acquired the status of an independent specialty. Many prestigious institutions and universities around the world now offer postgraduate or doctoral programs in epidemiology.

As noted in a previous chapter, while clinical practitioners deal with individual patients, public health works with populations. Just as a clinician diagnoses the illness before treating the patient, epidemiologists diagnose health problems of a population. They quantify burden of a disease, find its causes, and devise ways to manage it. Epidemiology is, therefore, the diagnostic discipline of public health.

Dr. John M. Last, an eminent public health scholar and epidemiologist, provided the following definition of epidemiology in his book *A Dictionary of Epidemiology*:

> *Epidemiology is the study of the distribution and determinants of health-related states or events in specified populations, and the application of this knowledge to the control of health problems.*

This definition may appear complex at first, but it is meaningful. This will become clear in the succeeding sections.

SCOPE AND USES OF EPIDEMIOLOGY

In his definition, Dr. Last purposefully uses the phrase "health-related states or events" in place of "diseases." This is accurate, since clinicians and epidemiologists are not only concerned with diseases but deal with all sorts of health-related problems, such as road accident injuries, dog bite, obesity, and poisoning.

Estimating Burden of Health-Related Problems

Epidemiology plays an important role in quantifying health problems in a population. This data is needed to plan for health services. For example, if we know the number of diabetes cases in a population, we can work out the requirements for diabetes clinics and laboratories, endocrinologists, and laboratory technicians and technologists. We can estimate the demand for diagnostic testing and common medicines. A budget to fight the disease can be worked out.

At the same time, if people of a region are exceptionally healthy, it is of great interest to epidemiologists, who try to understand why this is so and how this knowledge can be applied to improve the health of other communities.

Identifying Causes of Diseases

Another important function of epidemiology is to identify the causes, or etiology, of diseases and their risk factors. This information is critical for the treatment, control, and prevention of diseases.

Recall that Dr. Last defines epidemiology as "the study of the distribution and determinants of health-related states or events." Why should we study the distribution of diseases? What do we gain from it? The basic premise of epidemiology is that diseases do not occur randomly in a population;

DOI: 10.4324/9781032644257-10

they arise due to specific reasons. By studying the distribution of a disease, we can get vital clues about its cause(s), as will become clear through the following example.

Example 1

During the 1950s, public health authorities in the United States noted an alarming increase in cases of coronary heart disease, which was leading to a high number of premature deaths. Further, it was observed that the disease was more common among Americans than among Asian immigrants. A study was conducted to understand the reasons behind this. One of the findings was that Americans consumed higher quantities of meat and dairy products compared to other groups. This provided a vital clue about the role of diet in coronary heart disease. Subsequent studies confirmed the correlation between diet and coronary heart disease and also identified additional risk factors. Thus, by studying the distribution of coronary heart disease among different communities, researchers were able to identify a key risk factor of the disease.

In addition to understanding the distribution of a disease, we need to know its determinants. This is vital to control and prevent the disease. Determinants of an infectious disease include its causative agent, source(s), and mode(s) of transmission. In case of COVID-19, for example, scientists determined that the disease is caused by the SARS-CoV-2 virus, which transmits through saliva droplets when an infected person coughs or talks. This information helped in the development of prevention strategies for COVID-19.

Control and Prevention of Health-Related Problems

As stated by Dr. Last, the knowledge gained from epidemiological investigations is applied to control health problems. Note that epidemiology's role is generally limited to diagnosing and measuring health problems in a population and finding their solutions. Based on this knowledge, the broader domain of public health takes over the function of designing and managing health programs. Recall that epidemiology is the diagnostic discipline of public health.

Applications in Clinical Practice

Epidemiology describes the natural history of diseases: How a disease is expected to behave if left untreated and what prognosis or clinical outcomes are expected. Some diseases have serious consequences. A classic example is that of HIV/AIDS, which devastated many African countries, killing millions of people, orphaning children, and ruining economies. Others, such as osteoarthritis, may not be fatal, but they significantly affect quality of life. By learning the natural history of diseases, we can identify diseases that are likely to become severe or fatal, or cause disability, or worsen quality of life. Based on this knowledge, we can prioritize certain conditions, plan resources, and allocate funds.

Additionally, epidemiology helps to define normal ranges for health indicators.[1] We know that high blood sugar harms multiple organs, so it is important to maintain healthy blood sugar levels. But what is the normal range for blood sugar and who decides it? Epidemiology plays a central role in defining normal ranges for indicators such as blood sugar, blood pressure, pulse rate, and blood cholesterol level. To ascertain healthy blood sugar values, epidemiologists study health outcomes in people with different blood sugar levels and identify the values with favorable outcomes. At what level of blood sugar should antidiabetic treatment be started? Again, epidemiological studies answer such questions.

If multiple treatments or therapies are available for a disease, epidemiological studies can help identify the ones that are most effective.

Example 2

As a woman ages, the production of sex hormones in her body declines. This can lead to osteoporosis and increase the risk of fractures. In the 1990s, hormone replacement therapy (HRT) was found to be effective in preventing osteoporosis in older women. Gradually, it became a norm to prescribe HRT to older women. However, subsequent epidemiological studies found that, although HRT reduced the risk of osteoporosis and fractures, it increased the risk of heart disease, stroke, and even Alzheimer's disease. As a result, HRT is no longer a first-line option for preventing osteoporosis.

Application of the principles and methods of epidemiology to answer questions pertaining to diagnosis and treatment of diseases is known as Clinical Epidemiology.

Evaluating Health Programs and Disease Prevention Programs

Epidemiological studies play an important role in evaluating health programs and prevention programs.

Example 3

By the time some women seek treatment for breast cancer, the disease has often progressed to an advanced stage. Naturally, the clinical outcome in these cases will be poor. Breast cancer can be treated effectively if identified early, but how can we ensure timely detection of cases? Screening for breast cancer is one way to identify cases in communities. Self-examination and mammography are the two main screening methods for breast cancer. In low-income countries, where mammography is costly and access is limited, self-examination of breast was thought to be a practical option. Accordingly, this method was widely promoted. Meanwhile, many high-income countries continued with periodic mammography. Subsequent epidemiological studies found that mortality from breast cancer was reduced in communities where women underwent periodic mammography but not where breast self-examination was promoted. As a result, physicians no longer promote breast self-examination. This example demonstrates how epidemiological studies provide evidence of the effectiveness, or lack thereof, of public health programs.

It might be worthwhile to investigate what went wrong with breast self-examination—whether the technique itself was flawed (i.e., it failed to identify breast cancer early), whether we could not train women to properly conduct self-examination, or if poor access to breast cancer treatment rendered the intervention futile.

Epidemiological studies are also used to determine the cost-effectiveness of interventions, enabling program managers to choose the most appropriate interventions.

Support to Policy Development

Policies and programs should be based on need and evidence. Opioid use disorder is a public health problem in many states in the United States. Effective medicines are available for its treatment, but their utilization has been poor. Studies show that the requirement of prior authorization by insurance companies has been a key barrier to the uptake of services. As a result, many US states have passed laws prohibiting insurance companies from insisting on preauthorization. In this way, epidemiological studies contribute to formulating evidence-based laws and policies.

EPIDEMIOLOGICAL APPROACH

Being a diagnostic discipline, epidemiology approaches a health problem by:

1. Raising questions
2. Collecting data
3. Making comparisons

Raising Questions

To understand health problems in a population, epidemiologists ask questions such as:

What	What is the health problem? What is its magnitude? What is its cause? What are the consequences?
Who	Who are the people affected—what is peculiar about them? How are they different from others?
Where	Where is the disease distributed geographically? Where did people contract the disease? Was there any new exposure in that area?
When	When did the problem begin? Were all the people affected together or one after another? What was the sequence of events?
Why	Why did the disease occur? Why are some people affected and not others?
How	How can the disease be controlled? How can it be prevented?

Collecting Data

To answer these questions, epidemiologists collect information and data. To begin with, they decide what type of data will be needed to determine the scale of the health problem, its causes, modes of transmission, and the effectiveness of treatment. They then identify sources from which this data can be obtained and develop methods for data collection. In an outbreak of an infectious disease, for example, data is collected to know how many people contracted the disease, how many among them were exposed to a suspected agent or risk factor, how many were treated or cured, and how many died. The collected data is analyzed to draw conclusions.

Making Comparisons

To make sense of data, we compare it with similar data. This can be done in two ways:

Cross-Sectional Comparison

In this method, we compare data from two or more geographies at a specific point in time. For example, a comparison of all US states in 2021 revealed that death rate from cancer was the highest in West Virginia and lowest in Utah. Efforts are underway to identify the reasons for this disparity. Corrective interventions will be made based on the findings.

Longitudinal Comparison

Longitudinal studies compare data from a population or geographical area over a period of time. In the above example, once interventions are implemented in states with higher rates of cancer-related deaths, the government, through a longitudinal study, will want to closely monitor the performance of each state year on year to see if death rates from cancer reduce.

NOTE

1. A health indicator is a characteristic of a population that is measurable and describes its health status.

9 Disease Transmission

How do diseases spread? Some diseases transmit from person to person. These are known as infectious or communicable diseases. The flu, pneumonia, diarrhea, malaria, HIV/AIDS, and scabies are infectious diseases. However, not all diseases are infectious; they are noncommunicable, meaning they do not spread from one person to another. One does not get diabetes, coronary heart disease, cancer, or asthma from others even if there is close physical contact.

Occasionally, some infectious diseases get transmitted from animals to humans. COVID-19 is believed to have originated from animals.

In the following sections, we will discuss common modes of transmission of infectious diseases, which are:

1. Airborne
2. Fecal–oral
3. Vector-borne
4. Sexual contact
5. Blood-borne
6. Physical contact

AIRBORNE TRANSMISSION

Respiratory infections primarily spread through the air. They can be caused by a range of bacteria, viruses, or fungi. Infections that affect the throat or adjacent tissues are known as upper respiratory tract infections (URTI), and infections that involve the lungs are known as lower respiratory tract infections (LRTI). Lower respiratory tract infections can be particularly severe. They cause significant mortality in children and older adults.

Airborne transmission of respiratory pathogens occurs through saliva droplets or aerosols.

Droplets

We release saliva droplets into the air when we talk, cough, or sneeze. Saliva droplets of a person with a respiratory infection can contain pathogens that can infect others who inhale these droplets. Due to their large size, droplets cannot remain suspended in the air for long and usually fall to the ground within a short distance of around 1 meter. Therefore, for droplet transmission to occur, close-range contact between an infected person and a susceptible host is necessary. Settings such as several people living in a small room, school children in a classroom, or crowded public transportation offer favorable conditions for such transmission.

Aerosols

Aerosols are very fine and lightweight respiratory particles that can remain suspended in the air for a considerable time and can travel long distances with wind. Pathogens of TB, chickenpox, and measles can get transmitted through aerosols, although droplet transmission is more common.

Examples of Upper and Lower Respiratory Tract Infections

Common cold, sinusitis, tonsillitis, and pharyngitis are common URTIs. Measles, mumps, rubella, and diphtheria generally start as URTI but can spread to other parts of the body. Measles can spread

DOI: 10.4324/9781032644257-11

to lungs, mumps can cause complications in testes, and diphtheria can cause complications in heart. These diseases commonly affect children, particularly in low-income settings, and have caused many outbreaks and significant mortality in the past. Immunization has played a key role in controlling these infections, and some have been eliminated in developed countries.

Pneumonia and TB are LRTIs. Pneumonia kills a large number of children in low-income countries. In high-income countries, mortality from pneumonia is higher in older people. Fortunately, a vaccine for pneumonia is now available and has been included in immunization programs in many countries. Deaths from pneumonia are expected to reduce in the coming years.

Transmission through Touch

Respiratory infections primarily spread by air, but they can also transmit through touch. When an infected person coughs or sneezes, he may cover his mouth and nose with his hands, contaminating his hands with pathogens. These pathogens can get transferred to objects like doorknobs, electrical switches, and taps. Others who touch these objects can inadvertently transfer the pathogens to their eyes, nose, or mouth and become infected. However, if the pathogens dry out during this chain of events, they may lose their potency. So transmission of respiratory infections through touch should not be common.

Preventing Airborne Transmission

Preventing airborne transmission can be challenging since, in many diseases, people become infectious two to three days before displaying symptoms. This means that an apparently healthy person can be a potential source of infection.

During an outbreak, anyone whose infection status is not known should be considered potentially infected. Wearing face mask reduces the risk of airborne transmission.[1] Both infected and healthy individuals should wear face masks. A minimum distance of 2 meters should be maintained when talking to others, and interactions should be kept brief. Overcrowded places should be avoided to minimize the risk of exposure.

FECAL–ORAL TRANSMISSION

Gastrointestinal tract infections are a major burden in low-income settings. They are transmitted through fecal–oral contamination. Diarrhea, dysentery, typhoid, hepatitis A, and helminthic infestations transmit through the fecal–oral route. Poliomyelitis and cholera also spread in this way, but poliomyelitis has been eliminated from most countries and cholera is largely under control. Fecal–oral transmission occurs when fecal matter of an infected person is inadvertently ingested by another person. This may sound unrealistic, but it is rampant.

People with a gastrointestinal infection have large quantities of pathogens in their feces. In low-income settings, basic hygiene is often compromised. People may not consistently wash their hands after defecation or before handling food and eating meals. This may lead to fecal–oral transmission. Helminthic infestations are common in communities where open defecation is common and people walk barefoot. Additionally, food can become contaminated by exposure to flies or dust.

Example 1

By the early twentieth century, typhoid had virtually disappeared from the West. However, in 1906, a doctor in New York City was surprised to receive several cases of typhoid fever in his clinic within a few weeks. By this time, it was known that typhoid was caused by unhygienic conditions. But these cases had occurred in affluent households, where the likelihood of poor hygiene was expected to be low. Among those affected was the only daughter of a wealthy couple, who succumbed to the illness. Her parents hired a private investigator to find the reason behind this tragedy. The investigator found that the only common factor among the affected families was their cook, Ms. Mary Mallon. Mary was apparently a healthy woman. Although the concept of a healthy carrier[2] was not known at the time, the investigator suspected Mary's role in the outbreak and reported her to the health department. When Mary refused to provide her urine and stool samples for testing, she was arrested and admitted to the Willard Parker Hospital, where lab tests confirmed that her stool was full of typhoid bacteria. However, Mary refused to accept that anything was wrong with her and sued the New York health department, but the case was dismissed by the New York Supreme Court.

Since antibiotics were not available at the time, Mary could not be treated to eliminate her carrier state. Hence, she was forcibly quarantined on North Brother Island, far from the city. Not all medical experts supported the idea of forced isolation, but no new cases of typhoid were reported in the city after her incarceration. After three years, Mary was freed on the condition that she would no longer work as a cook. She started working as a laundress, earning much less than she did as a cook. After some time, she disappeared and could not be traced by health authorities. Some years later, a typhoid outbreak erupted at the Sloane Hospital in New York, affecting 25 people and resulting in two deaths. The same investigator was called in, who found that Mary was working at the hospital as a cook under an assumed identity. Once again suspected as the source of the infection, Mary was deported to the same island, where she remained until her death 23 years later.

Prevention of Fecal–Oral Transmission

Handwashing is the single most important measure to break the chain of fecal–oral transmission. Hands should be washed with soap and running water before handling food or eating meals, after defecation, and after handling dirty objects. Alcohol rub is equally effective. Food and drinking water should be kept covered and protected from dust, insects, and rodents. Food handlers should be particularly careful about personal hygiene. Kitchen cleanliness is important. Western countries have virtually eliminated diarrheal diseases through these measures.

VECTOR-BORNE TRANSMISSION

Vectors are insects that feed on blood and, in this process, transmit pathogens of infectious diseases. Mosquitoes are the most common vectors that transmit numerous diseases. When mosquitoes suck human blood, pathogens are injected into host tissues. Infective female *Anopheles* mosquitoes transmit malaria. Infective female *Aedes* mosquitoes transmit dengue fever, chikungunya, lymphatic filariasis, yellow fever, and Zika. The sand fly transmits leishmaniasis. Ticks transmit rickettsia disease, relapsing fever, tick-borne encephalitis, tularemia, and Lyme disease. Lice can transmit typhus and louse-borne relapsing fever. Tsetse flies transmit sleeping sickness.

Dengue and chikungunya are on the rise in some low-income countries. Lymphatic filariasis is endemic in some parts of the world. Yellow fever and Zika were previously limited to some African countries, but recently a few Zika cases have been reported in other regions. Malaria is declining globally.

Prevention of Vector-Borne Diseases

The discovery of insecticidal properties of dichloro-diphenyl-trichloroethane (DDT) in 1939 played a key role in the control of malaria and other vector-borne diseases during and after the Second World War. DDT was so effective that scientists initially believed it could eradicate malaria. But that did not happen. The vector developed resistance to DDT and malaria bounced back in the 1970s. The fact remains that we can never defeat a disease by chemicals alone.

Since mosquitoes breed in water, eliminating stagnant-water points is the most important strategy to prevent mosquito-borne infections. Unfortunately, this is not always done in low-income settings, where it is common to find stagnant water due to leaking taps, open sewers, or blocked drains. These sites become breeding grounds for mosquitoes. Insecticide-impregnated mosquito nets have been instrumental in reducing malaria in African countries. Installing insect screens on doors and windows, wearing clothes that provide maximum coverage, and applying mosquito repellent to exposed skin also provide some protection. Icaridin, DEET, and IR3535® are some common insect repellents. Insecticidal spray or fog can temporarily reduce mosquito population. This is helpful in controlling outbreaks. But long-term use results in development of resistance in the vector.

SEXUALLY TRANSMITTED INFECTIONS

Sexually transmitted infections (STIs) are reproductive tract infections that result from unprotected sexual intercourse. Many types of bacteria, viruses, and protozoa cause these infections. Chlamydia, trichomoniasis, gonorrhea, syphilis, hepatitis B, genital herpes, HPV, and HIV are some examples of STIs.

An STI transmits through contact with genital mucous membranes during sexual activity or through exchange of semen, vaginal secretions, or blood. Infectious mononucleosis is peculiar in that it can transmit through saliva while kissing.

Unprotected sex with multiple partners increases the risk of acquiring an STI. Certain groups, such as commercial sex workers, truck drivers, and LGBTQIA+ individuals, are considered high risk due to various factors. Anal sex causes minute injuries, increasing the risk of STI. Intravenous drug users who share syringes are at risk of contracting HIV, hepatitis B, and syphilis.

While many STIs can be treated, social stigma, lack of familial support, and poor access to healthcare services prevent people from seeking treatment.

Prevention of Sexually Transmitted Infections

Using a condom, a reliable barrier method for safe sex, and limiting the number of sexual partners can help prevent STIs. Promoting condom use has been an important strategy in HIV/AIDS control programs worldwide.

BLOOD-BORNE TRANSMISSION

Blood-borne transmission can occur through the following routes:

Blood Transfusion

Blood transfusion can be lifesaving in postpartum, intraoperative, or postoperative hemorrhage. When falciparum malaria or dengue causes internal hemorrhage, blood transfusion can save lives. People with blood disorders, such as thalassemia, also require periodic blood transfusions. However, if the donated blood is infected with pathogens of hepatitis B, hepatitis C, HIV, malaria, or syphilis, there is risk of blood-borne transmission. To prevent such transmission, donated blood units are tested for the presence of pathogens before use. Only contamination-free units are used for transfusion and others are destroyed.

Invasive Clinical Procedures

Use of contaminated instruments or needles during a surgical or invasive procedure can transmit infection.

Example 2

In 1989, a young woman named Kimberly Bergalis in Florida, United States, was diagnosed with AIDS. Ms. Bergalis had no history of contact with an HIV-positive person; however, investigators from the Centers for Disease Control and Prevention (CDC) discovered that she had received dental treatment in 1987 from a dentist named Dr. David Acer, who had AIDS. Laboratory tests revealed that the HIV strains of Ms. Bergalis and Dr. Acer were closely related, raising the suspicion that Ms. Bergalis contracted the infection from her dentist. This was a serious concern, as the dentist may have potentially infected other patients. The CDC then contacted all patients of Dr. Acer. Over a thousand people were counseled and tested for HIV, and two more positive cases were found. This raised the alarm that other HIV-positive healthcare professionals could be transmitting the infection to their patients. Extensive investigations followed, but no other such cases were found; the dentist was an exception.

To prevent infection during a surgery or other invasive procedure, service providers use sterile syringes, needles, and surgical instruments. They use no-touch technique[3] to further minimize the risk of contamination.

Mother-to-Child Transmission

A mother who is HIV-positive can pass the infection to her fetus in gestation. Antiretroviral treatment of the mother can prevent such transmission.

TRANSMISSION THROUGH PHYSICAL CONTACT

Diseases such as scabies,[4] ringworm,[5] and lice infestation[6] spread through direct physical contact. They are more common where people share overcrowded housing or live in unhygienic conditions. Head lice affect people who sleep in close proximity or children who play together. Body lice are similar to head lice, but they live on clothing. Pubic lice are found in pubic hair and can be transmitted through sexual contact. Proper personal hygiene and better housing conditions can help prevent these diseases.

NOTES

1. Double- or triple-layered cotton masks that cover the nostrils and mouth are generally effective, provided air passes through those layers only.
2. A healthy carrier is a person who has pathogens in his body but displays no sign or symptom of the disease.
3. In no-touch technique, sterile gloved hands and sterile instruments are not allowed to touch any unsterile object or surface.
4. Scabies is a skin disease caused by the mite *Sarcoptes scabiei.*
5. Ringworm is a skin disease caused by the fungus *Microsporum sp.*, *Trichophyton sp.*, or *Epidermophyton sp.*
6. The scientific name of head louse is *Pediculus humanus capitis.*

10 Natural History of Diseases

Natural history of a disease explains how the disease is expected to progress in a person if no treatment is provided. When HIV was first identified in the 1980s, no one knew how the disease would progress—whether it would subside on its own or become severe or cause death. With no treatments available, scientists learned the natural history of HIV through follow-up of patients. Now, when a person tests positive for HIV, doctors have a fair idea of how the disease is likely to progress. Natural history of HIV tells us that it is a lifelong condition that does not directly harm body organs. Instead, it weakens the immune system, increasing one's susceptibility to other infections like diarrhea, pneumonia, and TB.

Why should we know the natural history of diseases when treatments are available for most diseases? First, the natural history of a disease can tell us whether it will regress on its own or is likely to persist, whether it will cause mild discomfort or become severe, and whether it could lead to organ failure, disability, or death. For instance, we know that common cold is a self-limiting condition that normally subsides in a week without any treatment. In contrast, pneumonia can be fatal if not treated. Second, we can measure the effectiveness of a treatment only if we know how a disease behaves in the absence of treatment. Third, if more than one treatment or therapy is available for a disease, we can compare their relative effectiveness by using the natural history of the disease as a baseline.

It must be remembered that the same disease can manifest differently in people and generate unique responses. But on the whole, diseases tend to follow a pattern, and that is what natural history of diseases is all about.

STAGES OF A DISEASE

Figure 10.1 shows four stages through which an infectious disease commonly proceeds:

1. Biological onset
2. Preclinical stage
3. Clinical stage
4. Outcome

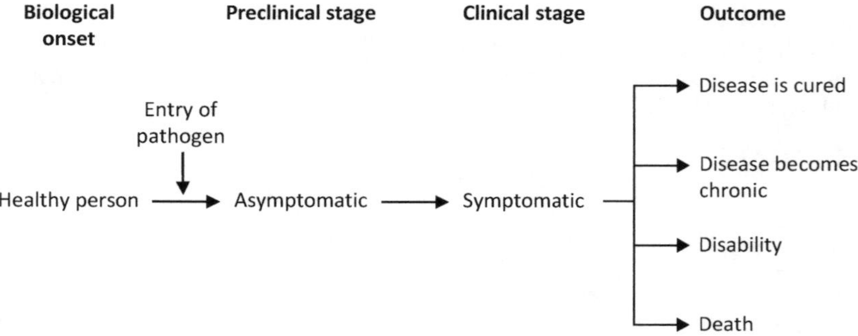

FIGURE 10.1 Natural history of an infectious disease: A schematic diagram.

DOI: 10.4324/9781032644257-12

Biological Onset of Disease

Some diseases or health problems have a clear-cut onset. For example, a case of food poisoning can often be traced back to a specific meal taken at, say, a street stall or a party. However, many health problems arise insidiously, making it difficult to pinpoint exactly when the problem started. People with TB, for instance, may have no clue when and from whom they contracted the infection.

Predicting the onset of noncommunicable diseases (NCDs) is even more difficult. A heart attack, in most cases, occurs suddenly and causes excruciating pain, but these people would not know when the gradual narrowing of their coronary arteries began that eventually led to the attack. Similarly, by the time people learn that they have diabetes or osteoarthritis, the disease process or pathology[1] may have been progressing in their bodies for several years or even decades.

Preclinical Stage

After pathogens of an infectious disease enter a host, it takes some time for the disease to manifest.

The time interval between a pathogen's entry into the host body and the appearance of signs and symptoms of the disease is known as incubation period.

Different diseases have different incubation periods. For example, malaria has an incubation period of around two weeks. Therefore, we can assume that a person who develops fever and tests positive for malaria may have been bitten by an infected female *Anopheles* mosquito around two weeks prior. Diphtheria has an incubation period of two to five days. In contrast, HIV takes considerably longer to manifest. Following unprotected sex with an HIV-positive person, it may take six months to several years for one to develop symptoms. NCDs have even longer latency periods.

Clinical Stage

Clinical stage is when the disease manifests with signs and symptoms. Some diseases begin with mild symptoms and progress to become full-blown or overt. Malaria typically starts with fever. In a day or two, it may progress to high-grade fever with chills and rigor, severe body ache, and extreme weakness. Some patients can bleed from the nose or intestines, and some develop altered sensorium.[2]

Outcome

A disease may culminate in one of the following outcomes:

- Disease is cured: Some diseases regress spontaneously. For example, most cases of acute diarrhea subside on their own without treatment. Of course, dehydration has to be prevented.
- Disease becomes chronic: HIV/AIDS and diabetes are likely to remain lifelong.
- Disability: Leprosy, cataract, and stroke generally result in disability.
- Death: Heart disease, chronic respiratory disease, TB, and dengue hemorrhagic fever cause many premature deaths.

The proportion of people who die from a disease is known as case fatality rate of the disease.

A study found that case fatality rate of TB in India is 12%, which means that nearly 12% of all people who develop TB die from it. Case fatality rate of a disease depends on the virulence of the causative pathogen.

SPECTRUM OF A DISEASE

Within a population, patients of a particular disease can be at different stages of illness. Let us again take the example of TB. At one end of the spectrum can be people who recently contracted the infection but have not yet exhibited symptoms. Others may have mild symptoms such as occasional cough, but are well enough to carry out their daily activities. Then there may be patients with pronounced symptoms such as cough with sputum, fever, weight loss, or weakness and who may not be in a condition to do their usual tasks. Some patients may be bedridden with severe illness and extreme debility. Lastly, there can be moribund cases with complications.

PROGNOSIS

Prognosis refers to predicting the course and outcome of a disease. In case of a young child with an isolated fibula shaft fracture, the prognosis is favorable. If the broken parts of the bone are properly aligned and stabilized for six weeks, they are very likely to join and lead to full recovery.

Prognosis of cancer is often expressed in terms of *five-year survival* or *ten-year survival*. In localized breast cancer, the five-year survival rate is 99%, which means 99% of cases will live for at least five years. After the disease has spread to other organs, five-year survival rate reduces to 27%.

Survival rate of patients with coronary heart disease has been increasing steadily. From this, we can infer that the effectiveness of CHD treatment has been improving over time.

EXAMPLES

A few examples are given here to illustrate how knowledge of the natural history of a disease can help physicians in predicting its prognosis.

Hepatitis B

Hepatitis B, a blood-borne infection, is one of the most common causes of chronic liver disease and liver cancer. The incubation period is generally 30–180 days, with an average of 75 days. While most people with hepatitis B remain symptom-free, a small proportion develop symptoms, such as loss of appetite, weakness, vomiting, and yellow discoloration of skin and urine. Less than 5% of hepatitis B infections culminate in chronic liver disease. Even in chronic stage, some people remain asymptomatic, although they may still be capable of transmitting the virus to others. Worldwide, there is a huge burden of chronic hepatitis B carriers. Around 20%–30% cases of chronic liver disease can end up in acute liver failure or hepatocellular carcinoma, leading to premature death.

From the natural history of hepatitis B, we know that the patient was likely exposed to the virus through an injection, dental procedure, or blood transfusion a few months prior to diagnosis. We can reassure the patient that they have a very high chance of spontaneous recovery, with a small likelihood (around 5%) that the condition will turn chronic. Even if this happens, they may remain symptom-free for years or even decades. There is 1% risk that the disease may progress to liver failure or carcinoma and turn fatal.

Osteoarthritis

Osteoarthritis is a degenerative disorder associated with aging that causes pain and stiffness in joints. From our knowledge of the natural history of osteoarthritis, we can explain to the patient that the disease will progress very slowly and is likely to remain lifelong. In between, there will be natural remissions and exacerbations. Regular exercise or physiotherapy can improve quality of life.

Malaria

When a female *Anopheles* mosquito carrying malaria parasites (*Plasmodium spp.*) bites a human, the parasites are injected into host tissues. Within an hour, the parasites reach the host's liver through blood circulation and start multiplying there. In around two weeks, they mature into large-sized schizonts. The schizonts eventually burst, each releasing thousands of small parasites into peripheral blood, where they invade red blood cells, obtain nutrients from them, and continue to multiply. The affected red blood cells are destroyed in this process. Destruction of a significant number of red blood cells causes symptoms like fever and chills. Every 48 hours, a fresh stream of parasites is released from the liver into peripheral blood, causing spikes of fever. The host's body develops immunity in response to the infection. A strong immune response can kill the parasites and clear the infection. Otherwise, the disease progresses and becomes severe.

Plasmodium is of several types. A *P. vivax* infection classically manifests with fever, chills, and rigor, with temperature spikes on alternate days. In a few days, the liver and spleen become enlarged and tender. A *P. falciparum* infection is more dangerous. In this case, red blood cells infected with the parasite adhere to the inner lining of blood vessels in the brain, kidneys, liver, lungs, and intestines, impairing blood flow. This can lead to multiple organ failure. Fever in *P. falciparum* infection may not follow a pattern, and even patients who seem stable can deteriorate rapidly. Affliction of the brain, known as cerebral malaria, can be fatal. The patient should be closely monitored and readiness of blood transfusion should be ensured.

From the natural history of malaria, we know that a person diagnosed with malaria may have been bitten by an infected mosquito around two weeks prior. Since different malarial parasites have different prognoses and treatments, it is important to identify the specific parasite through a laboratory test. Effective antimalarial treatment is available for each type of parasite, and a majority of cases can be cured. In case of *P. vivax*, relapse can occur, so it is important to complete the full course of treatment.

Poliomyelitis

Poliomyelitis is a viral disease that almost always affects children. The virus multiplies in the child's intestines and passes out through feces. Other children can become infected through fecal–oral transmission. Around 75% of infected children remain asymptomatic and recover spontaneously. The other 25% develop symptoms, such as fever and headache, after an incubation period of seven to ten days. A majority of symptomatic cases also recover spontaneously within a few days. In less than 1% of infected children, the virus enters the spinal cord and damages nerve cells that control certain muscles, resulting in paralysis. Leg muscles are commonly disabled. In many cases, the affected muscles regain strength in subsequent weeks. But if weakness or paralysis persists beyond one month, it is likely to remain lifelong. Reinfection with polio virus virtually does not occur, and death from polio is an exception.

There is no specific treatment for poliomyelitis. When a physician comes across a child diagnosed with polio, she can use her knowledge of the natural history of polio to reassure the family that the child has a very high chance (around 99%) of full recovery without any treatment. The child needs to be closely observed for any difficulties in standing, walking, or running. Even if these issues arise, there is still a good chance of recovery. But if weakness persists beyond a month, the child is likely to remain disabled for life. Apart from this, polio will not harm other organs or tissues. After a few weeks, the child will be free of the infection and is not likely to get it again.

It should be known that infected children can continue to transmit the polio virus through their feces for several weeks after symptoms appear. Therefore, measures should be taken to prevent fecal–oral transmission to other children.

NOTES

1. Pathology refers to the effects of a disease on the structure and functions of body tissues and organs.
2. Altered sensorium refers to changes in brain function, such as disorientation or unconsciousness.

11 Measuring Mortality

How do we measure the health of a population? We do it by assessing the burden of major diseases and the average lifespan of the people. If many people in a population suffer from heart diseases or chronic respiratory diseases, or many children die from pneumonia or diarrhea, or many women die during delivery, this indicates that the population's health status is poor. Note that burden of disease encompasses both morbidity and mortality.

Morbidity is the number of people in a population who experience sickness, injury, or deformity.

Mortality is the number of deaths that occur in a population from disease or injury.

Mortality is relatively easier to measure than morbidity. Crematoriums and burial grounds maintain a record of deaths. Government regulation requires compulsory registration of deaths. Family members of the deceased seek a proper death certificate for legal purposes. So, mortality data is relatively reliable.

Mortality has serious consequences for the family of the deceased, but it also has an impact on the community and country. To know whether the number of deaths in a country is normal or high, we can compare its mortality data with similar data from other countries. For this, we use an indicator known as crude death rate.

CRUDE DEATH RATE

Crude death rate (CDR) is the number of deaths from all causes in a population of 1,000 people in one year.

$$\text{Crude death rate} = \frac{\text{Number of deaths from all causes in a year}}{\text{Mid-year population}} \times 1000$$

In 2022, the United States had a CDR of 10, while India's CDR in the same year was 9.[1] Does this mean that Indians are at a lower risk of dying? Certainly not. The United States has a higher proportion of older people, so naturally there will be more deaths. To compare mortality rates in populations of different sizes or demographic compositions, we need standardized mortality rate. It is explained later in this chapter.

Note that CDR provides an overall estimate of mortality. If we want to know mortality risk for specific groups such as children or mothers, we will need to study mortality rates among neonates, under-five children, and mothers. These are also explained in succeeding sections.

LIFE EXPECTANCY

Life expectancy at birth is the number of years a person is expected to live at the time of birth.

Life expectancy is a highly reliable indicator of a population's health status. Death from old age is a natural phenomenon, but when many people die prematurely from disease or injury, the population's average life expectancy is reduced.

While life expectancy can be determined at any age, life expectancy at birth is the most commonly used indicator in epidemiological studies since it takes into account the risk of death during childhood, which is quite high in low-income countries.

DOI: 10.4324/9781032644257-13

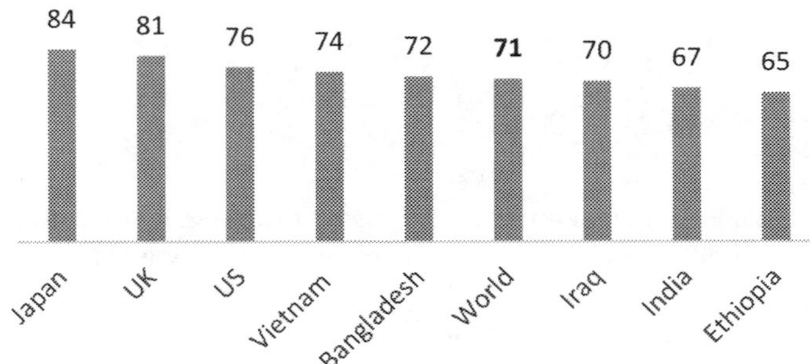

FIGURE 11.1 Average life expectancy at birth in select countries (2021).

Source: https://data.worldbank.org/indicator/SP.DYN.LE00.IN

As Figure 11.1 shows, low-income countries have a considerably lower life expectancy at birth than high-income countries. This is primarily because many young people in these countries die from heart diseases, chronic respiratory diseases, TB, malaria, or injuries, and many children die from pneumonia or diarrhea.

Gender Differentials

Interestingly, women in general live six to eight years longer than men. This could be partly due to women's relatively lower tendency to engage in risk-taking behaviors, as well as their lower rates of smoking and alcohol consumption.

NEONATAL MORTALITY RATE

Neonatal mortality rate (NMR) is the number of deaths of children within the first 28 days of birth per 1,000 live births.

We can see in Figure 11.2 that lower-income countries have higher neonatal mortality. Preterm birth is the leading cause of neonatal mortality worldwide.

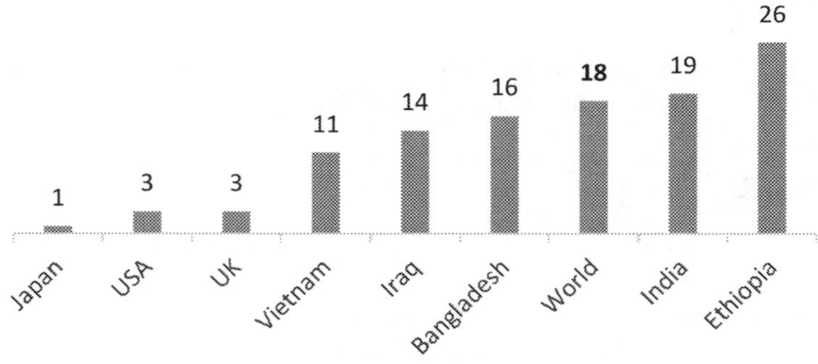

FIGURE 11.2 Neonatal mortality rate in select countries (2021).

Source: https://data.worldbank.org/indicator/SH.DYN.NMRT

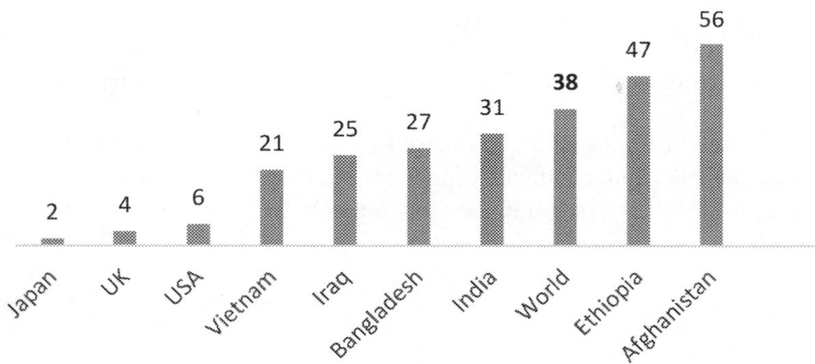

FIGURE 11.3 Under-five mortality rate in select countries (2021).

Source: https://data.worldbank.org/indicator/SH.DYN.MORT

UNDER-FIVE MORTALITY RATE

Under-five mortality rate (U5MR) refers to the number of children who die before reaching the age of five per 1,000 live births. This includes neonatal and infant deaths.

In Figure 11.3, we can see that low-income countries have higher under-five mortality. Pneumonia and diarrhea are leading causes of under-five mortality.

MATERNAL MORTALITY RATIO

Maternal mortality ratio (MMR) is the number of women who die from complications of pregnancy or delivery per 100,000 *live births. This includes deaths that occur during pregnancy, during childbirth, or within 42 days of termination of pregnancy (by delivery or abortion).*

As seen in Figure 11.4, low-income countries experience significantly higher maternal mortality than developed countries. Postpartum hemorrhage is the most common cause of maternal deaths worldwide.

FIGURE 11.4 Maternal mortality ratio in select countries (2020).

Source: https://data.worldbank.org/indicator/SH.STA.MMRT?view=chart

PROPORTIONATE MORTALITY RATIO

Proportionate mortality ratio (PMR) is the proportion of deaths from a given cause.

PMR informs the contribution of various diseases in causing mortality in a population. It tells us which diseases cause a higher number of deaths. For example, in many low-income countries, infectious diseases took maximum toll in the past, but now NCDs account for more deaths. The top ten causes of mortality worldwide are:[2]

1. Ischemic heart disease
2. Stroke
3. Chronic obstructive pulmonary disease
4. Lower respiratory infections
5. Neonatal conditions
6. Trachea, bronchus, lung cancers
7. Alzheimer's disease and other forms of dementia
8. Diarrheal diseases
9. Diabetes
10. Kidney diseases

An understanding of PMR can help in prioritizing public health problems and making budget allocations.

INDICATORS USED BY VARIOUS AGENCIES

The following health indicators are used by various bodies to assess, improve, and rank health status of countries and states:

MILLENNIUM DEVELOPMENT GOALS

In a meeting at the UN headquarters in September 2000, world leaders agreed to adopt eight Millennium Development Goals (MDGs) aimed at reducing extreme poverty and hunger, promoting education, and empowering women. While MDGs 4 and 5 emphasized reducing child mortality and improving maternal health, MDG 6 aimed to combat major diseases like malaria, TB, and HIV.

SUSTAINABLE DEVELOPMENT GOALS

In 2015, the UN General Assembly reviewed countries' progress on MDGs and adopted Sustainable Development Goals (SDGs) 2030, a set of 17 global goals that emphasize social, economic, and environmental equity. Among these, SDG 3 focuses on health and proposes the following targets:

• Neonatal mortality rate	<12 per 1,000 live births
• Under-five mortality rate	<25 per 1,000 live births
• Maternal mortality ratio	<70 per 100,000 live births

The Sustainable Development Report ranks countries on the basis of their achievement of SDGs. In 2023, the top three positions were taken by Finland, Sweden, and Denmark. The United Kingdom ranked 11, and the United Sates 39. India, Ethiopia, and Afghanistan ranked at 112, 141, and 158, respectively, among 163 countries.

Human Development Index

The United Nations Development Program (UNDP) monitors development of countries with a tool called the Human Development Index (HDI). The HDI assesses countries on three parameters: Income, literacy, and health. Health is measured by *life expectancy at birth*. In HDI 2020, India ranked 132 out of 191 countries.

STANDARDIZED MORTALITY RATE

We saw previously that India has a lower CDR than the United States. But this can be misleading as CDR does not take into account the differences in demographic compositions of these countries. For a realistic comparison between two populations, we use age-standardized mortality rate, which adjusts for variations in age distribution between populations by applying age-specific mortality rates of each population to a standard population.

For this purpose, the WHO provides a standard population with predetermined age and sex distribution. We apply age-specific mortality rates of the two populations on the standard population. This provides us expected crude mortality rates for both populations if they have standard age and sex distribution, which can then be compared. This is known as *direct standardization*.

Another method of standardization is *indirect standardization*, where we apply the standard population's age-specific death rates to the populations being compared. Indirect standardization gives more stable results and is more commonly used.

When we use standardized mortality rate to compare mortality rates of India and the United States, we find that India has a higher mortality rate than the United States.

NOTES

1. https://data.worldbank.org/indicator/SP.DYN.CDRT.IN
2. https://www.who.int/news-room/fact-sheets/detail/the-top-10-causes-of-death

12 Measuring Morbidity

As discussed earlier, we need morbidity statistics to plan for healthcare services. How do we quantify a disease in a population? A simple way is to count the number of cases of that disease. For example, in the United States, around 610,000 people have a first-time stroke every year.[1] How can we know whether this is high, normal, or low? We can compare this data with similar data from other countries; however, since countries' populations differ in size, a simple comparison would be meaningless. Therefore, we convert these raw numbers into *rate*.

There is another concern with measuring morbidity: While we want to know the existing number of cases of a disease, we also want to know how many new cases of the disease are added each year. In this context, two measures are used to quantify morbidity:

- Incidence rate
- Prevalence

INCIDENCE RATE

Incidence rate is the number of new cases of a disease appearing in a specified population at risk in a specific time interval.

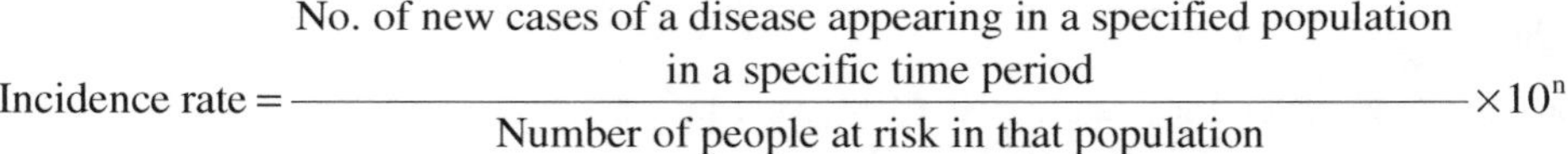

$$\text{Incidence rate} = \frac{\text{No. of new cases of a disease appearing in a specified population in a specific time period}}{\text{Number of people at risk in that population}} \times 10^{n}$$

Note that the denominator in this formula is not the entire population but only the people who are at risk of contracting or developing the disease. For example, to calculate incidence rate of measles in children in a population, the denominator will naturally be the child population and not the entire population. Second, the multiplication factor is 10^n, which means that it can be any multiple of 10, such as 100, 1,000, or 100,000. We choose the multiplication factor based on convention, which generally depends on the burden of the disease under study. For example, malaria is generally expressed as number of cases per 1,000 population. Incidence rate of malaria in Nigeria is 313 new cases per 1,000 people at risk (2020).[2] Birth rate and death rate are also normally expressed as number of births or deaths per 1,000 population. Incidence of leprosy is expressed as number of cases per 10,000 population. Incidence of TB is expressed as number of cases per 100,000 population.

If a population is not stable—that is, if there is significant inward or outward migration or a considerable number of deaths during a given period—the sum of person-years at risk should be taken as the denominator. But this is difficult in practice, so we normally take midyear population (as on July 1) as the denominator.

Incidence rate measures the risk of a disease in a population and informs the speed at which the disease is occurring. It can be used for both acute and chronic diseases.[3] Dengue, typhoid, and Japanese encephalitis are examples of acute infectious diseases. Diabetes, breast cancer, and TB are chronic diseases. Incidence rate of TB in India is 191, compared to 2.2 in the United States.[4] This gives us a fair idea of the magnitude of the problem in India.

Other health-related events, such as road accidents, drowning, or poisoning, can also be expressed in terms of incidence rate. In 2020, incidence rate of fatal road accidents in the United States was 17 per 100,000 licensed drivers, compared to 27 in 1990.[5]

DOI: 10.4324/9781032644257-14

PREVALENCE

Prevalence is the total number of cases of a disease in a specified population at risk at a given time.

Note the difference between incidence and prevalence: While incidence informs the new cases of a disease appearing in a defined time period, prevalence represents all current cases of the disease at a particular point in time, including both existing and new cases.

For the purpose of comparison, prevalence can also be expressed as rate.

$$\text{Prevalence rate} = \frac{\text{Number of cases of a disease in a specified population at a point in time}}{\text{Number of people at risk in the population at that time}} \times 10^{n}$$

Prevalence of a disease depends on its incidence rate and the average duration of illness: If a disease takes a long time to be cured or is incurable, and if its case fatality rate is low, the cases will keep adding up in the population over time, increasing its prevalence. Diabetes is a classic example of this phenomenon. Prevalence of diabetes has been increasing because it continues lifelong for most people and does not directly result in death. In 2014, 8.5% of adults worldwide had diabetes.[6]

While incidence rate can be used for both acute and chronic diseases, prevalence is used only for chronic diseases. For a chronic disease like TB, we would like to know both incidence (number of new cases added each year) and prevalence (total number of cases in the population). On the other hand, acute conditions such as Japanese encephalitis and dengue hemorrhagic fever are expressed only in terms of incidence rate, as there is no question of their prevalence. People affected by these diseases either recover within a few weeks or succumb to the disease; they do not continue to live with the disease for long.

Point Prevalence versus Period Prevalence

If there is an outbreak of jaundice in a hostel with 500 students, it may be possible to examine all 500 students or conduct blood tests for all of them in one to two days. In other words, prevalence of a disease in a small population can be measured at a point in time. This is known as point prevalence. But in a larger population, such as a province or a country, cases will be staggered over several months. In such situations, the total number of cases recorded throughout the calendar year are used to calculate prevalence, with midyear population as the denominator. This is known as period prevalence.

EXAMPLES

Table 12.1 presents the measures used to quantify morbidity for common health problems.

CHALLENGES IN MEASURING MORBIDITY

Measuring morbidity is more challenging than measuring mortality. Where can we get data on heart diseases or leishmaniasis or prostate hypertrophy? Hospitals maintain patient statistics, but not all cases of a disease visit a hospital. Further, it can be challenging for authorities to collect data from numerous hospitals and providers. Despite these constraints, some critical diseases are systematically measured in many countries. Many countries maintain a national cancer registry. Cancer patients are generally diagnosed and treated at cancer hospitals or tertiary care hospitals, which are linked to the cancer registry. This allows for systematic tracking and documentation of cancer cases. Similarly, cases of HIV, TB, and COVID-19 are systematically accounted for due to their significance and impact.

TABLE 12.1
Common Health Problems and Their Morbidity Measures

Health Problem	Incidence Rate	Prevalence Rate
Pneumonia	√	
Diarrhea	√	
Dengue hemorrhagic fever	√	
Malaria	√	
Typhoid	√	
Dog bite	√	
Road accident	√	
Acute myocardial ischemia	√	
Tuberculosis	√	√
Breast cancer	√	
Diabetes		√
Hypertension		√
Obesity		√
Stunting		√
Anemia		√

NOTES

1. https://www.cdc.gov/stroke/facts.htm
2. https://ourworldindata.org/malaria
3. Acute diseases have a sudden onset, and the patient either recovers or succumbs within a short time. Chronic diseases persist for years or even a lifetime.
4. https://www.cdc.gov/tb/statistics/tbcases.htm
5. https://www.statista.com/statistics/191660/fatality-rate-per-100000-licensed-drivers-in-the-us-since-1988/
6. https://www.who.int/news-room/fact-sheets/detail/diabetes

13 Indirect Indicators of Health

As stated in preceding chapters, we can assess the health of a population from its morbidity and mortality statistics. We can also get valuable insights into the health status of a population from certain other indicators. These indicators are particularly important in low-income countries.

FERTILITY-RELATED INDICATOR

Total fertility rate (TFR) is a key indicator of fertility.

Total fertility rate is the average number of children a woman is expected to have in her lifetime.

If TFR of a country is high, its maternal, neonatal, and child health outcomes are likely to be poor. There may be many maternal deaths occurring during childbirth and many children dying at an early age.

NUTRITION-RELATED INDICATORS

If children in a population are undernourished, it is a clear indication of their poor health. Similarly, high prevalence of anemia in adolescent girls reflects their poor health. Many of these children and adolescents will grow into physically weak and vulnerable adults. A large number of obese people in a population is indicative of the population's poor health status. Health indicators used in the context of nutrition are:

- Proportion of children short in height (stunted[1]) compared to most children of their age
- Proportion of children with lower weight (wasted[2]) compared to most children of their height
- Proportion of adolescent girls or reproductive-age women who are anemic
- Proportion of people with obesity

SOCIOCULTURAL INDICATORS

If many girls in a population are married before 18 years of age, they are likely to have poor health outcomes in pregnancy and childbirth. The indicator is:

- Proportion of girls married before 18 years of age

Gender bias also plays a significant role in poor health of girls and women. It contributes to female feticide, which distorts sex ratio. An important indicator of gender bias is:

- Sex ratio at birth

WATER- AND SANITATION-RELATED INDICATORS

If people in an area do not have access to clean drinking water and basic sanitation facilities, they are likely to have poor health. The indicators are:

- Proportion of population not having access to safe drinking water
- Proportion of population not having access to septic latrines

DOI: 10.4324/9781032644257-15

INDICATORS OF HEALTHCARE UTILIZATION

Poor utilization of healthcare services can affect health outcomes. Unvaccinated children are at a higher risk of developing vaccine-preventable diseases. In populations where many deliveries happen at home, maternal mortality will be high. Health indicators in this regard are:

- Proportion of children who are not fully vaccinated
- Proportion of deliveries occurring at home

NOTES

1. Children are defined as stunted if their height-for-age is more than two standard deviations below the WHO Child Growth Standards median.
2. Children are called wasted if their weight-for-height is more than two standard deviations below the WHO Child Growth Standards median.

14 Disease Surveillance

Surveillance refers to monitoring the occurrence of a specific health problem in a specified population. This also involves scrutinizing the factors that influence the occurrence and distribution of that disease.

Surveillance aims to provide early warning about a potential outbreak. This is accomplished by the systematic collection of health-related data, followed by in-depth analysis and interpretation of the data. This allows decision-makers to make prompt interventions when needed. For ground-level surveillance to be effective, healthcare providers must be sensitized to suspect an impending outbreak. They must have access to diagnostic facilities for common diseases. Diseases such as dengue, malaria, typhoid, and cholera can be diagnosed in peripheral facilities. Others require specialized laboratories for diagnosis. There should be a mechanism to transfer samples from peripheral facilities to these laboratories. Additionally, health facilities must have computers and Internet access to rapidly transmit information about an unusual occurrence of a disease to higher authorities. The higher office should then take corrective actions. If needed, they may send a team of experts to assist in diagnosing and managing the outbreak.

Surveillance can be organized in two ways:

- Routine surveillance through existing health information systems (HIS) in hospitals or healthcare systems
- Special surveillance specifically designed to monitor an emerging health problem in an area

ROUTINE SURVEILLANCE

Hospitals and clinics collect patient information on a day-to-day basis. Data generated by outpatient clinics, inpatient wards, operating rooms, delivery rooms, and others is compiled. Monthly statistics are submitted to the district health office. The district health office compiles the information received from all facilities under its jurisdiction and forwards it to the provincial health office, which further processes and transmits the information to the national health ministry.

Hospitals that commonly treat cases of a specific disease are usually the first to detect the appearance of that disease or a sudden surge in the number of cases. Such hospitals are called sentinel centers for that disease. Outbreaks of measles, diphtheria, hepatitis, and HIV are often reported by sentinel centers.

In areas where risk of HIV is high, pregnant women who visit antenatal clinics are routinely tested for HIV. The HIV positivity rate in antenatal women generally reflects the HIV status of the general population. A few decades ago, when the HIV epidemic was at its peak, HIV positivity rate in antenatal women was an important source of information for understanding the burden and trend of HIV infection.

National cancer registries provide information about the number and types of new cancer cases diagnosed in healthcare institutions.

Diarrhea is a common problem in children in low-income settings. However, a sudden surge in the number of diarrhea cases in adults might indicate the start of a cholera outbreak. In such cases, laboratory testing of stool samples should be started without delay.

Surveillance of fatal road accidents over the years informs the trend. Surveillance of environmental factors in specified areas informs air pollution levels as well as the types of primary pollutants. Study of seasonal fluctuations in pollution levels may provide clues about the sources of pollution.

DOI: 10.4324/9781032644257-16

SPECIAL SURVEILLANCE

In some situations, a special surveillance system is set up for a limited period to monitor an emerging health problem. During the COVID-19 pandemic, governments monitored the number and distribution of cases through surveillance systems. Laboratories conducting RT-PCR tests were required to feed data of the total number of tests conducted and positive results to a national portal. This provided authorities with real-time information on positivity rate, distribution of cases, and trend of the disease. Hospitals closely monitored and reported the proportion of cases that became severe or resulted in death. International travelers were tested to identify potential sources of infection.

In times of famine, a surveillance system may have to be set up to monitor the nutritional status of children in the affected area. Similarly, during floods, drinking water should be tested periodically.

Section III

Applied Epidemiology

15 Screening of Diseases

Screening is the process of identifying undetected cases of a disease in a population.

THE ICEBERG PHENOMENON

Normally, only a fraction of sick people seek treatment from formal healthcare facilities. There can be several reasons for this. In the case of diabetes, for example, many people may be unaware of their condition because they never had their blood sugar levels tested. Others may find it difficult to accept their diagnosis, or try home remedies, or seek help from unqualified or traditional practitioners. Yet others may not have access to proper treatment. As a result, local health authorities may not know about these *hidden* cases of diabetes. In public health, this is known as the *iceberg phenomenon*. Similar to an iceberg, where only a small part is visible above the water surface while the larger part remains submerged posing a threat to ships, hidden cases of a disease in a population can be problematic. Their condition may worsen over time, reducing their productivity and burdening their families and the country's healthcare system. If the disease is infectious, it can spread to others. This is where disease screening becomes crucial.

CRITERIA FOR SCREENING

Due to the costs involved, it is not feasible to conduct large-scale screening for every disease. Then which diseases should be screened? Health authorities use the following criteria to prioritize diseases for screening:

Burden of Disease

If the disease causes significant morbidity, mortality, or disability in a population, and if there are indications of many hidden cases in the community, screening can be useful.

Example 1

In India, cervical cancer is the second most common cancer in women and is a leading cause of cancer-related deaths. However, a large number of women with cervical cancer do not seek treatment, either due to ignorance or due to limited access to healthcare services. Many women feel uncomfortable discussing the problem or undergoing a clinical examination. As a result, many cases of cervical cancer remain undiscovered. This makes cervical cancer a candidate for screening.

Natural History of the Disease

Screening is possible only if there is a significant time interval between the onset of a disease and the disease becoming clinically overt. This allows for timely detection and treatment.

Example 2

Breast cancer is the most common cancer in women globally. It starts as a small nodule or lump in the breast that grows insidiously over several years without causing any pain. As a result, many women fail to seek treatment during this stage. After several years, the lump may burst,

DOI: 10.4324/9781032644257-18

causing a wound. Many women seek treatment at this stage, but it is too late as the disease may have spread to other parts of the body, making it difficult to treat. In some developed countries, women aged 45 years and above are advised to undergo periodic mammography screening for breast cancer. Those diagnosed with the disease are provided treatment. Early treatment of breast cancer has a better outcome. Early diagnosis and treatment of a disease is known as *secondary prevention*. It is explained in the chapter "Disease Prevention."

Screening is not normally possible for acute diseases as they appear without warning and progress rapidly. Malaria is a good example. It may present with a sudden onset of fever and body ache. Depending on the type of pathogen, the host's immune response, and the treatment provided, the disease may be cured, become complicated, or result in death. All this happens within a few weeks. Events move so fast, there is barely any time for screening. Therefore, screening is not practically possible for acute diseases like malaria, typhoid, acute pancreatitis, and Japanese encephalitis.

Screening Test

Screening is possible only when a simple and cost-effective diagnostic test is available that can be used on a large scale.

Example 3

Anemia is widespread in low-income countries, yet a majority of the affected people remain unaware of their condition. Anemia can be detected by a simple blood test that measures blood hemoglobin levels. Portable digital hemoglobinometers are now available, enabling convenient door-step assessment. The cost of diagnostic strips for these devices is currently a limiting factor, but they may become affordable in the coming years.

Treatment

There is no point in screening for a disease if we cannot treat the identified cases. For example, anemia can be effectively treated at scale with iron-folic acid (IFA) tablets and deworming tablets. Thus, the availability of a simple and affordable remedy makes anemia a suitable candidate for screening. Let us take another example.

Example 4

Sore throat is a common illness in children. In some cases of repeated infection with *Streptococcus pyogenes*, the child's immune system responds aggressively, causing damage to the heart valves and leading to rheumatic heart disease. While the child's sore throat heals in a week or two, her heart valves may remain permanently impaired. With reduced heart capacity, the child experiences dyspnea (breathlessness) on running or exertion.

A physician can suspect rheumatic heart disease by auscultating heart sounds with a stethoscope. An echocardiography (ultrasound of the heart) can confirm the diagnosis, but this requires access to a tertiary-level hospital. Further, although heart valve defects can be corrected by surgery, the procedure is expensive and is typically available only in tertiary care hospitals. Therefore, despite the need to screen children in low-income settings for rheumatic heart disease, screening is not done as the treatment is not easily accessible. As a result, many children in low-income countries continue to live with rheumatic heart disease.

APPROACHES TO SCREENING

Mass Screening

Mass screening is useful for health issues with a high prevalence, such as anemia in adolescent girls and women in low-income settings.

Targeted Screening

If a problem is localized to a specific group, screening can be focused on that group. For example, breast cancer screening can be focused on women aged 45 years and above. Professionals in sedentary IT jobs can be screened for backache. Targeted screening is more cost-effective.

Opportunistic Screening

People who visit a clinic or hospital for routine treatment can be screened for common diseases. Adult patients visiting medical OPDs are often screened for hypertension and diabetes. Women visiting antenatal clinics are screened for anemia and HIV. In pediatric OPDs, children are screened for growth faltering and vaccination.

COMMON SCREENING PROGRAMS

Screening of School Children

Many schools organize screening for common health problems like dental caries and vision defects. Every child is examined once a year by a doctor or a trained nurse. If a problem is identified, appropriate medical advice is given to the parents.

Screening of Preschool Children

In countries where undernutrition is rampant, community health workers screen preschool children for growth faltering. A health worker measures the height and weight of all children in her assigned area and records this information on a prescribed card. Children found to have any deficiencies are referred for supplementary nutrition.

Screening for Cancer

Screening for breast cancer can reduce mortality from breast cancer. The United States Preventive Services Task Force recommends that women aged 50–74 years undergo mammography every two years. In low-income settings, cervical cancer can be screened by visual inspection with acetic acid or by PAP smear.

Screening for Osteoporosis

Osteoporosis, a common problem of old age, increases the risk of fractures. A bone scan can be used to diagnose osteoporosis, but it is generally available at specialized hospitals. This makes large-scale screening unfeasible in low-income settings. In developed countries, women over 65 are recommended to undergo regular bone density testing. Those identified with osteoporosis are advised to take calcium and vitamin D supplements.

Screening for Diabetes and Hypertension

Some hospitals and NGOs organize screening camps in residential areas to identify older people with high blood pressure or high blood sugar. Early treatment of hypertension is known to reduce the risk of coronary heart disease and stroke. Similarly, early treatment of diabetes can reduce the risk of vascular and neurological complications.

Screening for Cataract

Cataract is a common cause of blindness in low-income countries. People in remote areas are often unaware that cataract can be treated by a simple surgery. In some countries, charitable eye hospitals and NGOs organize cataract screening programs in villages, targeting older individuals. Ophthalmic assistants or health workers are trained to examine eye lenses with a torch to identify opacity, a key feature of cataract. They conduct doorstep visits to reach people who may not have access to health facilities. Those found to have cataract are referred for surgery at an eye hospital in a nearby city. Some organizations also provide transportation to the patients.

Newborn Screening

In the United States, infants are screened for birth defects such as hypothyroidism, phenylketonuria, and sickle cell anemia. In low-income countries, newborns are screened for low birth weight.

16 Disease Prevention

Public health's thrust is on prevention of diseases, injuries, and disabilities. The worldwide eradication of smallpox and, more recently, the elimination of poliomyelitis from most countries are classic examples of disease prevention. Measles, mumps, rubella, and diphtheria are virtually eliminated from developed countries. Maternal and neonatal tetanus, yaws, and Guinea worm disease (dracunculiasis) have also been eliminated from many developing countries.

Both infectious diseases and noncommunicable diseases (NCDs) can be prevented through public health interventions.

Example 1

Earlier, automobile accidents took a heavy toll globally. In 1983, the United Kingdom passed a law mandating the use of seat belts in cars, which led to a drastic reduction in fatalities from car accidents. The scientific evidence provided by the United Kingdom encouraged many other countries to replicate the intervention. Thus, a simple intervention now prevents hundreds of thousands of deaths worldwide. This is the power of prevention.

At what stage can a disease be prevented? Is it necessary to make the intervention before the disease or injury occurs? Interventions made before the onset of a health problem will undoubtedly have greater impact; however, measures can be taken at any stage of a disease to reduce or prevent harm—it is never too late. Disease prevention can be done at four levels:

- Primary
- Secondary
- Tertiary
- Primordial

PRIMARY PREVENTION

As the name suggests, primary prevention is undertaken before a disease or injury occurs. This involves one or more of the following strategies:

Eliminating the Source of Infection

Diarrheal diseases are caused by intake of contaminated food or water. Ensuring food and water hygiene can help prevent these diseases. Rodents are reservoirs of plague, and controlling their population helps prevent outbreaks. This can be done by ensuring basic sanitation in kitchens, homes, and restaurants; closing rodent hideouts; covering sewer holes and drains; and clearing municipal waste regularly.

Reducing Transmission

Proper handwashing is key to preventing fecal–oral transmission. Use of face masks and social distancing can help prevent airborne transmission of respiratory infections. Use of condom can prevent STIs. Insecticide-treated bed nets reduce transmission of malaria.

DOI: 10.4324/9781032644257-19

Strengthening Host Immunity

Certain diseases can be prevented by strengthening the host's immune system. Similarly, immunization is vital in preventing vaccine-preventable diseases. Early initiation of breastfeeding gives newborns immunity against several diseases. Adequate nutrition helps maintain immunity in children.

Preventing Exposure to Risk Factors

Many NCDs can be prevented by avoiding exposure to their risk factors. Adopting a low-fat diet, proper management of hypertension and diabetes, and regular exercise can reduce the risk of coronary heart disease. Abstinence from smoking reduces the risk of lung cancer.[1]

Preventing Physical Injury

Use of helmet and seat belt can prevent head injuries and other serious injuries in road accidents. Avoiding recapping of needles and using auto-disable syringes can protect healthcare workers from needle-prick injuries. In factories, installing safety devices in machines can protect workers from injuries.

SECONDARY PREVENTION

What can we do if a disease has already occurred? We can slow down or stop its progression through early diagnosis and treatment. This is known as the secondary level of disease prevention.

Secondary prevention can prevent complications, disability, or death. In case of infectious diseases, it can prevent transmission to others. However, note that secondary prevention is only possible for diseases that can be diagnosed early by a simple test and for which effective treatment is available.

Example 2

Hypertension is a risk factor for coronary heart disease and stroke, particularly in middle-aged and older adults. However, many people are unaware of their high blood pressure. Screening of at-risk age groups can help identify hidden cases of hypertension in communities. Blood pressure can be easily measured using a simple blood pressure apparatus, and those diagnosed with hypertension can be prescribed anti-hypertensive medicines and advised to undergo periodic check-ups. They can be educated on the benefits of weight control, physical exercise, and low-fat diet. Early diagnosis and treatment of hypertension can significantly reduce the risk of CVDs.[2] Similar secondary prevention programs can be useful for other NCDs such as dental caries, diabetes, breast cancer, and cervical cancer.

Example 3

Leprosy is an infectious disease that begins with one or more white patches on the skin. As these patches do not cause pain or itching, many people do not take them seriously. Social stigma further prevents people from accepting that they could have leprosy. In the absence of treatment, the disease continues to progress, damaging nerves and causing limb deformity and disability. It may spread to others. In leprosy-endemic areas, health workers conduct doorstep screening to identify people with white skin patches or limb deformities. They are able to identify most cases of leprosy by inspection. For confirmation, a sample of skin smear is collected at the doorstep and sent for testing at the district hospital laboratory. Confirmed cases are provided treatment.

Leprosy is curable, and its early detection and treatment can prevent complications and transmission to others. Other common infectious diseases like malaria, typhoid, and TB can also be controlled through secondary prevention.

TERTIARY PREVENTION

If a disease has progressed considerably and has resulted in disability, can something still be done? Tertiary prevention aims to reduce the impact of disability caused by stroke, cataract, arthritis, and other diseases. People with stroke-related disability can benefit from physiotherapy. Surgery can help restore vision in cataract, and knee-replacement surgery can help people with severe knee arthritis.

Where disability cannot be reduced or eliminated, rehabilitation can help the person gain some level of independence and lead a productive life. People with irreversible blindness can be provided with aids such as white cane for walking and braille for reading. Those with an interest in music or art can be given training to excel in their area of interest and improve their quality of life.

PRIMORDIAL PREVENTION

Recall that primary prevention aims to *control* the causative agent or risk factors of a disease. Primordial prevention comes a step before primary prevention. Taking a proactive approach, it focuses on *preventing* the emergence of these risk factor(s) in a community.

Although primordial prevention precedes all other types of disease prevention, in this chapter we have changed the sequence and presented the more familiar terms first.

Example 4

Colorectal cancer is the third leading cause of cancer deaths in the United States. Obesity, physical inactivity, and overdependence on processed meat in diet are some of the risk factors. In contrast, India has a relatively low risk of colorectal cancer. This is likely due to the cultural practice of consuming freshly prepared homemade meals and a relatively lower consumption of processed meats. But with changing dietary habits, the risk of colorectal cancer is rising in India. How can this be stopped?

Primordial prevention can help prevent the development of risk factors for colorectal cancer in India. People can be educated to lead a physically active life, maintain their body weight, and continue their traditional dietary habits, particularly the practice of consuming fresh, homemade meals. Harmful consequences of consuming processed or preserved foods can be explained. These efforts can reduce the emergence of risk factors for colon cancer to some extent.

In the United States, where risk factors for colorectal cancer already exist, people can be educated to avoid those risk factors. That would be primary prevention.

NOTES

1. Despite a significant reduction in cigarette smoking in many countries, evidence of reduction in incidence of lung cancer is yet to be established. This could be an interesting area for research.
2. Remember, cardiovascular diseases include coronary heart diseases and stroke.

17 Epidemiological Study Designs
An Introduction

To control an infectious disease, we need to know its cause(s), source(s), mode(s) of transmission, and treatment options. In case of NCDs, we should at least know the risk factor(s). Epidemiological studies, also known as epidemiological methods, are used to investigate such matters. They are also used to assess the safety and efficacy of medicines and vaccines.

Additionally, epidemiological studies can evaluate the effectiveness of public health programs and preventive interventions. For example, in developed countries, older women are advised to undergo periodic mammograms for early detection of breast cancer. However, repeated mammography carries the risk of radiation. Through epidemiological studies, it was determined that the benefits of reducing breast cancer deaths far exceeded the risks of radiation exposure. Therefore, periodic mammography continues to be recommended as a preventive measure for breast cancer.

There are broadly two types of epidemiological studies: Observational and experimental. In an experimental study, the researcher, or investigator, makes an intervention and measures its effects on the health of participants. In observational studies, the investigator does not make any intervention. Instead, she makes interpretations by carefully observing the existing situation.

Figure 17.1 illustrates common epidemiological study designs.

Observational studies can be descriptive or analytical. In a descriptive study, the investigator examines the distribution of a disease in terms of person, place, and time to identify factors that are consistently associated with the disease and may have a role in causing it. Cross-sectional and ecological studies are the two common types of descriptive studies. While cross-sectional studies measure prevalence of diseases, ecological studies examine the impact of environmental factors on health. The unit of study in ecological studies is the *community* rather than the *individual.*

Once a descriptive study has identified an association between a factor and a disease, an analytical study goes a step further by measuring the strength of this association. This helps us to know whether the identified factor could be a cause of the disease.

Case-control and cohort studies are the two main types of analytical studies. A case-control study is retrospective, meaning it examines historical data to determine if cases of a disease were exposed to a suspected risk factor. Cohort studies are prospective—they follow healthy individuals over a period of time to see if those who were exposed to the suspected risk factor go on to develop the disease under study.

These study designs are explained further in succeeding chapters.

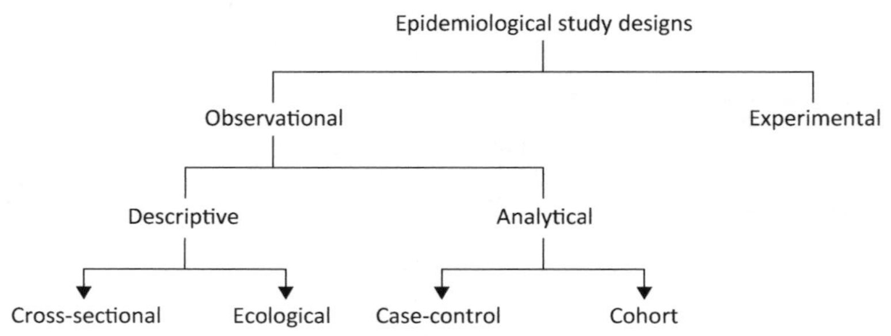

FIGURE 17.1 Epidemiological study designs.

DOI: 10.4324/9781032644257-20

18 Descriptive Study

Descriptive study is the most common method of epidemiological research. These studies have been instrumental in discovering the causes of diseases, solving public health mysteries, and formulating research questions. In this study design, investigators try to identify factors that are consistently associated with a disease. With this intent, they examine the situation from three angles:

- Person
- Place
- Time

PERSON

The investigator examines people having the disease to understand how they differ from others. Factors such as age, sex, socioeconomic status, lifestyle, immunization status, recent travel, and any new exposure may provide vital clues. For example, if an outbreak has mainly affected children, the investigator thinks of diseases that primarily afflict children, such as Japanese encephalitis, poliomyelitis, measles, mumps, or diphtheria. If the affected people recently traveled overseas, the investigator rules out any link to major outbreaks in other countries. If the affected people have multiple sex partners, a sexually transmitted disease is suspected. If obese or older adults are mostly affected, they are investigated for NCDs.

PLACE

The investigator tries to find out where the affected people may have contracted the disease. Was there exposure to an agent or a risk factor? With this intent, the investigator examines the places where the affected individuals live, work, study, or visit. For example, if they work in mines or factories, suspicion goes to occupational hazards. If they consumed food at the same party, feast, or restaurant, a foodborne disease is suspected. If residents of a locality are affected regardless of their age, sex, or lifestyle, a local factor such as water contamination or mosquitoes could be responsible. Geographical distribution of the disease may also give some clues about its origin.

TIME

When did the affected people get the disease? How did the events unfold? How fast did the disease spread? If families are affected, were all members affected at the same time or one after another? In the former scenario, the entire family may have been infected by a common source. In the latter, the infection may have spread from one family member to another.

Thus, by in-depth examination of person-place-time, the investigator tries to identify any common factors among the affected people that are absent in healthy people. This is done with the assumption that these factors may have some role in causing the disease. The following example further illustrates this point.

Example 1

In 1854, a cholera outbreak in London caused more than 500 deaths. At that time, it was not known what cholera was or how it was caused. In fact, microorganisms had not yet been discovered.

DOI: 10.4324/9781032644257-21

To find the cause of the illness, a local physician named Dr. John Snow studied the situation in detail and analyzed it in terms of person-place-time.

Person: Dr. Snow found that people of all ages and backgrounds were affected. He also found that these individuals had not eaten at a common place, and there had been no feast or celebration around that time. This ruled out the possibility of a foodborne infection.

Place: Dr. Snow created a map of the area, marking roads, buildings, community resources, and open spaces. He then marked the homes of the affected people. In those days, there was no direct water supply to homes. People took water from the community water pump in their area. Dr. Snow observed that the affected houses were clustered around a single water pump located on Broad Street. People living near other water pumps were mostly unaffected.

Time: Most people had fallen ill within a short period, and in most cases, family members were all affected at the same time.

So what was common among the people who had taken ill? Dr. Snow found that they all consumed water from the same water pump. He could not identify any other common factor. This led him to conclude that water from the Broad Street pump was the likely cause of the illness. At a time when the existence of microorganisms was still unknown to humankind, this was a major breakthrough in understanding the causation of diseases.

Here, two questions arise. First, why did people suddenly fall ill after years of drinking water from the same water pump? Second, how could water from one particular pump cause the illness when all pumps drew water from the same river, the Thames? While these questions remained unanswered at the time, it was later realized that the outbreak had occurred shortly after sewage from the city was released directly into the Thames. However, only the Broad Street water pump was affected because it was located downstream from the point of contamination, while the other pumps were located upstream.

Thus, careful examination of person, place, and time by Dr. John Snow led to the discovery of the cause of the outbreak, which was later named *cholera*.

A distinct advantage of descriptive studies is that they can be conducted quickly. As seen in the above example, a single investigator completed the study in a short time. Further, since no interventions are made, the cost remains low. However, a downside of descriptive studies is that, with no comparison group involved, a cause-and-effect relationship is not established. In the above example, Dr. Snow's study found that the people who took ill had consumed water from a particular pump. That is to say, the illness was associated with consumption of water from a particular pump. However, we cannot say with certainty that the illness was caused by the water from that pump.

Next, we briefly discuss the two types of descriptive study designs.

CROSS-SECTIONAL STUDY

A cross-sectional study, also known as a prevalence study, provides a snapshot of the prevalence of a disease at a specific point in time. In other words, it determines how many people in a specified population are currently suffering from a disease and how many are exposed to a suspected agent or risk factor. For example, if we want to know the prevalence of chronic kidney disease among diabetics or the prevalence of hepatitis B infection among intravenous drug users, a cross-sectional study is an option.

Example 2

A cross-sectional study was conducted to measure the prevalence of dental caries in school children (disease) and to know whether the problem was associated with eating chocolate (exposure). A dentist examined the students and recorded their history of eating chocolate. Among students who were found to have dental caries, some ate chocolates regularly, while others did not eat chocolates. Similarly, among the students who did not have dental caries, some ate chocolates regularly and others did not eat chocolates. Figure 18.1 depicts this scenario.

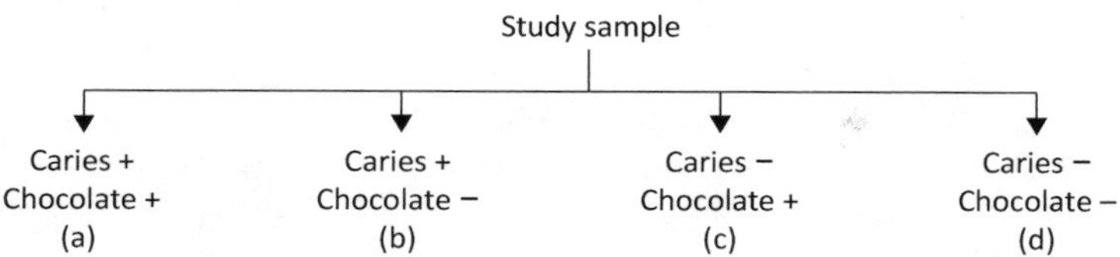

FIGURE 18.1 Cross-sectional study of dental caries in school children.

TABLE 18.1
A 2 × 2 Table Depicting Findings of a Cross-Sectional Study of School Children

		Dental Caries	
		Present	**Absent**
Chocolate consumption	Yes	a	c
	No	b	d

These findings are presented in Table 18.1.

$$\text{Prevalence of dental caries among all students} = \frac{a+b}{a+b+c+d}$$

To know whether the problem is associated with eating chocolate, we calculate the prevalence of dental caries in two groups: Students who ate chocolates regularly (exposed group) and students who did not eat chocolates (unexposed group). Comparing the two values will tell us whether there is an association between eating chocolate and dental caries.

$$\text{Prevalence of disease in exposed group} = \frac{a}{a+c}$$

$$\text{Prevalence of disease in unexposed group} = \frac{b}{b+d}$$

Let us assume that $\frac{a}{a+c} = \text{x}$ and $\frac{b}{b+d} = \text{y}$.

If x clearly exceeds y, we can interpret that children who eat chocolate regularly have a higher prevalence of dental caries. However, this does not establish regular chocolate consumption as a cause of dental caries. This is because we do not know whether the affected children developed dental caries after they started eating chocolate or if they had the problem already. In other words, we do not know the temporal relationship between the exposure and the disease.

ECOLOGICAL STUDY

An ecological study is a descriptive study where the unit of study is the community and not the individual. Health consequences of environmental factors like air pollution are mostly examined through ecological studies.

Example 3

For good dental and skeletal health, drinking water should have an optimum level of fluoride. In the 1940s, water of the Hudson River in the United States was found to be deficient in fluoride. Two cities in New York State, Kingston and Newburgh, sourced their water from the Hudson. To address the problem, the authorities decided to add fluoride to the municipal water supply. However, since excess fluoride in drinking water can also be harmful, a study was undertaken to test the impact of the intervention. At the start of the study, school children in both cities were clinically examined for tooth decay, and its prevalence was found to be similar in both groups. Starting 1945, fluoride was introduced into the municipal water supply of Newburgh. When school children in both cities were examined again after ten years, the prevalence of tooth decay, missing teeth, and filled teeth was found to be nearly twice as high in Kingston compared to Newburgh. Further, investigators found no adverse effects of fluoride among school children in Newburgh. Therefore, it was concluded that adding fluoride to drinking water in areas where water is deficient in fluoride can reduce tooth decay.

This is an example of a study that is both experimental and ecological. It is ecological because the unit of investigation is the population and not individual participants—we do not have information regarding individual consumption of fluoridated water; only population-level data is available.

Similar to cross-sectional studies, ecological studies do not establish a true association between cause and effect. Nevertheless, they can suggest areas for further research that may provide more conclusive evidence.

19 Case-Control Study

A case-control study is an analytical study. It is undertaken when we want to measure the strength of association between a known risk factor and a disease. This is a step toward understanding the risk factor's role in causing the disease.

As the name suggests, in this study, we take two groups of people—cases and controls—and compare their respective histories of exposure to the suspected risk factor. Cases are people who have the disease under investigation. Controls are people who are similar to the cases but do not have the disease. Through in-depth interviews, we examine the participants' exposure to the suspected risk factor during a specified time period in the past. Then we compare the findings from both groups.

Figure 19.1 shows two groups of a case-control study. Within each group, some people have a history of exposure to the suspected risk factor and others do not.

Example 1

During 1959–60 in Germany, an unusually high number of children were born with limb deformities. A descriptive study was undertaken to find the cause. Investigators conducted in-depth interviews with mothers of the affected children, examining person-place-time characteristics such as their age, education, income, occupation, medical history, lifestyle, place and time of delivery, and places where they lived, worked, and visited. As they looked for commonalities among the women, they found that 41 of the 46 women whose babies had deformities had taken a painkiller called thalidomide during their pregnancy. In those days, thalidomide was commonly prescribed for morning sickness. Thus, this study established an association between birth deformities and intake of thalidomide during pregnancy.

To determine the strength of this association, the study was continued as a case-control study. A second group of women were recruited as the control group. These were mothers who had given birth to healthy babies in the same region during the same period. Interviews revealed that only one of the 50 women in this group had taken thalidomide during her pregnancy. The findings are summarized in Table 19.1, where thalidomide intake is the *exposure*.

To measure the strength of association between an exposure and a disease, we calculate odds ratio.

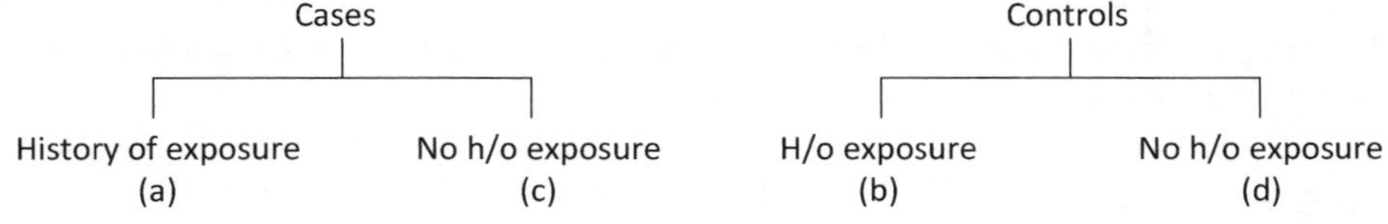

FIGURE 19.1 Case-control study design.

TABLE 19.1
A 2 × 2 Table Depicting Exposure in a Case-Control Study

		Cases	Controls
History of exposure	**Yes**	41 (a)	1 (b)
	No	5 (c)	49 (d)

DOI: 10.4324/9781032644257-22

ODDS RATIO

Odds ratio is a measure that compares the odds (likelihood) of exposure among cases to the odds of exposure among controls. Let us calculate odds ratio for the data in Table 19.1.

$$\text{Odds Ratio} = \frac{a}{c} \div \frac{b}{d} = \frac{\text{ad}}{\text{bc}}$$

Out of 46 cases, 41 had exposure and 5 did not.

$$\text{Therefore, odds of exposure among cases} = \frac{41}{5}$$

Out of 50 controls, 1 had exposure and 49 did not.

$$\text{Therefore, odds of exposure among controls} = \frac{1}{49}$$

$$\text{Odds Ratio} = \frac{\text{Odds of exposure among cases}}{\text{Odds of exposure among controls}} = \frac{41/5}{1/49}$$

$$= 401$$

An odds ratio of 1 means that there is no association between the exposure and the disease. An odds ratio of greater than 1 indicates a positive association, and an odds ratio of less than 1 implies a negative association.

In the above example, an odds ratio of 401 means that the cases were 401 times more likely than controls to have had exposure (i.e., thalidomide intake). This odds ratio is exceptionally high and suggests a strong association between thalidomide intake and birth deformities.

Subsequent to this study, thalidomide was withdrawn from Germany and other countries. Thereafter, no similar cases of birth deformity were reported in the region, which further strengthened the possibility of a causal relationship between thalidomide intake and birth deformity.

An advantage of case-control studies is that they can be taken up even for rare diseases. No matter how rare the disease, if some cases are available, a case-control study can be conducted. Even if cases are scattered in different locations or occurred at different points in time, a case-control study can still be designed. However, a key challenge in these studies is to find controls who are similar to the cases but do not have the disease. We will have to match them for age, sex, education, economic status, lifestyle, and more. Even with the best possible matching, some unknown characteristics may still remain unmatched.

Example 2

Till the early twentieth century, lung cancer was extremely rare worldwide. In the 1930s, a renowned American surgeon named Dr. Alton Ochsner observed a sudden increase in lung cancer cases in his practice. From history of his patients, Dr. Ochsner found that virtually all his lung cancer patients had been heavy smokers. This led him to suspect that cigarette smoking might have something to do with lung cancer. But this was an informal observation; evidence was needed to show that cigarette smoking was causing lung cancer.

Years later, in 1947, British researchers Richard Doll and Bradford Hill conducted a case-control study to investigate the causes of lung cancer. They identified lung cancer patients in 20 hospitals and selected control patients from the same hospitals who were similar to the cases but did not have lung cancer. Through in-depth interviews, they found that the cases were mostly heavy smokers, while smoking was less common among the controls. Their analysis yielded an exceptionally high odds ratio of 20, which suggested a strong association between cigarette smoking and lung cancer. There are not many examples of such a high odds ratio in public health. This finding led to the recognition of tobacco smoking as a serious health hazard and a risk factor for lung cancer.

To summarize, in a case-control study, we form two groups and compare their histories of exposure to a suspected risk factor. The resulting odds ratio informs us how strongly the risk factor is associated with the disease.

While a case-control study begins with people who have the disease, a cohort study starts with healthy individuals, as we will see in the next chapter.

20 Cohort Study

A cohort is a group of people with similar characteristics. A cohort study is an analytical study in which a group of healthy people are followed up over time—generally for years or decades—to see if they will develop the disease under study. Within this cohort, some people have exposure to the suspected risk factor and others do not. For example, if smoking is the suspected risk factor, study participants should include both smokers and nonsmokers. Also note that exposure to the risk factor occurs naturally; the investigator has no role in causing it. However, she is aware who all in the group are exposed. Over a period of time, some members of the cohort may develop the disease. By comparing the incidence of disease among exposed and nonexposed participants, we can know whether the risk factor is associated with the disease.

It should be noted that at the start of a cohort study, no one in the cohort has the disease. Some members are expected to develop the disease in future. Therefore, cohort studies are also called prospective studies.[1]

This study design is particularly suitable for diseases with a high incidence—of course, only then can we expect some of the exposed individuals to develop the disease.

Cohort studies have played an important role in identifying risk factors for various NCDs. The Framingham study is a classical cohort study that will help you understand this study design.

FRAMINGHAM STUDY

In the early twentieth century, cardiovascular disease (CVD) was surging in the United States and Europe, but its cause remained unknown. In 1948, a cohort study was commissioned in Framingham, Massachusetts, to investigate the cause. Over 5,000 healthcare professionals aged 30–65 years, including doctors and nurses, were enrolled for the study. Before enrollment, each participant's detailed medical history was taken, followed by a physical examination and laboratory tests. Only those without any evidence of heart disease or stroke were included in the study. Lifestyle factors such as smoking, alcohol consumption, and dietary habits were also documented. The participants were then followed up through the same process of interviews, physical examinations, and laboratory tests every three to five years.

Eventually, some members of the cohort developed CVD. Researchers investigated what was common among these people and how they differed from others who did not get the disease. It was found that many of those who developed CVD were smokers, obese, hypertensive, or habitual of consuming high-lipid foods.

Popularly known as the Framingham Heart Study, this was a landmark study that identified the risk factors for CVD. Interestingly, the study is still ongoing. The cohort was expanded twice to include children and then grandchildren of the original participants. Thus, three generations are now part of the study.

Figure 20.1 shows the analysis plan of a cohort study.

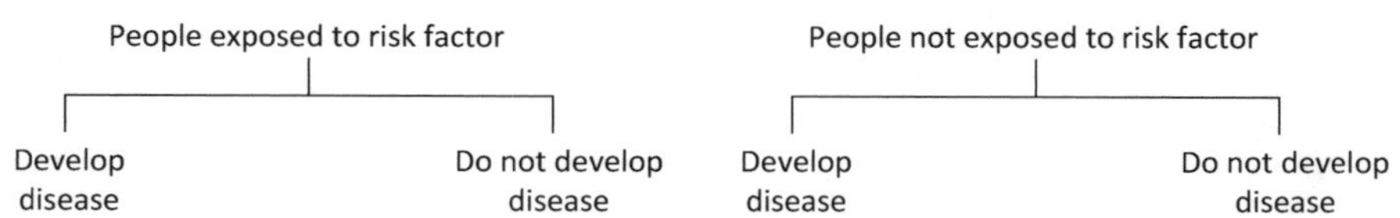

FIGURE 20.1 Cohort study design.

DOI: 10.4324/9781032644257-23

ADVANTAGES AND LIMITATIONS OF COHORT STUDIES

A prospective cohort study provides stronger evidence than a case-control study. Why? Since there is no control group involved, there is no possibility of selection bias. Another advantage of a cohort study is that we can estimate the incidence rate of the disease by observing how many participants develop the disease. Third, a cohort study may give some clues about the time factor. For example, if smoking is the suspected risk factor, we will know after how many years of smoking the participants develop the disease. Fourth, sometimes a cause that was never thought of may be identified.

A disadvantage of cohort studies is that they take a long time, sometimes several decades, to give results. This increases the cost. Further, cohort studies cannot be taken up for rare diseases, as the disease may not develop in any participant even over a long period.

In a cohort study, the strength of association between the risk factor and the disease is measured by calculating relative risk.

RELATIVE RISK

Relative risk compares the incidence rate of a disease in people who were exposed to a risk factor with the incidence rate in people who were not exposed to that risk factor.

The following example illustrates how to calculate relative risk.

Example 1

A cohort study was undertaken to measure the association between cigarette smoking and coronary heart disease. The cohort consisted of 5,000 men above 40 years of age, among whom 800 were regular smokers and the rest were nonsmokers. The cohort was followed up for 20 years, during which time some members developed coronary heart disease. Some of the members died before completing the observation period. The collected data is summarized in Table 20.1.

$$\text{Relative risk} = \frac{\text{Incidence rate of disease among exposed}}{\text{Incidence rate of disease among not exposed}}$$

$$= \frac{3.9}{1.5}$$

$$= 2.6$$

A relative risk of 1 means that there is no association between the risk factor and the disease. A value greater than 1 indicates a positive association, while a value less than 1 suggests a negative association. In our example, a relative risk of 2.6 means that men who smoke are 2.6 times more likely to develop coronary heart disease compared to nonsmokers. Since a relative risk of more than 2 indicates considerable risk, smoking is a substantial risk factor for coronary heart disease.

TABLE 20.1
Coronary Heart Disease in Smokers versus Nonsmokers

Smoking Habit	No. of Persons	Person-Years Observed	No. of Persons Who Developed Coronary Heart Disease	Incidence Rate Per 10,000 Person-Years
Smokers	800	15,200	06	$(6/15{,}200) \times 10{,}000 = 3.9$
Nonsmokers	4,200	79,200	12	$(12/79{,}200) \times 10{,}000 = 1.5$
Total	5,000	94,400	18	

Another long-term study, called the Nurses' Health Study, found a relative risk of 1.5 for breast cancer among hormonal contraceptive users. This means that the use of hormonal contraceptives was associated with a higher risk of breast cancer. This raised alarm; however, subsequent studies showed a lower relative risk between hormonal contraceptives and breast cancer. As a result, hormonal contraceptives continue to be in use.

In another study of over 22,000 US physicians, the relative risk of acute myocardial infarction (MI; commonly known as heart attack) among men taking aspirin was found to be 0.5. This indicates a negative association, meaning that taking aspirin reduces the risk of acute MI. Therefore, physicians continue to prescribe aspirin as a preventive measure for MI.

ODDS RATIO VERSUS RELATIVE RISK

Recall that in a case-control study, we calculate odds ratio and not relative risk. To calculate relative risk, we need to know the incidence of the disease under study, but this information is not available in case-control studies since we do not know the total number of people exposed to the risk factor. For example, in the thalidomide study, we knew that 46 women had babies with deformities, and 41 of them had taken thalidomide during their pregnancy. But we do not know how many pregnant women in the region took thalidomide, which means that we do not have the denominator to calculate incidence of deformities among the exposed. Therefore, relative risk cannot be calculated.

In cohort studies, we can calculate both relative risk and odds ratio. They are roughly equal when the disease under study occurs infrequently.

To distinguish between odds ratio and relative risk, remember that odds ratio is about how many of the cases had exposure to the risk factor, while relative risk is about how many of those who had exposure to the risk factor later developed the disease.

NOTE

1. There are also retrospective cohort studies, but to keep the text simple we have not included them here.

21 Experimental Study

Experimental studies are also called intervention studies. In this study, investigators recruit a group of people with similar characteristics and divide them into two subgroups. They then make an intervention in one subgroup. Measurements are taken in both subgroups before and after the intervention. At the end of the study, if changes are observed only in the intervention group, we can say that they were caused by the intervention.

A randomized controlled trial (RCT) is a type of experimental study commonly used in medical science.

RANDOMIZED CONTROLLED TRIAL

This study design is used to assess the safety and efficacy of a specific drug against a disease. Investigators enroll a group of people who have the disease under study. Then they create two subgroups—intervention group and control group—and randomly assign participants to each group. This process, known as randomization, helps ensure that the two groups are similar.

The intervention group receives the drug being tested, and the control group is given a placebo that is similar in appearance but does not contain the active chemical. Figure 21.1 depicts this process.

Clinical outcomes of the intervention are measured at specified intervals, such as how many members in each subgroup experienced relief and how many were cured. Any side effects are also recorded. Results of the two subgroups are then compared to determine the effectiveness of the drug.

BLINDING

Some participants of an RCT may report feeling better because they think they are receiving the new drug. To eliminate this psychological effect, participants are not informed whether they are receiving the drug or the placebo. This is known as a single-blind trial. Similarly, if service providers (doctors or nurses) know which participants are receiving the drug, they, too, may succumb to bias. They may examine those receiving the drug more frequently or may inquire about their well-being. To eliminate such influences, details of group allocation are also withheld from the service providers, and the study is then called a double-blind study.

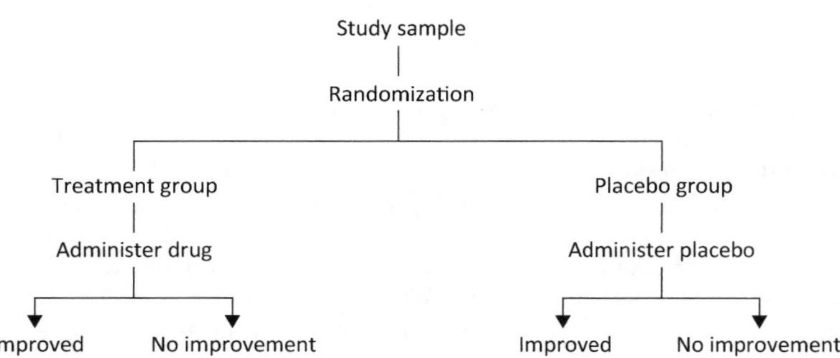

FIGURE 21.1 Randomized control trial: Study design.

DOI: 10.4324/9781032644257-24

ETHICAL CONSIDERATIONS

Ethical issues are a key consideration in experimental studies. For example, in a study to test the efficacy of a new cancer drug, participants who have cancer cannot be denied conventional treatment. Similarly, it would be wrong to ask people not to wear a face mask to see if it increases their risk of contracting COVID-19.

These examples may make you think that an experimental study may not be possible for many research questions. This is true. Experimental studies are only undertaken when the intervention is expected to benefit the participants. Second, ethical clearance from an approved Institutional Review Board (IRB) is necessary to conduct an experimental study. Many reputed research organizations have an IRB. Lastly, we cannot administer a new drug or vaccine to people without their consent. Each participant must give their written consent to be enrolled in the study.

CLINICAL TRIAL PHASES

A new drug, before it is sold commercially, is subjected to rigorous testing to evaluate its safety and efficacy. This includes in-vitro testing, animal trials, and human trials. Human clinical trials are conducted in phases. In phase one, the drug is given to a small group of 20–80 people, mainly to test its safety. If the drug is found safe, the trial moves to phase two, where a larger group of, say, 100–300 people, receives the drug. In phase three, the trial is further expanded to include 1,000–3,000 people. In all three phases, participants are assigned to two groups by random selection and monitored for outcomes. On satisfactory completion of the trial, the drug is made commercially available. A mechanism for reporting and documenting any side effects is put in place.

Example 1

In 2009–10, a clinical trial was conducted in India to test a new human papillomavirus (HPV) vaccine developed to prevent cervical cancer. Several thousand adolescent girls received the vaccine in phase three of the trial. Unfortunately, there were many reports of adverse reactions, including seven deaths. This led to massive public outcry, and the trial was terminated midway.

EXPERIMENTAL STUDIES VERSUS COHORT STUDIES

Experimental studies share one similarity with cohort studies. In both studies, we follow up to see how many of the exposed participants experienced a change. But note a key difference: In a cohort study, exposure occurs naturally, whereas in experimental studies, the investigator creates the exposure. Randomization is the essence of experimental studies. It makes this study design more powerful and provides stronger evidence of a causal relationship.

Example 2

In early 1980s, an experimental study was conducted in Brazil to test the efficacy of a new vaccine against cutaneous leishmaniasis, a common disease in the Brazilian army at that time. New army recruits were randomly assigned to two groups. One group was administered the vaccine and the other a placebo. After a few months, all participants were tested for the presence of antibody titer against leishmaniasis. It was found that soldiers who had received the vaccine had developed antibodies. This raised hope for the vaccine's effectiveness. However, in a follow-up to the study, incidence of leishmaniasis was found to be similar in both groups. Therefore, the vaccine was considered ineffective in preventing cutaneous leishmaniasis and was discontinued.

22 Association and Causation

When Edward Jenner developed the smallpox vaccine, he did not know what caused smallpox. A popular folklore that people with a history of cowpox did not get smallpox sparked an idea that led him to develop the smallpox vaccine. This vaccine played an important role in eradicating smallpox.

During the cholera epidemic of London, no one knew the nature or cause of the disease. Concepts of microorganisms and infection were not yet known. There were no antibiotics. Then how did Dr. John Snow control the outbreak? His observation that the disease affected only those who consumed water from a specific source gave him a vital clue. The outbreak died out when water supply from the suspected source was stopped.

Tuberculosis was controlled in the West long before its causative agent was known or antitubercular drugs became available. Improved socioeconomic conditions, better nutrition, and better sanitation and housing contributed to this achievement.

These are some examples of diseases being controlled before their causes could be known. But this is not common. Normally, to prevent or control a disease, we need to know its cause(s) and treatment options. For infectious diseases, we also need to know how the disease spreads.

In December 2019, an outbreak of a respiratory infection was reported in China. Testing of swabs taken from nasopharynx and oropharynx of the affected individuals revealed a new strain of a known virus, the SARS coronavirus. This new strain was named SARS-CoV-2. In this case, the causative pathogen was identified without much difficulty, but that does not happen always, as we will see in the following example.

Example 1

In June 2019, over 150 children in Muzaffarpur, India, succumbed to a mysterious illness. The disease manifested with fever, vomiting, disorientation, and coma, similar to Japanese encephalitis or acute encephalitis syndrome. Most cases had hypoglycemia. Muzaffarpur is famous for the cultivation of lychee, and there were rumors that impoverished children who consumed lychee on an empty stomach were particularly affected. National and international scientists visited the site to investigate the cause, but no pathogen could be isolated from the blood, cerebrospinal fluid, or other body fluids of the patients. Affected children were managed symptomatically, and the outbreak subsided on its own in a few weeks. With the cause of the disease still unknown, there is currently no way to prevent future outbreaks.

How can we find the cause of a disease? One approach is to observe its associations and identify the factors with which it is commonly associated.

ASSOCIATION

The history of medicine offers many examples where a scientist identified the cause of a disease by observing its associations. Dr. Alton Ochsner's observation that most of his lung cancer patients were heavy smokers pointed to an association between lung cancer and smoking. Subsequent epidemiological studies confirmed that smoking was a strong risk factor for lung cancer. Similarly, Dr. John Snow's association of cholera with consumption of water from a particular source helped in identifying the disease. Clinical practitioners are often in a position to notice such associations in their practice.

DOI: 10.4324/9781032644257-25

Spurious Association

We must remember that not every observed association between a risk factor and a disease is causative, as will become clear from the following examples.

Example 2

Iodine deficiency disorders (IDDs) were once more common in mountainous regions than in the plains. Originally, it was believed that this had something to do with dietary practices of the people living in these areas. But this association was proved spurious when it was discovered that iodine primarily comes from seawater, seafood, and sea plants. As we move away from the sea, the iodine content in plant and animal foods decreases, which explains why IDD was more prevalent in hilly areas. Now that iodine is readily available through iodized salt, occurrence of IDD is reducing everywhere, including in mountainous areas.

Example 3

In 2012, a scientist made an astounding observation: Countries that produced a higher number of Nobel laureates had higher per capita chocolate consumption. Examples included Switzerland, Norway, Sweden, Denmark, the United Kingdom, and others. Conversely, China, Japan, and Brazil had lower chocolate consumption and fewer Nobel winners. From this, can we conclude that higher chocolate consumption is associated with greater chances of winning a Nobel prize? No, because we do not know whether the Nobel laureates from countries with higher chocolate consumption actually consumed more chocolate, or if they consumed chocolate at all. Therefore, the perceived association between chocolate intake and winning a Nobel prize is a spurious one.

Exploring Association

Presence of one or more of the following factors increases the possibility of an association between a risk factor and a disease.

Plausibility

Plausibility is the likelihood of a scenario, statement, or explanation to be true or believable. For example, it is a scientifically established fact that a high-lipid diet increases blood cholesterol levels, leading to deposition of plaque in blood vessels. This narrows blood vessels, which ultimately leads to coronary heart disease. This means that there is a plausible association between a high-lipid diet and coronary heart disease. In other words, the association is logically possible.

It is worth noting that a current belief or knowledge that appears logical and is widely accepted may not always be true. When Dr. John Snow suspected the role of water in causing the cholera outbreak, the prevailing beliefs did not support his hypothesis. At that time, diseases were thought to be caused by evil spirits or supernatural forces, and people had difficulty accepting that something as pure and holy as water could cause illness. Of course, this belief was later proved incorrect.

Consistency

In the context of research, consistency refers to getting similar results in different situations or at different times.

Example 4

Breast cancer seems to be less common in communities where women liberally breastfeed their children. A researcher analyzed the findings of 27 epidemiological research studies that aimed to identify the risk factors for breast cancer. These studies had been conducted in different countries at different times and collectively included over 13,000 women with breast cancer. Pooled results revealed an inverse relationship[1] between breastfeeding and the risk of breast cancer. This means that increased breastfeeding is associated with a lower risk of breast cancer, and vice versa. When we get similar results across different situations and time periods, reliability (believability) of the findings increases.

Dose-Response Relationship

If greater exposure to a risk factor leads to more severe disease, this strengthens the possibility of the risk factor's role in causing the disease.

Example 5

An observational study was conducted to examine the effects of noise on hearing. Researchers measured noise levels in factories that produced a lot of noise. Workers employed in these factories for 10 or more years were invited to participate in the study, and their hearing acuity was measured. It was found that hearing loss was greater in workers (a) who worked in factories with higher levels of noise and (b) who had been working there for a longer duration.

In other words, the study found a positive relationship between dose of noise and hearing loss.

Time Relationship

Time relationship, also known as temporal relationship, requires that a cause must come before an effect. After seat belt usage was made mandatory in the United Kingdom, there was an immediate reduction in the number of deaths from car accidents. This sequence of events suggests that wearing seat belt leads to fewer deaths in car accidents.

Reversibility

If removing a suspected risk factor reduces the risk of the disease, this reinforces the risk factor's role in causing the disease. When thalidomide was banned in Germany, birth defects stopped occurring.

EVIDENCE OF CAUSATION

The process of establishing causation is also known as *causal inference*. We know that infectious diseases are caused by specific pathogens, whereas NCDs are caused by one or more risk factors. The final evidence of causation comes from epidemiological studies, some of which have been discussed in preceding chapters. They are summarized here.

Descriptive Studies

Indication of a potential association between a risk factor and a disease mostly comes from descriptive studies. Indication about the role of smoking in causing lung cancer came from a descriptive study. Association between a water source and the cholera outbreak in London was also discovered through a descriptive study.

Ecological studies: Detrimental effects of low fluoride in drinking water on dental health were learned through an ecological study. Similarly, role of air pollution in respiratory diseases was learned from ecological studies.

Case-Control Studies

Case-control studies have provided evidence of causation for many diseases. The thalidomide study in Germany is a notable example. Evidence of the role of smoking in causing lung cancer also came from a case-control study.

Cohort Studies

Cohort studies can provide compelling evidence on causation, but their long duration and high cost make them unaffordable. The Framingham Study, a cohort study that identified the risk factors for coronary heart disease, is a classic example. It is admirable that the authorities invested in this study despite knowing that it would take 20–30 years to get meaningful results. Such examples are not common.

Experimental Studies

Randomized control trials (RCTs) provide strong evidence of a causal relationship between a risk factor and a disease, but their contribution in this area has been limited. In many situations, it is not possible to conduct an RCT due to ethical considerations. Nevertheless, RCTs have played a critical role in proving the efficacy and safety of new drugs and vaccines.

Meta-Analysis

A meta-analysis is a statistical process that combines data or findings from multiple research studies to arrive at a conclusion.

A meta-analysis strengthens the evidence by summarizing results of studies conducted by different investigators in different places at different points in time.

Example 6

Several studies were conducted to examine the role of beta-blockers[2] in preventing death following a heart attack. These studies compared the risk of death between people who took beta-blockers after a heart attack and those who did not. Findings from 11 studies revealed a relative risk of 0.5–1.1 when beta-blockers were used after a heart attack. A meta-analysis pooled these results and arrived at a combined relative risk of 0.65. As a relative risk of less than 1 suggests a negative association between two variables, it was concluded that taking beta-blockers after a heart attack reduces the risk of death.

NOTES

1. Two variables are said to be inversely associated when an increase in one causes a decrease in the other.
2. Beta-blockers are a group of medicines for treating hypertension. Bisoprolol, metoprolol, and propranolol are some examples of beta-blocker medicines.

23 Bias and Confounding

When conducting epidemiological studies, we cannot completely eliminate errors, but we can reduce them considerably by selecting the right study design. For instance, in most studies, we rely on sample statistics to estimate population parameters, but findings from a sample may differ from the true values of the population. Ensuring an adequate sample size can minimize this error.

Errors in epidemiological studies can be random or systematic.

RANDOM ERROR

Random errors occur occasionally and by chance alone. For example, an investigator may inadvertently record a value as 25,000 instead of 2,500. This is a simple mistake, but it can make a big difference in the results. To reduce the impact of such errors, we exclude any outliers[1] when analyzing the data.

SYSTEMATIC ERROR

Systematic error, also known as bias, occurs repeatedly—that is, the same mistake occurs every time a process is repeated. Consequently, the findings are systematically different from actual values. For example, when measuring mid-upper arm circumference in children, if the investigator holds the measuring tape too loose, the measurements will be higher than actual values. The difference may be more or less consistent across all readings.

Two types of systematic errors can be seen in epidemiological studies:

Selection Bias

This refers to an error in selecting the right participants for a sample. When the sample is not representative of the study population, we get biased results.

Example 1

A study was conducted to assess patient satisfaction in a hospital. A team of investigators stood outside the outpatient clinic in the morning and interviewed the first 30 patients leaving the clinic after availing services. Do you see the error in selecting the sample? It is possible that patients who left the clinic early were more satisfied than others. Patients who left later might have faced delays or other problems that could have affected their satisfaction. This bias in sample selection may give erroneous results.

Measurement Bias

This refers to an error in taking measurements.

Example 2

In a case-control study that explored the association between an exposure and a disease, investigators interviewed two groups of people: Those who had the disease (cases) and those who did not have the disease (controls). Generally, people having a disease are able to recall when and where they were exposed to a suspected risk factor, whereas many of those who do not have the disease may fail to recall their exposure. This error in measurement may lead to incorrect results.

DOI: 10.4324/9781032644257-26

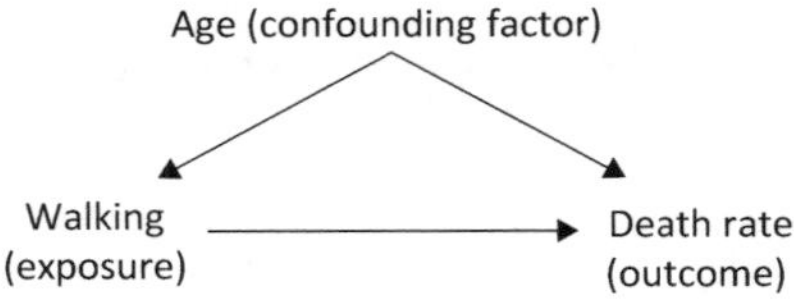

FIGURE 23.1 Age as a confounding factor in a study of the effect of walking on mortality.

CONFOUNDING

A study was conducted in the United States to examine the effect of walking on mortality. Over 600 men aged 61–81 years who were physically fit to walk were enrolled for the study. The participants' daily walking distance was recorded over the next 12 years. Findings showed that the mortality rate among men who walked less than one mile per day (let us call it Group A) was nearly twice that among the men who walked two or more miles per day (let us call it Group B). From this, can we conclude that men who walk two or more miles a day live longer? No, because the study design appears to have some weaknesses. There is possibility of confounding. It is likely that the men in Group B could walk more because they were younger than the men in Group A. And since younger people are likely to live longer, this could be the reason for the lower mortality rates in Group B.

Confounding is a phenomenon in research where the accuracy of findings is compromised due to the influence of an extraneous factor that is associated with both the exposure and the disease.

In the above example, age is a confounding factor.

As we can see in Figure 23.1, age is associated with walking: With advancing age, people may walk less. Age is also associated with death rate, and they share a causal relationship: As age increases, risk of death also increases. So, age is a confounding factor in measuring the effect of walking on mortality.

There can be many more confounders in this study. For example, people who are more physically fit than others are likely to take more interest in walking. They may have lower mortality due to their general fitness. Conversely, those who eat high-lipid foods, take excessive alcohol, smoke, or have a sedentary lifestyle are likely to walk less and may have higher mortality due to diseases.

A confounder creates a problem when it is unevenly distributed in the two groups being compared. In the above study, participants should have been matched by their age, dietary habits, smoking, alcohol intake, and other characteristics. This would have neutralized the effects of any confounders. Therefore, when designing a study, we must look for possible confounders and control them to the extent possible.

Age, social class, and lifestyle can be confounding factors in epidemiological studies.

NOTE

1. An outlier is an odd value in a dataset that is very different from other values. It is explained further in the chapter "Analyzing Data."

24 Epidemic Management

Some diseases persist in certain populations, while others occur occasionally. For example, malaria occurs regularly in many African countries, but it is rare in Western countries. Due to its persistent occurrence, we can say that malaria is endemic in some African countries. In Guyana, around 20,000 malaria cases are reported each year, and this trend has continued for many years. If, in a given year, the number of cases suddenly shoots up to, say, 30,000, it will be called an epidemic.

An epidemic refers to a sudden spurt in the number of cases of a disease in a population that is clearly in excess of past trends.

Another example is of poliomyelitis. It has been eliminated from most countries and we expect to find no new cases. Therefore, even a single new case of polio in any of these countries will amount to an epidemic as it would be a significant increase from their previous status of zero cases.

When an epidemic is limited to a specified geographical area, it is called an outbreak. The cholera outbreak of London is an example. When an epidemic spreads to multiple countries and affects vast populations, it is called a pandemic. COVID-19 is a pandemic. When a disease is persistently present at a high level in a population, it is called hyperendemic. Tuberculosis is hyperendemic in India.

COMMON EPIDEMICS

The following infectious diseases have been occurring as epidemics:

- Waterborne or foodborne diseases: *E. coli* infections, typhoid, cholera
- Vector-borne diseases: Malaria, dengue, chikungunya, Japanese encephalitis, plague
- Respiratory diseases: Influenza, measles, diphtheria

Epidemics of SARS, SARS-CoV-2, and Zika have occurred in recent past. These diseases have a short incubation period, due to which they can cause significant loss of life in a short time. Diseases with longer incubation periods, such as HIV, viral hepatitis, and leishmaniasis, also occur as epidemics. Lately, many NCDs such as obesity, diabetes, cardiovascular diseases, and cancer have taken the form of an epidemic.

Many other health catastrophes can also be classified as epidemics, such as the high incidence of pollution-related respiratory diseases in the population of Shanghai, China, in 2013. The Bhopal gas tragedy of 1984 in India was an epidemic. Poisoning or death from consumption of spurious alcohol, which is not uncommon in low-income settings, is an epidemic.

CONFIRMING AN EPIDEMIC

To confirm an epidemic, we compare the current number of cases of a disease with statistics from the same month(s) in previous years. A considerable increase amounts to an epidemic.

How do we get information about an epidemic? Local hospitals, clinics, and healthcare professionals are often in a position to alert health authorities to a sudden spurt in cases. Delay in reporting an epidemic can have serious consequences, as is believed to have happened with the COVID-19 epidemic in Wuhan, China. However, declaring an epidemic is generally a political decision, and governments sometimes hesitate to acknowledge an epidemic fearing it might be construed as their failure. Media reports following public outcry are often the first source of information about an epidemic.

DOI: 10.4324/9781032644257-27

MANAGING AN EPIDEMIC

Epidemic management involves three key aspects:

1. Investigation
2. Control
3. Prevention

If the disease or its etiology is not known, the first step is to find this out. We need to know from where the disease originated and how it spread. We need to understand why it occurred and what can be done to prevent it from reoccurring. Second, care and treatment are provided to the affected people. Third, interventions are made to prevent further spread. Table 24.1 enumerates the main activities under these three components.

Diagnosis

The first step in epidemic investigation is to diagnose the disease or health problem that caused the epidemic. This is done by examining some of the affected people through detailed history-taking, physical examination, and laboratory tests. Cases may be available in hospitals, or we may have to find them in the community.

Care and Treatment

To control an epidemic, the first step is to start care and treatment of the cases. This can be done based on our understanding of the disease thus far. If the disease seems to be infectious, cases may have to be isolated to prevent further spread.

Constructing a Case Definition

Based on the information collected, epidemiologists construct a case definition—a set of criteria to define a typical case. This helps healthcare workers diagnose cases and differentiate between cases and non-cases. In an epidemic of Japanese encephalitis, the case definition can be: "acute onset of fever with change in mental status." Confusion, disorientation, inability to talk, and coma are signs of change in mental status.

TABLE 24.1
Main Activities in Investigation, Control, and Prevention of an Epidemic

Investigation	Control	Prevention
Diagnosis	Care and treatment of reported cases; isolation if needed	Preventing further transmission
Constructing a case definition	Active detection of hidden cases; isolation of positive cases if needed	Protecting vulnerable populations
Developing clinical protocols	Contact tracing; quarantine of positive cases if needed	Increasing community awareness
Environmental assessment	Setting up a monitoring system	
Gathering local opinion		
Describing the epidemic		
Hypothesis testing		

Note: For obvious reasons, many activities pertaining to investigation, control, and prevention go side by side.

Developing Clinical Protocols

Protocols are developed for history-taking, physical examination, laboratory tests, and treatment. This is to bring uniformity in case detection and management. In a suspected cholera epidemic, health workers particularly inquire about the source of drinking water. In suspected hepatitis A, the clinician checks for liver enlargement by palpating the abdomen. In suspected Japanese encephalitis, testing of cerebrospinal fluid (CSF) is mandated. Treatment protocol involves specifying whether antibiotic or antiviral medicines are to be given or if cases should be managed symptomatically.

As our understanding of a disease develops, case definitions and clinical protocols can be revised from time to time.

Environmental Assessment

An environmental factor is examined if its role is suspected. In a suspected cholera epidemic in West Bengal, India, water samples from local ponds were tested and some were found to be contaminated. Similarly, in a vector-borne disease, investigators look for vector-breeding sites and inspect the water for presence of larvae.

Example 1

In 1976, an organization of US war veterans called the American Legion held a four-day convention at a hotel in Philadelphia. Within a month of the event, 152 cases of a respiratory disease were reported among the attendees who had stayed at the hotel. There were also a few cases of people who had not participated in the event but had been working in or around the hotel during that time. Twenty-two people died from the illness. Since nothing was known about the disease, including its cause or source, the CDC's assistance was sought to investigate and control the outbreak. When the affected people were examined, no microorganism or toxic chemical could be identified in their blood or body fluids. After several months, investigators successfully identified a new type of bacterium in some of the samples. The bacterium was named *Legionella* and the disease was termed Legionnaires' disease. To find the source of the bacterium, investigators combed the hotel environment—water, food, air, carpets, toilets, and others. Cooks and other staff were examined. Eventually, the bacterium was found in the water of the hotel's air-cooling tower. Later, scrutiny of past records revealed that similar outbreaks had occurred at other places in the country, including one in 1965 at a psychiatric hospital in Washington, DC, that had affected 81 patients, 14 of whom had died.

Following the Philadelphia outbreak, air-conditioning regulations were made more stringent to prevent similar incidents in future.

Gathering Local Opinion

Interactions with local healthcare workers and community members can provide useful information about the factors that led to the epidemic. Unfortunately, this information is often missed out or ignored.

Describing the Epidemic

To prevent future epidemics, we need to understand why an epidemic occurred and what factors supported it. We can use a descriptive study to understand the dynamics of the epidemic. Recall that a descriptive study examines person-place-time.

Person

We look for common characteristics among the cases. How are they different from non-cases? Did they have any new exposure?

Place

A spot map is prepared to understand the geographical distribution of cases. Where could people have contracted the disease? What is peculiar about that place? Was any exposure present in that location?

Time

An epidemic curve is prepared to show the number of new cases against time: How many new cases appear each day? An epidemic curve can tell us about the magnitude of the epidemic and whether it is growing or regressing. Two types of epidemic curves are given here to explain their utility.

Figure 24.1 shows an epidemic curve of an infectious disease. As we can see, all cases contracted the disease within a short span of eight days, raising the possibility that the disease spread from a single source. This pattern, known as a *point source epidemic*, is typically seen in waterborne or foodborne diseases. The epidemic curve also shows that this was a minor outbreak that affected around 26 people.

Figure 24.2 depicts an outbreak that began with a few cases but gradually gained momentum. This pattern hints at person-to-person transmission, or a *propagated epidemic*. From the curve, we can make out that this was also a minor outbreak that peaked at nine cases in a single day and started to subside from day 15.

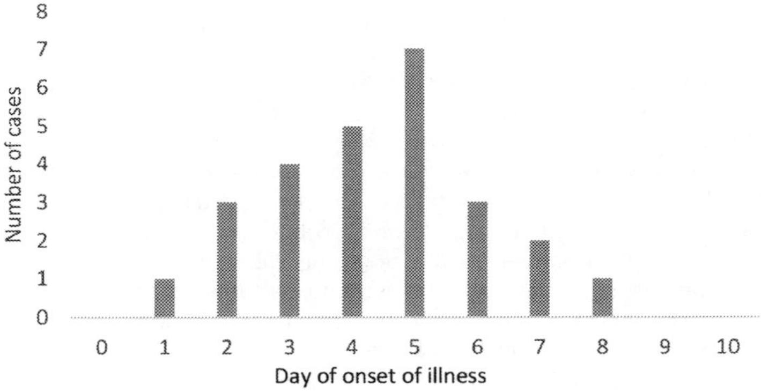

FIGURE 24.1 Point source epidemic.

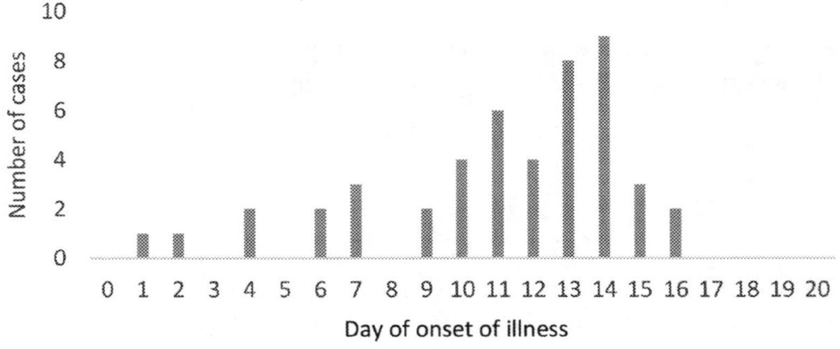

FIGURE 24.2 Propagated epidemic.

Note that these are simple graphs prepared for beginners; actual epidemic graphs can be much more complicated.

Hypothesis Testing

Based on the findings of the descriptive study, a hypothesis is developed explaining the causative agent, its source(s), mode(s) of transmission, and so on. The hypothesis is then tested by a case-control study wherein cases of the disease are compared with controls.

Detecting Active Cases

Generally, only a fraction of the people who develop a disease report to healthcare facilities. Many asymptomatic or mild cases remain hidden in the community. To prevent further spread of an infectious disease, it is important to identify and isolate hidden cases and provide them treatment.

Contact Tracing

In highly infectious diseases like SARS-CoV-2 or Ebola, people who came in contact with the cases are traced. Healthcare workers visit the contacts and arrange for their testing.

Quarantine

Asymptomatic contacts are quarantined on the assumption that they may be in incubation period. Duration of quarantine is equivalent to the maximum known incubation period of the disease. For example, quarantine period of COVID-19 is 14 days. People in quarantine are tested, and positive cases are placed in isolation and provided treatment.

Quarantine is similar to isolation, except quarantine is for a fixed duration. Duration of isolation depends on the patient's recovery.

Preventing Further Transmission

Depending on the type of disease, measures are taken to prevent its further transmission. During the COVID-19 pandemic, lockdowns were imposed to interrupt transmission. In a waterborne-disease epidemic, existing water sources are sealed and safe drinking water is provided to the people.

Protecting Vulnerable Populations

If a vaccine is available, susceptible people should be immunized. In a Japanese encephalitis epidemic, children in and around the affected area are immunized. In a chemical accident, such as leakage of radiation or toxic gas, people are evacuated to safer places.

Example 2

Between 1989 and 1991, several epidemics of measles were reported in schools across the United States. This was surprising, as virtually all children in the country had received primary immunization. Upon investigation, health authorities found that immunity against measles withered with advancing age. Accordingly, all adolescents in the country received an extra booster dose of measles vaccine. This intervention helped prevent further epidemics.

Increasing Community Awareness

Programs are developed to raise community awareness about the disease. People are educated on how to protect themselves, how to identify a case, which laboratory tests are required to confirm diagnosis, what initial care and support can be given to a suspected case at home, and at what stage the patient should be hospitalized.

Setting Up a Monitoring System

A system is set up to track the number of new cases detected every day, number of hospitalizations, number of deaths, and other critical data. Effectiveness of control measures is monitored.

CONTROLLING CHRONIC-DISEASE EPIDEMICS

Chronic diseases such as obesity, diabetes, heart diseases, cancer, and Alzheimer's disease are called "slow killers." These diseases progress slowly and take years to cause disability. Older people are more commonly affected. Since many chronic diseases do not cause sudden sickness or death, they do not attract much interest from stakeholders. Further, their causation is multifactorial, so their prevention and control are relatively complicated. Nevertheless, as our understanding of diseases grows, many chronic conditions can now be prevented. This is discussed in detail in the chapter "What Are Noncommunicable Diseases?"

Section IV

Biostatistics

25 What Is Biostatistics?

To understand biostatistics, we must first have a basic understanding of research.

RESEARCH

The process of systematic inquiry to answer a pertinent question is called research.

Research involves defining a research question, designing a methodology to answer the question, collecting data, analyzing the collected data, and interpreting the results to answer the research question.

STATISTICS AND BIOSTATISTICS

Data: Any collected information or facts can be called data.

Numerical data consists of numbers. For example, India has a high burden of TB—this is information, which can be substantiated with numerical data: 2.7 million new cases of TB are registered in India every year.

When data is collected from a large number of people, it can be difficult to analyze. Statistics provides us the tools and techniques to analyze large volumes of complex data.

Statistics is the science of organizing, analyzing, and interpreting data so that we can draw meaningful conclusions from it.

Additionally, knowledge of statistics helps us to determine the right sample size and the most appropriate sampling technique for a research study.

Biostatistics: It refers to the application of statistics in healthcare.

RESEARCH QUESTION

What is a research question? Let us understand this with an example.

Example 1

During the COVID-19 pandemic, some people developed severe illness while others were affected mildly. Why this difference? In other words, what factors contributed to the severity of illness in COVID-19 patients? This is a research question. Research studies can be designed to answer this question. A comparison of mild and severe cases might give us some clues. There can be many more research questions: Which COVID-19 treatment regimen is the most effective? Does early use of steroids improve clinical outcomes? Who are the people who develop post-COVID complications? Some people died from the disease despite being fully vaccinated. How were they different from those who remained protected after vaccination?

After a research question is answered, it may lead to new questions. For example, if we find that the severity of COVID-19 illness is linked to comorbidities, the next question will be: Which comorbidity

DOI: 10.4324/9781032644257-29

makes a considerable difference: diabetes, hypertension, history of myocardial ischemia, or others? If diabetes is identified as a risk factor, we will want to know at what level of blood sugar the risk increases significantly. This cycle of questions can go on endlessly.

HYPOTHESIS

A hypothesis is an assumption we make to answer a research question. The hypothesis will be proved or rejected through a research study.

Example 2

Osteoarthritis of the knee was once considered rare, but now it is common in older adults. Why have knee problems increased in people? This is a research question. To answer it, we can begin by making some assumptions. For example, we know that in the past people habitually walked or cycled long distances. Now they walk much less and rely more on motorized vehicles. From this, we can make a hypothesis: Physical activity of lower limbs protects from knee disability. A research study can be undertaken to determine whether this is true.

Let us design a research study to test this hypothesis.

STEPS OF A RESEARCH STUDY

Study Design

To test our hypothesis, we will select a sample of older adults and divide them into two groups: Those with a knee disability and others with healthy knees. We will interview participants in both groups to know whether they lived a physically active life. If we find that a large proportion of the people with knee disability did not have an active lifestyle, whereas a large proportion of those with healthy knees had been physically active, we can infer that physical inactivity is associated with knee disability.[1]

Research Protocol

For systematic execution of a research study, we develop a research protocol and define what exactly we want to measure and how. In this case, we need to specify the criteria by which we will differentiate people with knee disability from those with healthy knees. These criteria could be:

- Presence of pain in both knees for at least five years
- Inability to squat, sit cross-legged, or walk half a kilometer at a stretch

Second, we need to define *physical activity*. On what grounds shall we determine that a person has lived a physically active life? One possible criterion could be:

- History of walking around 2 kilometers at a stretch at least once a week during the last ten years

Third, we specify the people from whom we will collect the information. We may characterize them by age, sex, body weight, socioeconomic status, location, and so on. The study population for this study could be:

- Men and women aged 50–70 years, weighing 60–80 kilograms, belonging to middle-income families residing in an upscale neighborhood in Paris

Fourth, we decide the sample size—that is, the number of people from whom we will collect the information. Knowledge of statistics can help us calculate an appropriate sample size, or we can seek the help of a statistician. Assuming that a sample size of 300 is determined, the next step is to specify the sampling technique—the method we will use to select 300 candidates from the identified neighborhood.

Methodology

This involves collection of data, for which we may have to engage a few investigators. To ensure uniformity of information, we develop a questionnaire that may include questions such as:

1. Do you have a knee problem? Yes/No
2. If yes, is it painful? Yes/No
3. If yes, does the problem stop you from squatting, sitting cross-legged, or walking half a kilometer at a stretch? Yes/No
4. If yes, for how many years have you had this problem?
5. Did you walk regularly before you had a knee problem? Yes/No
6. If yes, how much distance did you cover in a day? Less than 1 kilometer/1–2 kilometers/ more than 2 kilometers
7. How often did you walk? Almost daily/at least thrice a week/at least twice a week/at least once a week/occasionally
8. For how many years did you follow this routine? 1–5 years/6–10 years/11–15 years/16 years or more

Analysis

We analyze the collected data to see if there are significant differences between the walking patterns of participants with a knee disability and those with healthy knees.

Conclusion

Based on our findings, we can conclude whether or not physical inactivity is associated with knee disability.

WHY SHOULD PUBLIC HEALTH PROFESSIONALS LEARN BIOSTATISTICS?

There are several reasons. Many public health programs include a research component, and biostatistics is central to research. Public health professionals need to write research proposals, collect data, and prepare reports, and knowledge of biostatistics is required at various stages of this process. Some public health programs involve the collection of copious amounts of data from field units. An understanding of biostatistics can be invaluable in analyzing this data and making decisions.

NOTE

1. Note that this study will not prove that physical inactivity is the cause of knee disability. It can only prove whether or not there is an association between physical inactivity and knee disability. If an association is found, further research will be needed to measure the strength of this association.

26 Organizing Data

To analyze large amounts of data, we must first organize it systematically. In this chapter, we will discuss two important methods of organizing data:

- Preparing a master table
- Frequency distribution

Example 1

Tubal ligation is a popular method of terminal contraception among women in Asia and Latin America. However, this service is not regularly available in hospitals. It is generally provided through periodic family planning camps conducted at district hospitals and some health centers. A medical team from the district headquarters visits these facilities to provide the service.

Every client who registers for tubal ligation surgery is required to undergo a medical examination and laboratory tests to assess her fitness for the procedure. Findings of the preoperative check-up are recorded in a comprehensive five-page form known as a client record, in addition to details such as the client's name, age, address, education, medical history, number of children, age and gender of each child, and name and occupation of the husband. Before the client is taken for surgery, the surgeon reviews her records to ensure that she is fit for the procedure.

After the camp concludes, all client records are sent to the district health office. The district office receives thousands of such records each month from various facilities. What can they do with this information? They can analyze the data to answer research questions. In the context of family planning, some of these questions can be:

1. At what age do women generally opt for terminal contraception?
2. After having how many children do women generally go for tubal ligation?
3. What is the education level of women who undergo this surgery?
4. Is there a difference in fertility rates of literate and illiterate women?
5. What proportion of clients are rejected for tubal ligation surgery in these camps, and on what grounds?

Insights gained from this data can be used to improve services. For example, until a few decades ago, women in India opted for terminal contraception after having three or more children, but nowadays many women stop childbearing after having one or two children. Program managers can use this information to design communication campaigns that target the right clients.

Now, imagine a scenario in a district health office—thousands of client records piled up on racks or in computer files. Before this data can be analyzed, it has to be organized. How can this be done?

MASTER TABLE

This is a simple method of data organization wherein data from multiple individual forms is compiled into a single spreadsheet known as a master table or line list. Let us take the example of a family planning camp where 30 women came for tubal ligation. Thirty forms were filled, and some of the data was transferred to a master table. As shown in Figure 26.1, each row in the spreadsheet represents an individual client and each column represents a specific variable.

DOI: 10.4324/9781032644257-30

I	II	III	IV	V	VI	VII	VIII	IX
Client	Age	Education (Grade)	No. of children	Hb g/dL	Urine Pregnancy Test	Medical Examination	Fitness for Surgery	If Rejected, Reason
A	25	5	4	8.4	N	N	Fit	-
B	24	3	3	9.2	N	N	Fit	-
C	20	8	2	10.4	N	N	Fit	-
D	21	Illiterate	3	8.6	N	N	Fit	-
E	21	8	3	7.8	Positive	N	Unfit	Pregnancy, Anaemia
F	22	6	2	7.6	N	N	Unfit	Anaemia
G	27	2	3	10.2	N	N	Fit	-
H	22	2	3	11.0	N	N	Fit	-
I	30	Illiterate	3	9.8	N	N	Fit	-
J	22	Illiterate	5	10.2	N	N	Fit	-
K	30	Illiterate	3	6.4	N	N	Unfit	Anaemia
L	29	3	3	9.2	N	N	Fit	-
M	28	5	3	11.6	N	N	Fit	-
N	30	5	5	11.0	N	N	Fit	-
O	23	4	4	12.2	N	N	Fit	-
P	26	8	3	10.4	N	N	Fit	-
Q	23	12	2	11.8	N	N	Fit	-
R	21	Graduate	1	12.0	N	N	Fit	-
S	22	Illiterate	4	7.8	Positive	N	Unfit	Pregnancy, Anaemia
T	22	8	2	8.8	N	N	Fit	-
U	28	5	2	13.2	N	N	Fit	-
V	28	2	3	12.4	N	N	Fit	-
W	29	4	4	10.0	N	N	Fit	-
X	52	5	4	8.4	N	PID	Unfit	PID
Y	25	Illiterate	4	12.2	N	N	Fit	-
Z	26	8	2	10.4	N	N	Fit	-
ZA	28	5	3	8.4	N	N	Fit	-
ZB	26	5	4	9.2	N	N	Fit	-
ZC	26	8	3	7.8	N	N	Unfit	Anaemia
ZD	29	7	3	10.4	N	N	Fit	-

N: In urine pregnancy test, N denotes negative; in medical examination, N means normal. PID: pelvic inflammatory disease.

FIGURE 26.1 Master Table of 30 Tubal Ligation Clients

Variable

A variable is a characteristic that differs from person to person. For example, people may differ in their age, sex, blood hemoglobin level, education, or number of children. These variables allow us to distinguish people from one another.

Value

Each variable can take more than one value. In the given example, if a client has two children, the variable is *number of children* and its value is *2*. Another client who has three children will have a value of *3* for this variable. Note that the value of a variable can change over time—one's age or hemoglobin level or number of children can change with time.

A master table allows us to see pertinent data at a glance and makes it easier to analyze data.

FREQUENCY DISTRIBUTION

We can further simplify data using frequency distribution, a method that condenses data of individual variables.

Frequency is the number of times a value occurs in a dataset.

Column III of Figure 26.1 provides the education level for each client. We can see that seven women are educated up to Grade 5. Therefore, we can say that the frequency of clients with education up to Grade 5 is 7.

Let us use frequency distribution to answer a research question.

Research question 2: After having how many children do women generally go for tubal ligation?

Column IV of Figure 26.1 provides the number of children for each client. If we want to know how many clients have three children each, we will have to go through the entire column and locate cells having the value *3*. We will have to repeat this process to know the number of clients with two children, and so on. Instead, we can generate a frequency distribution table, which provides ready answers by summarizing the occurrence of each value in the column.

In Table 26.1, we can see that 14 clients have three children each. Since 14 is the highest frequency in the table, we can infer that the most common number of children for women who opt for tubal ligation is three. This answers research question 2: Most women opt for tubal ligation after having three children.

TABLE 26.1
Frequency Distribution of Number of Children for 30 Tubal Ligation Clients

No. of Children	Frequency (No. of Women)
1	1
2	6
3	14
4	7
5	2
Total	**30**

TABLE 26.2
Percentage Frequency Distribution of Number of Children for 30 Tubal Ligation Clients

No. of Children	Frequency (No. of Women)	% of Women $\frac{\text{Frequency}}{30} \times 100$
1	1	3
2	6	20
3	14	47
4	7	23
5	2	7
Total	**30**	**100**

PERCENTAGE OF FREQUENCY

Frequency becomes easier to interpret when expressed as a percentage. Let us add a column for percentages to Table 26.1 and see how it helps.

As we can see in Table 26.2, nearly half of the clients (47%) have three children each. One-fifth (20%) of clients have two children each. In this way, percentage frequency distribution makes it easier to interpret and compare data.

Let us use percentage of frequency to answer a research question.

Research question 5: What proportion of clients are rejected for tubal ligation surgery in these camps, and on what grounds?

To answer this question, we will compute the percentage frequency for each reason for rejection listed in column IX of Figure 26.1.

Table 26.3 provides the answer to research question 5: Approximately one-fourth of clients (27%) are rejected for tubal ligation surgery, with anemia (Hb less than 8 g/dL) being the most common reason for rejection (17%). Other reasons include pregnancy (7%) and pelvic inflammatory disease (3%). Two of the clients had more than one reason for rejection.

TABLE 26.3
Reasons for Rejection for Tubal Ligation Surgery

Reason for Rejection	Frequency (No. of Women)	% of Women: $\frac{\text{Frequency}}{30} \times 100$
Anemia	5	17
Pregnancy	2	7
PID	1	3
Total	**8**	**27**

TABLE 26.4
Class Intervals of Education Levels of 30 Tubal Ligation Clients

SN	Education Class Intervals	Frequency (No. of Women)	% of Women: $\frac{\text{Frequency}}{30} \times 100$
1	Illiterate	6	20
2	1–5	14	47
3	6–10	8	27
4	11–12	1	3
5	Graduate	1	3
	Total	**30**	**100**

FREQUENCY INTERVAL

To simplify complex data, we can organize it into various groups, or classes. The width of each class is known as frequency interval or class interval. Let us use frequency interval to answer a research question.

Research question 3: What is the education level of women who undergo tubal ligation surgery?

Column III of Figure 26.1 provides the education level for each client, ranging from illiterate to graduate. To simplify this data, we can group it into class intervals.

From Table 26.4, we get the answer to research question 3: The highest proportion of clients (47%) are educated up to Grade 5. A fifth (20%) of the clients are illiterate, and only 3% are graduates.

Next, we will learn various methods of analyzing data.

27 Analyzing Data

Refer to research question 1 in the preceding chapter: *At what age do women generally opt for terminal contraception?*

To answer this question, we need to calculate the average age at which women opt for terminal contraception. Column II of Figure 26.1 provides ages of 30 clients, reproduced below as Data A.

Data A: 25, 24, 20, 21, 21, 22, 27, 22, 30, 22, 30, 29, 28, 30, 23, 26, 23, 21, 22, 22, 28, 28, 29, 52, 25, 26, 28, 26, 26, 29.

How can we use this data to answer our research question? We can express the dataset in terms of its central value. There are three measures of central value: Mean, median, and mode. These measures provide a single value that best represents the dataset. Let us calculate the mean, median, and mode for Data A.

MEAN

The mean, also known as arithmetic mean or average, is one of the most widely used measures to summarize data. It gives us an overall idea of the values we are dealing with. To calculate the mean, we add up all the values in a dataset and then divide the sum by the number (count) of values.

$$\text{Mean} = \frac{x_1 + x_2 + x_3 + \ldots + x_n}{n}$$

where $x_1, x_2, x_3 \ldots$ are individual values in the dataset and n is the number of values.

Therefore, mean of Data A:

$$\begin{aligned}\text{Mean} &= \frac{\begin{matrix}(25+24+20+21+21+22+27+22+30+22+30+29+28+30+23+\\26+23+21+22+22+28+28+29+52+25+26+28+26+26+29)\end{matrix}}{30}\\ &= \frac{785}{30}\\ &= 26.16 \approx 26\end{aligned}$$

This answers research question 1: The average age at which women opt for terminal contraception is 26 years.

OUTLIER

On scrutinizing the values in Data A, we can see that one value, 52, is quite different from others. It is an outlier.

An outlier is an extreme or odd value in a dataset that is very different from other values.

DOI: 10.4324/9781032644257-31

TABLE 27.1
Fertility of 30 Clients with Different Literacy Levels

Education Class Interval	Frequency (No. of Women)	Number of Children for Each Education Category of Women	Mean No. of Children
Illiterate	6	3+3+5+3+4+4 = 22	22/6 = 4
1–5	14	4+3+3+3+3+3+5+4+2+3+4+4+3+4 = 48	48/14 = 3
6–10	8	2+3+2+3+2+2+3+3 = 20	20/8 = 3
11–12	1	2	2/1 = 1
Graduate	1	1	1/1 = 1
Total	**30**		

Let us remove the outlier and then calculate the mean for Data A:

$$\text{Mean} = \frac{733}{29}$$
$$= 25.27 \approx 25$$

As you can see, the mean has changed. Presence of an outlier alters the mean, and if a dataset has many outliers, the mean can change considerably. Therefore, when dealing with a dataset that may potentially contain outliers, we avoid using the mean and use the median instead. It is discussed in the next section.

Let us use the mean to answer another research question from the previous chapter.

Research question 4: Is there a difference in fertility rates of literate and illiterate women?

For this, we will use data from Figure 26.1 to compute the mean number of children for each education category of clients.

From Table 27.1, we can deduce that women with higher levels of education tend to have fewer children. This answers research question 4.

MEDIAN

The median is the preferred measure of central tendency for datasets that may contain one or more outliers. The median is the middle value when data is arranged in ascending or descending order. It divides the data into two equal parts.

Let us calculate the median for Data A.

Data A: 25, 24, 20, 21, 21, 22, 27, 22, 30, 22, 30, 29, 28, 30, 23, 26, 23, 21, 22, 22, 28, 28, 29, 52, 25, 26, 28, 26, 26, 29.

First, we organize the values in ascending order. Let us call it Data B.

Data B: 20, 21, 21, 21, 22, 22, 22, 22, 22, 23, 23, 24, 25, 25, 26, 26, 26, 26, 27, 28, 28, 28, 28, 29, 29, 29, 30, 30, 30, 52.

Then we identify the middle value.

Data B: 20, 21, 21, 21, 22, 22, 22, 22, 22, 23, 23, 24, 25, 25, **26**, **26**, 26, 26, 27, 28, 28, 28, 28, 29, 29, 29, 30, 30, 30, 52.

Since this dataset has an even number of values, there are two middle values. Therefore, we take the mean of the two middle values as median. Their mean $= \frac{26+26}{2} = 26$.

Hence, the median age of women who opt for terminal contraception is 26 years.

Note that the outlier, 52, has no impact on the median. If we replace this outlier with another value, say, 20, the median will remain the same. This is because the median is completely insensitive to outliers.

Age is generally expressed in terms of median. The median age of marriage for girls in India is approximately 19 years (2021). Since the median represents the middle value in a dataset, this means that half of all girls in India get married by age 19. Interestingly, the mean (average) age of marriage for girls is 22 years (2021). This is because there are many girls who get married at an older age, and these outliers impact the mean.

Height, weight, and income are also commonly expressed in terms of median.

MODE

Mode is the most frequently occurring value in a dataset. Let us calculate the mode for Data A.

Data A: 25, 24, 20, 21, 21, 22, 27, 22, 30, 22, 30, 29, 28, 30, 23, 26, 23, 21, 22, 22, 28, 28, 29, 52, 25, 26, 28, 26, 26, 29.

Arranging the values in ascending order, we get Data B.

Data B: 20, 21, 21, 21, 22, 22, 22, 22, 22, 23, 23, 24, 25, 25, 26, 26, 26, 26, 27, 28, 28, 28, 28, 29, 29, 29, 30, 30, 30, 52.

Then we identify the value that occurs the maximum number of times. In this case, 22 is the most repeated value; it occurs five times.

Data B: 20, 21, 21, 21, **22**, **22**, **22**, **22**, **22**, 23, 23, 24, 25, 25, 26, 26, 26, 26, 27, 28, 28, 28, 28, 29, 29, 29, 30, 30, 30, 52.

This means that the maximum number of women in this group are 22 years old. So, the modal age of women who opt for terminal contraception is 22 years.

Let us use the mode to analyze literacy levels for this group. By assigning values from 0 to 15 to the education data of 30 clients (0 for illiterate, 1 for Grade 1, … 15 for graduate), we get Data C.

Data C: 5, 3, 8, 0, 8, 6, 2, 2, 0, 0, 0, 3, 5, 5, 4, 8, 12, 15, 0, 8, 5, 2, 4, 5, 0, 8, 5, 5, 8, 7.

Organizing this data in ascending order, we get:

Data D: 0, 0, 0, 0, 0, 0, 2, 2, 2, 3, 3, 4, 4, **5**, **5**, **5**, **5**, **5**, **5**, **5**, 6, 7, 8, 8, 8, 8, 8, 8, 12, 15.

Here, 5 is the most repeated value; it occurs seven times. This means that the maximum number of women in this sample are educated up to Grade 5. In other words, the modal education level in this dataset is Grade 5.

To know the quality of faculty in a teaching institution, we may like to know whether most faculty members have a doctorate degree. That would be the mode. The mode is used in specific situations and is employed less often than other measures of central tendency.

28 Measures of Dispersion

Examine the datasets given below:

Data E:	17	22	25	29	**30**	33	34	39	41
Data F:	2	11	19	22	**30**	42	42	44	58

You can see that the two sets have very different values. In Data E, values range from 17 to 41 and are close to one another. In Data F, they range from 2 to 58 and are quite dispersed. However, both sets have the same mean and median, 30. This shows that very dissimilar datasets can have the same mean or median.

To get a better sense of data, besides the mean or median, we should also know the dispersion of values, meaning the degree to which they are scattered around the central value. The above datasets are quite small, so we can easily see the dispersion. To know the dispersion of values in a large or complex dataset, we use standard deviation and range.

STANDARD DEVIATION

Standard deviation (SD) informs the dispersion of values in a dataset around its mean. In other words, it tells us the average distance of values from the mean.

Let us calculate SDs for datasets E and F and see how they differ.

Exercise 1

Calculate standard deviation for Data E.

Data E:	17	22	25	29	30	33	34	39	41

$$SD = \sqrt{\frac{\Sigma (x_i - \overline{x})^2}{n-1}}$$

where $\Sigma = summation$

$x_i = value$

$\overline{x} = mean$

$n = number\ of\ values.$

First, we calculate the mean of this data.

$$Mean = \frac{17+22+25+29+30+33+34+39+41}{9} = \frac{270}{9} = 30$$

Now we will find out the extent to which each value is dispersed around the mean. Let us begin with the highest value, 41. Its deviation from the mean is 41 − 30 = 11. In this way, we calculate deviation of each value from the mean, as shown in Table 28.1.

To calculate SD, we divide the sum of deviations by the number (count) of values in the dataset. However, in this case, the sum of deviations is zero. This is because some values are greater than the mean while others are smaller, and they cancel each other. To prevent

DOI: 10.4324/9781032644257-32

TABLE 28.1
Deviation of Values in Data E from the Mean

Value	Mean	Deviation from Mean (Value − Mean)
17	30	−13
22		−8
25		−5
29		−1
30		0
33		3
34		4
39		9
41		11
270	**Total**	**0**

cancellation of negative and positive deviations, we first square the deviations, as shown in Table 28.2. We then calculate the mean of the squared deviations. The square root of this value will give us the SD.

$$\text{Sum of squared deviations} = 486$$

$$\text{Mean of squared deviations} = \frac{\text{Total}}{(\text{Number of values} - 1)}$$

$$= \frac{486}{(9-1)}$$

$$= \frac{486}{8}$$

$$= 60.75$$

TABLE 28.2
Squared Deviations of Values in Data E

Values	Mean	Deviation from Mean (Value − Mean)	Squared Deviation
17	30	−13	169
22		−8	64
25		−5	25
29		−1	1
30		0	0
33		3	9
34		4	16
39		9	81
41		11	121
		Total	**486**

Square root of the mean gives us SD:

$$\text{Standard deviation} = \sqrt{60.75}$$
$$= 7.79 \approx 8$$

This implies that the average distance of values from the mean is 8.

Note that we use $n - 1$ and not n as the denominator when calculating SD of a sample. There is a reason behind this, which you can learn in an advanced course of biostatistics.

Exercise 2

Calculate standard deviation for Data F.

Data F:	2	11	19	22	30	42	42	44	58

Table 28.3 gives squared deviation for each value in this dataset.

$$\text{Mean of squared deviations} = \frac{2598}{(9-1)}$$
$$= 324.75$$
$$\text{Standard deviation} = \sqrt{324.75}$$
$$= 18$$

The SD for Data F is 18, which indicates that the average distance of values from the mean is 18. Compare this to the SD of Data E, which was 8. It is evident that values in Data F are more dispersed than those in Data E.

Why do we need to calculate standard deviation? Besides giving us a sense of dispersion of values in a dataset, standard deviation is also needed to perform tests of significance. These are covered in a later chapter.

TABLE 28.3
Squared Deviations of Values in Data F

Values	Mean	Deviation from Mean (Value – Mean)	Squared Deviation
2	30	–28	784
11		–19	361
19		–11	121
22		–8	64
30		0	0
42		12	144
42		12	144
44		14	196
58		28	784
		Total	**2598**

RANGE

Range is another measure of dispersion. It gives the difference between the highest and lowest values in a dataset.

Exercise 3

Data A provides the ages of 30 women. Calculate the range for this data.

Data A: 25, 24, 20, 21, 21, 22, 27, 22, 30, 22, 30, 29, 28, 30, 23, 26, 23, 21, 22, 22, 28, 28, 29, 52, 25, 26, 28, 26, 26, 29.

Arranging the values in ascending order, we get:

Data B: 20, 21, 21, 21, 22, 22, 22, 22, 22, 23, 23, 24, 25, 25, 26, 26, 26, 26, 27, 28, 28, 28, 28, 29, 29, 29, 30, 30, 30, 52.

To get range, we subtract the lowest value in the dataset from the highest value.

$$\begin{aligned} \text{Range} &= 52 - 20 \\ &= 32 \end{aligned}$$

Although we can see that most values in this dataset lie between 20 and 30, the outlier, 52, has distorted the range. Therefore, like mean, range is not a suitable measure when there are outliers in the data.

PERCENTILE

A percentile indicates the percentage of values that fall below a particular value in a dataset. So, if a dataset is divided into 100 equal parts, the 99th percentile is the value that has 99% of the values below it. This method is commonly used to rank performance in examinations. If a student scores in the 75th percentile, it means that 75% of the students who took the exam scored less than her and are therefore below her on the merit list. Thus, without knowing this student's actual marks, we can get an idea of her performance compared with other test-takers. Remember, the median is the 50th percentile.

29 Presenting Data

In previous chapters, we dealt with numbers and tables. Data can also be presented visually as a graph or chart, which makes it easier to compare two or more datasets and identify trends and patterns. The following types of charts are commonly used to present data:

- Bar diagram
- Pie diagram
- Line diagram
- Histogram

Besides these, there are also scatter plots and bubble charts, which are used in specific situations.

BAR DIAGRAM

A bar diagram uses rectangular bars to visualize data. The length of each bar is proportional to the value it represents.

Refer to research question 4 in Chapter 26: *Is there a difference in fertility rates of literate and illiterate women?*

Recall that Table 27.1 provided the mean number of children for 30 women grouped by their education levels. It is consolidated and reproduced here as Table 29.1.

Figure 29.1 shows a bar diagram of this data. We can see at a glance that women with higher literacy levels have fewer children.

TABLE 29.1
Fertility of 30 Women with Various Literacy Levels

Education Class Interval	Frequency (No. of Women)	Mean (No. of Children)
Illiterate	6	4
1–5	14	3
6–10	8	3
11–12	1	2
Graduate	1	1
Total	**30**	

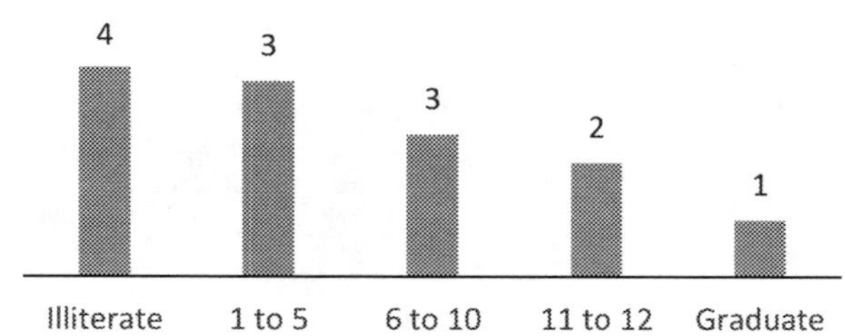

FIGURE 29.1 Average number of children for 30 women with various literacy levels.

DOI: 10.4324/9781032644257-33

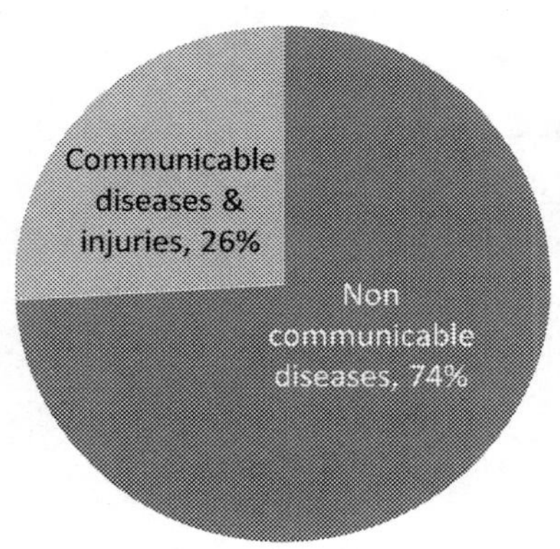

FIGURE 29.2 Causes of death globally.

Source: WHO, 2019: https://www.who.int/news-room/fact-sheets/detail/the-top-10-causes-of-death

PIE DIAGRAM

A pie diagram presents the breakup of a whole as slices, or sections, where each slice represents a specific variable. The size of the slice is proportionate to the frequency of that variable.

The pie diagram in Figure 29.2 shows causes of global mortality, categorized into noncommunicable diseases (NCDs) and communicable diseases and injuries. We can easily make out that NCDs account for nearly three-fourths of all deaths. Alarmingly, share of NCDs in global mortality has been increasing over time.

Figure 29.3 illustrates the top five causes of global mortality. We can see that ischemic heart disease causes maximum deaths, followed by stroke and chronic obstructive pulmonary disease (COPD). Pneumonia and neonatal conditions also contribute to mortality, but their share is decreasing. Notably, share of deaths from ischemic heart disease has increased rapidly in recent decades.

LINE DIAGRAM

A line diagram is a useful tool to study the trend of a disease or health problem over time. A simple line graph shows a single line representing one variable, as illustrated in Figure 29.4.

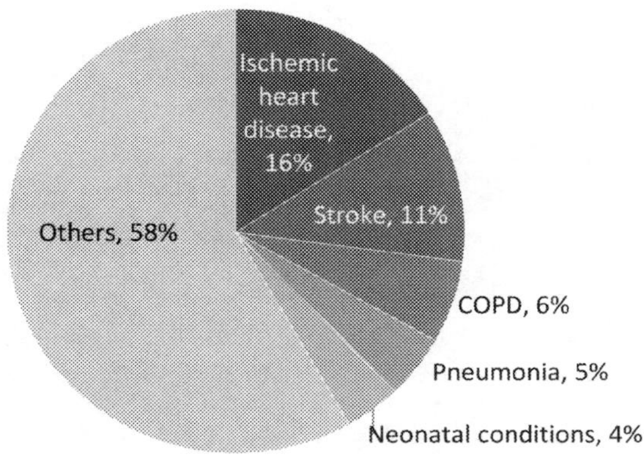

FIGURE 29.3 Top five causes of global mortality.

Source: WHO, 2019: https://www.who.int/news-room/fact-sheets/detail/the-top-10-causes-of-death

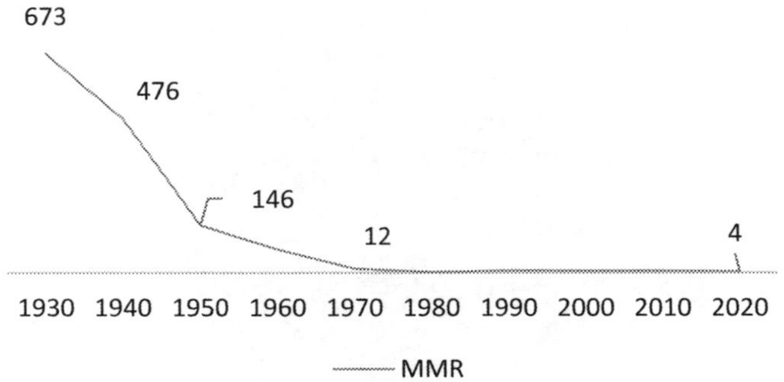

FIGURE 29.4 Finland's maternal mortality ratio.

Figure 29.4 shows that Finland's maternal mortality ratio (MMR) reduced from 673 to 146 in 20 years (1930–1950). In the next 20 years, it reduced from 146 to 12. This gives an idea of the speed with which countries can aim to reduce their MMR.

HISTOGRAM

A histogram is similar to a bar diagram, but with no gaps between the bars. Let us see which type of data can be presented as a histogram.

Data can be discrete or continuous. Discrete data consists of distinct values. For example, educational qualifications like *primary school*, *high school*, *graduate*, and *postgraduate* are distinct values. One can either be a graduate or not—there is no in-between. In contrast, continuous data can take on any value within a range. For example, in a group of children aged 4–5 years, one child may be four years old, another may be four years and one month old, and yet another may be four years, one month, and one day old. Continuous data is commonly presented as a histogram.

As we learned in the chapter "Organizing Data," large or complex data can be organized into frequency (class) intervals. The frequency distribution can then be presented as a histogram. Age, height, weight, and other continuous data are often visualized as a histogram.

Example 1

In a hospital, birth weights of 30 newborns were recorded. The measurements are given in Table 29.2.

TABLE 29.2
Birth Weights of 30 Newborns

SN	Birth Weight (kg)	SN	Birth Weight (kg)	SN	Birth Weight (kg)
1	2.2	11	3.5	21	2.9
2	2.8	12	2.1	22	2.7
3	2.8	13	2.3	23	2.4
4	2.4	14	2.9	24	3.1
5	2.9	15	3.1	25	2.9
6	3	16	2.4	26	2.7
7	2.3	17	2.7	27	3.1
8	3	18	2.9	28	3.5
9	3.3	19	3.1	29	3.2
10	2.6	20	3.2	30	2.7

TABLE 29.3
Birth Weight of 30 Infants Grouped into Class Intervals with Corresponding Frequency Percentages

Birth Weight (kg)	Frequency (No. of Children)	Frequency % $\frac{\text{Frequency}}{30} \times 100$
2.0–2.4	7	23%
2.5–2.9	12	40%
3.0–3.4	9	30%
3.5–4.0	2	7%
Total	**30**	**100%**

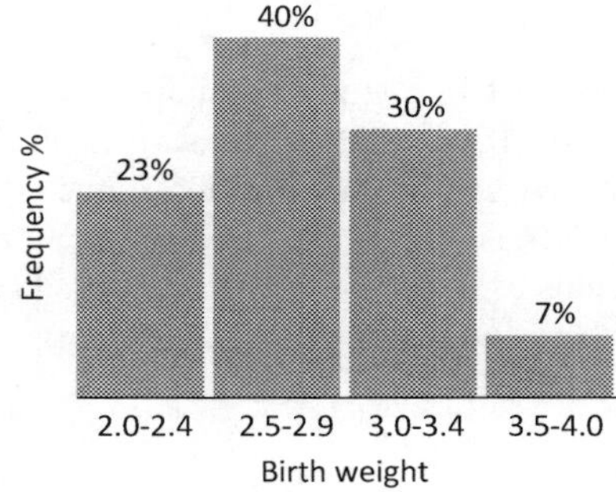

FIGURE 29.5 Histogram of birth weight frequency.

This is a small dataset, but you can see that it is not easy to analyze. Let us group the values into class intervals. On what basis should we fix the class intervals? The primary consideration is that we should be able to distinguish LBW babies from others. A newborn weighing less than 2.5 kg is considered LBW. Additionally, we may like to know if there are children with very low (less than 1.5 kg) or very high (more than 4.5 kg) birth weight. We can define the class intervals accordingly, as shown in Table 29.3.

Figure 29.5 displays a histogram prepared from this data. We can see at a glance that the maximum proportion of children have a healthy birth weight. However, nearly one-fourth (23%) of the children are LBW. There are no children with very low or very high birth weight in this sample.

SCATTER PLOT

Scatter plot is described in the chapter "Correlation and Regression."

30 Sampling Methods

To understand sampling methods, we must first be familiar with the terms commonly used in this context.

STUDY POPULATION

It is the complete set of individuals who can be examined in a research study. It is commonly referred to as *population*. If we want to know the incidence of pneumonia in under-five children in a district, for example, the study population will consist of all under-five children in that district.

SAMPLING FRAME

It is the list of all persons of interest in a study population, with each person assigned a unique numerical identifier. For example, if we want to measure inpatient satisfaction in a hospital, all patients admitted on a particular day can be the sampling frame. This information would be readily available at the hospital. However, it is not always possible to enumerate every person of interest in a study population. In our previous example, it may not be possible to list all under-five children in a district due to their large numbers and distribution across a large area. In such situations, we draw conclusions from one or more samples.

SAMPLE

It is a group of people selected from the study population that represents the entire population.

Why do we use a sample when, ideally, we should study every person in the study population? This is because covering the entire population is rarely possible. For instance, if we want to know the immunization coverage of children aged 12–23 months in a district, it is virtually impossible to reach every child in the district. What we can do is take a representative sample of children from the district and find out their immunization status. To ensure that findings from the sample are applicable to the entire district, the sample must meet certain criteria:

- The sample should include the right participants. This means that every child included in the sample should be between 12 and 23 months old.
- Participants should be drawn from the study population by a valid sampling technique. This is discussed in succeeding sections.
- An adequate sample size should be taken as determined through statistical methods.

Sample size plays an important role in research outcomes. If we increase the sample size, findings will become more and more accurate, but only up to a certain point. Any further increments in sample size will not make a significant difference in the results. Additionally, a larger sample size increases the study's duration and cost. Therefore, it is important to have a sample size that is just sufficient. The discipline of statistics provides methods to determine the optimal sample size for research studies.

STATISTIC

A finding obtained from a sample is called a statistic. If we measure blood hemoglobin levels in a sample of 100 women, the finding can be referred to as a statistic.

DOI: 10.4324/9781032644257-34

SAMPLING VARIATION

If we draw several samples of the same size from a population, the statistics derived from these samples are likely to vary. This is known as sampling variation.

PARAMETER

In some situations, we may need to study the entire population. For example, a national census collects data on every citizen of that country. Similarly, to assess visual acuity of students in a school, we may need to examine every student in the school. A finding derived from the entire population is called a parameter. It is the true value of the phenomenon being studied.

SAMPLING METHODS

Sampling methods can be classified as random and nonrandom.

RANDOM SAMPLING METHODS

In random sampling, everyone in the sampling frame has an equal chance of being selected for the sample. This makes the sample a true representative of the study population. A sampling frame is a prerequisite for random selection—if we do not have a list of all persons of interest in the study population, we cannot make random selection.

There are several methods of random selection:

1. Simple random sampling
2. Systematic sampling
3. Stratified sampling
4. Multistage sampling
5. Cluster sampling

Simple Random Sampling

This is an ideal method of random selection. A sampling frame is prepared, and a unique serial number is assigned to each person. For example, if the study population consists of 200 people, they can be numbered 1–200. Let us say we need a sample size of ten from this population. Which ten people should we include in our sample? We can draw the sample using a random number table, such as the one shown in Figure 30.1.

To use this table for random sampling, we first randomly select a starting point. Let us say we pick the number 61718 as the starting point. For our sample, we need ten numbers between 0 and 201. But the numbers in this table have more digits than we need. We can ignore the extra digits. So, our first number would be 61 (first two digits of 61718). Similarly, we will take the first two digits of the subsequent nine values: 69, 28, 20, 13, 72, 52, 01, 06, and 83. The people who were assigned these numbers in the sampling frame will constitute our sample.

Random number tables can be found in statistics textbooks. To avoid duplication when drawing multiple samples from the same random number table, we take a different starting point each time. Computer programs are also available to generate random numbers.

Systematic Sampling

In this method, we use a fixed pattern to draw a sample from a sampling frame. For example, if we want to draw a sample of 40 people from a sampling frame of 200, we can choose every fifth person in the sampling frame (200/40 = 5). Therefore, the sampling interval in this case is 5. The first person

23157	54859	01837	25993	76249	70886	95230	36744
05545	55043	10537	43508	90611	83744	10962	21343
14871	60350	32404	36223	50051	00322	11543	80834
38976	74951	94051	75853	78805	90194	32428	71695
97312	61718	99755	30870	94251	25841	54882	10513
11742	69381	44339	30872	32797	33118	22647	06850
43361	28859	11016	45623	93009	00499	43640	74036
93806	20478	38268	04491	55751	18932	58475	52571
49540	13181	08429	84187	69538	29661	77738	09527
36768	72633	37948	21569	41959	68670	45274	83880
07092	52392	24627	12067	06558	45344	67338	45320
43310	01081	44863	80307	52555	16148	89742	94647
61570	06360	06173	63775	63148	95123	35017	46993
31352	83799	10779	18941	31579	76448	62584	86919
57048	86526	27795	93692	90529	56546	35065	32254
09243	44200	68721	07137	30729	75756	09298	27650
97957	35018	40894	88329	52230	82521	22532	61587
93732	59570	43781	98885	56671	66826	95996	44569
72621	11225	00922	68264	35666	59434	71687	58167
61020	74418	45371	20794	95917	37866	99536	19378
97839	85474	33055	91718	45473	54144	22034	23000
89160	97192	22232	90637	35055	45489	88438	16361
25966	88220	62871	79265	02823	52862	84919	54883
81443	31719	05049	54806	74690	07567	65017	16543
11322	54931	42362	34386	08624	97687	46245	23245

FIGURE 30.1 An example of a random number table.

can be selected randomly from 1 to 5. Suppose we choose 3 as the first number, the subsequent numbers in the sample would be 8, 13, 18, 23, and so on. Due to this predictability in systematic sampling, randomization becomes slightly weaker.

Stratified Sampling

This method is useful for large study populations consisting of two or more strata. For example, if we want to study anemia in adolescents, there are two distinct strata in this population: Male and female. Since anemia is more prevalent in females, a sample drawn from a mixed population of both sexes may not give meaningful results. A more effective approach would be to take an equal number of male and female participants. This would allow us to compare the two groups.

Similarly, if we want to study vision defects in school children, it might not be logical to include students from all grades in our sample as there can be differences in vision of senior and junior students. A better approach would be to draw separate samples for different grades.

If a district has both urban and rural areas, people in these areas may differ in certain characteristics. If the district's entire population is the sampling frame for a study, it might be better to draw separate rural and urban samples.

Multistage Sampling

When a population is very large, multistage sampling is an option. This technique is often used for country-level studies. First, some districts are randomly selected from every province. Then a few villages are randomly selected from each district. This is followed by selection of a few houses from each village. This method is convenient, but it may give less accurate results than simple random selection.

Cluster Sampling

When a study population is very large and scattered over a vast geographical area, it might be possible to identify geographic clusters that are identical in the characteristics we want to study. However, each cluster may be internally heterogenous.

The UNICEF uses cluster sampling method to measure immunization coverage in districts. On a map of the district, 30 villages (clusters) are randomly selected that are apparently similar. To draw the required sample size of 210, seven children from each selected village are included in the sample. Investigators start at any point in a village and, moving in a single street or direction, conduct a doorstep survey to identify children aged 12–23 months. The children's immunization status is determined by checking their immunization cards and through interviews with the mothers. After collecting this data for seven children, investigators move to the next selected village. In this way, they cover 210 children across 30 villages. The findings obtained from the 30 clusters apply to the entire district.

If we want to compare immunization coverage in urban and rural areas of a district, we will have to take 30 clusters from each area.

Nonrandom Sampling Methods

Nonrandom sampling methods include the following:

1. Convenience sampling
2. Purposive sampling

Convenience Sampling

A postgraduate medical student conducting a study on pancreatitis for her thesis may choose to examine the first 50 cases of pancreatitis she comes across in her unit. This technique is known as convenience sampling or opportunistic sampling. Of course, the findings of this study will not represent the entire population of pancreatitis cases in the city or state, but the student cannot help it; she cannot reach all those cases. This method is convenient and saves time and cost. Even though it is not representative, it can provide useful information.

Purposive Sampling

During the second wave of COVID-19, there was a sudden spurt of mucormycosis (black fungus) cases. The exact cause of the infection was not known. A study can be undertaken for this purpose: We can interview subject matter experts—intensivists, pulmonologists, ophthalmologists, ENT surgeons—from ten prestigious hospitals in the city to know their opinions on possible causes of the infection. In this sampling technique, researchers use their judgment to select study participants. Here again, the sample is not representative, but it can provide useful information that can be used to design further clinical studies.

CALCULATING SAMPLE SIZE

Many web-based sample size calculators are available to use both online and offline; however, we generally take the help of a statistician to calculate sample size for a research study. Logistical, financial, and time constraints often come in the way of sample size determination.

31 Tests of Significance

Let us understand tests of significance with an example.

Example 1

An experiment was conducted to know if iron-folic acid (IFA) tablets increase blood hemoglobin levels in anemic women. Two hundred women with below-normal blood hemoglobin were identified and divided into two groups of 100 each. Women in Group A were given one IFA tablet daily for 100 days. Women in Group B received one placebo tablet daily for the same period. The placebo tablets were similar to IFA tablets in appearance but did not contain iron. After 100 days, 80 women in Group A showed an increase of at least 1 g/dL in their blood hemoglobin levels, whereas only 20 women in Group B showed a similar improvement. From the vast difference in outcomes, we can interpret that IFA tablets are effective in raising blood hemoglobin.

When the same experiment was conducted for a different set of participants, 40% of women in Group A and 30% of women in Group B showed an improvement in their hemoglobin levels. Can we still conclude that IFA is effective in raising blood hemoglobin? Possibly not, because in this case the difference in results does not appear to be significant and could have occurred by chance. If the trial is repeated, this difference may reduce even further, or the results may even reverse.

To know whether the difference in findings from two samples is real or by chance, we apply tests of significance.

HYPOTHESIS TESTING

A hypothesis is an unproven statement.

When conducting research, we begin by formulating a null hypothesis and an alternative hypothesis. For Example 1 above, the null hypothesis is that IFA is not effective in raising blood hemoglobin. The reason we formulate a null hypothesis is that research begins with a skeptical mind. The alternative hypothesis is that IFA is effective in raising blood hemoglobin. To test which hypothesis is correct, we apply an appropriate test of significance on the findings of the study. The null hypothesis is maintained until the test of significance provides evidence against it. If it does, the null hypothesis is rejected and the alternative hypothesis is accepted.

There are many tests of significance, among which Z-test, T-test, and Chi-Squared test are commonly used. Selection of a suitable test depends on what we want to test, the sample size, and our knowledge of the population's distribution.

To apply a test of significance, we need to be conversant with some statistical concepts:

1. Normal Distribution
2. Standard Error
3. Confidence Interval

NORMAL DISTRIBUTION

Let us take an example to understand the concept of normal distribution.

DOI: 10.4324/9781032644257-35

TABLE 31.1
Frequency Distribution of Heights of 408 Men

Height (cm)	Frequency	Relative Frequency: $\frac{\text{Frequency}}{408}$
155	7	0.02
157	10	0.02
159	18	0.04
161	45	0.11
163	80	0.20
165	100	0.25
167	80	0.20
169	38	0.09
171	17	0.04
173	9	0.02
175	4	0.01
Total	**408**	**1.00**

Example 2

A random sample of 408 men aged 25–50 years was drawn from a specified population of men and their heights were measured. The findings are presented in Table 31.1. The last column provides the relative frequency[1] for each value.

This data is presented as a bar diagram in Figure 31.1, where heights are plotted on x-axis and relative frequencies on y-axis. Each bar represents the proportion of people of that height. We can see that the maximum proportion of people are 165 cm tall. A smaller proportion are taller or shorter by 2 cm; a still smaller proportion are taller or shorter by 4 cm; and so on. By joining the tips of the bars with a line, we get a symmetric curve, as shown in Figure 31.2.

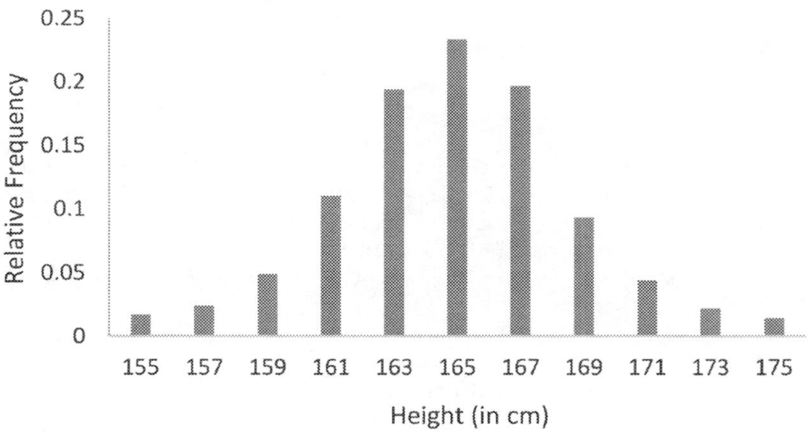

FIGURE 31.1 Relative frequency distribution of heights of 408 men.

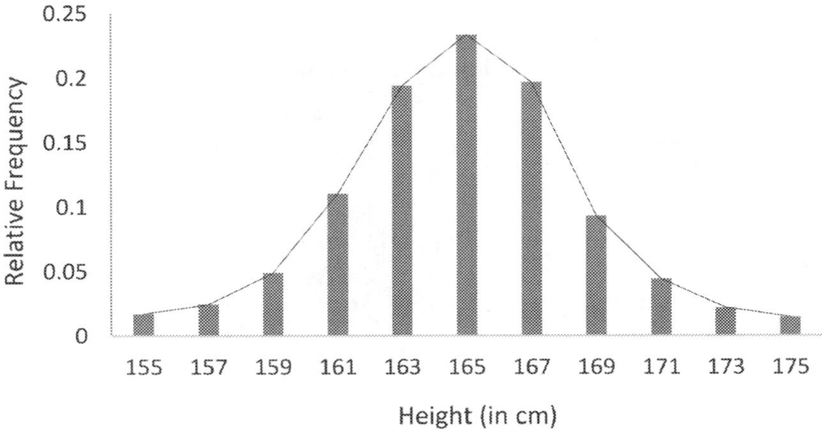

FIGURE 31.2 Relative frequency distribution curve of heights of 408 men.

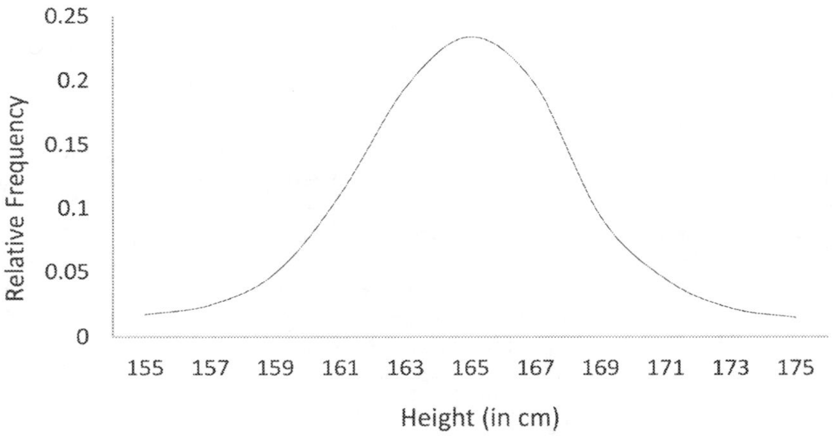

FIGURE 31.3 Normal curve of heights of 408 men.

If we increase the sample size, this curve will take a smooth and symmetric bell shape, as depicted in Figure 31.3. Such a curve is known as a normal curve, or normal distribution. A vertical line passing through the mean splits a normal curve into two equal and identical halves.

Interestingly, many biological measures like body weight, blood pressure, and blood hemoglobin are normally distributed in large samples, though the shape of the curve may vary. Let us see how.

If the majority of adults in a population have average body weight, the frequency distribution of their weights will be a normal curve, as shown in Figure 31.4.

If a large number of adults in the population are underweight, the curve deviates to the left, or becomes positively skewed, as shown in Figure 31.5. As you can see, with fewer people weighing 66 kg or more, the right tail of the curve has become elongated.

Conversely, if a large number of adults in the population are overweight or obese, the frequency distribution curve deviates to the right, or becomes negatively skewed, as shown in Figure 31.6. In this case, the left tail of the curve is elongated because fewer people weigh 60 kg or less.

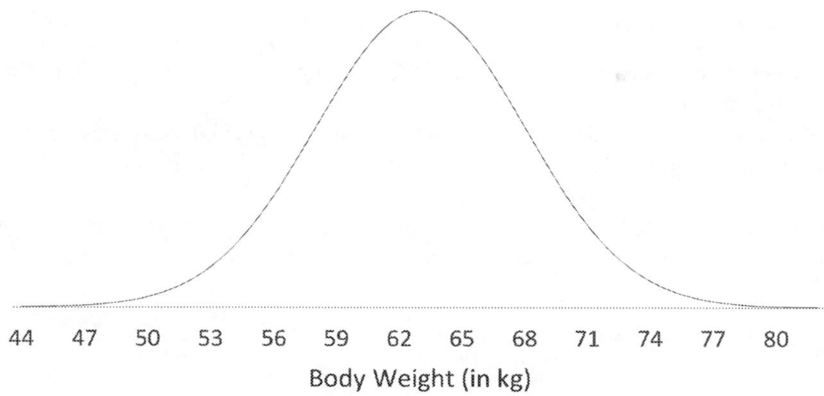

FIGURE 31.4 Normal frequency distribution curve of body weights in a population.

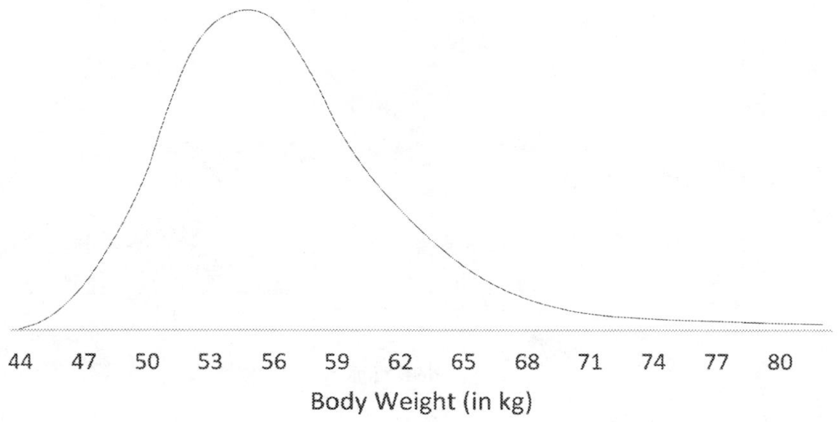

FIGURE 31.5 Positively skewed frequency distribution curve of body weights in a population.

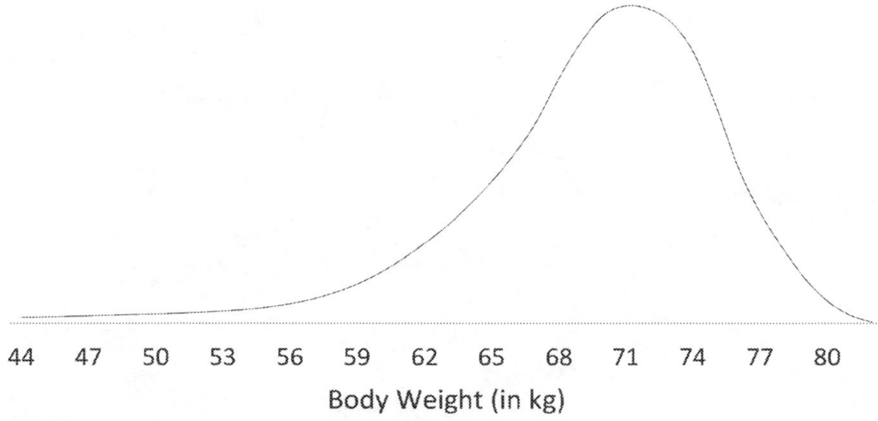

FIGURE 31.6 Negatively skewed frequency distribution curve of body weights in a population.

Area under a Normal Curve

In Table 31.1, the sum of relative frequencies is 1. Accordingly, the area under the normal curve is 1, or 100%, as shown in Figure 31.7.

The spread of a normal curve depends on its standard deviation (SD). Another interesting feature of normal distribution is that 95% of the total area under the curve lies between 1.96 times the SD on either side of the mean, as shown in Figure 31.8.

Let us understand the application of this feature using Example 2. The mean height for this sample of 408 men was calculated to be 164.8 cm, which can be rounded to 165 cm. The SD was found to be 3.7 cm.

Now,

$$1.96 \times \text{SD} = 1.96 \times 3.7 = 7.2 \text{ cm}$$

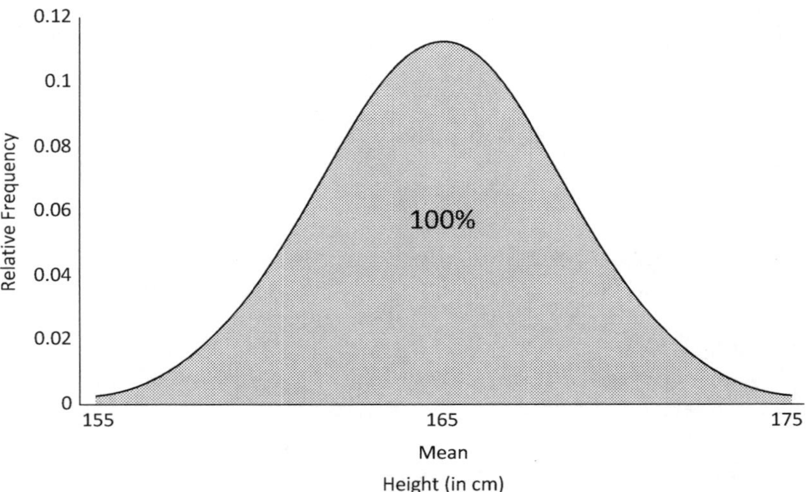

FIGURE 31.7 Area under a normal curve.

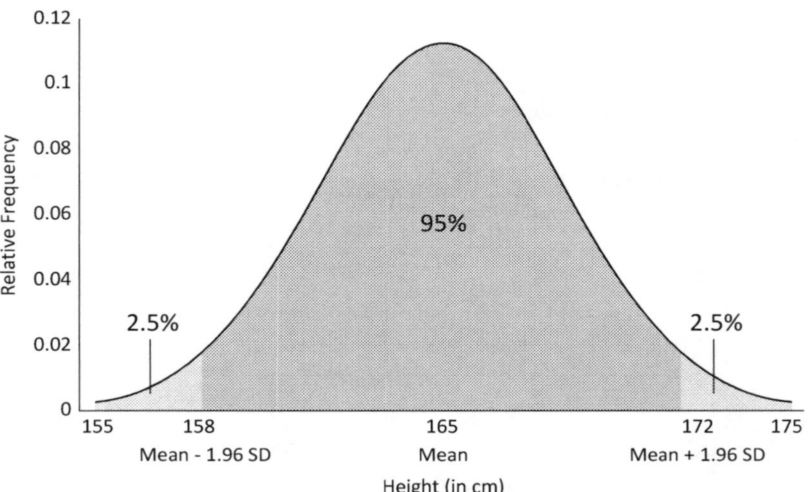

FIGURE 31.8 Area under a normal curve (1.96 SD around mean).

This means that heights within 7.2 cm on either side of the mean constitute 95% of the curve's area.

$$\text{Height on left side of the mean: } 165-7.2=157.8\approx 158 \text{ cm}$$

$$\text{Height on right side of the mean: } 165+7.2=172.2\approx 172 \text{ cm}$$

That means that heights of 95% of men in this sample lie within the range of 158–172 cm.

The concept of normal distribution can be applied to determine whether two values of a variable are significantly different from each other. In the above example, men whose height is between 158 cm and 172 cm will be considered similar to others in the sample; any deviation is by chance. However, men whose height is below 158 cm or above 172 cm will be considered significantly different from others in the sample.

It should be known that many statistical tests and calculations are applicable only if we presume that the population data is normally distributed.

STANDARD ERROR

When we draw several samples of a particular size from a population, it is normal for them to differ from each other. Naturally, the statistics calculated from these samples, be it the mean or SD, will also differ. As previously stated in the chapter "Sampling Methods," this is known as sampling variation.

Regardless of how a population is distributed, the means of the samples drawn from it will always follow a normal distribution. The SD of the mean values of the samples is called standard error (SE) of the mean. SE is typically smaller than the SD of individual values.

$$\text{Standard error of mean} = \frac{\text{SD}}{\sqrt{\text{n}}}$$

where SD = standard deviation

n = sample size

$$\text{In our example, standard error of mean} \approx \frac{3.7}{\sqrt{408}} \approx \frac{3.7}{20.2} \approx 0.18 \text{ cm}$$

This means that if we draw several samples of men from the specified population, the means of these samples will differ from the population mean by 0.18 cm on average.

Standard error is a useful tool for calculating confidence intervals and for testing hypotheses, as we will see in the next sections.

CONFIDENCE INTERVAL

We estimate the population mean from the sample mean, but if we draw several samples of equal size from a population, their means can differ. So, a range of values may better express the population mean. This range is known as confidence interval. The population mean is likely to lie within this interval.

$$\text{Confidence interval of the mean} = \text{sample mean} \pm (1.96 \times \text{standard error})$$

Note: Since 95% of a normal distribution lies in the range "mean ± 1.96 SE," our calculations below give us the 95% confidence interval of the mean.

Let us find the confidence interval for the mean height in Example 2. The mean height is 165 cm, and SE of the mean is 0.18 cm. Therefore, confidence interval of mean height:

$$165 \pm (1.96 \times 0.18)$$
$$= 165 \pm 0.35$$
$$= (164.65,\ 165.35)$$

This means that if we draw some more samples from the population, the mean for most samples will lie between 164.65 and 165.35. It can be assumed that the population mean also lies in this range.

EXAMPLE

Let us see how a test of significance can be applied to accept or reject a null hypothesis.

Example 3

In a specified population, the mean fasting blood sugar level was reported to be 90 mg/dL. A researcher who wanted to test this finding randomly selected 100 people from this population and measured their fasting blood sugar levels. She obtained a mean fasting blood sugar of 96 mg/dL, with an SD of 40 mg/dL. Was this finding different from previous knowledge? To answer this question, the researcher applied a test of significance.

Null hypothesis: Difference between the new measured value (96 mg/dL) and previous knowledge (90 mg/dL) is by chance.

Alternate hypothesis: The new value (96 mg/dL) is significantly different from previous knowledge (90 mg/dL).

It is known that blood sugar level is normally distributed in a population, and since a sample size of 100 people is sufficiently large, a Z-test can be used.

For a mean blood sugar level of 90 mg/dL, we know that the area within 90 ± 1.96 SE should cover 95% of the area under a normal curve. The SD is 40 mg/dL.

$$\text{Therefore, standard error} = \frac{\text{SD}}{\sqrt{n}} = \frac{40}{\sqrt{100}} \approx 4 \text{ mg/dL}$$

$$\text{Confidence interval} = 90 \pm (1.96 \times 4) = (82.2,\ 97.8)$$

Since the calculated sample mean of 96 lies within this range, the null hypothesis can be accepted at a 95% level of confidence. That means, in this situation, the difference observed between the measured value (96 mg/dL) and previous knowledge (90 mg/dL) is due to chance.

If we had a smaller sample, we could have used a T-test instead. Students can learn about T-test and Chi-squared test in an advanced course of biostatistics.

P-VALUE

Statistical methods also allow us to calculate the probability of observed differences being due to chance. This probability, known as P-value, is the probability of obtaining a particular value of the statistic if the null hypothesis is true. If P-value is high, the null hypothesis is true, and the observed difference is due to chance. Conversely, a low P-value indicates that the difference is real and so the alternative hypothesis is true.

Some readers may find these concepts difficult to understand. This is expected, as these concepts are actually complicated. The author recommends that you use the information provided in these chapters to become familiar with the terminologies commonly used in statistics. In the future, when you conduct research and seek the help of a statistician, familiarity with these terms will be useful in communicating the help you need.

NOTE

1. Relative frequency informs us how often a particular event occurs relative to the total number of events in a given sample. It is calculated by dividing the frequency of the specific event by the total number of events.

32 Correlation and Regression

CORRELATION

When children grow in height, we expect their weight to increase as well. But to what extent? Correlation is a metric that measures the strength of association between two variables. It is expressed as the correlation coefficient r, which can take values from −1 to +1.

SCATTER PLOT

A scatter plot is a visual representation of the correlation between two variables. It shows whether the correlation is positive or negative and gives an idea about the strength of association between the variables. However, note that a scatter plot only provides a qualitative assessment and not a precise measurement of the correlation between variables.

POSITIVE CORRELATION

When an increase in the value of one variable is accompanied by a corresponding increase in the value of the other, the two are said to be positively correlated. The strength of this relationship can be measured using the correlation coefficient.

When $r = +1$, the correlation is perfectly positive. This means that an increase in one variable will be accompanied by a proportional increase in the other. The closer the value of r is to +1, the stronger the degree of positive correlation. Figure 32.1 illustrates an almost perfect positive correlation between the lengths and weights of children.

When r is between 0 and +1, the correlation is imperfect but positive, as shown in Figure 32.2.

When $r = 0$, there is no correlation between the two variables.

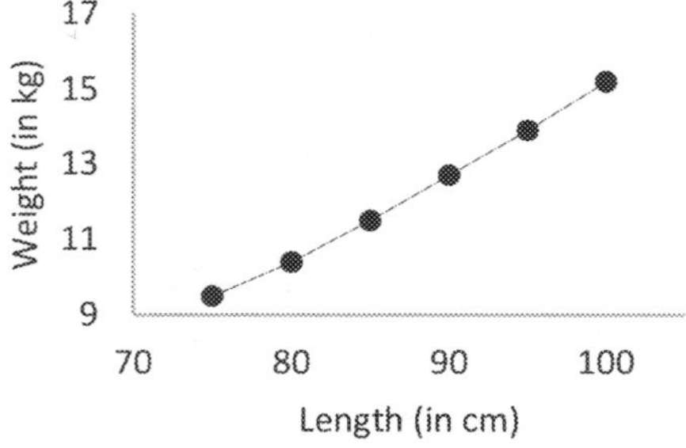

FIGURE 32.1 Perfect positive correlation.

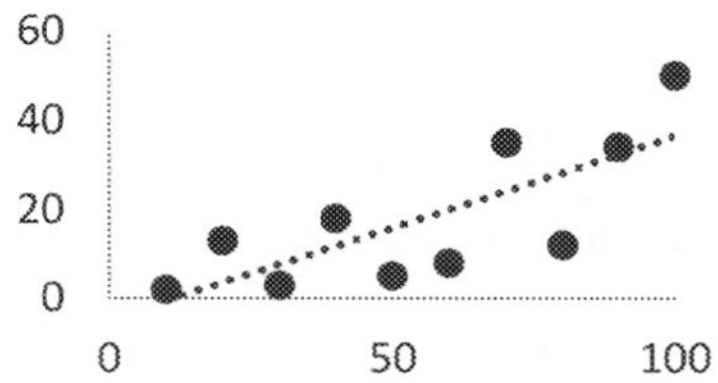

FIGURE 32.2 Imperfect positive correlation.

DOI: 10.4324/9781032644257-36

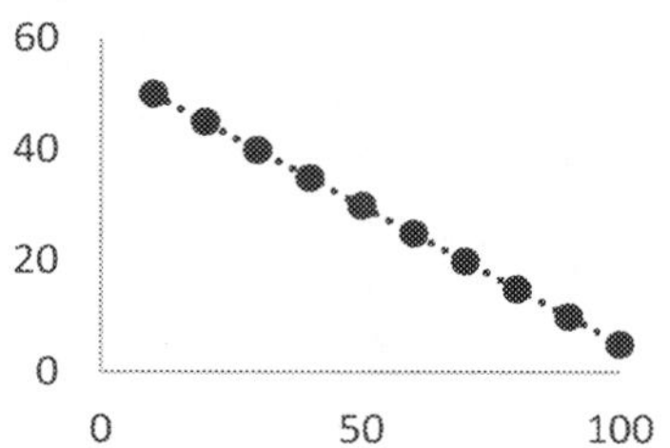

FIGURE 32.3 Perfect negative correlation.

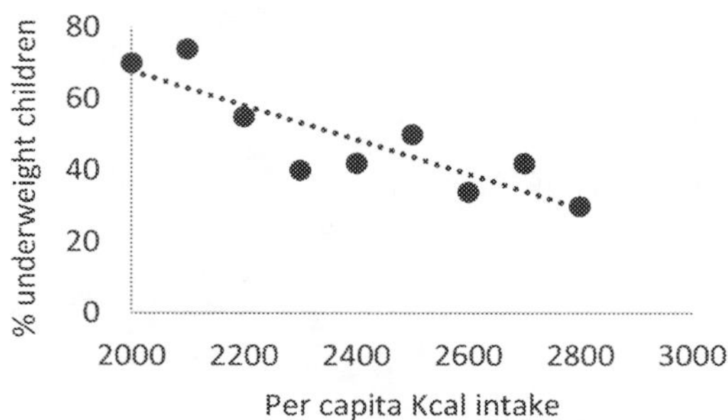

FIGURE 32.4 Imperfect negative correlation.

Negative Correlation

When an increase in the value of one variable is accompanied by a corresponding decrease in the value of the other, the two are negatively correlated. For example, as age of older women increases, their bone mineral density (BMD) decreases.

In a perfect negative correlation, $r = -1$. The closer the value of r is to -1, the stronger the degree of negative correlation. Figure 32.3 illustrates a perfect negative correlation.

When r lies between 0 and -1, the correlation is imperfectly negative. Figure 32.4 shows an imperfect negative association between per capita energy intake and the prevalence of underweight children in selected populations.

It may be known that an association between two variables does not necessarily indicate a cause-and-effect relationship. For example, high blood cholesterol level is often associated with hypertension, but this does not mean that high blood cholesterol causes hypertension.

REGRESSION

Regression analysis goes a step further than correlation. It quantifies the association between a dependent variable and an independent variable. We can predict the value(s) of the dependent variable based on the value(s) of the independent variable.

A linear regression is commonly used for this purpose, as illustrated below.

Example 1

Figure 32.5 shows a scatter plot of the association between age and BMD of 36 women aged 40–80 years. Here, age is the independent variable (plotted on *x*-axis) and BMD is dependent on age (plotted on *y*-axis). As we can see, an increase in age is associated with a decrease in BMD. But to what degree? We can find this out using linear regression.

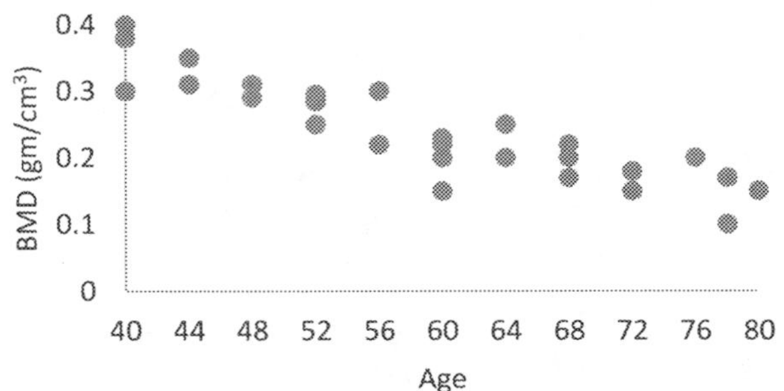

FIGURE 32.5 Scatter plot of ages and BMD of 36 women.

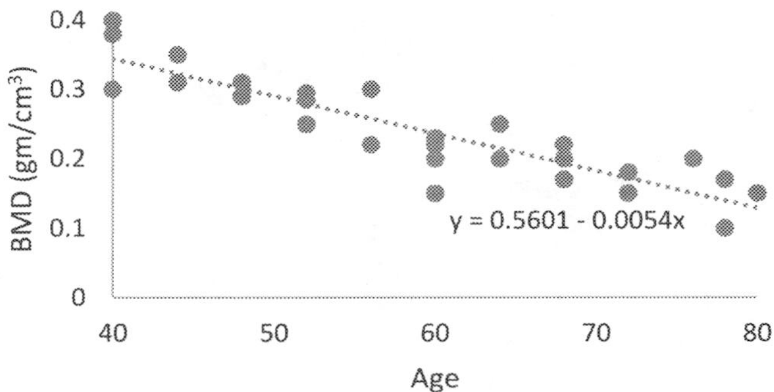

FIGURE 32.6 Linear regression line of ages and BMD of 36 women.

By drawing a linear regression line through the dots, we get the best estimate for the average BMD for a given age; see Figure 32.6.

$$\text{Equation of linear regression line: } y = a + bx$$

where y = dependent variable (plotted on y-axis)

x = independent variable (plotted on x-axis)

a = constant or intercept value of y for x = 0

b = slope of linear regression line.

Note that a and b are also called regression coefficients. We can find the value of BMD for any age if we know the values of the regression coefficients.

$$\text{BMD} = \text{a} + (\text{b} \times \text{age})$$

The values of regression coefficients can be computed using data management software, such as the Statistical Package for the Social Sciences. In the above example, we found that, on average, a one-year increase in age corresponds to a BMD decrease of 0.0054 gram per cubic centimeter.

Section V

Public Health Nutrition

33 Nutrition and Nutrients

We need energy to perform physical activities. Even when we are at rest, our internal organs use energy to function.

Basal Metabolic Rate (BMR) is the amount of energy our body needs to maintain its basic functions while at rest.

We get energy from food. The quantity of food we need depends on factors such as age, gender, and level of physical activity. For instance, a laborer who digs earth needs more food than someone in a desk job. Further, nutritional requirement increases in certain stages of life. A pregnant woman needs additional nutrition to support the growing fetus in her womb; lactating women need extra nutrients for milk production; and children and adolescents need additional nutrition for their growth and development.

TYPES OF NUTRIENTS

All foods, whether they come from plants or animals, contain biochemical substances known as nutrients. These are broadly classified into two groups: Macronutrients and micronutrients.

Carbohydrates, proteins, and fats are macronutrients. They are our primary sources of energy and we need them in large quantities. Vitamins and minerals are micronutrients. These nutrients do not produce energy but they facilitate the utilization of macronutrients and regulation of metabolic functions in the body. We need micronutrients in relatively smaller quantities.

CARBOHYDRATES

Carbohydrates (or carbs) provide the bulk of energy for our day-to-day activities. Each gram of carbohydrates provides four calories. Sugar and starch are the two main energy-producing carbohydrates. Starch is made up of several units of sugar.

While cereals and pulses are the main sources of starch, roots and tubers also contain considerable starch. Sugar mostly comes from cane sugar and fruits. Among foods of animal origin, milk contains lactose, a type of sugar. Other animal foods, such as meat, fish, and egg, are virtually devoid of carbohydrates.

Our body converts dietary carbohydrates into glucose for immediate energy. Any excess carbs are converted into glycogen and are stored mainly in the liver and muscles for future use.

Glycemic Index

Some types of carbohydrates are absorbed more rapidly by the body when consumed, causing a quick spike in blood glucose levels. Glycemic index (GI) ranks carbohydrates on a scale of 0–100 based on how much and how quickly they raise blood sugar.[1] Foods such as cane sugar, watermelon, potato, and some varieties of rice have high GI scores. People with diabetes should take these foods in moderation. Conversely, pulses and a majority of cereals have medium GI. Meat, fish, vegetables, and fruits mostly have low GI.

DIETARY FIBER

Fiber,[2] also called roughage, is a type of carbohydrate that cannot be digested by the human gut and therefore provides no nutritive value. Despite this, we should include fiber in our diet as it aids

DOI: 10.4324/9781032644257-38

bowel cleaning. Commensal bacteria in the colon break down fiber, where it forms the bulk of feces and helps in its evacuation.

Fresh vegetables and fruits are rich sources of fiber. Unrefined cereals and whole pulses also contain some fiber.

Some studies suggest that a high-fiber diet may have a role in preventing obesity by slowing the absorption of carbs and fats. It may also have a role in reducing the risk of colon cancer. More evidence is needed to reach definite conclusions.

FATS

Fats are also known as lipids. Fats that are liquid at room temperature are called oils. Besides edible oil, butter, and clarified butter, many other foods like fresh milk, nuts, and meat contain fat, although it may not be visible to the eye. Most cereals and pulses contain traces of fat. Majority of fats are insoluble in water.

After carbohydrates, fats are the second-most important source of energy. While carbs provide us immediate energy, fats serve as long-term reserves. In starvation, the body uses fat reserves to produce energy. Fats have the highest energy density; they provide nine calories per gram.

Fats have many other functions. They aid the absorption of fat-soluble vitamins and act as precursors to various hormones, including adrenocortical hormones and sex hormones. Essential fatty acids are necessary for certain metabolic processes. Fats in meals slow down gastric emptying, giving us a sense of satiety and reducing the urge to overeat. Fats improve palatability of foods; foods are often tastier when cooked in oil or butter than when boiled or steamed. The layer of fat beneath our skin serves as a cushion, protecting us from extreme cold.

Dietary fats are of three types: Saturated fats, unsaturated fats, and trans fats.

Saturated Fats

Foods of animal origin, such as milk, butter, clarified butter, cheese, paneer, mutton, pork, and beef, contain saturated fats. Fish and chicken are exceptions as they mostly contain unsaturated fats. An advantage of animal fat is that it contains vitamins A and D, which are not typically found in vegetable fats.

Saturated fats tend to solidify at room temperature. They are considered unhealthy as they increase low-density lipoproteins (LDL), the "bad cholesterol" associated with cardiovascular diseases (CVDs).

Interestingly, despite being plant products, coconut oil and palm oil are predominantly saturated fats. Coconut oil is a common cooking medium in the Indian state of Kerala. It might be interesting to study whether this has any implications on the occurrence of CVDs in the region.

Unsaturated Fats

Unsaturated fats mainly come from plant sources. They are liquid at room temperature. There are two types of unsaturated fats:

- Monounsaturated fats: Mustard oil, groundnut oil, rice bran oil, rapeseed oil, olive oil, nuts, and chicken meat are some examples.
- Polyunsaturated fats: Safflower oil, sunflower oil, corn oil, cotton seed oil, and walnuts are high in polyunsaturated fats. Fish is a major source of these fats.

Unsaturated fats are good for health. They increase high-density lipoproteins (HDL), the "good cholesterol" that transports cholesterol from peripheral tissues to the liver for elimination. Polyunsaturated fats also provide essential fatty acids.

It may be noted that repeated heating of vegetable oils degrades their quality and renders them harmful.

Trans Fats

Trans fats are unhealthy fats that increase LDL. They come from both natural and industrial sources. Industrial-produced trans fats are created by passing hydrogen gas through vegetable oil, which solidifies the oil. Due to their adverse effects on health, the WHO recommends eliminating trans fats from diet.

Body Fat

Fat exists in two forms in our bodies:

- Triglycerides: Most of the fat we consume in our diet is stored as triglycerides, serving as an energy reserve for future use.
- Cholesterol: While cholesterol does not provide us energy, it is an essential constituent of cell membranes, steroids, and sex hormones. We need cholesterol in small amounts; excess cholesterol is harmful for health as it gets converted into LDL.

PROTEINS

Protein is an important constituent of cell membranes. The bulk of our muscles are made up of two proteins, namely actin and myosin. We also need proteins for growth, tissue repair, injury recovery, and production of hormones and antibodies.

Proteins are made up of amino acids. Twenty amino acids make a variety of proteins by various combinations. Nine of these amino acids, known as essential amino acids, cannot be produced in the body and must be obtained through diet.

While protein is not our primary source of energy, the body can use it to generate energy when its carbohydrate and fat reserves are depleted.

Animal-based foods such as milk, eggs, chicken, fish, and meat are excellent sources of high-quality proteins that are easily digestible. These foods contain around 20% protein, and their protein is considered to be of high biological value due to the presence of many essential amino acids.

Plant foods such as pulses, legumes, and cereals also contain protein, but in relatively smaller amounts (around 10%). Wheat contains 12% protein. Rice contains 7% protein, but its protein quality is relatively better. Soybean, with 40% protein, is one of the best protein sources, but many people do not like its taste. Fruits, vegetables, roots, and tubers are poor sources of protein. Plant-based proteins lack essential amino acids and are therefore considered to have lower biological value than animal-based proteins. They also have lower digestibility. Cooking improves their digestibility.

VITAMINS

Vitamins A, B, C, D, E, and K are the main vitamins. Among these, vitamins B and C are water-soluble and vitamins A, D, E, and K are fat-soluble. Vitamins A and D are of particular importance in public health as their deficiencies are common. Deficiencies of vitamins B1, B2, B3, B12, and C have become less common over time.

Our bodies can synthesize vitamins A, B3, and D; for others, we depend on our diet.

MINERALS

The human body needs a number of minerals. Among them, iron, zinc, iodine, fluoride, and calcium are particularly important from a public health perspective.

NUTRITIONAL DEFICIENCIES

People living in poverty cannot afford vegetables, eggs, or meat products. They survive mainly on carbohydrates. Such a diet lacks essential micronutrients, particularly iron, zinc, vitamin A, and calcium. This is "hidden hunger," wherein people suffer from micronutrient deficiencies despite getting enough calories from their diet.

The following nutritional deficiencies are common in low-income settings:

- Protein-energy malnutrition
- Iron-deficiency anemia
- Iodine deficiency disorder
- Vitamin A deficiency
- Calcium deficiency

These are explained in subsequent chapters.

NOTES

1. Pure glucose is given an arbitrary value of 100 glycemic index.
2. Fiber is technically cellulose, hemicellulose, gum, or pectin.

34 Nutritional Assessment

Nutritional assessment refers to measuring the nutritional status of a population to identify common nutritional deficiencies and the affected groups. The findings are used to implement targeted interventions that address the specific nutritional needs of the affected people.

While the nutritional status of individuals can be assessed by clinical examination and laboratory tests, measuring the nutritional status of an entire population requires methods that can be applied on a large scale. Assessment of vulnerable groups such as children, adolescent girls, and women of reproductive age gives us a fair idea about the population. The following methods are commonly used.

ANTHROPOMETRIC EXAMINATION

Anthropometry is the practice of measuring body dimensions, such as height, weight, arm circumference, and skin thickness. It is a valuable tool for assessing nutritional status of children.

Inadequate nutrition leads to growth retardation in children. The child fails to gain weight or grow in height. Accordingly, the two most common measures of nutritional deficiencies in children are the following:

1. Height-for-age
2. Weight-for-height

Height for Age

Stunting: Children are considered stunted if their height is significantly below the height of normal children of the same age and sex.

Stunting is a sign of chronic undernourishment, meaning that the child did not receive adequate nutrition for a long period of time.

How can we measure stunting? The WHO Child Growth Standards provide median heights for normal male and female children at different ages, along with corresponding values of standard deviation (SD) from median height. A child whose height is 2 SD below median height is identified as stunted (mild to moderate stunting). A child whose height is 3 SD below the median height is considered severely stunted. Note that we use median height for this purpose and not mean (average) height. Table 34.1 shows a slice of the WHO growth chart for height-for-age.

As we can see, the median height for 24-month-old girls is 85.7 cm. Two SD below median height is 79.3 cm. Therefore, a 24-month-old girl whose height is less than 79.3 cm will be considered stunted. A 24-month-old girl whose height is below 76 cm (or 3 SD below median height) will be considered severely stunted.

Weight for Height

When children do not get adequate food, they fail to gain weight and even lose weight. This is called wasting. Wasting can occur in a short time.

Wasting: In clinical parlance, wasting refers to reduction in a person's muscle mass. Children are considered wasted if their weight is significantly below the weight of normal children of the same height and sex.

DOI: 10.4324/9781032644257-39

TABLE 34.1
A Sample of WHO Child Growth Standards: Height-for-Age

Sex	Age (Months)	Median Height (cm)	−1 SD (cm)	−2 SD (cm)	−3 SD (cm)
Girl	24	85.7	82.5	79.3	76.0
Boy	24	87.1	84.1	81.0	78.0

Source: https://www.who.int/tools/child-growth-standards/standards/length-height-for-age.

TABLE 34.2
A Sample of WHO Child Growth Standards: Weight-for-Height

Sex	Height (cm)	Median Weight (kg)	−1 SD (kg)	−2 SD (kg)	−3 SD (kg)
Girl	65	7.2	6.6	6.1	5.6
Boy	65	7.4	6.9	6.3	5.9

Source: https://www.who.int/tools/child-growth-standards/standards/weight-for-length-height.

The WHO Child Growth Standards provide weight-for-height references for normal male and female children at different ages. A child whose body weight is 2 SD below median weight is identified as wasted. A child whose weight is 3 SD below median weight is considered severely wasted. Table 34.2 provides median weights for boys and girls of 65 cm in height.

As you can see, here body weight is correlated with height and not age. There is a reason for this: If a child is tall for his age, his weight should be proportionate to his height and not his age.

Height-for-age and weight-for-height are sensitive indicators. Many international organizations, including the UN and UNICEF, use these indicators to rank countries on undernutrition or hunger indices.

Mid-Upper Arm Circumference

In a large survey, where it might not be feasible to measure the heights and weights of all children, mid-upper arm circumference (MUAC) can be an alternative. A special measuring tape is used for this purpose. The child inserts his left arm into the tape's loop, and the health worker tightens the tape around the mid-upper arm and takes the reading while the arm hangs loosely at the side. The tape is color-coded, with green indicating a normal reading, yellow indicating borderline, and red indicating acute malnutrition. In a large group of children, malnourished children can be identified readily with this method. Figure 34.1 shows how MUAC is measured.

An MUAC measurement of less than 11.5 cm in children aged six months to five years indicates severe acute malnutrition. There is risk of tissue atrophy and death. In such cases, the child should be immediately admitted for therapeutic feeding.

For up to five years of age, MUAC remains relatively independent of height and age. It is a particularly useful method to assess the nutritional status of children in famine-affected areas and to monitor the progress of large-scale nutritional interventions aimed at children.

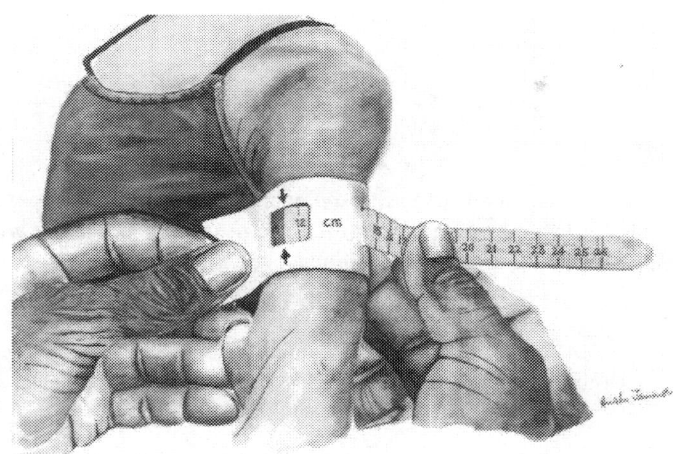

FIGURE 34.1 Measurement of mid-upper arm circumference.

Others

Skin thickness,[1] head circumference, and chest circumference are other indicators of children's nutritional status, but they are not commonly used nowadays as height-for-age and weight-for-height are more reliable measures.

BIOCHEMICAL TESTS

Iron-Deficiency Anemia

A large number of adolescent girls and reproductive-age women in low-income settings are anemic. Anemia can be easily identified by clinical examination. Inspection of inner surface of eyelids, nailbeds, palms, or tongue shows pallor (paleness). But this method is not suitable for large-scale surveys, where many field investigators are involved in data collection. To avoid subjectivity in measurements, we need a reliable diagnostic test. In community programs, a portable digital hemoglobinometer can be used for blood hemoglobin estimation. For larger populations, serum ferritin level is a useful indicator of iron deficiency.

Vitamin A Deficiency

Clinical signs such as night blindness and Bitot spots indicate vitamin A deficiency in populations. Night blindness during pregnancy is particularly common in low-income countries. To assess subclinical vitamin A deficiency, which is more widespread, serum retinol concentration can be used in population-level surveys. But note that this method is not suitable for individual assessments.

Iodine Deficiency

Urinary iodine concentration is a simple and sensitive test to detect iodine deficiency at community level. It can be used across age groups. By comparing test results to the median urinary iodine concentration, the extent of iodine deficiency can be determined.

Vitamin D Deficiency

Vitamin D deficiency can be assessed by measuring blood level of 25-hydroxy vitamin D.

BODY MASS INDEX

Body mass index (BMI) is calculated by dividing a person's body weight in kilograms by the square of their height in meters. It is a commonly used measure of obesity in adults, with BMI above 25 indicating obesity and BMI below 18.5 indicating undernutrition.

NOTE

1. Skin thickness is measured over the triceps muscle, on the posterior side of the upper arm.

35 Protein-Energy Malnutrition

Protein-energy malnutrition (PEM), also known as protein-calorie malnutrition, mainly affects children. It occurs when a child gets inadequate food or virtually gets no food over a long period of time.

Normally, a child deprived of food would be deficient in all nutrients and not just protein. So why the name *protein-energy malnutrition*? It is true that a malnourished child can be deficient in all nutrients; however, the primary concern in such cases is that the child does not get the minimum energy to sustain basic body functions (i.e., basal metabolic rate). This can lead to irreversible physical and cognitive damage and even death.

BURDEN

According to WHO estimates, over 50% of all childhood deaths are due to undernutrition. The problem is endemic in sub-Saharan Africa and South Asia, where there is no respite from mild to moderate PEM. Severe PEM is now less common in peaceful regions, but it can be seen during times of famine, civil unrest, or war.

CAUSES

Undernutrition is the primary cause of PEM. Undernutrition weakens immunity, increasing the risk of infections like diarrhea, measles, and malaria. Repeated infections deplete the body's nutritional reserves. Recurring episodes of diarrhea can lead to chronic inflammation of the small intestine, impairing its capacity to absorb nutrients. Helminthic infestations, common in communities where basic sanitation is compromised, can cause blood loss and potentiate nutritional deficiencies. This interplay of food inadequacy, infections, and infestations worsens PEM in children.

In low-income settings, many children are born preterm or LBW. These infants have low immunity and poor nutritional reserves. Their inability to suckle further increases their risk of PEM.

Sociocultural and economic factors also have an important role in causing PEM. Breastfeeding is a common practice in low-income communities, but underage or undernourished mothers may not produce enough milk. In extreme poverty, children are often weaned on diluted rice water or other starch solutions that barely contain any nutrients. Gender inequalities and gender-based discrimination in some communities further compound the problem for girl children.

MANIFESTATION

PEM manifests in the following ways:

Stunting

As mentioned in the preceding chapter, stunting, or reduced linear growth, is a consequence of long-term nutritional inadequacy. To plan appropriate interventions, public health experts should know the age groups in which stunting is prevalent. A newborn has some nutritional reserve that can sustain her for nearly two months after birth, and with breastfeeding being a common practice in low-income communities, nutritional deficiencies generally start to develop after weaning. However, if breastfeeding is inadequate, growth faltering can start as early as the third month. Risk of stunting is particularly high from 12 to 24 months and remains considerable until age five.

DOI: 10.4324/9781032644257-40

FIGURE 35.1 Stunting in children.

Figure 35.1 shows three children of the same age. They all appear to be healthy, but we can see that two children are shorter in height—they are stunted. Stunting is a common problem in low-income countries, but not much attention is given to this problem.

Wasting

Wasting in absence of stunting reflects short-term nutritional inadequacy.

Severe Acute Malnutrition

In some cases, PEM can progress to severe acute malnutrition (SAM), a severe and potentially fatal condition that may take one of two forms:

Marasmus

In this condition, the child's weight drops to 3 SD below the median weight of children of same sex and height. When a child experiences starvation, her body utilizes fat deposits to maintain BMR and produce energy. After fat reserves are depleted, the body starts using proteins from muscles, which leads to muscle wasting. Eventually, the child is reduced to skin and bones, with virtually no fat or muscle in between. The ribcage becomes visible, the head appears disproportionately large, buttocks appear like baggy pants, and mid-upper arm circumference is reduced to less than 11.5 cm. The child becomes irritable and cries.

Kwashiorkor

This condition is characterized by bilateral swelling of feet (pedal edema). The cause of edema is debatable—it could be due to protein deficiency, electrolyte imbalance, or interference in functioning of the antidiuretic hormone. Second, there is associated infection. Skin lesions are typical, ranging from hyper- or hypopigmentation with or without ulcerations to weeping lesions. Scanty, lusterless hair is classic. The child loses appetite and interest in her surroundings. When protein reserves are entirely depleted, transportation of fats from the liver is impaired, and the liver becomes enlarged with fatty changes.

Note the differences between marasmus and Kwashiorkor. In marasmus, the child is emaciated. In Kwashiorkor, there is pronounced edema, and liver is enlarged. Second, in marasmus, the child is irritable and keeps crying, whereas in Kwashiorkor the child becomes quiet and withdrawn.

Marasmic Kwashiorkor

Characteristics of both marasmus and Kwashiorkor are present in this condition.

IMPLICATIONS

Mortality is alarmingly high in cases of PEM, especially in those with SAM. Death is generally due to infection.[1] If the child survives, her motor functions, such as sitting, walking, and running, are delayed. Cognitive functions, such as learning in school, are impaired. These impairments are irreversible. Children who survive PEM may also have shorter attention spans, lower self-esteem, and other issues.

Childhood stunting has long-term implications for both individuals and society. Adults with a history of childhood stunting tend to be short-statured, physically weak, and less productive. They face a higher risk of morbidity and mortality from chronic diseases like diabetes, hypertension, and CVD. These health issues have far-reaching consequences for a country's socioeconomic development as they increase healthcare costs and reduce productivity.

MANAGEMENT

Mild to moderate PEM can be managed at home. Exclusive breastfeeding for first six months of life followed by appropriate complementary feeding is crucial—of course, the mother herself should be well nourished. Breastfeeding may be continued for two to three years. The child should receive routine immunization, and deworming is advised in areas where worm infestations are common. Hygiene and sanitation should be maintained to prevent diarrheal diseases.

Children with SAM need hospitalization. Hypothermia (low body temperature), hypoglycemia (low blood sugar), electrolyte imbalance, and infection are key issues to be addressed. Hypothermia and hypoglycemia often occur together and are generally caused by infection. Hypothermia is treated by placing the child in an incubator or a warm area. Intravenous glucose and saline are administered to treat hypoglycemia and restore electrolyte balance. Intravenous antibiotics are given to treat infection. Breastfeeding and/or complementary nutrition is continued.

NOTE

1. Cellulitis, sepsis, meningitis, hepatitis, and TB are common infections in SAM.

36 Iron-Deficiency Anemia

Red blood cells (erythrocytes) transport oxygen from lungs to tissues. Hemoglobin, a constituent of red blood cells, plays an important role in this process. Every hemoglobin molecule contains four subunits, each made up of a pigment called *heme* and a protein called *globin*. Each heme unit contains one iron atom that binds with a single oxygen molecule. Therefore, each hemoglobin molecule can transport four oxygen molecules.

Anemia is a condition in which the blood's capacity to transport oxygen is impaired. Iron deficiency is the most common cause of anemia. Iron-deficiency anemia is characterized by hypochromic (pale) microcytic (small-sized) red blood cells. Other causes of anemia include inadequate or defective production of red blood cells, excessive destruction of red blood cells, and blood loss.

We get iron from food. Leafy greens, vegetables, egg yolk, fish, and sheep liver and kidney are good sources of iron. Around 60% of the iron in our body exists in the form of hemoglobin, and the rest is stored in the liver.

BURDEN

Iron deficiency is the most common nutritional disorder globally, and iron-deficiency anemia is the most prevalent form of anemia. Under-five children, adolescent girls, and pregnant and lactating women are more commonly affected. Alarmingly, 40% of under-five children and 30% of women aged 15–49 years are anemic globally. This proportion is around 50% in some South Asian countries.

CAUSES

Iron deficiency has two primary causes: Inadequate dietary intake of iron and poor absorption of iron by the body.

Inadequate intake of iron-rich foods can be due to poverty or due to lack of awareness. People may not be able to afford common iron-rich foods such as green vegetables and meat products, or they may be unaware of the nutritive value of these foods. Further, taste often takes precedence over nutrition. Cultural beliefs also influence dietary habits; for example, some cultures prohibit the consumption of meat or eggs.

Iron-deficiency anemia is known to be more common in people who do not eat animal-based foods. This could be because iron from meat products is more readily absorbed in the intestines than iron from plant-based foods. In fact, one school of thought proposes that poor iron absorption has a key role in the widespread iron deficiency seen in low-income settings. Diets in these populations are mostly cereal-based, and cereals contain phytate, a compound that impedes iron absorption.[1]

There are many other causes of iron deficiency. Helminthic infestations and frequent infections lead to iron deficiency. Hookworm infections, and schistosomiasis in particular, cause significant blood loss. Repeated diarrhea in children causes intestinal inflammation, which impairs iron absorption. Malaria leads to the destruction of red blood cells (hemolysis), and this is one of the causes of anemia in some African countries. Demand for iron increases in certain stages of life, which, if not met, results in anemia. Adolescents need more iron to support their rapid growth. The onset of menstruation in young girls increases their need for iron. In pregnancy, a substantial portion of the mother's iron is deposited in the fetus and placenta, and there is blood loss during delivery, increasing her risk of iron deficiency. While milk as such is a poor source of iron, human breast milk contains some iron, causing lactating women to lose some iron. Interestingly, absorption

DOI: 10.4324/9781032644257-41

of iron from breast milk is much better than from cow's milk. Sociocultural practices such as early marriage of girls, early motherhood, and less spacing between births further compound the problem of anemia in some communities.

Full-term healthy babies are born with sufficient iron stores that can sustain them for the first six months of life. After this, they must get iron and other micronutrients from complementary feed. Accordingly, complementary feed should include a variety of foods and not just cereals. Preterm and LBW babies are born with low iron reserves and need a higher daily intake of iron.

Certain natural mechanisms help conserve iron during pregnancy. First, menstruation stops. Second, the body's capacity to absorb dietary iron increases. But this is not enough; to prevent anemia, pregnant and lactating women must get additional iron from their diet.

MANIFESTATIONS AND IMPLICATIONS

Besides its role in transporting oxygen, iron has many other functions in the body. Therefore, iron deficiency can have severe implications. Iron deficiency in children under 24 months of age can have irreversible effects on their brain development.[2] It increases the risk of poor cognitive and motor development, which may impair learning and school performance later in life.

Iron deficiency during the third trimester of pregnancy can have implications on the motor and cognitive development of the baby. Additionally, anemic women are at a higher risk of preterm delivery, which is a common problem in low-income settings. They also face a higher risk of postpartum hemorrhage, the leading cause of maternal mortality in developing countries.

In adults, anemia manifests with fatigue, weakness, and lethargy. In severe anemia, one may feel breathless while climbing stairs or when doing strenuous work. Work capacity and productivity are reduced. High prevalence of anemia adversely impacts a country's social and economic development.

ASSESSMENT

Moderate to severe anemia can be identified by examination of inner eyelids (conjunctiva), tongue, nail beds, or palms for signs of pallor. In severe anemia, pulse becomes rapid as the heart beats faster to compensate for reduced oxygen supply.

Anemia in individuals is diagnosed by estimating blood hemoglobin level. The WHO provides reference values below which a person is considered anemic:

Category	Hb (g/dL)
• Men	13
• Women (nonpregnant)	12
• Women (pregnant)	11
• Children below age five	11

To assess iron deficiency in populations, serum ferritin level is a suitable indicator. It informs total iron stores in the body.

DAILY IRON REQUIREMENT

Red blood cells have an average lifespan of 120 days, after which they break down. Most of the iron released in this process is reused by the body. As a result, our daily requirement of iron is relatively low. Men need around 1 mg iron per day, and adolescents and reproductive-age women need around 2 mg iron per day. Pregnant women in their third trimester and lactating women need around 3 mg iron per day. Infants older than six months need around 1 mg iron per day.

Our body absorbs only 10% of the iron we get from food, so our diet should contain ten times our daily requirement of iron. This means that an adolescent girl or a woman of reproductive age should get around 20 mg iron per day from her diet.

PREVENTION

First, people need to be educated that cereals alone cannot fulfill their nutritional needs; they must include green vegetables and animal-based foods in their diet. Eggs are an affordable and excellent source of iron, calcium, and many other micronutrients. Those who do not have reservations about eating eggs should routinely include them in their diet.

Most cereals and pulses contain some iron. In fact, we can fulfill up to half of our daily iron requirement by adding fresh lemon juice to dishes prepared from these foods, as vitamin C improves iron absorption. Pearl millet and finger millet are good sources of iron and other nutrients. Once a staple food among low-income communities, these grains have now largely been replaced by wheat. Efforts may be made to popularize them again. Roasted Bengal gram with jaggery is another affordable source of iron. Paired with boiled egg, it can be an ideal midday meal in schools in low-income countries.

It is worth noting that interventions to educate people to improve their dietary choices and eat more iron-rich foods have met with limited success. This is not surprising, as many poor families cannot afford such a diet. Also, it is not easy to change our dietary habits—we like to eat what we relish.

Besides health education, the three main approaches to anemia prevention are: Iron supplementation, deworming, and food fortification.

Iron Supplementation and Deworming

Iron-folic acid supplementation is recommended for the following vulnerable groups:

- *Adolescent girls:* One IFA tablet[3] per week and deworming[4] every six months
- *Women of reproductive age:* One IFA tablet per week throughout reproductive years
- *Women, pregnant or lactating:* One IFA tablet daily for 100 days beginning from second trimester of pregnancy
- *Children (6–23 months):* 10 mg elemental iron daily through IFA syrup;[5] deworming every six months for children older than 12 months
- *Children (24–60 months):* 30 mg elemental iron daily through IFA syrup; deworming every six months

Food Fortification

Studies by the WHO show that regular consumption of iron-fortified foods can reduce anemia in populations. Many countries have been able to reduce their anemia rates by fortifying their staple foods with iron. The Philippines fortified rice with iron; Chile fortified wheat flour; the United States, the United Kingdom, and Sweden fortified maize flour and wheat flour.

Fortified wheat flour and rice are now available in many low-income countries; however, they are either unaffordable or not easily available to the masses. This is one of the reasons for widespread anemia in these countries.

Others

Access to safe drinking water and practice of basic hygiene are crucial for preventing gastrointestinal infections and worm infestations. This can then help reduce anemia in populations.

NOTES

1. Tannins in tea also reduce iron absorption.
2. https://www.who.int/news/item/20-04-2020-who-guidance-helps-detect-iron-deficiency-and-protect-brain-development
3. One IFA tablet (for adults) contains 100 mg elemental iron and 500 mcg folic acid.
4. Deworming is done with a single dose of Albendazole 400 mg tablet. Children aged 12–24 months are given half a tablet.
5. One milliliter of IFA syrup contains 20 mg elemental iron and 100 mcg folic acid.

37 Iodine Deficiency Disorders

Iodine is essential for the production of thyroid hormones—namely, triiodothyronine (T3) and thyroxine (T4). Low iodine level reduces the production of T3 and T4, leading to an increase in the secretion of thyroid-stimulating hormone (TSH). Elevated TSH level, in turn, causes proliferation of cells in the thyroid gland, resulting in a condition called goiter.

Besides its effect on thyroid function, iodine deficiency can have many other adverse effects. In children, iodine deficiency affects early brain development and learning abilities. In adults, it can cause hypothyroidism. Disorders arising from iodine deficiency are collectively known as iodine deficiency disorders (IDDs).

Iodized salt is the most readily available source of iodine. Seawater, seafood, and coastal plants are naturally rich in iodine. As we move away from the sea, the iodine content in local produce reduces. Dairy products and eggs also contain some iodine.

A healthy adult has a reserve of around 20 mg iodine, stored primarily in the thyroid gland.

BURDEN

Iodine deficiency is a major nutritional problem worldwide, particularly in sub-Saharan Africa and South Asia.

CAUSE

Iodine deficiency is caused by insufficient intake of iodine in diet.

MANIFESTATIONS AND IMPLICATIONS

Iodine deficiency-induced hypothyroidism leads to weight gain, tiredness, and general weakness. It may cause depression. Edema in this condition is typically non-pitting and commonly affects the face, eyelids, hands, and feet. Hypothyroidism is more common in women.

Iodine deficiency in pregnant women has multiple implications. Thyroid hormones produced by the mother have a critical role in the growth and brain development of the fetus. Deficiency of these hormones (hypothyroxinemia) in the mother can lead to irreversible brain damage to the fetus. The child may be born with congenital hypothyroidism (formerly known as cretinism), mental retardation, dwarfism, deaf-mutism, squint, or neuromotor defects. Globally, iodine deficiency is the leading preventable cause of brain damage in infancy and childhood. It can also lead to miscarriage or stillbirth.

Breast milk of iodine-deficient women is low in iodine, which can affect the growth, motor functions, and cognitive development of their children. Some studies have informed that children living in areas where iodine deficiency is endemic have lower IQ scores.[1]

Deficiency of iron or vitamin A can exacerbate the effects of iodine deficiency.

ASSESSMENT

Nearly 90% of the iodine we get from food is eliminated through urine. This makes urinary iodine concentration a reliable indicator of iodine status in populations. It should be noted that goiter is not a good indicator of iodine deficiency as it manifests only in prolonged iodine deficiency.

DOI: 10.4324/9781032644257-42

PREVENTION

Universal iodization of salt has been one of the most cost-effective public health interventions. It has effectively reduced the prevalence of IDDs worldwide. Regular supply of iodized salt to the public is the mainstay of IDD control programs. Sale of non-iodized salt for human consumption is prohibited in most countries, although it may be permitted for industrial uses.

An adult needs around 150 mcg of iodine per day. Pregnant and lactating women need more. Common salt is iodized to 30 parts per million (ppm) with the intent that at least 15 ppm would be available to consumers after loss in processing and transit. Some iodine is also lost in cooking. Common salt can fulfill our daily iodine requirement. However, the WHO recommends limiting daily salt intake to less than 5 gm to reduce the risk of stroke and coronary heart disease.

Administration of iodine to pregnant women who are iodine-deficient can prevent congenital hypothyroidism.

Some foods are goitrogenic. They contain chemicals that compete with iodine for uptake by the thyroid gland. Cabbage, cauliflower, broccoli, sweet potato, cassava, and rapeseed oil are some examples. People with goiter and those at risk of iodine deficiency should avoid goitrogenic foods.

NOTE

1. https://saltcomindia.gov.in/NIDCCP_IodineDeficincy.html

38 Vitamin A Deficiency

Chemically, vitamin A is retinol. Its primary role is in the formation of rhodopsin, a visual pigment in the rods of the retina that is essential for night vision. Additionally, vitamin A strengthens immunity and is essential for healthy skin, bones, and teeth.

Foods of animal origin such as milk, cheese, egg, and shark liver oil are primary sources of vitamin A. Among plant foods, yellow and orange fruits and vegetables contain carotene, which is converted into retinol in the body. Mango, papaya, orange, tomato, yellow pumpkin, and carrot are high in carotene. Green leafy vegetables such as spinach and amaranth, as well as radish leaves, also contain vitamin A.

An adult needs 0.750 milligrams (2500 IU[1]) of vitamin A per day. Women need additional vitamin A during pregnancy and lactation, and children need more vitamin A daily during their growth years.

Vitamin A is mainly stored in the liver.

BURDEN

Vitamin A deficiency is rare in the developed world, but it is common in developing countries, especially in young children and pregnant women. It is a major cause of preventable childhood blindness.

CAUSES

Vitamin A deficiency occurs when we do not get enough vitamin A from food. However, adults in general are at low risk of vitamin A deficiency as the vitamin A reserve in their liver can sustain them for some period when their diet is deficient.

Pregnant women in their third trimester face a higher risk of vitamin A deficiency on account of accelerated fetal development. Exclusively breastfed infants are at risk if the mother is deficient in vitamin A. Further, illnesses such as diarrhea and measles can worsen vitamin A deficiency in children. Communities that predominantly consume rice are known to have a higher incidence of vitamin A deficiency.

MANIFESTATIONS

Vitamin A deficiency mainly affects the eyes, but it has many other health effects.

Ocular Manifestations

Vitamin A deficiency can cause a range of eye conditions. Collectively known as xerophthalmia, these conditions are characterized by dryness of conjunctiva and cornea. Night blindness is one of the first signs of xerophthalmia. A person with night blindness can see normally in adequate light but has difficulty seeing in darkness or dim light. Night blindness is more common in pregnant women and children in low-income communities. Bitot spots are another early sign of vitamin A deficiency. These are raised, silver-gray patches that form on the sclera, the white part of the eye, due to the accumulation of epithelial debris and secretions.

Xerophthalmia can progress to blindness. The cornea becomes soft and progresses to ulceration and necrosis, a condition known as keratomalacia,[2] ultimately resulting in blindness. Retina may also be damaged. Notably, nearly half of children who lose their vision to severe vitamin A deficiency die within a year.

DOI: 10.4324/9781032644257-43

Childhood Infections

Vitamin A deficiency weakens the immune system, increasing the risk of infections such as pneumonia, diarrhea, and measles in children. It also increases mortality from these diseases.

Growth and Development

Vitamin A deficiency slows down bone formation, which may lead to growth impairment.

Maternal Implications

Vitamin A deficiency is associated with poor pregnancy outcomes and maternal mortality.

ASSESSMENT

Vitamin A deficiency in populations can be assessed by estimating liver vitamin A reserves in a sample population. This is considered the gold standard for community-level detection; however, this method is not feasible in low-income countries.

Night blindness and Bitot spots are pathognomonic signs of vitamin A deficiency. Night blindness occurs before other ocular changes can be seen. When more than 5% of pregnant women in a population have night blindness, it is considered a moderate-level public health problem.

Serum or plasma retinol level can inform subclinical vitamin A deficiency in populations. A considerable number of cases with low serum retinol levels indicates a high prevalence of vitamin A deficiency. If more than 10% of preschool children in a population have low serum retinol, it is a moderate public health problem.

It should be known that serum retinol level is not a reliable indicator of vitamin A deficiency in individuals. Our bodies can maintain serum retinol levels until the liver reserve becomes dangerously low. As a result, blood test shows normal result in mild to moderate deficiency.

PREVENTION AND TREATMENT

Breast milk can fulfill an infant's vitamin A requirement during the first six months of life, provided the mother is not vitamin A-deficient. After six months, the child's supplementary diet should include some animal-based foods like cow milk, buffalo milk, or eggs. Plant-based foods are not helpful at this stage as conversion of carotene into vitamin A is not efficient in children.

The WHO recommends vitamin A supplementation in regions with high prevalence of vitamin A deficiency. In vitamin A prophylaxis programs, children aged 6–12 months are given 30 mg (100,000 IU) oral vitamin A solution twice a year. From the second year onward, 60 mg (200,000 IU) is given twice a year. These supplements are generally administered along with vaccine shots. Vitamin A supplementation is generally avoided in infants younger than six months as it may cause bulging of the fontanelle.

In the early stages of vitamin A deficiency, supplementation can completely resolve night blindness, Bitot spots, and conjunctival xerosis. However, corneal scarring and blindness are irreversible.

Benefits of vitamin A supplementation during pregnancy and lactation are being studied. The current recommendation is that pregnant women should get sufficient vitamin A from their diet. Around 100 gm of green leafy vegetables, or 100 gm of yellow fruits or vegetables, or one glass of milk, or one egg can fulfill the daily vitamin A requirement for adults, including pregnant and lactating women.

Packaged products like milk, edible oils, and ghee are fortified with synthetic vitamin A. Many are fortified with both vitamins A and D. Attempts to fortify common salt with vitamin A have not been successful.

VITAMIN A TOXICITY

Vitamin A toxicity is rare and is usually seen in children who accidentally consume large amounts of the vitamin. Symptoms range from skin irritation, abdominal pain, and vomiting in mild cases to increased intracranial pressure in severe cases. Once vitamin A intake is stopped, recovery is generally rapid. Prolonged overdose of vitamin A in pregnancy can lead to fetal abnormalities (teratogenicity).

NOTES

1. IU: international unit.
2. https://rarediseases.org/rare-diseases/keratomalacia/

39 Other Micronutrient Deficiencies

ZINC DEFICIENCY

Zinc plays an important role in basic cell functions, such as promoting cell growth, building proteins, and healing damaged tissues. It is also involved in senses of taste and smell. Zinc deficiency can lead to multiple dysfunctions in the body. Similar to iron, demand for zinc increases during childhood, adolescence, pregnancy, and lactation.

Iron-rich foods, such as green vegetables and animal products, are also good sources of zinc. Legumes, nuts, and wholegrain cereals also contain zinc. Recall that phytates present in many cereals impair absorption of iron. They also impair absorption of zinc.

Burden

Deficiencies of iron and zinc often coexist as their dietary sources are the same. However, unlike iron deficiency, zinc deficiency develops rapidly as there is no zinc reserve in the body.

Causes

Low dietary intake of zinc is the primary cause of zinc deficiency. Diarrhea and other infections precipitate the deficiency. Children born prematurely are prone to zinc deficiency due to their poor capacity to absorb nutrients.

Manifestations

Like protein-energy malnutrition, zinc deficiency also causes stunting and wasting in children. Immune functions are impaired, increasing the risk of diarrhea and other infections. Long-term effects of zinc deficiency include delayed sexual maturation, loss of hair, and impaired sensory functions.

Assessment

In individuals, zinc deficiency can be assessed by plasma or serum zinc concentration or urinary zinc concentration. Estimating zinc deficiency in populations is not practically possible. However, high prevalence of stunting in a population suggests widespread zinc deficiency.

Treatment and Prevention

Food diversification is an important long-term approach to improving zinc intake. Similar to iron, zinc is better absorbed from fermented foods. Research is needed to identify low-cost locally available and socially acceptable food sources of zinc. Food fortification is also being explored.

Exclusive breastfeeding can fulfill an infant's daily requirement of zinc, provided the mother is not zinc-deficient. Complementary feed should include foods rich in zinc.

In acute diarrhea, the WHO recommends zinc supplementation along with ORS. Zinc supplementation for two weeks reduces the duration and severity of diarrhea, as well as the risk of

DOI: 10.4324/9781032644257-44

reoccurrence. Studies are underway to examine the benefits of zinc supplementation in pneumonia and malaria. Some studies have indicated that zinc supplementation during pregnancy reduces the risk of premature birth, but more evidences are needed.

VITAMIN D DEFICIENCY

Vitamin D, chemically cholecalciferol, plays a critical role in maintaining bone health by facilitating the absorption of dietary calcium from the small intestine and its deposition in bones, in a process known as bone mineralization. It also helps improve immunity, reduce inflammation, and prevent infections.

Sunlight is the primary source of vitamin D. Ultraviolet rays in sunlight convert a cholesterol derivative in our skin to vitamin D. Fish liver oil is a good source of vitamin D, and egg yolk contains a small amount. Other commonly available foods do not contain vitamin D.

Burden

Once rare, vitamin D deficiency has increased to alarming rates in recent decades.

Causes

Reduced exposure to sunlight is the main reason for widespread vitamin D deficiency. Earlier, people habitually spent time soaking up sunlight. They also had some exposure while commuting to school or work or markets. Now they travel in cars, buses, or subways. Children used to play outdoors. Now they like to spend time with their mobiles.

Manifestations

Vitamin D deficiency impairs absorption of calcium. Prolonged or extreme deficiency of vitamin D or calcium can cause rickets, particularly in children aged 6–36 months. Rickets softens and weakens the bones. Teeth are poorly formed. Rib-costochondral junctions become enlarged. Muscles become weak, and skeletal deformities occur. Bowed legs from weight-bearing are common. Growth is delayed or stunted. Risk of infections increases.

In adults, this condition is called osteomalacia. Its characteristics are similar to rickets: Softening and fragility of bones and muscle weakness. There is pain in hip bone and other bones. Ribs, pelvis, spine, and legs become prone to fracture. The problem worsens in pregnancy and may distort the pelvis, causing difficulty in delivery.

Assessment

Serum 25-hydroxy vitamin D level can inform vitamin D deficiency in both individuals and populations.

Treatment and Prevention

Vitamin D deficiency is treated with supplementation of vitamin D and calcium.

Adequate sunlight exposure can help prevent vitamin D deficiency. Generally, about 15 minutes of exposure to midday sunlight three times a week is sufficient for people with lighter skin tones. People with darker skin tones need longer exposure as the melanin in their skin reduces the penetration of ultraviolet rays. Milk and edible oils fortified with vitamins A and D may also help in preventing vitamin D deficiency.

Excessive long-term vitamin D supplementation should be avoided as it can cause vitamin D toxicity and lead to hypercalcemia (abnormally high level of calcium in blood). Symptoms of vitamin D toxicity include recurrent vomiting, abdominal pain, dehydration, and confusion.

CALCIUM DEFICIENCY

Calcium is the most abundant mineral in the human body. It is critical to the formation and maintenance of the skeletal system and teeth. It is also involved in contraction of muscles, including heart muscles. It has a role in blood clotting. Deficiencies of calcium and magnesium are widespread in low-income countries and occur in all age groups.

We can get calcium from a variety of plant- and animal-based foods. Besides milk and other dairy products, leafy vegetables such as amaranth and fenugreek are excellent sources of calcium. Tapioca is a good source. Wheat contains some calcium, but rice is not a good source of calcium, which is a disadvantage for people who primarily consume rice. In many parts of India, people chew betel leaf coated with lime, which provides them some calcium. Of course, the tobacco consumed with it is harmful.

Requirement of calcium increases considerably in pregnancy and lactation. If not met, it can lead to depletion of calcium from bones.

Similar to vitamin D deficiency, calcium deficiency can lead to rickets or osteomalacia. There are some indications that calcium deficiency has a role in hypertension and stroke, but more evidences are needed.

Serum calcium level can inform calcium deficiency in individuals and populations. Additionally, bone mineral density (BMD) provides a snapshot of bone health. In the United States, women aged 65 years or above are advised to undergo periodic BMD testing.

Calcium deficiency is treated with supplements. The WHO recommends calcium supplementation to all pregnant women in areas where calcium deficiency is common.

FLUORIDE DEFICIENCY

Water is the main source of fluoride, and it is recommended that drinking water should contain 1–3 ppm fluoride. Studies show that low fluoride in drinking water can lead to dental caries. Adding fluoride to public water supply in areas where water is deficient in fluoride can reduce the occurrence of dental caries.

Excess fluoride in drinking water is equally harmful. It causes fluorosis, a condition characterized by mottling of teeth, hardening of bones, and skeletal deformities. Fluorosis is a public health problem in many pockets globally. Although fluoride levels in water can be reduced by special treatment, switching to an alternative source of water is cost-effective.

VITAMIN B1 DEFICIENCY

Deficiency of vitamin B1, or thiamine, is called beriberi. Thiamine is found in virtually all foods, particularly in the outer layers of cereals and pulses. Populations that predominantly consume thiamine-deficient foods, such as maize or polished rice, are at a higher risk of beriberi. Infections, pregnancy, diabetes, and starvation also increase the risk.

Beriberi manifests in two forms: Dry and wet. Dry beriberi affects the nervous system, causing symptoms such as weakness, reduced sensation in hands or feet, anorexia, and mental confusion. Wet beriberi is a severe form of thiamine deficiency that can be life-threatening. It affects the cardiovascular system, leading to fluid accumulation in the abdomen (ascites), lungs (pleural effusion), and feet (edema). If untreated, it may lead to heart failure.

Beriberi can be treated by oral or parenteral administration of thiamine. Once quite prevalent globally, beriberi is now rare, mainly because people now consume a variety of whole grains, which are a good source of thiamine.

Efforts are underway to fortify rice with thiamine.

VITAMIN B2 DEFICIENCY

Deficiency of vitamin B2, or riboflavin, is rare. It is mostly seen in people who live in extreme poverty and survive mainly on rice and salt.

Riboflavin is found in green leafy vegetables, wheat, pulses, and meat products. Its deficiency causes angular stomatitis (cracking at corners of mouth), oral ulcers, glossitis (inflammation of tongue), sore throat, and burning sensation in eyes.

VITAMIN B3 DEFICIENCY

Vitamin B3, also called nicotinic acid or niacin, can be synthesized in the body from tryptophan, an amino acid found in almost all dietary proteins. Whole cereals, pulses, nuts, and meat are rich in niacin, with groundnuts being a particularly abundant source.

Niacin deficiency is called pellagra, which literally means "rough skin." Pellagra was once prevalent in African countries where people primarily eat maize, which is deficient in tryptophan.[1]

Pellagra can be fatal if untreated. Until the early twentieth century, it was thought to be an infectious skin disease similar to leprosy. Four *D*s are characteristic of pellagra: Dermatitis, diarrhea, dementia, and death. Dermatitis mainly occurs on pressure points such as elbows and knees and on skin exposed to sunlight.

Pellagra is diagnosed by identifying typical symptoms and reviewing the patient's dietary history. Rapid response to niacin supplementation further confirms the diagnosis.

VITAMIN B12 DEFICIENCY

Vitamin B12 is peculiar in not being available in any plant food. It can be obtained from milk, eggs, and meat. It is not well understood why people who do not eat animal-based foods do not develop B12 deficiency. It is believed that the vitamin is synthesized by commensal flora in the intestine, which likely fulfills the B12 requirement for those with vegetarian diets.

Inadequate intestinal absorption is the most common cause of B12 deficiency. Fish tapeworm infection can lead to severe B12 deficiency.[2]

B12 deficiency over a long period can cause megaloblastic anemia and neuropathy. In megaloblastic anemia, the bone marrow produces abnormal, oval-shaped red blood cells that die early. The condition manifests like other forms of anemia. Neuropathy causes tingling or numbness in hands and feet. There can be muscle weakness.

Deficiencies of vitamin B12 and folic acid often occur together and can be diagnosed by blood tests. Blood picture is similar in both cases. Treatment involves simultaneous administration of B12 injections and folic acid tablets.

VITAMIN C DEFICIENCY

Vitamin C, or ascorbic acid, is a strong antioxidant (reducing agent). It participates in collagen synthesis and calcification of bones and teeth. Importantly, it helps in the absorption of dietary iron by keeping it in reduced (ferrous) state.

Nearly all fresh fruits[3] and vegetables,[4] including some tubers such as potato, contain vitamin C. Heating or drying vegetables destroys their vitamin C content, but gooseberry retains some vitamin C even when dried. Cereals and pulses contain little or no vitamin C, although germinating pulses can acquire the vitamin. Sprouted green gram is a good source. Animal-derived foods do not contain vitamin C.

Deficiency of vitamin C is called scurvy. Historically, scurvy was seen in sailors who went without fresh food for months. In 1747, James Lind discovered that adding lemons or oranges to sailors' diet prevented scurvy. The condition is rare nowadays as most people get enough vitamin C from their diet.

Scurvy can develop within one to three months of stopping vitamin C intake. It manifests with weakness and fatigue. There can be severe pain in joints or legs. Gums are swollen and there can be minute bleeding or ulceration in oral mucosa. Red or blue spots form on the skin, particularly on shins. Wound healing is impaired. In severe cases, the disease can progress to extreme weakness, tooth loss, depression, neuropathy, and even death.

In infants and children, scurvy presents with tenderness of bones. The child avoids standing or crawling due to pain and may cry when her bones are touched.

Vitamin C deficiency is diagnosed by clinical picture or plasma vitamin C level.[5] X-ray of long bones is also useful.[6] Vitamin C supplementation provides rapid relief in scurvy.

NOTES

1. Maize does contain niacin, but in a form that is not readily bioavailable, meaning that it cannot be absorbed by the body. By treating the cereal in an alkaline solution, niacin becomes bioavailable.
2. Fish tapeworm competes with the host for dietary B12.
3. Orange, lemon, sweet lemon, apple, black plum, gooseberry, guava, lime, and papaya are particularly good sources of vitamin C.
4. Among vegetables, amaranth, cabbage, radish, tapioca, and turnip have good amounts of vitamin C.
5. Leukocyte vitamin C concentration is a better measure, but it is technically difficult to perform.
6. X-ray of long bones shows ground-glass appearance in the shaft due to trabecular atrophy.

40 Diet Planning

As noted in previous chapters, poverty and ignorance are the main causes of undernutrition. On the other hand, affluence combined with ignorance can lead to overnutrition. Cultural beliefs also influence our food choices. Although dietary habits differ across the world, a basic understanding of nutrition can help us plan a balanced diet.

A balanced diet is one that provides all the necessary nutrients in the right proportions.

To plan a diet, we should first know an individual's daily caloric requirement. Then we apportion these calories among various macronutrients while ensuring sufficiency of iron and other essential micronutrients.

CALORIC REQUIREMENT

People's daily caloric requirement depends on their age, sex, and level of physical activity. Table 40.1 provides an example.

In this table, we can see that caloric requirement varies by physical activity. Additionally, men require more calories per day than women.

One school of thought is that our daily caloric requirement is lower than the recommended values. It proposes that a sedentary male needs only around 2,100–2,200 kcal per day.

PROPORTION OF MACRONUTRIENTS

Ideally, fats should not exceed 30% of an adult's daily calorie intake,[1] and carbohydrates should not exceed 65% of daily calorie intake. The recommended proportion of macronutrients in total daily calorie intake is:

• Fats	15%–30%
• Carbohydrates	45%–65%
• Proteins	10%–12%

KEY ISSUES WITH POOR MAN'S DIET

Poor people's diet, being overly dependent on plant foods, has three limitations:

- Low iron content
- Poor-quality proteins
- High proportion of carbohydrates

Let us see how these issues can be addressed.

TABLE 40.1
Daily Caloric Requirement in Kilo Calories for Adult Men and Women

	Sedentary Work (kcal)	Moderate Work (kcal)	Strenuous Work (kcal)
Adult male	2,400	2,600	2,800
Adult female	1,900	2,100	2,300

DOI: 10.4324/9781032644257-45

Increasing Iron Content in Diet

Our diet should provide us 10–30 mg iron per day. However, the poor man's diet tends to be deficient in iron as it is largely cereal-based and lacks leafy greens, eggs, and meat products.

Animal foods are an excellent source of heme iron, which is more easily absorbed by the body. Those who are not opposed to eating these foods must include eggs, fish, or meat in their diet. Eggs are particularly affordable.

Among plant sources, leafy greens[2] are abundant in iron. Seasonal greens are generally affordable, so people should consume them more often and build their iron reserves. Around 100 gm of leafy greens per day can fulfill an adult's daily iron requirement. Leaves of radish, Bengal gram, cauliflower, and turnip are also high in iron, but they are mostly discarded; people can be educated to utilize them. Many other vegetables[3] contain nominal amounts of iron. They can be an alternative when iron-rich vegetables are not available.

Cereals[4] and pulses contain considerable iron, but the phytate in these foods interferes with iron absorption. Adding a few drops of lemon juice (vitamin C) to prepared dishes can enhance iron absorption from these foods. Potatoes also contain some vitamin C. Germination and fermentation reduce phytate content in foods, improving iron absorption. Whole pulses can be germinated. Germinated pulses should preferably be consumed raw, but they are beneficial even in cooked form. Cooking in iron utensils is advantageous as some iron from the utensil is absorbed by the food.

Milk products interfere with iron absorption, so curd, tea, or coffee should be avoided during meals. They can be taken separately after some time.

Enhancing Quality of Proteins

Eggs and other animal-based foods provide high-quality protein; conversely, the quality of protein in plant foods is generally low. Those who do not eat animal-based foods should particularly diversify their diet with a variety of pulses and legumes. This will improve the quality of their protein intake. Many types of lentils can be mixed and cooked together.

Rice has less protein than wheat, so those who mainly eat rice should eat more lentils and other pulses. Alternating between wheat, rice, and maize is a good way to increase protein intake.

Reducing Proportion of Carbohydrates

Wheat and rice are staple foods in many low-income families. Replacing some of these carbohydrates with seasonal vegetables and eggs can enhance the nutritive value of meals.

AFFLUENT DIET

A key issue with affluent diet is that it is often high in calories and fats, which increases the risk of lifestyle diseases (NCDs). Overeating is a major problem and needs to be avoided. Fat intake should be limited, and saturated fats (e.g., red meat) should be replaced by polyunsaturated or unsaturated fats (e.g., fish and chicken). Processed foods and deep-fried snacks should be avoided or taken in moderation.

The WHO recommends consuming at least 400 gm of fresh fruits and vegetables every day, as it can reduce the risk of NCDs. The WHO also recommends limiting daily sugar intake to less than 5% of total calorie intake and daily salt intake to less than 5 gm.[5] Potassium in fresh fruits and vegetables can reduce the adverse effects of excess sodium in meals.

Calcium deficiency is increasing rapidly in affluent communities. It can be prevented by regular exposure to sunlight and by including milk products or eggs in diet.

SPECIAL DIETS

Some health conditions call for modifications in diet. For example, people with diabetes are advised to follow a sugar-free and low-carbohydrate diet. Those with obesity are advised to follow a low-fat and low-calorie diet. In renal impairment, filtration of certain waste products is impaired. To prevent accumulation of this waste in the body, people with compromised renal function are asked to limit their intake of protein, sodium, potassium, and phosphorus. Patients with hepatic dysfunction are asked to avoid alcohol and restrict their intake of salt, sugar, and fats. Those who are unable to chew or digest solid foods are advised to follow a liquid-based diet.

ROLE OF DIETICIAN

The treating doctor advises patients on the dietary precautions they need to observe. Based on the doctor's advice and the patient's preferences, a dietician helps in diet planning, such as how much rice one can eat, how much oil to use in cooking, or which fruits and vegetables can be eaten.

NOTES

1. Children need more fat, typically 30%–40% of their total daily calorie intake.
2. Amaranth, mustard leaves, spinach, fenugreek leaves, lamb's quarters, and cabbage contain considerable iron.
3. French beans, cauliflower, brinjal, bitter gourd, bottle gourd, tomato, cucumber, ladies' finger, capsicum, round gourd, jackfruit, drumsticks, green onion stalk, and potato contain nominal iron.
4. Cereals, particularly Bengal gram, pearl millet, finger millet, cowpea, red lentil, and dry peas, contain considerable iron.
5. In South Asia, people generally consume 10–15 gm of common salt per day.

41 Food Fortification and Food Additives

FOOD FORTIFICATION

Fortification refers to the addition of certain micronutrients to food items without tampering with their taste, color, odor, or palatability.

Deficiencies of iron, zinc, iodine, and vitamin A are common in low-income settings. The WHO has determined that fortification of common foods like wheat flour, rice, maize, pulses, edible oil, milk, and salt can reduce these deficiencies. Universal iodization of salt is a classic success story of food fortification that helped to reduce iodine deficiency disorders globally. Many countries have successfully reduced micronutrient deficiencies in their populations by fortifying wheat or rice. Many others have made it mandatory to fortify wheat, rice, and maize with iron.[1] Milk, edible oils, and baby formula foods are generally fortified with vitamins A and D. Salt can be double-fortified with iodine and iron.

FOOD ADDITIVES

Food additives are substances that are added to food products to enhance their appearance, taste, texture, or freshness. These additives can be natural or synthetic.

Internationally, the Joint FAO[2]/WHO Expert Committee on Food Additives evaluates the safety of food additives for human consumption. The Codex Alimentarius Commission, a body of the FAO/WHO, has developed the Codex Alimentarius, a framework of standards, guidelines, and codes that governs the international trade of food.

There are thousands of food additives, some of which have been in use for centuries. Turmeric has been traditionally used as a natural colorant and preservative. Pickle is preserved by salt and oil. Jam is preserved by sugar. Dried meat and fish are preserved by salt.

Broadly, food additives are grouped into three categories:

Flavoring Agents

These are added to food products to enhance their taste or aroma. For example, fruit or spice extracts are added to soft drinks, cakes, and yogurt.

Enzymes

Enzymes are proteins sourced from microorganisms, plants, or animals. They break down large molecules into smaller molecules and are used in processes such as dough fermentation, brewing, and winemaking.

Others

This includes additives used for a variety of purposes, such as preservation, coloring, or sweetening.

NOTES

1. https://www.bioanalyt.com/flour-fortification-icheck-iron-fluoro
2. FAO is the Food and Agriculture Organization of the United Nations.

DOI: 10.4324/9781032644257-46

42 Meat Hygiene and Mushroom Poisoning

Humans can get infested with certain helminths by consuming meat that contains cysts or ova of the parasite. Infection with *Taenia solium*, *T. asiatica*, *Trichinella spiralis*, and some other *Trichinella* species can occur from eating raw or undercooked pork. Infection with *Taenia saginata* occurs from eating raw or undercooked beef.

Liver fluke (*Fasciola hepatica* or *F. gigantica*) is found in sheep, goat, and other cattle. Eggs of these flukes are discharged through the animal's stool, contaminating vegetation or snails. Humans get infected by eating contaminated vegetation, fish, crab, or crayfish.

Fish that inhabit water contaminated by industrial waste have higher levels of heavy metals or chemicals in their flesh. They can be harmful when consumed. Several outbreaks of mercury poisoning from eating contaminated fish are on record.

MUSHROOM POISONING

Some mushroom varieties of the genus *Amanita* are poisonous and can cause vomiting or diarrhea within minutes or hours of ingestion. A high dose may cause miosis (constriction of pupils), muscular incoordination, convulsions, or coma.

DOI: 10.4324/9781032644257-47

Section VI

Environmental Health

43 What Is Environment?

Environment refers to both living beings and nonliving elements or conditions in our surroundings that affect us. Interestingly, Hippocrates highlighted the role of environment in causation of diseases as early as the fourteenth century. We took six centuries to acknowledge it.

Environmental factors can be broadly classified into:

- *Physical factors:* Air, water, food, housing, vehicles on the road, sitting arrangements in school or workplace, etc.
- *Biological factors:* Bacteria, viruses, fungi, or parasites in air, water, food, clothing, bedding, or furniture; insects, birds, stray or pet animals; etc.
- *Chemical factors:* Air pollutants; excessive chemicals in water; preservatives, coloring agents, pesticides, and insecticides in our food; etc.
- *Social factors:* Family members, friends, relatives, neighbors, colleagues, people who travel with us in public transport; pets; etc.

Note that the above factors are all physical in nature. There is yet another aspect of our environment that affects us.

Sociopsychological factors: Peer pressure faced by adolescents, harassment of girls in public places, marital discord, unpleasantness at work, conflict with a neighbor, or inappropriate behavior by a co-passenger in public transport are some examples of sociopsychological factors that can affect our mood or well-being.

CLIMATE

Climate refers to the average weather pattern of an area over a long period of time. The World Meteorological Organization considers a 30-year period to describe the climate of a place, taking into account aspects such as average local temperature, rainfall, wind, and sunshine.

Climate is an integral part of our environment that significantly affects our health and well-being. The climatic changes observed in recent decades are largely due to human activities. They are a cause of concern.

GREENHOUSE EFFECT

A greenhouse is a glass structure used in colder regions to grow plants. During the day, sunlight warms the air inside the greenhouse. This heat remains trapped inside the greenhouse and gets absorbed by plants. The greenhouse effect works the same way. Gases liberated by human activity envelop the earth, trapping heat, which causes global warming. These gases are called greenhouse gases (GHGs). Although plants absorb carbon dioxide and release oxygen, it is no longer enough to counter the effects of GHGs. Oceans also absorb some excess carbon dioxide from the atmosphere, but this makes ocean water acidic and harms aquatic life.

Over the last century, the earth's average temperature has increased by about 1 degree Celsius. This has led to serious changes in global weather patterns. Ice in the Antarctic and Greenland is melting. Glaciers are retreating. Since the 1880s, global sea levels have risen by about 8 inches. However, climatic changes are not uniform across the planet. While some places are seeing more rainfall, flooding, storms, and hurricanes, others are seeing frequent heatwaves, wildfires, or draughts. With rising global temperatures, mosquitoes and other vectors are increasing, and so are vector-borne diseases.

DOI: 10.4324/9781032644257-49

Global temperatures are predicted to rise further, mainly due to the GHGs produced by human activity. Interestingly, despite the economic slowdown caused by the COVID-19 pandemic, the two main GHGs, carbon dioxide and methane, have continued to increase.

ENVIRONMENT PROTECTION

Protecting and sustaining the environment requires collective effort from governments and people. Below are some fundamental measures that can be implemented:

- Increase the use of renewable energy
- Increase energy efficiency to reduce gas emissions
- Conserve water sources by efficient use of water and rainwater harvesting
- Reduce waste generation and promote waste recycling
- Prohibit deforestation, plant more trees, and increase forest coverage
- Implement population-control measures
- Design and construct eco-friendly buildings
- Raise awareness on environmental issues and advocate with governments

At the 2015 United Nations Climate Change Conference in Paris, all 196 participating countries agreed to pursue efforts to limit global warming to 1.5 degrees Celsius above preindustrial levels. The Industrial Revolution (1760–1840) benefited developed countries but led to a dramatic increase in GHG emissions. Global warming caused by GHGs reduced agricultural yields worldwide. The Paris Agreement emphasized the responsibility of developed countries to provide financial assistance and technological support to less developed countries to reduce their GHG emissions.

At the 2022 Climate Change Conference in Egypt, countries were expected to demonstrate how they were implementing their commitments under the Paris Agreement. It was realized that the international community is falling far short of Paris goals.

44 Air Pollution

Air pollution refers to the presence of toxic substances, dust particles, or microorganisms in the air at a level that poses a health risk. Since we have no control over the air we breathe, it is important that the air in our surroundings is clean and free of pollutants. Both indoor and outdoor air pollution endanger our health.

Example 1

In 1952, a peculiar event occurred in London. Thick, dark fog covered the entire city. Visibility became so poor that fatal road accidents started to occur. Cases of respiratory and heart diseases began to rise. Some reports suggest that more than 4,000 people died in just five days. While the UK government initially dismissed the event as a natural phenomenon, massive public outcry forced the government to reconsider its stance and take corrective action. The phenomenon was later named smog (smoke plus fog).[1] Investigations revealed that the excessive smoke that led to the formation of smog mainly came from motor vehicles and industries. Similar crises were subsequently observed in many US cities, prompting the US government to pass the Clean Air Act of 1970. Strict emission norms were introduced for automobiles and factories. Many other countries followed suit. While air quality has since improved considerably in the Western world, air pollution continues to grow in developing countries.

HEALTH HAZARDS

Health hazards of air pollution range from minor to life-threatening depending on the type of pollutant, level of pollution, and duration of exposure. Minor effects include eye irritation, headache, dizziness, uneasiness, and low energy. In severe cases, there can be breathing difficulties or a choking sensation. Long-term exposure to air pollution reduces capacity of lungs and heart, worsening the health of people with asthma or CVD. It may be noted that while air pollution exacerbates these conditions, it is not likely to cause them.

TYPES OF AIR POLLUTANTS

Normal air contains around 75% nitrogen, 25% oxygen, and traces of carbon dioxide, argon, and other gases. The level of water vapor in the air varies by time and location. Following are the main pollutants responsible for health hazards of air pollution:

- Particulate matter
- Nitrogen oxides
- Sulfur dioxide
- Carbon monoxide
- Ozone

Particulate Matter

Particulate matter (PM) refers to very fine particles of dust, ash, smoke, soot, or liquid droplets that remain suspended in the air. Motor vehicles, factories, construction activity, thermal power plants, and domestic burning of wood and coal are major sources of PM.

DOI: 10.4324/9781032644257-50

PM is one of the main components of smog. It persists when the wind is calm; high-speed wind carries it away. Small particles with a diameter of 2.5 microns or less (PM 2.5) are the most hazardous, as they can bypass the body's natural defenses and penetrate lung tissues, where they get deposited in alveoli and cause chronic irritation. Preexisting cardiovascular or respiratory conditions may worsen. Coarse particles with a diameter of around 10 microns (PM 10) mainly come from construction activity and vehicular movement. They can irritate the eyes, nose, and throat but are relatively less harmful.

A study found that mortality from cardiovascular or respiratory diseases was higher in US cities with higher levels of PM pollution. Another study in India found an association between high PM pollution and low birth weight. Further research is in progress.

Nitrogen Oxides

Although nitrogen is a natural component of air, its oxides are hazardous.[2] Nitrogen oxides mainly come from motor vehicles and give the air a reddish-brown color. They irritate and constrict airways, aggravating symptoms of preexisting asthma or chronic obstructive pulmonary disease (COPD). Nitrogen oxides are also a constituent of smog.

When nitrogen oxides react with rainwater, they form nitric acid, leading to acid rain. Acid rain harms crops and forests, pollutes groundwater, and endangers aquatic life. In presence of sunlight and heat, nitrogen oxides combine with volatile organic compounds in the air to form ground-level ozone, which is hazardous.

Sulfur Dioxide

Sulfur dioxide is primarily generated by combustion of coal, diesel, or petrol. Thermal power plants, factories, and motor vehicles are major sources of this gas.

Like nitrogen oxides, sulfur dioxide also causes irritation and constriction of airways and worsens asthma and COPD. At high concentrations, sulfur dioxide reacts with water vapor in the air to form sulfuric acid, leading to acid rain. Sulfuric acid can settle down on airborne particles, increasing their potential to damage lung tissues.

Carbon Monoxide

Carbon monoxide is a colorless, odorless, and poisonous gas produced by incomplete combustion of fuels. In cities, it is mainly emitted by motor vehicles. In rural areas, it comes from domestic burning of wood, charcoal, or kerosene. When inhaled, carbon monoxide competes with oxygen to bind with hemoglobin in the blood, reducing the blood's capacity to carry oxygen. Carbon monoxide poisoning can cause visual disturbances and impair mental and physical functions.

Ozone

The protective role of ozone gas is well known—it forms a shield in the Earth's stratosphere that protects us from the sun's ultraviolet rays. However, ground-level ozone is hazardous. It is produced when nitrogen oxides react with volatile organic compounds in the presence of sunlight and heat. Since both nitrogen oxides and organic compounds come mainly from motor vehicles, ozone level rises in cities on days when there is heavy vehicular movement and the weather is hot and sunny.

Ground-level ozone irritates the respiratory tract, inflames airways, and aggravates acute symptoms of asthma and COPD. Lungs become susceptible to infection. Mortality from respiratory and cardiovascular disorders increases. Ozone is also harmful to plants.

PREVENTION

In a country, economic development and environmental sustainability have competing demands. Economic progress often means more industrial activity and higher demand for electricity, construction, and transportation. All these activities generate emissions that contribute to air pollution. However, development at the cost of the environment can have dangerous consequences. It is important for governments to strike a balance and implement measures that minimize air pollution from transportation, factories, thermal power plants, and other sources.

One such measure is to set up robust public transportation systems that offer last-mile connectivity, thereby reducing people's dependence on private vehicles. Airports should be located away from residential areas. Innovation of affordable electric vehicles and promoting the use of solar panels should be prioritized.

Efforts should be made to gradually replace thermal power plants with renewable energy sources such as solar power, wind energy, and hydroelectricity. Factories should be relocated away from habitation. Factories that produce toxic gases or other hazardous by-products may be provided with government assistance to treat their waste locally before releasing it into the environment.

In South Asia, stubble burning has emerged as a big menace. Modern agriculture technologies can address this problem, but they are capital-intensive. Governments may have to take the lead to resolve this impasse. Forming cooperatives, easing bank loans for purchase of stubble-clearing machines, reducing taxes on import of equipment, and promoting indigenous technology can be some measures.

To reduce dependence on electric generators and air conditioners, buildings should have an eco-friendly design. Wider availability of LPG and PNG in rural areas can reduce the use of cow dung, wood, and coal as cooking fuels. Trees and plants are critical to life. Concerted efforts should be made to plant more trees and increase forest coverage.

There is a need to educate people about their role in reducing air pollution. Environmental safety legislations should be enforced more diligently. Elimination of leaded petrol is a classic success story of such legislation. Lead is highly toxic; it can damage the nervous system, blood, and kidneys. It slows down learning in children. For nearly a century, use of leaded petrol caused catastrophic health problems globally. In 2021, after a decades-long campaign led by the UN Environment Program, leaded petrol was phased out from the world.

AIR QUALITY INDEX

Air Quality Index (AQI) is a scale to measure air pollution. It provides a composite number based on air concentration levels of five major pollutants: Particulate matter, nitrogen dioxide, sulfur dioxide, carbon monoxide, and ground-level ozone. Table 44.1 provides AQI values and the corresponding levels of health concern.

TABLE 44.1
Interpretation of AQI Values

AQI Values	Health Concern
• 0–50	Good
• 51–100	Moderate
• 101–150	Unhealthy for sensitive people
• 151–200	Unhealthy for all
• 201–300	Very unhealthy
• 301–500	Hazardous

Source: https://www.epa.gov/outdoor-air-quality-data/air-data-basic-information

While AQI in many cities around the world stays well within the safe limit of 50, in many cities in developing countries, it hovers around 200–400 for most part of the year.

NOTES

1. Under certain environmental conditions that are not yet fully understood, ozone, particulate matter, and nitrogen oxides combine to form smog.
2. Nitric oxide and nitrogen dioxide are the two most hazardous nitrogen oxides.

45 Water and Its Sources

We need water for drinking, cooking, personal hygiene, agriculture, and industry. Water is also used for recreational activities like swimming pools and water games. The WHO maintains that all people, regardless of their social or economic status, have a right to adequate supply of safe drinking water.

Around 97% of the earth's water is in the oceans, but it is unfit for human consumption. The rest is freshwater, with some of it frozen in high mountains or trapped in the Antarctic. Roughly 1% of the earth's water is available for consumption.

HYDROLOGICAL CYCLE

Surface water (oceans, rivers, lakes, ponds, etc.) evaporates and is carried away by the wind to different parts of the earth. On condensation, this vapor falls as rain and replenishes surface water and groundwater. Surface water evaporates again. Thus, a hydrological cycle continues.

REQUIREMENT OF WATER

People's water requirements vary by their vocation, economic status, lifestyle, location, and other factors. In areas where water supply is limited, people in middle- and lower-income groups use around 135 liters of water per person per day, nearly one-third of which is used for toilet flushing.

SOURCES OF WATER

Water for human consumption comes from three main sources:

1. Rainwater
2. Surface water
3. Groundwater

Rainwater

When surface water evaporates, the vapor produced is pure and free of contaminants. This vapor is carried by the wind to other places and condenses as rain. This is nature's mechanism to purify water. However, rainwater becomes contaminated when it passes through polluted air. Contaminated rain, in turn, pollutes surface water and harms crops.

Surface Water

Surface water includes oceans, rivers, lakes, ponds, and tanks. The saline nature of ocean water makes it unsuitable for consumption. Desalination can make it usable, but it is a costly process that few countries can afford.

Contrary to popular belief, surface water is not limitless. Over a long period, it reduces due to evaporation and by seeping into the earth's deeper layers.

Many cities depend on rivers or lakes as their primary water sources. Sadly, in some cities, human and animal excreta, domestic waste, and even industrial effluents are directly released into waterbodies. Again, nature has inherent mechanisms to purify surface water—exposure to sunlight

DOI: 10.4324/9781032644257-51

and air reduces some contamination in rivers, and impurities in lake water settle naturally at the base. However, the enormous amount of waste discharged into these waterbodies cannot be cleaned by nature alone. As a result, many rivers, lakes, and ponds in some low-income countries are heavily polluted. Some are akin to drains.

Many examples of surface water contamination can be found globally. The 1854 cholera outbreak in London was a turning point in the history of public health. After the outbreak's source was traced back to contaminated water from the Thames, authorities realized that similar incidents had occurred in the past but had gone unnoticed. In the United States, in 1969, industrial pollution led to a river fire in Ohio. In 1975, the James River in Virginia was found to be polluted with chlordecone, an insecticide. Investigators found that a factory had been discharging the chemical into the river for seven years. In Minnesota, water of Lake Superior was considered so clean that the municipality distributed it without any treatment. However, in the 1970s, human rights activists discovered an unusually high incidence of cancer in populations around the lake. A laboratory test in 1975 found that the water was contaminated with asbestos. A mining company had been dumping its waste into the lake for 16 years. Despite litigation and strong activism, it took several years for this to stop. Eventually, the mining company was shut down, leaving 3,000 people jobless. This was the first instance in the United States, and possibly the world, where an environmental issue led to the closure of a major industrial facility.

In subsequent years, growing public awareness led several countries to formulate regulations to safeguard their water sources. The situation has since improved significantly in developed countries, but not in many overpopulated countries.

Groundwater

Groundwater refers to water below the earth's surface. Quality of groundwater is generally better than that of surface water due to several reasons. First, it is not directly exposed to contamination from human activities. Second, rainwater percolating into the ground is naturally filtered through soil. Lastly, groundwater remains undisturbed, which allows suspended impurities to settle at the bottom.

There are three ways to draw groundwater:

Open Well

Open wells are generally wide, with a diameter of 6–12 feet. Water is drawn using a bucket and rope. Since the well is open at the top, there is risk of contamination from debris or waste. Constructing a parapet around the well can reduce such contamination. Using a pulley system with a common bucket to draw water can further help maintain cleanliness and hygiene.

Hand Pump

A borehole is dug using a drilling machine. A pipe is inserted into the hole, and a hand pump is fixed at the outlet. Water is drawn manually by operating the hand pump.

Tube Well

A tube well is similar to a hand pump, except water is pumped out by a motor powered by electricity or diesel.

Earth is composed of several porous and impervious layers. Shallow wells draw water from above the first impervious layer, while deep wells go into deeper layers. As we go deeper into the earth, both the quantity and quality of water improve.

Groundwater is generally cleaner than surface water, but in low-income settings, groundwater too gets polluted, especially in densely populated areas. Borehole latrines or septic tank latrines can contaminate the groundwater in their vicinity. Open sewage drains traverse the city to reach a treatment plant or a river. Enroute, sewage water seeps into the ground, contaminating groundwater.

In landfills, harmful chemicals percolate into groundwater. Ideally, there should be no potential source of contamination within a 50-foot radius of a groundwater source.

HARDNESS OF WATER

Hardness of water is caused by the presence of magnesium and calcium salts. Hard water is generally not harmful to human health; however, it is not suitable for washing as it does not lather well with soap. Additionally, it can harm domestic appliances such as water heaters and industrial devices such as boilers as its precipitate gets deposited in water pipes, clogging them sooner.

Total Dissolved Solids

Total dissolved solids (TDS) is a measure of water hardness. According to the WHO, the TDS level of drinking water should less than 600 mg per liter. However, reverse osmosis (RO) machines often reduce TDS to very low values. This serves no purpose and results in considerable wastage of water. This wastage can be reduced by adjusting the RO machine's TDS level to 400–500 mg per liter.

46 Water Pollution and Treatment

Safe drinking water is crucial for good health, yet roughly a quarter of the world's population does not have access to it. The SDG 6.1 calls for equitable access to safe drinking water. By efficiently managing their water resources, countries can improve the health of their populations. This can enhance their economic development and help reduce poverty.

Water pollution can stem from point sources or nonpoint sources. A factory routinely discharging its waste into a pond or a river is an example of point-source contamination. When contamination results from multiple sources, such as human and animal feces washing into a river all along its course, it is called nonpoint source contamination.

Microbes and chemicals are common sources of water contamination. Rarely, radiological contamination occurs.

MICROBIAL CONTAMINATION

Low-income countries bear a high burden of waterborne diseases caused by bacterial, viral, protozoal, or helminthic contamination. The greatest risk to the safety of drinking water comes from microbes present in human or animal feces. Some common waterborne diseases and their causative agents are given below:

- Diarrhea: Rotavirus, norovirus, adenovirus
- Dysentery (also known as bloody diarrhea): *Shigella spp.*, *Campylobacter spp.*, *Salmonella* (non-typhoidal), *E. coli*[1]
- Parasitic infection: *Entamoeba histolytica, Giardia intestinalis,* helminths; less commonly *Schistosoma*
- Cholera: *Vibrio cholerae* (now mostly restricted to endemic areas)

Non-fecal microbial contamination of water is caused under specific circumstances by organisms such as the Guinea worm (*Dracunculus medinensis*). When a person infected with Guinea worm (a case of dracunculiasis) enters a waterbody, the blisters on his skin burst, releasing thousands of Guinea worm larvae into the water. Water fleas (cyclops) swallow these larvae. The disease is transmitted to others when they drink water contaminated with these fleas. There is no specific treatment or vaccine for dracunculiasis, but the disease is on the verge of eradication.

Waterborne diseases can also spread through contaminated food.

CHEMICAL CONTAMINATION

Chemical contamination of water can occur from natural sources, such as underground minerals, or human sources such as agrochemicals, industrial effluents, and domestic sewage. Unlike microbes, chemical pollutants generally take longer to produce adverse effects on health. Indirect exposure can occur by consuming food contaminated with chemicals.

In some areas, naturally occurring minerals such as fluoride, arsenic, or nitrate pollute groundwater. Fluoride toxicity causes staining and mottling of teeth and may lead to skeletal deformities with pain and tenderness in bones. Groundwater in pockets of India and Bangladesh contains high levels of arsenic, a chemical element commonly called the "king of poisons." Drinking arsenic-contaminated water causes hardening of skin, painful sores, swollen limbs, and loss of sensation. Progressive neurological disorder can occur. Risk of cancer increases.

DOI: 10.4324/9781032644257-52

Example 1

In the 1970s, after recurrent outbreaks of cholera and other waterborne diseases in parts of West Bengal in India and neighboring Bangladesh, hundreds of wells were dug to provide safe drinking water to the people. However, incidence of diarrhea and vomiting increased after this intervention. Over a period of time, some people developed progressive neurological disorders. It was later found that groundwater in these areas had high levels of arsenic.

Pesticides, pharmaceuticals, microplastics, and PFAS[2] also pose significant risk to people's health. Many industries release untreated water into waterbodies, introducing contaminants such as asbestos, bisphenol, lead, mercury, nitrate, nitrite, polychlorinated biphenyls, trichloroethylene, vinyl chloride, and xylene. At times, municipal waste containing chemical contaminants also finds its way into waterbodies.

Earlier, lead-coated water pipes were used in buildings. Corrosion of these pipes over time contaminated the water supply. Consuming lead-contaminated water can delay physical and mental development in children and cause learning difficulties. It can damage kidneys. While most modern plumbing pipes are lead-free, some low-quality PVC pipes may contain lead as a stabilizer.

Asbestos is a naturally occurring mineral composed of microscopic fibers. Due to its poor conductivity of heat and electricity, asbestos is widely used in industrial production, such as fireproof coatings, insulation materials, roofing materials, automotive brake and clutch systems, and shipbuilding. Inhaling asbestos fibers can cause asbestosis, a lung condition. Asbestos is also a known carcinogen; consuming asbestos-contaminated water over a long period of time may cause gastrointestinal cancer.

Example 2

In the 1950s, over 2,000 residents of Minamata Bay in Japan reported mood and behavior changes. Their intelligence was impaired. Many children were born with mental retardation. Upon investigation, it was found that the local fisherfolk were mainly affected. Residents of Minamata obtained their water from several different sources, and mosquitoes and other vectors were not common in the area. This helped scientists to conclude that the condition was not waterborne or vector-borne. Additionally, since short-term visitors from other areas were not affected, it was construed that the disease was not communicable. The only common factor among the affected people was a staple diet of fish. After years of research, it was determined that the disease was caused by consuming fish with high levels of methylmercury in their flesh. Methylmercury is neurotoxic. It was found that a local chemical factory had been discharging wastewater containing methylmercury into the bay. Similar outbreaks, though less severe, were reported from other countries, and many of them were traced back to methylmercury contamination of water.

Example 3

In 1975, environmentalists in New York discovered polychlorinated biphenyls (PCBs) in waters of the Hudson River. The contamination was traced to two General Electric (GE) factories that used PCBs in the manufacture of electrical devices like capacitors and transformers. Although GE stopped discharging PCBs into the river after local protests, the chemical persisted in the riverbed even after 25 years. Eventually, the US Environmental Protection Agency (US EPA) ordered GE to clean up a 40-mile section of the riverbed by dredging. The process took six years.

Currently, PCBs are the most widespread chemical contaminants. In 1968, an accidental leakage of PCBs into rice-bran oil in a factory in Japan affected 1,800 people. A similar incident in Taiwan in 1979 affected 2,000 people. Notably, children born to Taiwanese mothers who had consumed PCB-contaminated rice oil were reported to have low birth weight. There are indications that PCBs may be carcinogenic. Epidemiological studies will inform the long-term effects of PCB contamination.

In 2001, ninety countries signed the Stockholm Convention on Persistent Organic Pollutants, a global treaty to end the production, use, and release of 12 persistent organic pollutants (POPs) such as DDT and aldrin.

Recently, adverse effects of some new chemicals[3] used in everyday products like plastic containers, soaps, and shampoos have come to light. When ingested, these chemicals can disrupt the endocrine system, which can lead to early puberty in girls, reduce sperm count in men, and increase the risk of diabetes and obesity. These health problems are increasing in populations, but due to lack of research, it is difficult to say to what extent chemical contaminants have contributed to this increase.

The rampant use of pesticides and chemical fertilizers in agriculture also contributes to water pollution. Nitrate is commonly used as a fertilizer, and it is also naturally present in human and animal waste. It is a major pollutant. Nitrate in drinking water converts into nitrite in the body, which binds with hemoglobin to form methemoglobin, a type of hemoglobin that is incapable of transporting oxygen. This is the most common cause of *blue baby syndrome* (infant methemoglobinemia), a potentially fatal condition. Unfortunately, in low-income countries, water is neither tested for pesticides nor treated to eliminate them.

In most cases of chemical contamination of water, switching to a different water source is the best solution as treating contaminated water is generally not cost-effective.

TREATMENT OF WATER

Water intended for drinking or cooking should be free from any contaminants known to have adverse effects on human health. Normally, water is treated on a large scale by municipalities. However, people can treat smaller quantities of water for their personal use. This is discussed in a later section.

Large-Scale Water Treatment

Municipal water treatment typically involves the following steps:

1. Coagulation-flocculation
2. Sedimentation
3. Filtration
4. Disinfection

Coagulation-Flocculation

This first step involves the removal of suspended particles. Larger particles present in water settle at the base on their own, but smaller particles remain suspended in the water. To remove these finer particles, a harmless and inexpensive chemical called alum (aluminum sulfate) is added to the water. Alum causes these particles to clump together and form large particles. This process is known as coagulation-flocculation.

Sedimentation

After treatment with alum, water is allowed to remain still for a time to allow suspended particles to settle at the base. This is called sedimentation. The material collected at the base, called sludge, is cleared periodically by mechanical devices. Sedimentation is an effective natural method of water purification.

When water is devoid of organic matter, it becomes largely free of microbes in around two weeks. However, prolonged stagnation may lead to growth of algae.

Filtration

Water from the sedimentation tank is passed through a sand filter or synthetic filter to remove smaller particles, parasites, and bacteria.

Disinfection

Chlorination: Filtered water is treated with chlorine gas to eliminate any remaining microbes. A regulated amount of chlorine gas is pumped into the water through a device called a chloronome, such as Peterson's chloronome. Chlorine acts by releasing hypochlorous acid, which is toxic to most microorganisms. However, some organisms, such as poliovirus, hepatitis virus, and cysts of *Giardia* and *Cryptosporidium*,[4] are resistant to chlorine.

Besides its antimicrobial action, chlorine has other benefits. It destroys constituents that produce taste, color, and odor in water; oxidizes iron, manganese, and hydrogen sulfide; and controls algae growth. The amount of chlorine required in water, known as chlorine demand, depends on the level of contamination. Around one hour of contact time is required for chlorine's microbial action to take effect. Generally, hyperchlorination[5] is done to maintain a residual effect in the distribution system. A free chlorine level of 0.5 mg/L is sufficient to maintain water quality in public distribution systems, and up to 4 mg/L is considered safe for drinking water. Chlorine test kits are available to assess the presence of free chlorine in water.

Chlorination is a cost-effective disinfection method commonly used in large-scale water treatment. Bleaching powder or bleaching solution (hypochlorite) can be used for chlorination on a smaller scale.

Alternative Technologies

Ozone

In many developed countries, ozone gas is used for disinfecting water. Ozone gas is produced by subjecting oxygen to a high-voltage electric field. Although the technology is costly, ozone is significantly more effective as a disinfectant than chlorine. It has the additional benefit of neutralizing pesticides and other chemicals, and, unlike chlorine, it does not persist in water for long, so it does not have a residual effect. However, ozone can have toxic effects if released into the environment, so its discharge should be regulated.

Ultraviolet Treatment System

In adequate doses, ultraviolet light is highly effective against most microbes. There are no chemicals involved, and a very short contact period of 20–30 seconds is sufficient. Like ozone, UV light does not leave a residual effect in water. Equipment for UV disinfection occupies a small space, but it is expensive.

Slow Sand Filter

A slow sand filter consists of a thick layer of sand supported by multiple layers of gravel of varying sizes. Water takes several hours to pass through the filter. After a few days, a layer of algae forms on the water's surface. Oxygen produced by the algae allows aerobic bacteria to break down organic contaminants in the water. The algae may also take up excess nitrogen and phosphorus. Because of these biological processes, slow sand filters are also called biological filters. To sustain the algae, use of alum is avoided. In the absence of coagulation-flocculation, suspended particles are removed through natural sedimentation. After filtration, water is disinfected by chlorination. Slow sand filtration is considered highly effective, but it is a time-taking process.

Water Testing

During the treatment process, water is tested at different stages to assess the effectiveness of treatment.

Water Treatment at Household Level

In areas where treated municipal water is not available or where extra precaution is required, water can be treated at household level using one of the following methods:

Boiling

Boiling water for 20 minutes kills most microorganisms except bacterial spores. Boiling also removes temporary hardness of water.

Filtration

A ceramic filter is generally used for this purpose. Micropores in a ceramic filter can eliminate helminths and protozoa, and they are moderately effective against bacteria such as *Campylobacter*, *E. coli*, *Salmonella*, and *Shigella*. However, ceramic filters are not effective against viruses, and of course they cannot remove chemicals. Depending on the level of contamination, pretreatment with alum followed by sedimentation might be necessary. Since chlorinated water cannot be fed into ceramic filters, chlorination can be done after filtration.

Advanced ceramic filters such as ultrafilters are moderately effective against viruses, and nanofilters can even remove chemicals. But these filters are expensive and not always commercially available.

Reverse Osmosis System

An RO machine has pre- and post-filters that can effectively remove bacteria and viruses. They also reduce hardness of water by eliminating calcium and magnesium.

Disinfection

Chlorine tablets are commonly available for small-scale water disinfection. It may be noted that chlorination is effective only if the water is free of suspended particles.

WATER QUALITY

Quality of water should be such that it does not harm people's health and that its appearance, taste, and odor are acceptable to consumers. For this, regular laboratory testing of treated water is essential. The most important water-quality checks are given here.

Turbidity

Turbidity (cloudiness) indicates the presence of suspended particles or organic matter in water. These particles can have microbes attached to them, making the water unsafe for consumption. The WHO recommends turbidity level below 1 NTU (Nephelometric Turbidity Unit). Generally, turbidity becomes visible to the naked eye at 4 NTU. If water appears turbid, it is unlikely to be safe for consumption.

Coliform Level

Presence of coliform bacteria in treated water is a sign that the treatment was ineffective. Additionally, it raises the possibility that other harmful pathogens may also have survived the treatment process.

Besides turbidity and coliform levels, TDS and pH (potential of hydrogen) are other measures of water quality. Water with TDS below 600 is considered safe. pH indicates the acidity or alkalinity of water on a scale of 1–14. Water with high pH level can damage hair. It can irritate the eyes, skin, and mucous membranes. Excessive pH or oxygen in water can corrode metal pipes.

WATER QUALITY STANDARDS

Water quality standards vary across countries. The following are bare minimum:

Coliform	Ideally, there should be no coliform in drinking water; however, water with up to 50 MPN[6] coliform per 100 mL can be used after disinfection.
pH level	6.5–8.5
Dissolved oxygen	6 mg/liter or more Water normally contains dissolved atmospheric oxygen. Bacteria or other microorganisms present in water decompose organic matter and consume oxygen in the process. This reduces the water's dissolved oxygen concentration, increasing its biological oxygen demand (explained below).
Biological Oxygen Demand (BOD)	2 mg/liter or less (after five-day incubation at 20 degrees Celsius) Biological oxygen demand, also called biochemical oxygen demand, is the amount of oxygen required by microbes to decompose the organic matter present in water over a specified period at a specified temperature. A higher BOD value means a higher amount of organic matter in water.

NOTES

1. *E. coli* is a fecal bacterium found in the guts of humans and animals. While most *E. coli* strains are harmless, some can cause severe disease. It may be noted that the presence of *E. coli* in water is not a threat in itself, but it is an indication of fecal contamination and the possible presence of pathogens in the water.
2. PFAS are per- and polyfluoroalkyl substances, a group of synthetic chemicals used widely in consumer and industrial products.
3. These include bisphenol A (BPA) and phthalates.
4. A microfilter with a pore size of 1 micron or less can eliminate cysts of *Giardia* and *Cryptosporidium*.
5. Hyperchlorination is a water-treatment method in which a high dose of chlorine is added to water for complete disinfection.
6. MPN is Most Probable Number.

47 Water Harvesting

Water is finite. If we continue to draw more water than nature can replenish through rain, our water sources will get depleted. Rainfall, too, is limited. Our ponds, lakes, and rivers are shrinking, and some have even disappeared. When shallow wells run dry, we bore deeper, but even the deepest wells will not last forever.

In light of these facts, water conservation is no longer an option but a necessity. Besides using water sensibly and efficiently, we should reuse it when possible. Additionally, we can set up systems to capture and harvest water from natural sources for future use. Common methods of water harvesting are explained here.

RAINWATER HARVESTING

Rainwater harvesting is an effective method of water conservation, wherein rainwater falling over rooftops is collected through a pipe or a semicircular channel and stored in a drum or tank. This method is particularly useful in places where rainfall is abundant. Many countries have made water harvesting compulsory for large buildings that meet certain criteria, though the implementation is not uniform.

In some rural areas, rainwater is collected in a natural or excavated pond or an underground tank. These reservoirs are strategically located to maximize catchment area. A natural slope or a specially dug open channel diverts the rainwater to the pond or tank. Underground water storage reduces water evaporation, making it particularly useful in deserts and arid regions. In areas with low rainfall, some of these tanks provide enough potable water to sustain native communities through the entire summer.

In forests or barren lands, "recharge pits" are dug to collect rainwater. These pits are typically 6–12 inches wide and 2–3 feet deep. The collected water gradually seeps into the ground and supports vegetation.

SURFACE WATER AND STORMWATER HARVESTING

To capture water from a stream or waterfall, a stone wall or tank is constructed on its path. Water collects in the enclosure and overflows to continue its journey downstream. The collected water is used during periods of reduced natural flow. In the case of a river, this structure is called a check dam. A barrier is constructed on one side of a low-lying area. Excess water from monsoon rains accumulates in the catchment area behind the barrier, from where it seeps into the soil, recharging groundwater, or is used for irrigation, livestock, and other activities.

Similarly, stormwater can be collected in tanks constructed strategically along the storm's natural course.

GROUNDWATER RECHARGING

As stated earlier, groundwater is naturally replenished through rainfall and through seepage of water from rivers and lakes. Groundwater can also be recharged by rainwater harvesting. Rainwater falling on rooftops or within a building's premises can be channeled into a borewell to recharge groundwater, as shown in Figure 47.1. Before the water enters the borewell, it passes through a storage tank or soak pit to filter trash and reduce impurities.

Rainwater collected in an underpass, a low-lying area, or a stormwater drain can also be directed into a borewell to replenish groundwater.

DOI: 10.4324/9781032644257-53

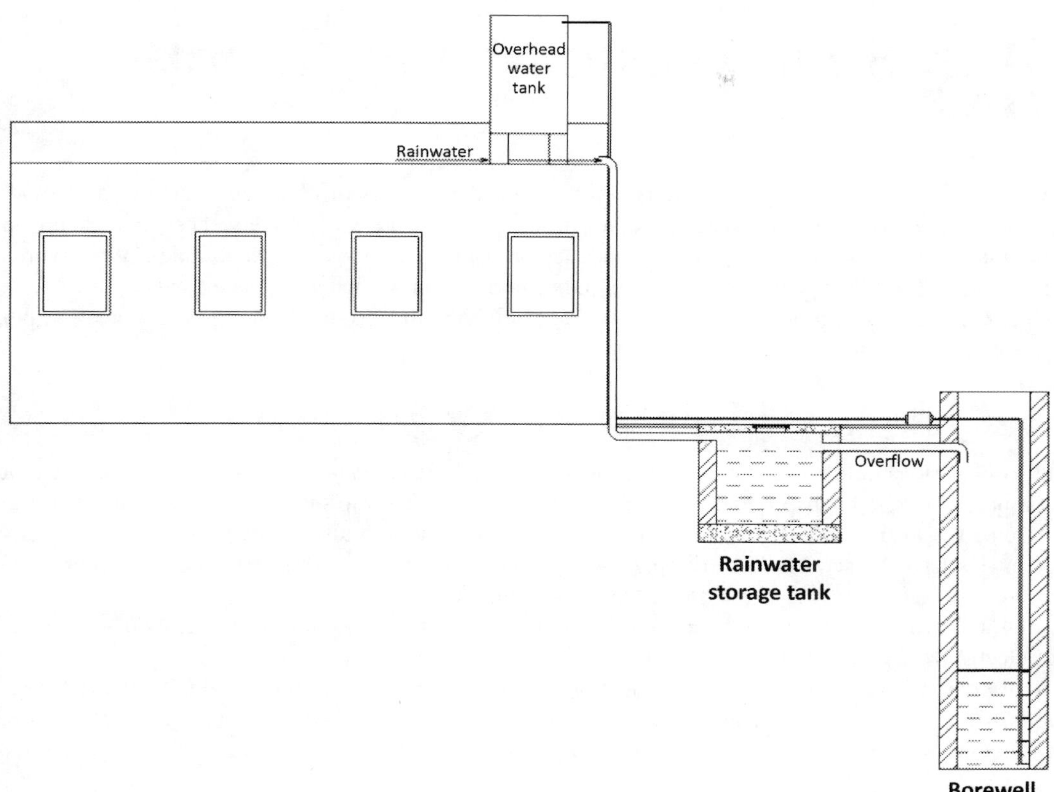

FIGURE 47.1 Groundwater recharging: A schematic diagram.

48 Solid Waste Management

Anything we no longer intend to use is waste. Every day, we discard kitchen waste, leftover food, packaging materials, paper, plastic, garden trimmings, and more. Collectively, these items make up municipal waste. With our growing dependence on packaged goods and disposables, along with a declining culture of *repair and reuse*, the quantum of waste we generate has grown exponentially. This is true globally. In low-income settings, urban inhabitants produce around 0.5 kg of waste per person per day. Affluent homes produce more.

WASTE DISPOSAL

Ideally, waste should be segregated where it is generated, and only waste that cannot be recycled or composted should be disposed of in municipal bins. Domestic scrap should have a separate disposal system. Waste from construction and industrial activities should also be treated separately. Many countries have passed laws prohibiting the disposal of untreated industrial waste into municipal waste or waterbodies, but enforcement remains a challenge.

Biomedical waste generated in hospitals is hazardous to human health. E-waste, such as batteries or electronic items, can also be harmful if not disposed of properly.

In areas where municipal waste collection is irregular, people often discard their waste on the roadside. Although this does not pose a direct threat to health, the nuisance value of littered waste cannot be overstated. It attracts flies, rodents, and stray animals.

MANAGING SOLID WASTE

There are four key strategies for solid waste management:

- Reduce waste generation
- Recycle paper, plastic, cloth, etc.
- Compost organic waste
- Safely treat and dispose of remaining municipal waste

Reducing Waste Generation

Stringent law enforcement and active public participation are both integral to reducing waste generation. To begin with, production and supply of single-use plastics and disposables should be curtailed. People should be encouraged to use reusable food containers and water bottles and to bring their own bags when purchasing groceries.

When millions of children are undernourished or starving, food wastage is no less than a crime. It should stop.

In some countries, citizens are required to pay a "waste fee" based on the amount of waste they generate. This is a good strategy to make people accountable, but its implementation in developing countries may be difficult.

Recycling

Plastic, paper, cloth, and e-waste can be recycled, provided they are not mixed with organic waste. Municipalities should encourage residents to segregate waste. Separate bins should be provided for recyclable items, and their collection and transportation should be separate from other types of waste.

DOI: 10.4324/9781032644257-54

Recycling creates jobs and reduces the cost of waste treatment. Many countries recycle a considerable portion of their municipal waste.

Composting

Organic waste, such as leftover food, vegetable and fruit peels, and garden trimmings, can be composted. The collected waste is buried in a deep trench or a compost bin, where it is broken down by microbes. In approximately 12 weeks, the waste converts into a stable and innocuous product that can be used as manure.

Some organisms, such as earthworms, aid composting in the presence of adequate moisture and oxygen. The technique of using earthworms to convert organic waste into manure is known as vermicomposting.

Many cities around the world have pioneered waste reduction, recycling, and composting, thereby substantially reducing the amount of waste they send to landfills.

Safe Treatment of Municipal Waste

Landfill

Landfilling is a simple and cost-effective waste disposal method used worldwide. A landfill is a piece of barren land designated by authorities for garbage dumping. It is typically located on the outskirts of a city, away from habitation and waterbodies. Bulldozers pile up the collected waste in layers up to 10–20 feet high. At the end of the day, the waste is covered with a layer of soil to avoid access by flies, rodents, and scavengers.

Over a period, pressure of the overlying waste raises temperature in the deeper layers, which promotes bacterial digestion and gradually reduces the volume of waste. Presence of moisture speeds up this process.

Large landfills can take around 10,000 tons of waste per day. Once a landfill reaches its capacity, it is closed off and covered with 2 feet of soil. After a few years, the area can be converted into a park, but permanent construction is avoided as decomposing waste can cause the ground to shift.

Landfills have certain disadvantages. Leachate, a liquid that forms underneath the waste, trickles down and contaminates the underlying soil and groundwater. In fact, leachate is a significant source of groundwater pollution. To prevent such contamination, the base of the landfill should be made of concrete or sealed with a thick plastic sheet. Alternatively, a system can be set up to extract leachate and dispose it of safely.

Second, volatile compounds and gases liberating from landfills give off bad odor and may cause respiratory irritation in the people living nearby. Methane liberated from landfills poses a fire hazard. Some developed countries have been able to capture methane from landfills and use it as fuel.

Incineration

Incineration is the process of burning waste at very high temperatures of 800–1,300 degrees Celsius. The high temperature significantly reduces the volume of toxic gases produced in combustion. The resultant innocuous ash can be used in brickmaking or other industries, or it can be disposed of in a landfill. The energy produced in the process of incineration can be used for electricity generation, although low-income countries mostly fail to tap it.

The main disadvantage of incineration is that it produces toxic gases as a by-product. Further, incineration equipment can be costly, and running an incinerator requires a continuous supply of fossil fuel or electricity. Despite these limitations, incineration is commonly used for treating biomedical waste. This is further described in the chapter "Hospital Waste Management."

49 Human Excreta Disposal

Until recently, open defecation was common in some low-income countries. What is wrong with this practice? First, people may not properly wash their hands after defecating in the open. Neglecting proper handwashing is an important cause of fecal–oral transmission of diseases, as human feces contain numerous microorganisms, some of which are pathogenic. Diseases like diarrhea, dysentery, typhoid, cholera, hepatitis A, and helminth infestation spread through fecal–oral route. Intestinal worms like hookworm or whipworm can be transmitted when a person comes into contact with soil contaminated by feces. This is common in areas where open defecation is prevalent and people walk barefoot. Flies can also transfer feces to food. Therefore, safe disposal of human feces is paramount.

Human urine is comparatively harmless, except in areas where urinary schistosomiasis is common. Schistosomiasis is a parasitic disease caused by the worm Schistosoma haematobium. Eggs of this worm are excreted through urine. When an infected person urinates in a waterbody or swimming pool, others can contract the infection through their skin.

Human excreta can be disposed of through temporary or permanent arrangements. Choice of latrine in a permanent disposal system depends on the availability of a sewage system. Common methods of human excreta disposal are explained below.

TEMPORARY ARRANGEMENTS

Laborers working in remote areas with no proper latrines and military personnel stationed away from their permanent establishments often make temporary arrangements for excreta disposal. This requires a large stretch of desolate land. The following temporary latrines are commonly used.

Shallow-Trench Latrine

A shallow trench is manually dug into the ground. The user squats on the edge of the trench to defecate and covers the excrement with soil to prevent access by flies, insects, and rodents. The site is changed every few days.

Dug-Well Latrine

Increasing the depth of a trench can extend its life. However, manually excavating a deep trench also increases its width, making it risky for the user. For safety and convenience, a squatting plate is fixed over the excavation. Depth of the trench depends on how safely the squatting plate can be fixed over it; around 10 feet may be good enough. When the trench nears its capacity with excreta, it is covered with a layer of soil and the area is secured to prevent accidents. A new latrine is commissioned.

Borehole Latrine

A deep hole with a diameter of 6–12 inches is dug using a drill machine. Care is taken not to dig too deep, or it could lead to groundwater contamination with excreta. A depth of 10–20 feet may be adequate. A borehole latrine is safer to use, and it is easier to fix a squatting plate over it. When used by five to six people, it may last for a year.

In temporary latrines, fecal matter spontaneously undergoes partial microbial digestion and gradually dries out by exposure to sunlight, transforming into a less harmful product. If it does not dry completely, the risk of pathogens remains.

DOI: 10.4324/9781032644257-55

PERMANENT ARRANGEMENTS

WHERE SEWAGE SYSTEM IS NOT AVAILABLE

A large proportion of the rural population in developing countries does not have access to a piped sewer network. A septic tank latrine is used in such areas.

Septic Tank Latrine

Construction of a septic tank latrine involves proper masonry work. An underground tank is built using bricks and cement, typically reaching a depth of 2 meters. A squatting plate or commode is fixed over the tank. To prevent the entry of flies and rodents, a water seal is inserted into the pipe connecting the toilet seat to the tank. With regular maintenance, the latrine can remain fairly clean and odor-free. However, flushing of feces through a water seal requires a substantial amount of water, which can be a drawback in places where water supply is inadequate.

Excreta accumulates in the septic tank along with urine and wastewater. The solid part settles at the base, forming sludge. The liquid, known as effluent, floats above it. Fecal matter contains a significant amount of fat, which forms a layer of scum over the effluent. A thick layer of scum cuts off air to the effluent and sludge. In the absence of oxygen, the sludge undergoes anaerobic digestion by bacteria present in the feces. This process reduces the volume of sludge and renders it less offensive. The gases produced in the process, namely methane and carbon dioxide, are safely released into the atmosphere above human height through a vent pipe.

When the effluent in the septic tank reaches a certain level, it is allowed to leave the tank through a perforated pipe and percolate into the surrounding soil at a designated distance or into a soak pit. Bacteria in the soil aerobically digest and decompose organic matter present in the effluent. Figure 49.1 shows a schematic diagram of a septic tank latrine.

A septic tank latrine can last several years. When the tank becomes full, sludge can be removed manually. For convenience of operation, the tank is constructed outside the four walls of the latrine, with a slanting pipe connecting the toilet seat to the tank. This allows easy removal of sludge through an opening on top of the tank, called a manhole. A lid is installed over the manhole for safety.

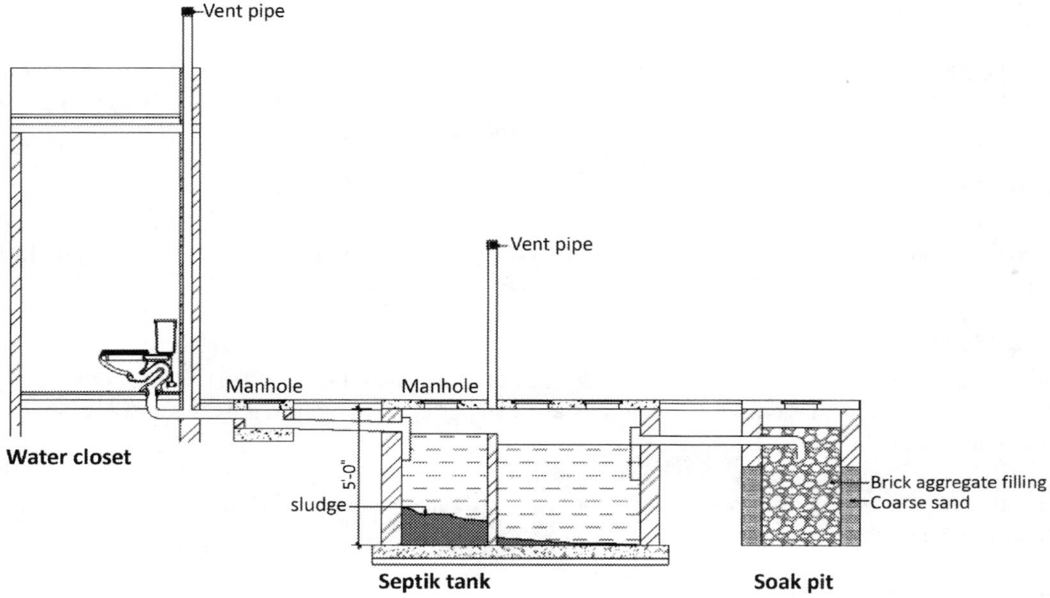

FIGURE 49.1 Septic tank latrine: A schematic diagram.

Preserving the natural microbial balance inside the tank is essential for proper functioning of this system. Therefore, soap and other disinfectants should not be used in this type of latrine as they can harm the microbial flora present in fecal matter.

Where Sewage System Is Available

A sewage system is a closed system of pipes that transports human excreta and wastewater from toilets, bathrooms, and kitchens to a sewage treatment plant. At the treatment plant, fecal matter is digested by bacteria and converted to an innocuous substance that can be used as manure. Water is separated from the waste and released into a waterbody after cleaning and disinfection.

In low-income countries, closed sewage networks are generally limited to residential colonies. Outside of these areas, sewage pipes discharge their contents into open drains that carry the waste over long distances to a treatment plant or river. A disadvantage with open drains is that the waste seeps into the ground along the way, contaminating groundwater. Further, rainwater and stormwater get added to the waste, increasing its volume. This causes additional strain on the treatment plant.

Design of Latrine in Sewage System

Latrines in a sewage system are similar to septic tank latrines. The only difference is the absence of an underground storage tank. The toilet seat is connected to sewage pipes through a water seal.

SEWAGE TREATMENT PROCESS

Sewage treatment plants can range from very basic to highly sophisticated depending on their capacity and technology. A large treatment plant can receive as much as 100–300 million gallons of waste per day and may be spread over several square kilometers of land.

Waste that reaches the treatment plant consists of fecal matter suspended in liquid (water and urine), along with other waste such as polythene, plastic, paper, rags, pieces of wood, and mud and sand from open drains.

Steps of the sewage treatment process are explained below.

Primary Treatment

Large objects, trash, and particles of mud and sand present in waste can overwhelm the treatment plant and damage machinery. Primary treatment involves removal of these inorganic materials by passing the waste through a screen and a grit chamber.

Screening

To remove large objects and trash, waste is passed through a vertical screen of iron bars spaced 4–6 inches apart. Trapped materials are periodically removed by mechanical devices and sent to a landfill. Waste that passes through the bars proceeds to a grit chamber.

Grit Chamber

In this chamber, waste moves at a very slow pace to allow mud and sand particles to settle at the base through sedimentation. These materials are also periodically removed by mechanical devices and sent to a landfill.

The fat in feces and kitchen waste forms a layer of scum over liquid waste. In advanced treatment plants, a mechanical scraper sweeps away the scum to a separate outlet. The remaining waste moves to the next chamber.

Secondary Treatment

This involves reduction of organic matter by bacterial action.

Aeration Tank

By this stage, the waste mainly consists of semisolid fecal materials suspended in water and urine. A network of perforated pipes pumps air into the waste, raising its oxygen content. This facilitates aerobic digestion of organic matter by the bacteria present in feces. Advanced plants also have a mechanism to swirl the waste, which aids decomposition.

To further increase bacterial population in the waste, a portion of activated sludge from the sedimentation tank is diverted back to the aeration tank. This is explained below.

Sedimentation Tank

After a few hours in the aeration tank, the waste moves to the sedimentation tank, where it remains still for several hours to allow the digested fecal matter and bacteria to settle at the base as sludge. The sludge is mechanically swept to one side and then shifted to another chamber through a conveyor belt. This collected sludge is rich in bacterial flora. Around 30% of it is sent back to the aeration tank to enhance the bacterial content of the waste. This is known as *activated sludge process*.

The effluent over the sludge is mostly water with some bacterial content. It is discharged from the sedimentation tank and directed to another tank for chlorination.

Sludge Dewatering

The sludge recovered from the sedimentation tank has high water content. It is centrifuged or belt-pressed to eliminate the water. The thickened, semisolid sludge thus formed is transferred to a drying bed or spread on open ground, where it dries naturally. As it dries, the sludge transforms into non-offensive material that can be used as manure.

Effluent Chlorination

Effluent from the sedimentation tank is chlorinated and released into a waterbody.

Depending on the type of treatment plant, the entire sewage treatment process takes 12–24 hours. If sludge is dried in the open, it takes a few more days.

Tertiary Treatment

Modern sewage treatment plants incorporate certain additional steps to further reduce the volume of sludge and purify the effluent. The sludge is subjected to anaerobic digestion in a closed tank. The temperature inside the tank is raised to promote bacterial multiplication. There can be a mechanism to swirl the waste. In the absence of air, anaerobic digestion by bacteria reduces the volume of sludge and converts it into innocuous granular material that is a higher-grade manure. Anaerobic digestion takes several weeks. The methane gas produced as a by-product can be captured. In many Western countries, it is utilized to heat buildings.

In advanced sewage treatment plants, the recovered effluent or water is treated with ozone gas or ultraviolet rays instead of chlorine. In some plants, after the water is treated with ozone, it is passed through sand filters before being released into a waterbody.

Testing

To ensure that the sewage treatment plant is working effectively, the waste is tested at various stages of the process. As we learned in the chapter "Water Pollution and Treatment," biological oxygen demand (BOD) is an important measure of water quality. It informs the amount of dissolved oxygen required by microorganisms to break down organic matter in a given sample of effluent at a specified temperature over a specified time period. A high BOD value indicates that the effluent has a high amount of organic matter. To release treated effluent or water into a waterbody, its BOD should be within a certain limit.

50 Hospital Waste Management

Waste generated in patient-care activities, mainly those related to diagnosis and treatment, is known as biomedical waste. This waste can be hazardous and requires careful handling and treatment.

Multispecialty hospitals produce 2–3 kg of waste per bed per day. This includes both biomedical waste and general, noninfectious waste.

TYPES OF BIOMEDICAL WASTE

Soiled	Cotton soiled with blood or body fluids, swabs, gauze, and dressings. These are typically generated in operating room, labor room, patient ward, and dressing room.
Sharps	Syringe needles, infusion set needles, scalpel blades, broken glassware, etc. These are used in virtually all patient-care areas.
Human anatomical	Tissues removed in surgery, placenta in delivery, tissues collected for histopathological examination, etc. This waste is generated in operating room, labor room, and histopathology laboratory.
Microbiological	Culture material; leftover samples of blood, urine, stool, and pus. These come from the microbiology lab.
Liquid	Leftover phenyl, acid, reagent, and other chemicals from housekeeping units and labs.

HAZARDS OF BIOMEDICAL WASTE

Among all types of biomedical waste, sharps and microbiological waste are especially hazardous as they can transmit infections to service providers and waste handlers. Serious chronic infections like HIV, hepatitis B, and hepatitis C can be transmitted through sharps. Nurses can get needle-prick injuries when attempting to recap needles (note that suture needles are less likely than syringe needles to transmit infection as they transfer a minimal amount of blood).

Laboratory waste, including leftover specimen samples and culture plates and slides, is full of pathogens and highly infectious. Despite this, there are not many known cases of infection resulting from lab waste. This is generally due to the exceptional care taken by laboratory staff in handling and disposing of hazardous waste.

NEED FOR WASTE SEGREGATION

Of the total waste generated in a hospital, only 10% is biomedical waste. Handling and treatment of biomedical waste is a costly affair, and failure to segregate it from general waste adds to the cost. Around 10%–15% of hospital waste is plastic, which cannot be treated alongside infectious waste as it produces toxic gases on burning. This makes waste segregation even more important, and it must be done at the point of generation. This means service providers should discard each type of waste in its designated container. To facilitate this, every service delivery point should be equipped with suitable waste containers for the specific types of waste generated in that area.

SEGREGATION GUIDELINES

To develop a common understanding among users, a color-coded system is adopted for waste segregation. An example is presented in Table 50.1.

DOI: 10.4324/9781032644257-56

TABLE 50.1
Color-Coded Segregation System for Hospital Waste

Color of Container	Type of Waste
Yellow	Soiled waste, anatomical waste, chemical waste, laboratory waste, discarded medicines, etc.
Puncture-proof container	Sharps (needles)
Red	Plastic waste such as tubing, plastic bottle, intravenous set, syringe, and vacutainer
Blue	Broken glass, metallic body implants, etc.
Black	General waste such as packing materials and paper

At a minimum, hospitals are required to segregate four types of waste: Sharps, soiled waste, plastic, and general waste. Separate containers for each type of waste are placed at all patient-care points, including the patient ward, operating room, labor room, and treatment room. Areas such as physiotherapy room or patient waiting room do not require containers for sharps or soiled waste.

Twice a day, the waste collected at various service delivery points is transferred to a central waste yard within the hospital. From this point, it is transported to a treatment facility located away from the city. This is generally done once a day. Throughout this entire process, measures are taken to prevent mixing of different types of waste.

COLLECTION

Sharps

Needles, blades, and broken glass are dangerous to handle, so no attempt should be made to decontaminate or mutilate them after use. Syringe needles should not be recapped. Sharps should be collected in a puncture-proof container. When the container is full, it should be sent for deep burial or incineration (explained in the next section).

Soiled Waste and Anatomical Waste

Soiled cotton, gauze, bandages, and anatomical waste can be treated by incineration.

Plastic Waste

Plastic waste generated in hospitals includes syringes, infusion sets, tubing, their wrappers, and other such items. Plastic cannot be incinerated as it produces carcinogenic gases like dioxin and furan on burning. It cannot be sent to a landfill as it does not decompose by bacterial action. Therefore, recycling remains the only option to manage plastic waste. Before plastic items are sent for recycling, they are soaked in 1% sodium hypochlorite solution for decontamination and then mutilated or cut into pieces to prevent reuse in their existing form.

Noninfectious Waste

Noninfectious waste in hospitals includes kitchen waste, packing materials, paper, and the like. This waste can be handled and treated like domestic or municipal waste, as explained in the chapter "Solid Waste Management."

Liquid Waste

Guidelines exist for treatment of liquid waste, but it is mostly disposed of in the sewage system.

TREATMENT METHODS

Incineration

An incinerator is a type of furnace consisting of two chambers lined by heat-resistant bricks. Each chamber has one or two burners that produce very high temperatures. Waste is loaded into the primary chamber, where it gets burned to ashes at a temperature of 850 degrees Celsius. Gases produced in the process are directed to the second chamber, where they are further heated to 1,050 degrees Celsius. This renders the gases relatively harmless. Next, the gases are passed through water to allow certain toxic products to dissolve in water. Finally, they are released into the environment through a chimney situated at a height of 30 feet above ground. At the end of the day, ash residue is removed from the primary chamber after the incinerator has cooled down.

Incinerators can be powered by electricity or diesel. Some models use electricity for ignition and then run on diesel.

The key feature of an incinerator is its ability to generate very high temperatures. If the required temperature is not reached, the gases produced may remain toxic. Overloading the chamber with waste is a common reason for this.

A major advantage of incineration is that it significantly reduces the volume of waste. The resulting ashes are sterile and can be disposed of safely and easily. They can be used in various industries. As human body parts are completely burned to ashes, there are no social or ethical concerns.

Disadvantages of incineration include high equipment and operating costs. Second, the smoke emitted by incinerators contains harmful pollutants, so they need to be installed away from habitation. Third, plastics and other waste items that have been treated with a hypochlorite solution cannot be incinerated as they produce toxic gases on burning.

Landfilling

Landfilling and deep burial are accepted methods for disposing of hospital waste in areas where desolate land is available and the site can be secured from access by ragpickers, animals, rodents, and flies. The process of landfilling is described in the chapter "Solid Waste Management."

Autoclaving

In hospitals, autoclaving is mainly used to sterilize surgical instruments and linen. Some laboratories use it for treating microbiological waste. An autoclave is a steel chamber that generates steam under high pressure. When steam is compressed at a pressure of 15 pounds per square inch, its temperature rises to 121 degrees Celsius. This kills all microbes, including bacterial spores, within 20 minutes. Thus, highly infectious microbiological waste can be rendered safe by autoclaving. No gases are produced as a by-product, and the entire process can be completed in around 30 minutes.

Autoclaving is a cost-effective method of sterilization. However, it is not suitable for treating items such as blood-stained cotton, pus-soaked gauze pieces, or human body parts, as their appearance and volume remain unchanged after treatment, posing a challenge for their disposal. Ethical concerns may arise when disposing of anatomical waste.

Microwaving

Microwaves are a type of electromagnetic radiation with a specific frequency. Microwaving is a suitable method for disinfecting microbiological waste. The equipment is similar to household microwave ovens but larger in size. Small quantities of waste can be treated quickly and easily by microwaving, compared to the more cumbersome process of autoclaving, which is more suitable for larger volumes. Other advantages and disadvantages of microwave treatment are similar to those of autoclaving.

OUTSOURCING

Most hospitals outsource their waste management to professional agencies. These agencies collect waste from the hospital, transport it, and treat it by appropriate methods. However, even when an external agency is involved, hospital management is still accountable for proper segregation, handling, treatment, and disposal of waste as per statutory guidelines.

51 Noise Pollution

Unwanted sound is noise. Industries, construction activities, and traffic produce noise. In some communities, neighborhood noise from festivals and celebrations is common.

Loudness of sound is measured in decibels (dB). Normal conversation produces 50–60 dB of noise, regular street traffic produces 60–80 dB, and a train passing close by may produce 100–110 dB. Noise level below 75 dB is generally considered safe. In schools, hospitals, and residential areas, noise below 40 dB is desirable.

Noise pollution is a growing problem, and it has both immediate and long-term effects on our health and well-being. In day-to-day life, it can cause annoyance, disturbance, or headache. It can interfere with communication, affect concentration, and reduce productivity. Long-term exposure to high-frequency noise can cause hearing impairment that may be irreversible. This is a common occupational hazard in noise-producing factories.

There is concern about the effects of noise on pregnant women and the developing fetus, but the evidence is lacking.

To reduce noise pollution in cities, train tracks, airports, factories, heavy road traffic, and celebration grounds should be situated away from hospitals, schools, and residential areas. Even with legislation in place, noise pollution remains a problem in many residential areas. There is a need to educate people about its dangers.

To reduce occupational risk for workers, noise-producing industries can provide their workers with hearing protection devices such as earplugs. Quieter machinery and equipment should be used where possible. Acoustic insulation may be possible in some cases.

DOI: 10.4324/9781032644257-57

52 Radiation

Radiation is energy in the form of electromagnetic waves. Radiation is constantly present in our environment, existing in air, water, soil, and all living organisms. Radioactive[1] materials, such as uranium, thorium, and radium, occur naturally in the Earth's crust, and they are also present in small amounts in water and air. Common home appliances like mobile phones, computer monitors, televisions, microwave ovens, and refrigerators produce electromagnetic field. Even the human body contains radioactive carbon and potassium.

All forms of electromagnetic radiation are fundamentally the same, but they differ in wavelength, frequency, and energy. The radiation we encounter in day-to-day life has long wavelength, low frequency, and low energy. Such radiation is nonionizing, meaning it lacks sufficient energy to harm human tissue or cause molecular changes in matter. Conversely, ionizing radiation has a short wavelength, high frequency, and high energy. Ionizing radiation can dislodge electrons from atoms and damage living tissue.

Radiation generated by human activities is more hazardous than naturally occurring radiation. The nuclear bombings of Hiroshima and Nagasaki and the Chernobyl nuclear disaster are well-known examples.

In hospitals, radiation is used for imaging and cancer treatment. It can be hazardous if protocols are not followed.

Lately, there have been concerns about the radiation emitted by mobile phones. Although early epidemiological studies have not found any harmful effects, long-term implications of mobile phone radiation are yet to be known.

ULTRAVIOLET RADIATION

Sunlight contains ultraviolet radiation (UVR), which is essential for the synthesis of vitamin D in our bodies. UVR is nonionizing at low frequencies and ionizing at high frequencies.

As UVR cannot penetrate deep into human tissues, its harmful effects are limited to the skin and eyes. Moderate exposure to UVR is necessary for the production of vitamin D; however, excessive exposure can cause pigmentation, sunburn, and skin aging. In some cases, it may cause skin cancer.[2] Melanin in the skin of people with darker skin tones provides natural protection from UVR. Wearing full clothing and applying sunscreen cream can further minimize exposure.

At higher altitudes, where the air is thin and there is less atmosphere to absorb radiation, intensity of UVR is much higher than it is in the plains. Exposure to high-intensity UVR can cause photo conjunctivitis or photokeratitis,[3] which may lead to temporary snow blindness. Long-term exposure to high-intensity UVR can cause cataract. At high altitudes, mountaineers use UV-protective goggles to protect their eyes.

RADIATION IN HOSPITALS

Roentgen's discovery of X-rays in 1895 revolutionized the diagnosis and treatment of bone fractures. In the 1930s, after X-rays had been in use for several decades, an epidemiological study in the United States made a concerning discovery: Radiologists lived five years less than other medical professionals. This finding underscored the potential harms of radiation exposure in hospitals. Some applications of radiation in hospitals and protective measures are discussed below.

DOI: 10.4324/9781032644257-58

Radiology (Imaging)

X-rays are used in multiple imaging procedures, such as dental X-rays, chest X-rays, computed tomography (CT) scans, fluoroscopy, and positron emission tomography (PET) scans. The radiation dose administered depends on the type of procedure. Dental or chest X-rays require a lower dose, while procedures like coronary angiography and CT scan need higher doses.

X-rays are classified as high-frequency ionizing radiation, which can be harmful to humans. Although the risk of cancer from radiation exposure is relatively low (<1 in 1,000,000), a radiology procedure should be carried out only when its benefits clearly outweigh the risks. For example, mammography for breast cancer screening was approved only after studies established that the benefits of early cancer detection far exceeded the risks of radiation exposure.

Radiotherapy

Radiotherapy is a cancer treatment method that involves the use of ionizing gamma radiation to destroy cancer cells. The radiation may be administered externally or internally. In external radiotherapy, cancer cells are exposed to radiation beams produced by a specialized machine such as a cobalt unit or a linear accelerator. In internal radiotherapy, known as brachytherapy, encapsulated radioactive sources are inserted directly into or near cancerous tissues. In cervical cancer, the implant is placed deep inside the vagina;[4] in prostate cancer, it is inserted in the prostate gland.

Nuclear Medicine

This discipline involves the use of radionuclides[5] to diagnose, stage, and monitor diseases.

Protection from Radiation in Hospitals

For patient safety, the minimum possible dose of radiation is used in imaging procedures. For safety of service providers, the duration and intensity of exposure are carefully managed. Providers are advised to spend minimum time near the radiation source and to maintain a safe distance. They should wear a lead shield or apron during the procedure. Radiographers are required to wear a dosimeter or personal monitoring device while on the job, which keeps a record of their radiation exposure. When exposure reaches a threshold level, the provider is temporarily removed from active duty in radiology.

ACCIDENTS IN NUCLEAR REACTORS

Since the advent of nuclear reactors in the 1940s, over 200 radiation accidents have occurred in various countries. The 1986 Chernobyl nuclear disaster is a tragic example of a radiation catastrophe caused by human error. It led to several thousand deaths from cancer.

Radiation emitted by nuclear reactors is extremely hazardous. Radioactive materials can enter the body through the skin, by inhalation, or by ingestion. The extent of damage depends on the dose and duration of exposure. Skin exposure can cause redness, burns, hair loss, or acute radiation syndrome.[6] Inhalation or ingestion of radiation can damage internal organs. In particular, cells that multiply rapidly, such as those in the skin, bone marrow, immune system, and epithelial lining of gastrointestinal and respiratory systems, atrophy quickly. Slow-multiplying cells, such as liver cells or vascular endothelium, atrophy slowly. Children are more sensitive to the effects of radiation.

Long-term exposure to low doses of radiation produces less pronounced effects, as the body simultaneously repairs some of the damage. But the risk of cancer remains, although it may take several years or decades for cancer to manifest. Leukemia and non-Hodgkin's lymphoma are common cancers associated with radiation exposure.

ATOMIC EXPLOSIONS

The atomic bombings of Hiroshima and Nagasaki killed hundreds of thousands of people within months. Deaths occurred initially from the force and intense heat of the explosions and later from the acute effects of radiation exposure.

Survivors of the explosions were followed up for several years and were found to have a higher occurrence of leukemia. Cases of leukemia began to surface in the second year after the bombings and peaked in the next five to six years. Solid cancers, such as cancers of thyroid, breast, and lungs, appeared after a decade.

When pregnant women are exposed to high levels of radiation, there is an increased risk of their children being born with birth defects, such as anencephaly,[7] cleft palate, or cleft lip. However, there are indications that these effects do not pass on to subsequent generations.

In the event of a nuclear reactor accident or a nuclear explosion, swift action can save lives. People should be promptly relocated to safer areas. Rescue teams should use personal protective equipment and respiratory devices.

NOTES

1. A substance that emits ionizing radiation is called radioactive.
2. Skin cancers caused by UVR are basal cell carcinoma and squamous cell carcinoma.
3. Welder's flash also causes similar effects on the eye.
4. The implant can be fixed by applying stitches.
5. A radionuclide is an unstable atom that becomes stable by releasing radiation.
6. Symptoms of acute radiation syndrome include nausea, vomiting, fever, and diarrhea. There can be seizures or coma.
7. Anencephaly is a serious congenital defect in which the child is born without parts of the brain and skull.

53 Pesticides

The term *pest* is commonly used for insects and other creatures that damage crops or vegetation, transmit diseases, or generally create a nuisance for people. Pesticides are chemical substances that are used to eliminate insects, fungi, weeds, and other pests that attack agricultural crops. They are also used against disease-carrying vectors. Sometimes, they are misused for suicide or homicide.

Insects belong to the phylum Arthropoda. They are characterized by a chitinous exoskeleton, a three-part body (head, thorax, and abdomen), compound eyes, three pairs of jointed legs, and a pair of antennae. Insecticides, a type of pesticide, kill insects by direct contact. The chemical dissolves in the fatty tissue in the insect's feet, paralyzing its legs and wings.

Pesticides are neurotoxic to humans. Severity of their effect depends on the dosage and duration of exposure. Acute pesticide poisoning causes headache, dizziness, nausea, salivation, sweating, tremors, and weakness. High dosage can paralyze respiratory muscles and cause death. Farmers and agricultural workers who handle pesticides, as well as their family members who live in proximity to pesticide use, are particularly vulnerable to pesticide poisoning.

Consuming crops sprayed with pesticides is harmful to health. When used extensively, these chemicals can be detected in plants, animals, fish, and water, from where they pass to humans. Around the world, pesticides have been found in human blood, breast milk, urine, and other bodily fluids.

TYPES OF PESTICIDES

There are hundreds of types of pesticides. Broadly, they can be classified into four major groups:

- Organophosphates
- Carbamates
- Organochlorines
- Pyrethroids

Besides these, plant-based pesticides such as neem oil are also in use.

ORGANOPHOSPHATES

Organophosphates, such as fenthion, malathion, sarin, and temefos, are extensively used in agriculture. These chemicals pose a significant health risk to humans. The infamous sarin gas attack in a Tokyo subway in 1995 caused multiple fatalities.

Organophosphates inactivate acetylcholinesterase, an enzyme that breaks down acetylcholine, the main neurotransmitter in the human body. In organophosphate poisoning, acetylcholine accumulates in the body, causing symptoms such as salivation, vomiting, diarrhea, miosis, muscle contractions, and confusion.

Atropine injection reduces the effects of acetylcholine. Being readily available in health facilities, it is commonly used in organophosphate poisoning. The antidote for organophosphate is pralidoxime (2-PAM), which binds with the chemical and stops its action in the body.

CARBAMATES

Carbamates are also commonly used as pesticides.[1] Their toxic effects include seizures, bronchospasm, respiratory paralysis, and coma. Airway management is lifesaving in carbamate poisoning.

 DOI: 10.4324/9781032644257-59

Organochlorines

These include DDT, HCH,[2] dieldrin, and others. After Paul Muller's discovery of the insecticidal properties of DDT in 1939, it was extensively used to control malaria and increase food production during and after the Second World War. However, in the 1970s, environmental activists in the United States detected DDT in the water of several lakes and ponds. It was also found in plants, animals, and fish, and even in humans who consumed DDT-contaminated foods. Recognizing its harmful effects, including its potential to cause cancer, the United States banned DDT in 1972. Many other countries followed suit.

Effects of organochlorine toxicity include sensory disturbances, nausea, vomiting, incoordination, confusion, and tremors. Prolonged exposure can lead to organ damage. Currently, no specific antidote is available for organochlorine poisoning. Stomach wash is helpful.

Pyrethroids

Pyrethroids are synthetic derivatives of pyrethrin, a naturally occurring insecticide found in chrysanthemum flowers. Deltamethrin, permethrin, and alpha-cypermethrin are commonly used pyrethroids.

Pyrethroids are less toxic to humans than they are to insects. Ingestion causes sore throat, nausea, vomiting, and abdominal pain. Treatment involves stomach wash. No specific antidote is currently available for pyrethroid poisoning.

PESTICIDE RESISTANCE

Pesticides have played an important role in improving agricultural yields and controlling disease-carrying vectors. However, when pesticides are used indiscriminately, pests develop resistance against them, necessitating higher doses and more frequent sprays. This leads to contamination of food crops and water sources, posing grave risks for human health. The need is to use pesticides judiciously and responsibly.

RODENTICIDES

Rodenticides are used to kill mice, rats, and other rodents. Commonly used rodenticides are anticoagulants, which means they inhibit blood clotting and may lead to spontaneous bleeding. There are also some non-anticoagulant rodenticides, such as cholecalciferol (activated vitamin D3), which acts by elevating calcium and phosphorus levels in the rodent's body, leading to acute renal failure. Cholecalciferol is generally safe for humans at doses of up to 10,000 IU per day, but very high doses can produce toxic effects.

Zinc phosphide is another non-anticoagulant rodenticide. When ingested, it releases phosphine gas in the rodent's body, leading to circulatory failure.

NOTES

1. Aldicarb, carbaryl, oxamyl, propoxur, and terbucarb are examples of carbamates.
2. HCH is hexachlorocyclohexane.

54 Housing and Family

HOUSING

The quality of our housing has a profound effect on our health and well-being, especially considering that we spend more time at home than at work. A house gives us shelter, security, and protection from adverse weather. It provides facilities for cooking, toilet, and rest.

Around the world, millions of low-income families live in poor housing conditions. The implications on their health and well-being are explained here.

Overcrowding

Living in overcrowded spaces exposes people to infections and diseases. Rural migrants, especially daily-wage workers, live in small houses in urban slums or shanty towns, with many people sharing a poorly ventilated room and a common toilet. This increases the risk of disease transmission. Respiratory infections, including TB, are known to be more common among those living in overcrowded spaces. Inadequate running water and poor toilet facilities increase the risk of fecal–oral contamination.

Indoor Air Pollution

Many poor families still use wood, coal, or kerosene oil as cooking fuel. This causes indoor air pollution, particularly in houses with no proper ventilation. With no separate space for a kitchen, food is cooked in the living area, which exposes the entire family to harmful smoke. Similarly, people who smoke tobacco indoors subject others to passive smoking. Indoor air pollution is particularly harmful for those with chronic respiratory or cardiovascular conditions.

Exposure to Vectors and Rodents

People who do not have proper housing cannot protect themselves from mosquitoes and other vectors. This increases their risk of vector-borne diseases like malaria, dengue, and chikungunya. Infestations of lice, ticks, or mites can occur.

Extreme Weather

Inadequate housing exposes people to weather extremities. In extremely cold weather, people burn wood or coal indoors, risking carbon monoxide poisoning.

Social Challenges

Lack of personal space increases people's risk of adopting unhealthy behaviors from one another, such as smoking, tobacco chewing, drug abuse, or unsafe sexual practices.

Others

In many areas, houses become submerged in water during monsoon. This not only makes life difficult for people but also increases their risk of waterborne diseases. In urban areas, extreme poverty forces people to live near railway tracks or factories, amidst high levels of noise or air pollution, or in hutments along sewer drains. This has severe health implications.

DOI: 10.4324/9781032644257-60

FAMILY

Family is the primary unit of society. Members of a family live together under one roof, eat from a common kitchen, and share resources. At the center of the family structure are the husband and wife, who share a relationship by marriage. Other family members are genetically related, with parents and children sharing a similar genetic constitution. All family members generally have a claim to ancestral property.

Types of Family

Nuclear Family

This is the fundamental family structure, consisting of two generations: The husband and wife and their children. When the children grow up and get married, they may leave their parental house and set up their own nuclear families. This is common in developed countries. Affluent societies in developing countries are also moving toward this practice.

Extended Family

When a married son continues to live in his parents' house with his wife and children, it is an extended family. Thus, three generations live under one roof—elderly parents, their son and daughter-in-law, and the grandchildren. Extended family is the most common family structure in many low-income countries. If the grandchildren continue to live in the same house after getting married, their children will constitute the fourth generation of the extended family.

A daughter, once married, ceases to be a member of her parents' family and becomes a member of her husband's family.

Joint Family

When two or more brothers live in the same house with their families, it is a joint family. When another generation gets added to a joint family, it becomes an *extended joint family*. Unmarried daughters may also be part of a joint family. This family structure is more common in East Asia and South Asia, followed by the Middle East and sub-Saharan Africa.

Others

A single-parent family consists of one parent raising one or more children. A person may be a single parent by circumstance (such as due to separation or death of spouse) or by choice. When two adults choose to live together without marriage, it is called a live-in relationship. They may or may not have children.

Family's Role in Health

Family provides its members a physical and social environment and a sense of safety and security. Adult members earn an income and run the family's affairs. They care for the children and support dependent elders. When a family member is sick, injured, or disabled, other members step in to assist with feeding, toilet care, and medical treatment.

Beyond these practical aspects, family plays an important role in shaping and regulating the behavior and conduct of its members. The process of socialization, whereby children learn socially acceptable behaviors and practices, begins with the family. Children learn sociocultural norms and practices by observing their parents and other family members. They adopt the family's dietary habits and sanitation practices. If the adults eat healthy meals, avoid overeating, wash their hands before and after meals, maintain personal hygiene, and keep their surroundings clean, their children will imbibe these habits. The tradition of education continues within a family; children of educated parents invariably pursue education.

Similarly, negative sociocultural practices, such as smoking, chewing tobacco, consuming alcohol, spitting in public, or improper garbage disposal, can also pass down from parents to their children.

A joint or extended family can be an exceptional source of psychological support for its members. Children feel secure in the presence of elders, and elders feel happy with children around them. Emotional support from each other helps family members cope with daily stresses and recover from illness.

Joint or extended families control many decisions that impact health. For example, it is generally the senior members who decide whether the family can consume certain foods like meat or eggs. They also decide about religious practices. In some families, the matriarch, generally the mother-in-law, decides whether a young couple can use contraception. After the couple has produced the desired number of children, it is again the mother-in-law who decides whether they can stop childbearing. In many cases, the mother does not permit her son to get a vasectomy; instead, the daughter-in-law is expected to undergo tubal ligation. In nuclear families, young couples make such decisions on their own.

As we can see, family has an important role in shaping people's physical, mental, and emotional health, as well as their dietary and lifestyle choices. Collectively, these influences impact the health status of a society.

Section VII

Sociocultural Dimensions of Health

55 Sociocultural Practices

As we learned in a previous chapter, our health is dependent on our genetic constitution, lifestyle, and living environment. Our living environment includes air, water, microbes, birds, animals, and our fellow human beings. How do other people influence us? What is their impact on our thoughts, attitudes, behaviors, and actions? This chapter explores these questions.

SOCIETY

As inherently social beings, we have an innate need to live among other people, communicate with them, and form relationships. We take pride in belonging to a group. A society is a group of people who live together, have a system of relationships, and follow a common way of life. For example, the inhabitants of a village are a society: They speak a common language, share similar dietary habits and dressing styles, celebrate the same festivals, follow the same rituals at birth, marriage, and death, and honor a code of relationships. Within a society, subgroups or communities emerge based on economic status, caste, religion, or occupation. These groups may have some differences in their lifestyles.

In this chapter, the terms *society* and *community* are used interchangeably, although sociologists make a distinction between the two.

CULTURE

Culture refers to the way people live and behave. It is culture that differentiates societies. For example, in some communities, girls drop out of school early, following which they are oriented to household chores before being married off. They rear children and look after their husband and in-laws. This is their culture. In other communities, girls pursue higher education and become financially independent; that is their culture.

SOCIOCULTURAL PRACTICES

In India, chewing tobacco and spitting in public are common. While some communities may see nothing wrong with these practices, others may find them unacceptable. Similarly, a girl who grows up in a community where women customarily wear a veil may perceive it as normal, while a girl raised in a progressive community may object to covering her face. That is the power of sociocultural practices.

To be a part of a society and be accepted by its members, we follow its sociocultural norms and practices. Gradually, these practices become embedded in our behavior and way of life, persisting through generations.

For the purpose of this discussion, the terms *culture*, *sociocultural*, and *sociocultural practice* are used interchangeably.

SOCIOCULTURAL PRACTICES AND WOMEN'S HEALTH

In the following sections, we explore some prevalent sociocultural practices related to reproductive health and hygiene and examine their impact on women's health.

Early Marriage

Child marriage is a widespread issue, with around 20% of girls getting married before 18 years of age. Although there has been a steady decline in this practice, progress has been particularly slow

DOI: 10.4324/9781032644257-62

in sub-Saharan Africa. South Asia has seen more rapid reductions, but in India, 23% of girls are still married before the legal age of 18. This is their culture.

What are the disadvantages of early marriage for girls? First, it robs them of their childhood, disrupts their education, and threatens their well-being. These young brides grow up to be financially dependent on others and ignorant of their rights. In some societies, married girls face pressure to prove their fertility and produce a male child. As a result, many girls conceive soon after marriage, before their reproductive organs are fully developed for childbirth. This increases their risk of preterm delivery and maternal complications. Young brides are also more likely to experience gender inequity and domestic violence. They may lack the emotional maturity and financial stability to raise a child.

Various factors contribute to early marriage. One important factor is girls dropping out of school, which prompts their parents to get them married. Again, girls leave school for various reasons. Some are unable to cope with their studies, and lacking support or guidance at home, they stop going to school. Many schools do not have a separate toilet for girls, or it is filthy or unusable. Adolescent girls drop out because there is no place to change their sanitary pads during menstruation. In many cases, social norms, financial constraints, or patriarchal influences[1] compel parents to arrange early marriage for their daughters. In some areas, lawlessness and fear of sexual violence force parents to make this decision.

Legislation against child marriage exists in many countries, but it is not sufficient to end the practice. Social interventions are necessary. To prevent girls from dropping out of school, school infrastructures need to improve. Education curriculums should be made more interesting and vocation-oriented. Teachers and parents should receive training and guidance on how to support girls, particularly during menstruation. For lasting change, there is a need to increase community awareness about gender equity and the importance of educating girls.

Adolescent Pregnancy

Adolescent pregnancy is a global concern, although there are significant variations between countries. While it is a public health problem in sub-Saharan Africa, it is relatively less common in Central Asia. Globally, adolescent pregnancies have been on the decline. South Asia has seen rapid reduction, but progress has been slower in sub-Saharan Africa, Latin America, and the Caribbean region.

It is seen that adolescent pregnancy is more common among those who are less educated or more economically deprived. In some societies, girls face societal pressure to marry and bear children. Limited employment opportunities for women add to the problem.

Roughly half of adolescent pregnancies are unintended, and adolescents' limited access to contraceptives compounds the problem. Further, more than half of all unintended pregnancies end in unsafe abortion, particularly in low- and middle-income countries. Both medical termination of pregnancy and the process of childbirth involve risks, and adolescents face an even higher risk of maternal complications.

If an adolescent pregnancy culminates in childbirth, the parents may not have the emotional maturity or financial stability to raise the child.

Female Genital Mutilation

Female Genital Mutilation (FGM) refers to partial or total removal of the female external genitalia. It is a grave violation of human rights. As per UNFPA estimates, four million girls in 31 countries are at risk of FGM, with Guinea and Somalia being particularly affected. In some communities, FGM is performed as a ritual, possibly to suppress a girl's sexuality or to "safeguard" her chastity. It may even be a prerequisite for marriage.

Genital mutilation can cause severe pain, hemorrhage, infection, and psychological trauma. It can have long-term effects such as infertility and complications during childbirth.

Medicalization of FGM, where the procedure is performed by a healthcare provider, is a dangerous trend emerging in some countries. It is unethical.

Eradicating FGM requires coordinated efforts to engage young people, parents of girl children, religious leaders, civil society activists, healthcare workers, teachers, and policymakers. As a result of joint efforts by UNICEF and UNFPA, 13 countries have passed legislation to ban this practice.

Violence against Women and Girls

Violence against women is a major public health issue worldwide. The WHO estimates that around 30% of all women experience violence at some time in their lives. Intimate partner violence and sexual violence are more common. Risk factors for violence against women include:

- Low literacy
- Community norms that ascribe higher status to men
- Harmful use of alcohol and other substances
- Unemployment or women's economic insecurity
- Witnessing family violence or maltreatment during childhood
- Antisocial personality disorder
- Inadequacies in law and order

Violence against women has far-reaching consequences on their physical, mental, and social well-being. It can lead to injuries, unintended pregnancy, miscarriage, preterm delivery, underweight infants, sexually transmitted infections, depression, sleep disorders, eating disorders, and suicide attempts. It can promote smoking and substance abuse in survivors. Children who witness violence in their homes may suffer from behavioral and emotional disturbances. There is also an enormous social and economic cost of such violence.

To address this issue, the WHO, UN Women, and other UN agencies jointly developed a framework called *RESPECT Women: Preventing Violence Against Women*. This framework guides policymakers in their efforts to prevent violence against women. The acronym RESPECT stands for seven strategies:

1. Relationship skills strengthened
2. Empowerment of women
3. Services ensured
4. Poverty reduced
5. Environments made safe, including schools, workplaces, and public places
6. Child and adolescent abuse prevented
7. Transformed attitudes, beliefs, and norms

Preference for Son

In many South Asian communities, there is a strong preference for male child. This stems from the belief that sons continue the family lineage and support their parents in old age, while daughters, once married, become a part of another family. Women who give birth to male children gain respect from their families and communities, while those who bear girl children are scorned. This is a sociocultural practice. In their pursuit of a male child, couples end up having many children, which harms women's health. Many resort to sex-selective feticide. This is often done in unsafe settings, posing a serious risk to women's health and survival.

Breastfeeding

Early initiation of breastfeeding is crucial for newborn health. Ideally, breastfeeding should begin within the first hour of birth. Initial breast milk, known as colostrum, provides essential nutrition and protects the newborn from many diseases. Further, being a clean and safe source of nourishment, breast milk eliminates the need for external feed or water, which could expose the newborn to infection.

In some Indian communities, breastfeeding is started several days after birth. What causes this delay? These communities adhere to the belief that the process of giving birth makes a woman "dirty" or "unholy." Interestingly, the child born to the same woman is considered clean and holy. Before the mother can breastfeed, she is required to undergo a "purification" ritual conducted by a priest. All this is done in a formal setting that can take a few days to organize. As a result, breastfeeding gets delayed.

Although most deliveries in India now take place in health facilities, early initiation of breastfeeding is still less common. This reflects poorly on the quality of services provided in these facilities. By developing a relationship of trust with the mother, healthcare providers can encourage her to start breastfeeding early. Advocacy with elderly women and religious leaders in the community can be helpful.

Responsibility for Contraception

In some communities, contraceptives are a taboo subject. The use of oral contraceptive pills and condoms is discouraged. Consequently, couples have two, three, or more children in quick succession before they decide to stop childbearing. Furthermore, contraception is generally considered the woman's responsibility. This is highly unjust when there are simple and safe contraceptive methods available for men.

Food Hygiene

In some societies, people can be careless about food hygiene. For example, instead of avoiding or discarding food that has been exposed to flies, they may just wave away the flies and eat the food. Young children imitate this behavior, perpetuating a sociocultural practice. Other basic hygiene practices, such as washing hands with soap, may also be neglected. Compromise with basic hygiene can lead to helminthic infestations, an important cause of anemia. As we know, anemia is particularly prevalent in women of reproductive age in low-income countries.

CHALLENGING SOCIOCULTURAL PRACTICES

Sociocultural practices are deep-rooted and difficult to change. However, a well-designed communication strategy, backed by legislation and the support of local opinion leaders, can bring about change. Of course, persistent efforts are needed.

A notable example of this is the successful elimination of smoking in public places despite strong lobbying by the tobacco industry and vested interests of authorities. Just a few decades ago, smoking in public was a cultural norm. People smoked on public transport, academics smoked during lectures, and doctors smoked while attending to patients in their clinics. These days, such behavior is met with condemnation. This cultural shift will hopefully discourage future generations from getting habituated to smoking.

GOOD SOCIOCULTURAL PRACTICES

Not all sociocultural practices are bad; there are some good traditions as well. India's joint family system, for example, has some advantages. Members of a joint family share resources and responsibilities and support each other in times of need. Children feel secure in such an environment, and the elderly are looked after. In many Western societies, the elderly retire to senior homes.

In many low-income countries, the institution of marriage is relatively stronger, leading to fewer broken homes. Again, there are social and cultural reasons for this: Financial dependence, family pressure, or concern for their children discourages women from pursuing divorce.

Women in low-income settings often breastfeed their babies for an extended period of up to two years. This is a good practice, although there is a need to promote early initiation of breastfeeding and exclusive breastfeeding.

Preference for fresh, homemade food over packaged or preserved products is again a good practice prevalent in many communities.

FACTORS INFLUENCING SOCIOCULTURAL PRACTICES

Why do sociocultural practices differ among societies? There are multiple reasons, though not all of them are understood. The following factors are known to shape sociocultural norms and practices.

Education

Literacy is the single most important factor to influence sociocultural practices. High literacy is associated with better hygiene, healthier dietary habits, and lower fertility rates. Educated women are mindful of their well-being and are more aware of their rights. They tend to be financially independent, enjoy better social status, participate in decision-making, and challenge gender-based conventions. They are also more likely to educate their children.

Economic Status

People's economic status directly or indirectly influences their access to health and education. Well-off individuals can afford nutritious food, basic sanitation, and education for their children. The very poor cannot even afford proper healthcare. They do not send their children to school as they need them to earn money.

Affluence can also negatively impact people's health. Wealthy people may have a sedentary lifestyle and may indulge in overeating or alcohol misuse, increasing their risk of NCDs.

Religion

Some sects or groups impose certain sociocultural practices on their members. For example, some communities are against immunization, while others oppose consumption of animal-based foods. There are some favorable practices as well: Some communities discourage the use of alcohol and tobacco.

Information and Communication

Radio, television, Internet, social media, and print media introduce people to sociocultural practices of other societies. People commonly adopt the sociocultural practices of economically and socially progressive societies, often without considering their merits or drawbacks.

Mobility

Increased mobility also helps transform sociocultural practices. Young people who migrate for work or children who travel for higher education bring back new sociocultural practices to their families and communities upon their return.

Others

Leadership, governance, law and order, employment, and industrialization are some other factors that influence sociocultural practices.

ASSESSING SOCIOCULTURAL AND ECONOMIC STATUS

How can we assess the sociocultural and economic status of a family? We can do this by observation and by interviewing the family members.

If we visit a family and find an unclean living space, many half-clad children playing or crying, or women with their faces covered, we can get clues about the status of women in the family, their fertility, and other aspects. In contrast, a clean home with fewer children, who are either dressed in school uniform or engaged in studies, gives a different impression. Observing the family at mealtime can tell us about their dietary and hygiene habits.

By interacting with family members, we can learn about their educational status. We can learn if the women have their own bank accounts, if they have access to Internet, and whether they participate in major decisions.

The family's economic status can be gauged from their assets and resources. Do they have piped water supply and a septic tank latrine? Do they cook using LPG, firewood, or cow dung? Do they have a source of information, such as a television or a mobile phone with Internet? Do they own a means of transport? Is it a bicycle, motorbike, car, or tractor? Ready-made scales are available to measure the socioeconomic status of individuals.

NOTE

1. Patriarchy is a system of society in which men hold power and force their opinions on women.

56 Gender and Health

Sex refers to the biological makeup of people—their physical attributes, reproductive organs, secondary sexual characteristics, and sex hormones. Gender is different from sex. While sex is about biology, gender is a social construct involving societal norms and expectations—what is expected of people or what is permitted to them as members of society. For example, in some societies, women cannot choose what they wear; society decides. The terms *sex* and *gender* are not interchangeable.

On attaining puberty, girls start menstruating. This is a natural phenomenon, yet in some conservative societies, menstruating girls and women are considered "impure." They are not allowed to enter the kitchen or participate in prayers. This is not natural. It is a societal norm and a gender issue. In other societies, girls may face no such restrictions. Thus, gender norms differ in societies. They also evolve with time. For example, in the past, girls were forbidden from engaging in vocations like military service or sports, but this has changed in many places.

Why are we concerned about *gender* in public health? This is because gender norms and roles fuel inequity, leading to unequal power and privileges for girls and women. This, in turn, increases their vulnerability to physical and mental health issues.

ROLE OF GENDER IN WOMEN'S HEALTH AND WELL-BEING

In some societies, discrimination against girls starts even before they are born. In previous chapters, we talked about female feticide, widespread anemia and undernutrition in young girls, and risks of early marriage. Besides these, girls and women face additional risks, such as unintended pregnancies, sexually transmitted infections, and cervical cancer. In some cases, when a woman in labor develops complications, her family members may not arrange for medical care. If she dies, the man can remarry and get more dowry.

Women and girls endure physical violence, stigma, and coercion. They face eve teasing and molestation. Studies show that nearly one-fourth of all girls experience gender-based violence before age 19. Unfortunately, many survivors do not disclose such incidents to their families or report them to law enforcement agencies. They fear being blamed for the assault. If the matter does reach the police or judiciary, the girl's family faces further harassment in the name of investigation. The girl's mobility is restricted on the pretext of safety, depriving her of education, skill development, and employment opportunities.

In traditional households, domestic work is the sole responsibility of women and girls. Most men consider it below their dignity to participate in household chores. Despite women's increasing participation in fields such as the armed forces, engineering, information technology, and governance, gender parity remains a distant goal. How can a country progress when half of its population faces poor workforce participation?

Gender inequity is also rampant at the workplace, with women workers receiving lower wages than their male counterparts for similar work.

Gender norms affect men as well. The notion of masculinity encourages boys and men to smoke or drink alcohol. Norms around "manhood" encourage risky behaviors such as unprotected sex and physical fights. These gender norms collectively contribute to an environment that encourages violence against women. Men are expected not to cry. They hesitate to seek help or healthcare when needed.

According to the United Nations, gender equity is a fundamental human right and is necessary for a peaceful, prosperous, and sustainable world.

DOI: 10.4324/9781032644257-63

WOMEN'S EMPOWERMENT

Women's empowerment refers to the elevation of women's status in society by creating an environment where they can recognize their self-worth, make their own choices, and exert their rights. Education is possibly the most powerful tool for women's empowerment. Studies show that educated women are more likely to be financially independent and have greater awareness of their rights.

Women's participation in governance is important, and progress is being made in many countries, albeit at a slow pace. Various initiatives have been implemented with varying degrees of success, such as setting up women's police stations and women's helplines, providing hostel facilities for female students and working women, encouraging women to have their own bank accounts, and extending financial support to women-owned businesses.

In addition to these measures, it is important to sensitize men about the importance of gender equity.

57 Poverty and Social Security

POVERTY

Poverty is the biggest enemy of health. This may prompt you to question why some manual laborers appear physically strong and healthy. It is true that people who do physical work and earn enough to afford adequate nutrition and basic sanitation can have good health and a strong, muscular physique. However, a majority of people living in rural, remote, or tribal areas in low-income countries either do not get consistent work or do not make enough money to support their basic needs. This directly or indirectly impacts their health. On what basis can a person be considered poor? Internationally, people who live on less than two dollars a day are identified as poor.

Poverty affects health in a number of ways. People living in poverty cannot buy adequate food, which leads to chronic hunger and nutritional deficiencies. Stunting and wasting are common in undernourished children. Their cognitive capabilities may be impaired. When they grow up, their capacity to earn a livelihood and lead a productive life may be compromised.

Impoverished people live in overcrowded and poorly ventilated houses with no proper facilities for bathing, washing, or cleaning. They consume unhygienic food and unsafe water. This exposes them to infections and diseases. They may get exposed to sociocultural practices detrimental to their health. Many low-wage workers work in unsafe conditions, which increases their risk of injuries and fatal accidents.

Poor families tend to have more children, increasing their risk of maternal and child morbidity and mortality. Many families lack the financial means to educate their children, which in turn limits their earning capacity as adults. These families may also have limited access to healthcare services. Even where free or subsidized healthcare is available, they may not be able to avail of it as they cannot afford to miss their daily wages. For the same reason, they may not get adequate rest to recover from illness.

Adding to the problem, public health facilities are frequently overcrowded. During emergencies, when the poor are compelled to seek treatment at private hospitals, the resulting out-of-pocket expenses push them further into poverty. Illness is one of the most common reasons for indebtedness among economically disadvantaged families.

SOCIAL SECURITY

In the past, family members supported each other in difficult times. With nuclear families becoming the norm, people need an alternative social support mechanism to cope with financial and other difficulties.

Social security is the assistance provided by the government or society to individuals or families in the event of a major illness, disability, job loss, or death of the primary earning member.

Social security is a mechanism that aims to reduce social inequity. In developed countries, a strong social security system safeguards citizens against adverse life events. Every citizen is assigned a social security number that gives them access to essential services like medical treatment, unemployment benefits, and disability allowance. In low-income countries, this system is either nonexistent or very weak. In some countries, social security primarily benefits government employees through retirement pension and medical benefits. Private employees can contribute to pension schemes during their youth to get returns in old age. Providing social security to the masses remains a big challenge, especially in countries with limited resources.

DOI: 10.4324/9781032644257-64

58 Health-Seeking Behavior

In a medical emergency, timely treatment can save life, while delay can cause death. In a critical situation, such as a road accident, heart attack, or stroke, people usually rush to a hospital for immediate care. But when a health problem is not so serious, some people delay seeking treatment, while others avoid it altogether. Some people turn to traditional healers, faith healers, or unqualified practitioners. Thus, health-seeking behavior differs among people.

What prevents people from seeking appropriate and timely healthcare services?

BARRIERS TO SEEKING HEALTHCARE

Poor Access

In low-income countries, remote areas lack proper healthcare facilities. Government hospitals in nearby cities or towns are often overcrowded, and private hospitals are unaffordable. As a result, some people avoid visiting these facilities and opt for local practitioners, who may or may not be qualified.

Financial Constraints

Those who cannot afford qualified doctors or private health facilities resort to less expensive options, such as local practitioners, pharmacies, or faith healers. Daily-wage earners face an additional challenge: They cannot afford to lose a day's wages to visit a busy hospital or clinic during regular hours. Their only alternative is to consult a pharmacist or local practitioner who is available after their working hours.

Ignorance

Diarrhea is a leading cause of child mortality. Despite the availability of a simple treatment, it kills over 400,000 children every year. South Asia and sub-Saharan Africa have a particularly high burden of diarrhea-related deaths, and lack of awareness is an important reason for this. Many people dismiss diarrhea as a minor illness, not knowing that it can cause fatal dehydration. They consult unqualified local practitioners, who may prescribe antibiotics or antimotility medicines, which are not indicated in simple cases of diarrhea. In fact, these drugs can harm the child. Administration of ORS and zinc is the recommended treatment in simple cases of diarrhea.

Further, the inability to differentiate between qualified and unqualified practitioners leads people to choose a practitioner who shares their language and sociocultural background. These practitioners may have good communication and persuasion skills, but their clinical competence may be lacking.

For conditions such as epilepsy or hysteria, many people turn to spiritual healers who claim expertise in treating these conditions. Similarly, there are practitioners offering remedies for fistulas, bone and joint problems, and snakebites. People avail of their services without realizing that these problems can be effectively treated by medical doctors.

Many people are uncomfortable discussing their sexual or genital health problems, such as vaginal discharge, sexually transmitted infection, unwanted pregnancy, or erectile dysfunction. Consequently, they avoid formal healthcare systems and seek treatment from unqualified practitioners who claim to be specialists of these problems.

DOI: 10.4324/9781032644257-65

Reluctance to Accept Diagnosis

Some people find it difficult to come to terms with a major illness like TB or leprosy. Seeking immediate relief, they turn to local practitioners, who prescribe some medicines and falsely assure them of a quick recovery. In the absence of proper antitubercular or anti-leprosy treatment, the patient's condition deteriorates. The disease may transmit to others.

Lack of Trust

In some communities, there is a false belief that modern medicine only provides symptomatic relief, whereas traditional systems like Ayurveda or Homeopathy address the root cause of the disease. Some people feel that doctors recommend unnecessary diagnostic tests or surgical procedures for their personal gain. These perceptions stop people from consulting qualified medical doctors.

Sociocultural Reasons

Villagers or tribals living in far-flung areas who have rarely interacted with outsiders may not be comfortable interacting with service providers in large hospitals.

IMPROVING HEALTH-SEEKING BEHAVIOR

To improve health-seeking behavior in populations, we need to address the barriers that stop people from using healthcare services.

First, there is a need to improve access to affordable healthcare. A notable example is the significant increase in institutional deliveries in India, which can be partly attributed to the revival of ambulance services in the public sector. With improved availability of ambulances in rural areas, more women in labor now reach the hospital in time and avail institutional delivery.

Second, it is important to increase public awareness about common health problems such as diabetes, hypertension, and TB. Educating people about the consequences of neglecting these diseases can help them realize the importance of proper and timely medical care.

Section VIII

Maternal and Child Health

59 Maternal Health

Maternal health refers to the health of women during pregnancy and childbirth.[1]

Why are we concerned about maternal health when there is no talk about paternal health? This is because women bear children, and the process of pregnancy and childbirth involves a risk to their lives and health. Many women die from complications of pregnancy or delivery.

MATERNAL MORTALITY

Maternal mortality refers to deaths of women from complications of pregnancy, delivery, or unsafe abortion.

Although pregnancy and delivery are natural processes, 10%–15% of pregnant women develop complications that may result in death. Maternal mortality includes deaths during pregnancy or delivery, deaths from unsafe abortion, and deaths within six weeks (42 days) of delivery. Why six weeks? This is because maternal complications do not always cause immediate death; some women struggle for weeks before succumbing.[2] Deaths from unsafe abortion are counted in maternal mortality because abortion is an outcome of pregnancy.

Until the early twentieth century, maternal mortality was high worldwide. Even in Western countries, deliveries were conducted by traditional birth attendants who were skilled in conducting normal delivery but often lacked the competence to identify and manage complications.

Example 1

Some vaginal bleeding is normal during labor, but occasionally there is excessive bleeding, and that is dangerous. Following a home birth, if the woman complains of bleeding, a traditional birth attendant lacking proper knowledge may incorrectly assure her that this is normal. As a result, the woman may keep bleeding excessively in her clothes with no one in her family knowing about it. She may quietly slip into a coma. Many such women die on their way to the hospital when they could have been saved by timely medical care. This is further explained in the section "Causes of Maternal Mortality."

Example 2

During labor, if the child is not getting delivered, a traditional birth attendant may ask the mother to push the baby out. This advice is incorrect if the child's head is not yet visible. If the fetus is stuck in an abnormal position in the womb, it will not proceed, and any exertion by the mother can aggravate the problem—she will get exhausted or she can bleed. A timely caesarean section can save both mother and child.

The above examples highlight that assisting birth is not a layperson's job; it requires clinical expertise. Realizing this, public health authorities in Western countries set up midwifery schools offering rigorous three-year courses. When trained and competent midwives started conducting deliveries, maternal mortality simply dropped in these countries. Middle-income countries followed suit in the late twentieth century. Meanwhile, low-income countries continued with their efforts to train traditional birth attendants for quite some time. India is a case in point. It was not until 2005 that the Indian government realized the futility of this approach and started promoting institutional

DOI: 10.4324/9781032644257-67

deliveries. Women were given cash incentives for delivering in public health facilities. This strategy seems to have worked, as most deliveries in India are now conducted by trained birth attendants. Sub-Saharan Africa is experiencing a similar but sluggish increase in institutional deliveries.

Maternal Mortality Ratio

Maternal mortality ratio (MMR) is the number of deaths of women resulting from complications of pregnancy, delivery, or unsafe abortion per 100,000 live births.[3]

Burden

Globally, sub-Saharan Africa and South Asia account for 87% of all maternal deaths. Nearly all of these deaths can be averted. Further, a notable difference is seen in MMRs of low-income and high-income countries. While MMR of most developed countries hovers between 10 and 20, in countries like India, Vietnam, and South Africa it ranges from 100 to 200. Guinea, Kenya, and Congo have extraordinarily high MMRs, reaching 500–600. The SDG for poor-performing countries is to reduce their MMR to less than 70 by the year 2030.

Causes

Hemorrhage, infection, hypertension, obstructed labor, and unsafe abortion are leading causes of maternal deaths in low-income countries, as illustrated in Figure 59.1. They are discussed in subsequent sections.

Postpartum Hemorrhage

Postpartum hemorrhage (PPH), or excessive bleeding after delivery, is the most common cause of maternal deaths globally. Uterine atony or trauma to reproductive organs can cause PPH.

Uterine atony: During pregnancy, the fetus receives nutrients and oxygen from the mother through the placenta. Following delivery, the placenta detaches from the uterus, leaving a raw and bleeding surface on the inner lining of the uterus. A natural mechanism controls this bleeding: Uterine muscles contract after delivery, which compresses the blood vessels passing through them and stops the bleeding. Failure of uterine muscles to contract adequately is known as uterine atony.

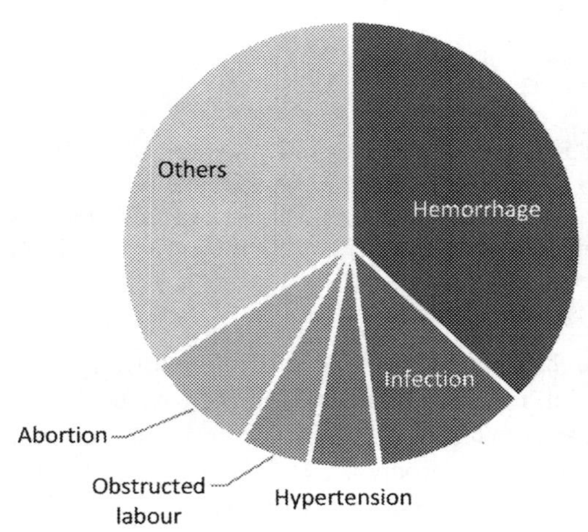

FIGURE 59.1 Causes of maternal mortality in low-income countries.

Why do uterine muscles fail to contract? During pregnancy, uterine muscles stretch to accommodate the growing fetus. In postpartum period (puerperium), which lasts for about six weeks after delivery, the uterus reverts to its normal, prepregnant state. However, with successive pregnancies, uterine muscles become weak due to repeated stretching. Women who have had five or more pregnancies (grand multipara) are at a relatively higher risk of uterine atony. Age also plays a role. Women in their twenties and thirties are generally physically fit to bear a child, and their uterine muscles are strong enough to contract after delivery. Underage women (below 20 years)[4] are at a higher risk of PPH since their reproductive organs are not fully developed. Similarly, women of advanced age (above 35 years) have an increased risk of PPH due to their weakened uterine muscles.

How is uterine atony managed? One method is the administration of injection oxytocin immediately after delivery. This injection induces uterine contractions and can control bleeding. Uterine massage after delivery of placenta may also help.

Trauma to reproductive organs: During labor, as the fetal head passes through the birth canal, the cervix or vagina may get injured. Vaginal tears extending to the perineum are not uncommon. Underage mothers are at a higher risk of such injuries due to their smaller organs. Timely suturing of injured tissues can stop the bleeding and facilitate healing. If there is considerable blood loss due to any reason, blood transfusion can be lifesaving.

Infection

Infection is the second most common cause of maternal deaths. Infection of the genital tract after delivery is called puerperal infection or puerperal sepsis. It can be caused by microorganisms already present in the genital tract. Therefore, any reproductive tract infections identified during antenatal checkups should be treated promptly. Second, tissues injured during delivery are prone to infection. Third, service providers can introduce infection by repeated pelvic examination if infection-prevention measures are not followed. There can be other reasons for puerperal infection, but they are less common.[5]

Infection is generally accompanied by fever. If a woman develops fever after delivery, especially on the second, third, or fourth day, puerperal infection is suspected. Purulent, foul-smelling vaginal discharge and lower abdominal pain further support the suspicion. Severe infection of uterus can spread to surrounding tissues and organs. If pathogens enter the bloodstream, it can result in a potentially fatal condition known as septicemia.

Bacterial infections are treated with antibiotics. In severe infection, intravenous antibiotics can be lifesaving.

Hypertensive Disorders of Pregnancy

Some women with no history of hypertension suddenly develop high blood pressure during pregnancy. This is known as gestational hypertension. A diastolic blood pressure of 90 mm Hg or higher or systolic blood pressure of 140 mm Hg or higher indicates hypertension. Gestational hypertension is more common in first pregnancy, particularly in the second half of the gestational period. Preexisting hypertension may also worsen during pregnancy. Regardless of the underlying cause, high blood pressure during pregnancy can be dangerous. As countries progress, an increase is observed in the proportion of hypertensive disorders of pregnancy.

Preeclampsia: Hypertension accompanied by proteinuria (excess protein in urine) is called preeclampsia. Preeclampsia can quickly worsen into eclampsia and become dangerous. Close observation is needed in such cases.

Eclampsia: Seizures in a preeclampsia patient are called eclampsia. Seizures pose a serious threat to both mother and fetus. The condition is managed with magnesium sulfate injections.

Definitive treatment of eclampsia or severe preeclampsia is termination of pregnancy by caesarean section. In some cases, this may have to be done preterm (before completion of normal gestation) to save the woman's life.

Hypertension and its associated risks generally resolve after delivery.

Obstructed Labor

When pregnancy culminates in labor, the woman starts experiencing pain due to the rhythmic contractions of uterine muscles. These contractions propel the fetus forward. The cervix dilates to allow the fetus to pass through.

Normally, the fetus lies in the womb with its head toward the cervix, which is favorable for easy descent. During labor, the birth attendant conducts periodic vaginal examination (typically every four hours) to check whether the cervix is fully dilated and the fetus is descending.[6] First-time mothers (primigravida) generally take longer to deliver. However, if the child is not delivered within 12 hours despite good uterine contractions and cervical dilatation, there is a problem. This is known as prolonged labor. Prolonged labor can be due to abnormal lie (position) of the fetus in uterus, which can be identified in the third trimester by palpating the uterus. If obstructed labor is confirmed, caesarean section is lifesaving.

Unsafe Abortion

People seek an abortion for various reasons. In low-income countries, unplanned pregnancies are common. This is often due to ignorance about contraception or poor access to contraceptives. Among married couples, some proceed with an unplanned pregnancy, calling it God's will, while others opt for termination of pregnancy, especially if they already have many children. If an unwed girl becomes pregnant, she has no choice but to terminate her pregnancy.

Here, it is important to distinguish between abortion and termination of pregnancy. Abortion can occur spontaneously, but when induced by medicines or surgical intervention, it is called medical termination of pregnancy (MTP). In many countries, approved clinics are legally allowed to conduct MTP under specific circumstances. Contraceptive failure is one such situation for which MTP can be availed.

Despite favorable legal provisions, utilization of MTP services in many low-income countries remains low. Overcrowding and poor quality of services are the main reasons for low uptake. In some cases, service providers may not behave appropriately with clients or may disregard their privacy and confidentiality. As a result, many clients prefer private providers, some of whom are unqualified practitioners who use crude methods to induce MTP that may cause injury to reproductive organs or introduce infection. Many women die due to such unsafe abortion practices.

REDUCING MATERNAL MORTALITY

Virtually all maternal deaths can be prevented. For this, birth attendants should be competent to recognize risk factors during a woman's pregnancy as well as complications during her labor and postpartum period. Second, there should be adequate facilities to either manage complications on-site or quickly shift the woman to an equipped facility, preferably within one hour.

Three pillars of safe motherhood are:

1. Antenatal care (safe pregnancy)
2. Intranatal care (safe delivery)
3. Postnatal care (support for six weeks after childbirth)

Antenatal Care

The aim of antenatal care is to identify and mitigate the risks of pregnancy and prepare the woman for safe delivery. The average duration of pregnancy is 40 weeks (280 days), or nine months plus one week, calculated from the first day of the last menstrual period (LMP). The expected date of delivery can be calculated using LMP.

The antenatal period is divided into three trimesters of nearly three months each. In normal cases, a minimum of eight antenatal checkups[7] are planned: One checkup every month for eight months. Antenatal care includes the following activities:

History-Taking

A woman's medical history can tell us whether she is underage, of advanced age, or grand multipara and if she has poor obstetric history.[8] These factors indicate a high-risk pregnancy. In such cases, women are counseled to make them aware of their risks. They are encouraged to attend regular checkups and plan their delivery in a well-equipped hospital.

General Physical Examination

Anemia can be identified by presence of conjunctival pallor on inner side of lower eyelids or by color of nail beds. Blood pressure should be measured carefully, as hypertension during pregnancy can have serious consequences.

Systemic Examination

Adequacy of birth passage can be gauged by pelvic examination. Tenderness of internal organs or foul-smelling discharge on gloved fingers indicates infection. Fetal heart sounds (FHS) can be heard at around 20 weeks by auscultating with a stethoscope over the abdomen. In advanced centers, fetal Doppler is used, which can identify FHS early, at around 12 weeks. Normal fetal heart rate is 120–160 beats per minute. The fetal lie can be identified by palpating the abdomen in the third trimester.

Laboratory Tests

Blood hemoglobin level is tested to check for anemia. During pregnancy, hemoglobin level below 11 g/dL indicates anemia. Hemoglobin below 7 g/dL is severe anemia, which may necessitate blood transfusion during or after delivery. Second, a urine test is conducted to check for presence of proteins and sugar. Protein in urine is a sign of preeclampsia, and presence of sugar indicates diabetes.

Antenatal Services

Every pregnant woman receives 100 IFA tablets to meet her increased demand for iron due to the growing fetus in her womb. One IFA tablet daily after a meal is recommended. Since any medicine should be avoided in the first trimester, IFA tablets are started from the second trimester. In postpartum period, the same dose should be administered for 100 days. Anemic women are prescribed a higher dose—200 IFA tablets for taking one tablet twice a day.

To eliminate a possible helminthic infestation, which is common in low-income settings, tablet albendazole 400 mg single dose can be given to pregnant women in their second trimester.

Since delivery involves some tissue injury, there is a risk of tetanus for the mother and newborn. Earlier, tetanus caused many maternal and neonatal deaths in many countries, but thanks to good vaccine coverage, it is now eliminated from most countries. It may be known that tetanus is still a problem in many African countries. The WHO recommends routine administration of Tdap (tetanus, diphtheria, and pertussis) vaccine to all pregnant women. In first pregnancy, two doses are administered one month apart at any time between 27 and 36 weeks. Immunization should be completed at least two weeks before delivery to ensure sufficient immunity at the time of delivery. In a subsequent pregnancy within a three-year period, one dose of Tdap vaccine will be sufficient.[9]

Nutrition is extremely important during pregnancy. On average, a pregnant woman needs 300 more calories per day than a nonpregnant woman. This amounts to around 2,400 calories per day during the third trimester. Accordingly, pregnant women are advised to increase their food intake.

To meet their increased demand for iron and folic acid, they are asked to include green leafy vegetables in their diet and take eggs, fish, and meat if possible. Milk and dairy products can fulfill their calcium requirement.[10] Exposure to sunlight helps in obtaining vitamin D.

For the safety of both mother and child, women are encouraged to have an institutional delivery. They are educated about the importance of early and exclusive breastfeeding, kangaroo mother care, and immunization. Experience shows that women are more receptive to such guidance during pregnancy and immediately after delivery.

Intranatal Care

Intranatal care refers to the support provided to a woman during labor and delivery. The birth attendant's role is important here. She alleviates the mother's anxiety and monitors progress of labor: Is cervical dilatation sufficient? Is fetal descent satisfactory? She also looks out for complications.

Active Management of Third Stage of Labor

Although delivery is a natural process that progresses on its own, a few things can be done to facilitate this process and reduce the risk. To prevent injury to vagina and perineum, a preemptive episiotomy[11] in the second stage of labor can be helpful. If despite this injury occurs to vagina, cervix, or perineum, it should be repaired by suturing. Additionally, when the fetal head is protruding from vagina, the birth attendant should provide support to prevent forceful extension. As soon as the child is delivered, the mother is given an intramuscular injection of oxytocin to prevent excessive bleeding.

Essential Newborn Care

Hypothermia is a leading cause of newborn mortality, especially in winter. Therefore, deliveries should be conducted in a heated room. A newborn's body is smeared with blood-stained amniotic fluid, which should be gently wiped off with a dry towel. No bath should be given. Cord clamping is delayed to allow the maximum transfer of cord blood to the child. The child is placed on the mother's bare chest for direct skin-to-skin contact. Both are then wrapped together in sheets and blankets to keep them warm. This is known as kangaroo mother care. The mother is encouraged to initiate breastfeeding as soon as possible, preferably within the first hour of delivery. After a few hours, the child is given polio-0 dose, BCG,[12] and hepatitis B vaccines.

Postnatal Care

After delivery, the mother and child are kept in the hospital for at least 24 hours, primarily to monitor for PPH. If the mother can rise from the bed and sit independently; if she can eat and drink; if she can walk to the toilet and pass urine—these are all positive signs indicating her well-being. Similarly, the newborn child suckling peacefully gives confidence that the child is all right.

After the mother and child are discharged from the hospital, a health worker should pay them at least two visits to assess their well-being and should particularly check for bleeding or fever.

MATERNAL MORBIDITY

While many women survive the complications of pregnancy or childbirth, some develop chronic and debilitating health problems afterward. Urinary tract infection, urinary or fecal incontinence, obstetric fistula, and vaginal or uterine prolapse are common postdelivery complications. Many women live with these problems their entire lives; some die prematurely after years of suffering. It is a tragedy that there is no account of such women, and there is no talk about them.

NOTES

1. Other health problems in women, such as breast cancer, coronary heart disease, or accidental injury, are not considered maternal health issues. Maternal health pertains specifically to pregnancy and its outcomes.
2. In some developed countries, death within one year of termination of pregnancy is counted as late maternal death.
3. This indicator differs from many other health indicators in that it is not expressed as per 1,000 live births. This is because MMR of high-income countries is so low that expressing it as per 1,000 live births would give fractional values. Further, readers may wonder why MMR is a *ratio* and not a *rate*. This is because the numerator and denominator in this case are different types of data. The numerator is *number of mothers*, while the denominator is *number of live births*.
4. The minimum age of marriage for girls is set at 18 years with a view that they will be at least 20 years old when they conceive.
5. Other causes of puerperal infection include early rupture of amniotic membranes and prolonged labor. Additionally, lochia, a fluid secreted by the uterus for about four to six weeks after delivery, provides a favorable environment for organisms to ascend from vagina to uterus, increasing the risk of infection.
6. A tool called the partograph can be used to monitor progress of labor.
7. The WHO recommends eight antenatal contacts. However, in resource-constrained settings, a minimum of four antenatal checkups are advised.
8. A woman has poor obstetric history if she had complication(s) in any of her previous pregnancies.
9. If the gap between pregnancies is more than three years, two doses of Tdap are recommended.
10. In some developed countries, pregnant women are routinely given oral calcium.
11. A surgical incision is made on posterior vaginal wall and perineum to expand the passage for the fetal head.
12. BCG protects against TB.

60 Adolescent Health

Adolescence, or teenage, is the transitional period between childhood and adulthood, from ages 10 to 19. If adolescents are supposed to be healthy, then why should we be concerned about their health?

While adolescence is generally a period of good health, not all adolescents are healthy. For example, many adolescent girls in low-income countries suffer from anemia, a condition that can be treated easily. Improving the health of adolescent girls is critical to improving maternal and child health. With adolescent population rising in low-income countries, adolescent health needs more attention.

Adolescents experience rapid physical and cognitive growth, and this affects how they think, feel, and make decisions. Girls normally attain puberty earlier than boys, between 10 and 14 years. During this phase, the hypothalamus in the brain causes the pituitary gland to secrete hormones called gonadotropins. In girls, these hormones stimulate the ovaries to release female sex hormones—namely, estrogen and progesterone. These hormones drive a range of biological and physiological changes collectively known as puberty. Secondary sexual characteristics, such as breasts and pubic and axillary hair, develop. This is followed by onset of menstruation. The ovaries start producing eggs.

In adolescent boys, gonadotropins stimulate the testes to secrete testosterone, the male sex hormone that drives secondary sexual characteristics such as growth of facial and body hair, development of muscles, and deepening of voice. Production of sperm begins, marking the onset of fertility. Boys start experiencing erections.

Besides these biological and physiological changes, adolescents also experience psychosocial changes. They become aware of their personal and social identities, gradually stepping away from a sheltered family environment to form close relationships with their friends. Their self-confidence grows, and they start thinking about their future—education, livelihood, and career prospects. They start to question familial and social norms, and some even challenge or defy these norms. Some adolescents engage in risky behaviors, such as reckless driving or experimenting with addictive substances. They experience sexual attraction and become physically capable of sexual intercourse.

FACTORS AFFECTING HEALTH OF ADOLESCENT GIRLS

Anemia and Undernutrition

As mentioned earlier, a large proportion of adolescent girls in developing countries suffer from anemia and malnutrition. Anemia is detrimental to the physical and cognitive development of adolescents. It lowers their resistance to infections and reduces productivity. Various factors contribute to anemia, such as poverty, food deprivation, poor dietary habits, helminthic infestations, frequent infections, and gender bias. Growth spurts during adolescence and the onset of menstruation further increase a girl's demand for iron, which often goes unmet in low-income settings.

Preventing Anemia

In many countries, clinics or community health workers provide IFA tablets to adolescent girls. Dose of supplementation is one IFA tablet per week. Second, deworming treatment is given twice a year to eliminate intestinal worms. A single tablet of albendazole 400 mg is given every six months. In some areas, deworming tablets are periodically distributed to school children.

DOI: 10.4324/9781032644257-68

In addition to addressing these health problems, there is a need to change sociocultural practices that contribute to malnutrition in girls. Families need to be educated about the importance of nutrition in adolescence. A wholesome diet includes adequate amounts of leafy greens and other vegetables. For those who eat animal-based foods, eggs, fish, and meat can provide valuable nutrition.

Menstrual Hygiene

Menstruation is a taboo subject in some societies. Girls in these societies may not have access to sanitary pads or safe toilets. This leads to poor menstrual hygiene and increases the risk of reproductive tract infections.

Promoting Menstrual Hygiene

Menstrual hygiene management involves the following interventions:

- Raising awareness about menstrual hygiene among adolescent girls, women, family members, and teachers
- Improving access to safe and affordable menstrual absorbents, such as sanitary pads and menstrual cups
- Ensuring functional toilets in schools with regular supply of water and soap
- Making provisions for safe disposal of used sanitary products

Early Marriage and Early Pregnancy

We know that many girls in low-income countries are married before age of 18 years. Many of them conceive soon after marriage. Pregnancy increases a woman's demand for iron, leading to anemia. As explained in the chapter "Maternal Health," underage and anemic mothers are at a higher risk of complications of pregnancy and childbirth.

Sexual and Reproductive Health

Unprotected sexual intercourse exposes girls and women to risks of unintended pregnancy and sexually transmitted infections (STIs). While adolescent boys are equally susceptible to STIs, it is girls who bear the burden of unintended pregnancy.

Unintended Pregnancy

Adolescents do not have the maturity to handle pregnancy and childbirth or the financial means to raise a child. To avoid the stigma of unwed motherhood, many girls seek abortion services from unapproved clinics or unqualified practitioners, often without informing their families. Tragically, many of these girls die due to unsafe abortion practices. Many others develop a chronic infection and subsequent infertility.

Preventing Unintended Pregnancies

Studies show that sex education in schools can help delay the initiation of sexual activity among students, and when they do become sexually active, they are more likely to use condoms. However, in many societies, sex education in schools faces strong opposition from social activists, religious leaders, and politicians, who argue that it would promote promiscuity among the youth.

Sexually Transmitted Infections

Sexually active adolescents are at a higher risk of contracting STIs. Data shows that HIV positivity rates are higher among young people. Adolescents should be educated to avoid premarital sex or to use condoms during sexual intercourse.

Human Papillomavirus Vaccination

Unprotected sex with multiple partners increases the risk of STIs, including HPV infection, which is associated with cervical cancer. The WHO recommends HPV vaccination in regions where preventing cervical cancer is a priority. Adolescent girls aged 9–13 years are given two doses six months apart.

FACTORS AFFECTING HEALTH OF ADOLESCENT BOYS

Some adolescent boys succumb to peer pressure and indulge in harmful practices, such as chewing tobacco, smoking, drinking alcohol, or engaging in unprotected sex. Some may get addicted to substance use. These behaviors harm the physical and mental health of adolescents and distract them from their academic and career pursuits.

Life skills training can empower children and adolescents to resist peer pressure. They can learn to say "No." Many NGOs provide life skills training to adolescents in schools and communities. Some NGOs work to sensitize adolescent boys on gender equity. Improving adolescents' access to contraceptives can reduce unwanted teenage pregnancies and STIs.

61 Child Health

As we learned in a previous chapter, children's health is dependent on their mothers' health. Interestingly, the health of a country's children is intricately linked to its economic development. As countries progress, their child health improves. It happened in Europe and America in the late nineteenth and early twentieth centuries and in Southeast Asian countries such as Singapore, Malaysia, and Thailand in recent decades. Vietnam, Cambodia, and Bangladesh are also showing improvement in their child health statistics.

In the past two decades, the most significant gains in global health have been in reducing child mortality. Despite this, child mortality rates in many low-income countries continue to be unacceptably high. In this chapter, we will understand the reasons behind this and how they can be addressed.

UNDER-FIVE MORTALITY

The maximum risk to a child's life is during delivery and immediately afterward. Although this risk reduces with time, it remains significant until the child turns five.

Under-five mortality rate (U5MR) refers to the number of child deaths within the first five years of life per 1,000 live births.

The U5MR of the Democratic Republic of the Congo is 79 (2021). In contrast, the United States has a U5MR of 6. As part of SDG 3, poor-performing countries are urged to reduce their U5MR to at least 25 by the year 2030.

International Comparison

As we saw in the chapter "Measuring Mortality," there is a significant difference in U5MRs of high-income and low-income countries.

CHILD MORTALITY: TWO FACETS

Nearly half of all under-five deaths occur during the neonatal period (first 28 days of life). The other half of under-five deaths occur in the postneonatal period (between 1 and 60 months of age). As the major causes of mortality differ for these two periods, they are analyzed separately.

NEONATAL MORTALITY

Neonatal mortality rate (NMR) refers to the number of child deaths within the first 28 days of life per 1,000 live births.

Sub-Saharan Africa leads in neonatal mortality, followed by South Asia and Central Asia. The NMR of Nepal is 16 (2021), while that of the United States is 3.2. The SDG 3 calls for all countries to reduce their NMR to at least 12 by the year 2030.

Gender Differentials

Globally, male neonates have higher mortality rates than female neonates. India stands out as the only country where female neonatal mortality is higher. Pervasive gender-based discrimination is likely the main reason for this anomaly.

DOI: 10.4324/9781032644257-69

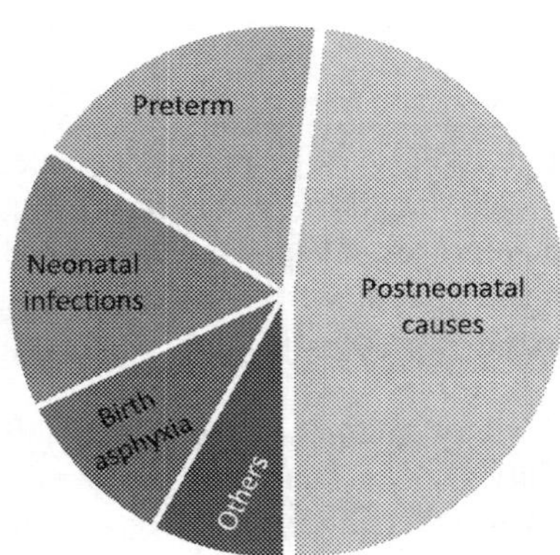

FIGURE 61.1 Causes of neonatal mortality.

Causes

Preterm birth is the most common cause of neonatal deaths in developing countries, followed by neonatal infections and birth asphyxia, as shown in Figure 61.1. Let us examine these conditions and their potential solutions.

Preterm Birth

A preterm birth is when a child is born before completing 37 weeks of gestation. The terms *preterm birth* and *prematurity* are sometimes used interchangeably. Preterm or premature newborns have low birth weight and are weak. Sometimes, even after full gestation, the child is born with low birth weight. This is due to faltered fetal growth in the womb, a condition known as fetal growth restriction (FGR) or intrauterine growth retardation (IUGR).

For many decades, India has been the epicenter of LBW births, accounting for 40% of the world's LBW children. Other South Asian countries are close behind, while countries in sub-Saharan Africa fare relatively better.

Why are preterm neonates at a higher risk of morbidity or mortality? First, these babies have a larger body surface area relative to their weight, with inadequate subcutaneous fat. This predisposes them to hypothermia, which can be fatal. Second, their organs are not fully developed to function optimally, which can cause difficulty in breathing or feeding. Third, their immune system is not fully matured, increasing their risk of infections. Preterm infants who survive may end up with permanent physical or cognitive disabilities.

Risk factors for preterm birth: Underage and anemic mothers are at a higher risk of preterm birth. Recall that many adolescent girls in low-income countries are anemic, and many are married before the age of 18 years. Such sociocultural factors, compounded by economic factors, contribute to the high number of preterm births. Medical causes of preterm birth are less common.[1]

Addressing preterm births: Interventions are needed on three fronts:

- Sociocultural practices: Communities should be encouraged to end the practice of early marriage. Coordinated efforts should be made to promote gender equity and raise awareness about proper nutrition and education of girl children.
- Public health interventions: IFA supplementation, anthelmintic treatment, and education on nutrition can help reduce anemia in adolescent girls. Young couples should be educated

about the benefits of delaying their first pregnancy and maintaining adequate spacing between births. They should have access to contraceptive methods.
- Medical care: Extremely preterm infants should be admitted to a neonatal intensive care unit (NICU) in a hospital, where they are placed in an incubator under controlled temperature and oxygen levels. Infants with respiratory distress may need assisted ventilation. Hydration should be maintained with intravenous fluids and breastfeeding should be encouraged. The environment should be scrupulously clean, and stringent infection-prevention measures should be followed.

Neonatal Infections

Neonatal infections are the second leading cause of neonatal deaths. The fetus can acquire infections from the mother's genital tract during gestation or delivery. Preterm babies are at a higher risk of neonatal infection.

The fetus lies in a protective sac of amniotic fluid, which maintains optimal temperature inside the womb. Normally, the amniotic sac ruptures during labor or just before it. This process is called rupture of membranes. If the amniotic sac ruptures prematurely, the risk of fetal infection increases. Prophylactic antibiotics are indicated in such cases.

Neonatal infection can be localized in the lungs (pneumonia), brain (meningitis), or other organs, or it can be systemic. Neonatal sepsis denotes serious infection involving abnormal host response. Organ function is impaired. If not treated promptly, it can progress to multiple organ failure or septic shock, resulting in death. Neonatal sepsis is most commonly caused by bacteria, but it can also be caused by other types of pathogens.

Neonatal infection can present with nonspecific signs and symptoms, such as fever or even hypothermia, lethargy, poor cry, inability to suckle, hypotonia (poor muscle tone), and respiratory distress.

Intravenous antibiotics, oxygen therapy, intravenous fluids, and a thermoneutral environment are the mainstays of management of neonatal infections. Assisted ventilation may be necessary in some cases. Studies in community settings show that early administration of oral antibiotics can reduce fatality in suspected cases of neonatal infection.

Birth Asphyxia

Birth asphyxia is the third leading cause of neonatal mortality. Normally, a newborn starts breathing spontaneously, prompted by a drop in air temperature or exposure to light or sound. Failure of the neonate to initiate breathing is called birth asphyxia. Preterm birth is an important cause of this condition. Timely intervention can prevent many birth asphyxia deaths.

Management of birth asphyxia: First, effort is made to stimulate breathing by touch, such as gently wiping the baby with a towel. If there is no response, the child's airway is cleared with a bulb syringe. If this does not help, in community settings, artificial ventilation is provided with a bag-and-mask device (ambu-bag). Many infants start breathing with this intervention. Experience of various countries shows that birth attendants and community health workers can be trained to resuscitate cases of birth asphyxia. In hospital settings, intubation and assisted ventilation can save virtually all such newborns.

Occasionally, when health workers fail to revive a child with birth asphyxia, they may incorrectly label it as stillbirth. It is important to differentiate between the two conditions. In stillbirth, heartbeat is absent at birth.

POSTNEONATAL MORTALITY

Postneonatal mortality refers to the number of child deaths within 1 and 60 months of age per 1,000 live births.

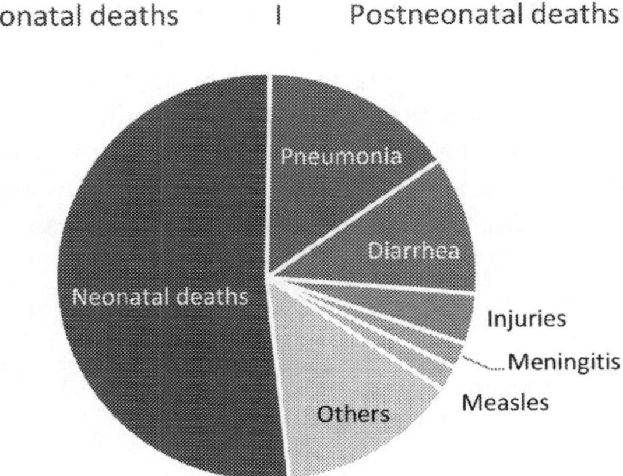

FIGURE 61.2 Causes of postneonatal mortality.

Causes

Pneumonia and diarrhea are the most common causes of death in postneonatal period, as depicted in Figure 61.2. Together, they account for roughly one-fourth of all under-five deaths.

Evidence suggests that community health workers can be trained to manage pneumonia, diarrhea, and malaria. This can improve health outcomes and significantly reduce under-five mortality. Let us see how.

Pneumonia

Pneumonia is an acute infection of the lower respiratory tract (lungs). It is the single largest cause of infection-related deaths in children, leading to over 700,000 deaths globally every year. Fatalities are highest in South Asia and sub-Saharan Africa.

Streptococcus pneumoniae is the most common cause of pneumonia, followed by *Hemophilus influenza* type b (Hib). However, pneumonia can be caused by a variety of bacteria, viruses, or fungi. The infection spreads through droplets released while coughing, sneezing, or talking. Environmental factors such as overcrowded housing, poor ventilation, and close physical contact increase the risk of transmission.

Symptoms and signs: Pneumonia presents with fever. In children, the disease progresses rapidly in absence of treatment. Severe damage to lung tissues prompts the child to breathe rapidly in an effort to obtain enough oxygen. Rapid or labored breathing indicates an emergency and the child should be promptly admitted to a hospital.

Diagnosis: Chest auscultation reveals crepitations (crackling or popping sounds). In a hospital setting, X-ray chest shows opacity or consolidation in the affected lung area. Elevated white blood cell count supports the diagnosis. In severe pneumonia, blood oxygen saturation may drop, which can be measured by a pulse oximeter.

In rural or remote areas of low-income countries, where diagnostic facilities may be limited, community health workers can be trained to diagnose pneumonia by looking for symptoms such as high fever and rapid breathing.

Treatment: On suspicion of pneumonia, the health worker should start treatment with oral antibiotics. Ampicillin and amoxicillin are common first-line antibiotics for pneumonia; however, selection of antibiotics may vary based on the sensitivity of the causative pathogen to certain antibiotics.

Health workers can be trained to assess when to refer a case of pneumonia to a hospital. High fever, respiratory rate exceeding 60 breaths per minute,[2] and indrawing of chest are indications for referral. A seriously ill child may not accept oral medication, necessitating intravenous antibiotics. Additionally, intravenous fluids may be needed to maintain hydration. Some cases may need oxygen therapy. Referral should be made to a hospital where these facilities are available.

Prevention: Pneumococcal conjugate vaccine (PCV) is effective in preventing pneumonia. It is included in immunization programs of many countries.

Diarrhea

After pneumonia, diarrhea is the second leading cause of death in children. In 2020 alone, diarrhea accounted for over 500,000 deaths globally.[3] It is also a leading cause of childhood malnutrition.

Three or more liquid stools per day is defined as diarrhea (WHO). Acute diarrhea can be caused by a range of bacteria or viruses, with *E. coli* and rotavirus being two common etiological agents in low-income settings. The pathogens spread by fecal–oral transmission resulting from consumption of contaminated food or water or poor hygiene practices.

Diagnosis: History provided by the child's mother or caregiver forms the basis for diagnosis. The primary consideration in a case of diarrhea is to assess whether the child is dehydrated. Signs of dehydration include irritability, refusal to eat or drink, reduced urine output, and sunken eyes. Physical examination may reveal rapid pulse and low blood pressure.

Treatment: Most cases of acute diarrhea are self-limiting and do not require medication. However, fluid loss must be replaced to prevent dehydration as dehydration can be life-threatening. Replenishing water and electrolytes is essential.

The WHO and UNICEF recommend ORS as the mainstay of diarrhea treatment. Early administration of ORS in right concentrations can prevent dehydration. Zinc treatment alongside ORS reduces the severity and duration of illness. Once loose stools stop, ORS can be discontinued but zinc should be continued for 14 days. There are indications that zinc treatment protects against reinfection for an additional two to three months. Feeding, whether breast milk or solid food, should be maintained throughout the illness as it helps in absorption of fluids from the gut. Cereals or homemade fluids with sugar and salt can be given, but it should be known that once dehydration sets in, these fluids alone are not sufficient.

Diagnosis and treatment of diarrhea are straightforward. However, a study in India (NFHS-5, 2021) reported that only 60% of children with diarrhea received ORS, and only a third received zinc. There is a need to increase public awareness on home management of diarrhea. ORS and zinc should be readily available.

If a dehydrated child stops accepting oral fluids, she should be immediately referred to a hospital for administration of intravenous fluids (such as Ringer's lactate or normal saline). Presence of fever or blood in stools also warrants hospitalization for administration of antibiotics.

Prevention: Exclusive breastfeeding for first six months of life may help prevent diarrhea in young children. Water and food hygiene are important.[4]

NEONATAL MORTALITY VERSUS POSTNEONATAL MORTALITY

From the foregoing discussions, it may be clear that reducing postneonatal mortality is relatively easier than reducing neonatal mortality. Vaccines are available for both pneumonia and diarrhea, the two main contributors to postneonatal deaths. Moreover, these conditions can be effectively managed by trained community health workers at the local level. Hence, nearly a fourth of all under-five deaths can be prevented by control and management of pneumonia and diarrhea.

In contrast, preventing or reducing neonatal mortality requires addressing complex sociocultural and economic barriers—a challenging and slow process. Second, intensive neonatal care facilities are cost-intensive, and not accessible in many low-income settings.

With declining postneonatal mortality, the proportion of neonatal mortality as a cause of under-five deaths has been rising.

NOTES

1. Medical causes of preterm birth include diabetes, hypertension, infection, and multiple pregnancies.
2. In adults, respiratory rate of more than 30 breaths per minute is considered a severe problem.
3. https://www.who.int/news-room/fact-sheets/detail/diarrhoeal-disease
4. Cholera also causes diarrhea, but cholera is rare these days and mostly occurs as an outbreak. Rice-water stools are characteristic of cholera. It can be treated with common antibiotics. Typhoid may also cause diarrhea. Vaccines for both cholera and typhoid are available, but they are not routinely administered in many countries.

62 Integrated Management of Childhood Illness

For low-income countries where under-five mortality is high and the public health infrastructure is weak, the WHO developed a strategy known as the Integrated Management of Childhood Illness (IMCI). The main objective of IMCI is to strengthen the capabilities of community health workers to identify, diagnose, and treat common childhood illnesses, particularly in rural and remote areas where diagnostic facilities and specialized care are lacking. The IMCI provides a series of algorithms and flowcharts that guide health workers in diagnosing and managing conditions such as fever, pneumonia, diarrhea, and malaria. Additionally, a list of danger signs helps health workers decide when to refer a child to a hospital. Multiple studies have shown that using IMCI tools leads to better outcomes for childhood illnesses.

Some examples of decision-making protocols for common childhood illnesses are given in Figure 62.1.

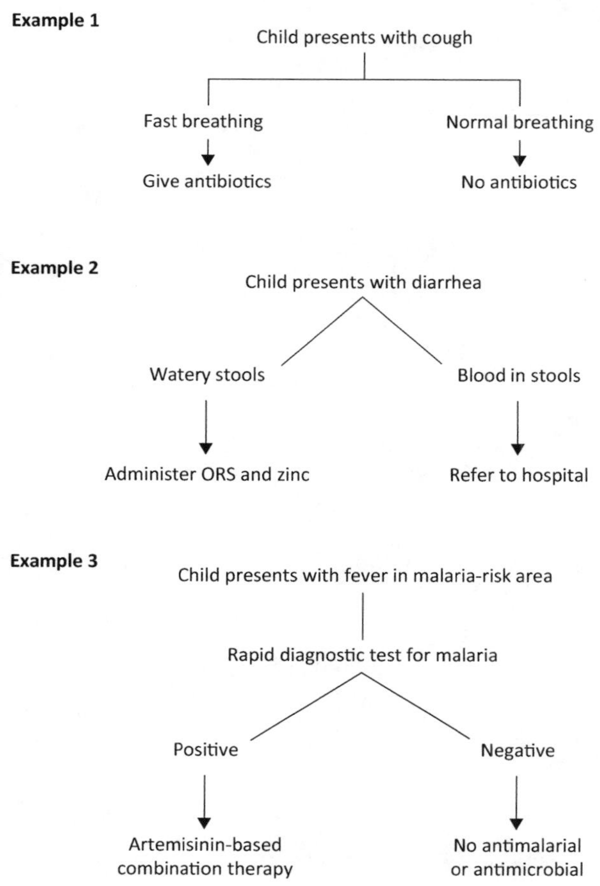

FIGURE 62.1 Examples of IMCI algorithms.

DOI: 10.4324/9781032644257-70

DANGER SIGNS

Community health workers are required to refer a child to a hospital after observing one or more of the following danger signs:

- The child does not move or moves only on stimulation
- Body temperature above 100 degrees Fahrenheit or below 96 degrees Fahrenheit
- Respiratory rate of 60 breaths or more per minute
- Indrawing of chest
- Convulsions
- Difficulty in feeding the child
- Malnourishment with persistent symptoms

63 Immunization

Encouraged by the success of the smallpox immunization program, the WHO launched the Expanded Program on Immunization (EPI) in 1974 to reduce the occurrence of vaccine-preventable diseases. In its early stages, the EPI provided vaccination against six diseases: Tuberculosis (BCG);[1] poliomyelitis; measles; and diphtheria, pertussis (whooping cough),[2] and tetanus (DPT).

However, despite efforts, vaccine uptake in low-income countries remained low, particularly in rural areas. Uptake of the measles vaccine was especially poor, and there was a reason for this: Although parents initially took interest in immunizing their newborns, their enthusiasm waned after the first three or four months and they failed to complete the entire vaccination schedule. As a result, the measles vaccine, administered at nine months, was commonly missed out.

IMMUNIZATION SCHEDULE

The WHO's recommendations for immunization programs (2021) are given in Table 63.1. Countries can adapt these guidelines to their needs. Many vaccines can be given in combination with other vaccines.

Certain vaccines are recommended in specific regions. These include vaccines against Japanese encephalitis, yellow fever, tick-borne encephalitis, typhoid, cholera, meningococcal infections, hepatitis A, rabies, dengue, mumps, seasonal influenza, and varicella.

TABLE 63.1
Immunization Schedule for Routine Immunization Programs

Vaccine	Recommendation
BCG	Single dose at birth.
Hepatitis B (HepB)	First dose at birth, followed by three doses (each four weeks apart).
Polio	Bivalent oral polio vaccine (bOPV) at birth, followed by at least three primary doses of bOPV (each four weeks apart) and one dose of inactivated polio vaccine (IPV).
DPT	Beginning at six weeks of age, three primary doses at least four weeks apart.
Tetanus + adult diphtheria (Td)	Diphtheria boosters in combination with tetanus toxoid boosters at 12–23 months, 4–7 years, and 9–15 years.
Hemophilus influenzae (Hib)	Three primary doses starting from six weeks of age.
Pneumococcal conjugate vaccine (PCV)	Three doses starting from six weeks of age.
Rotavirus	Three doses, each at least four weeks apart.
Measles	Two doses, first at nine months and second at an interval of at least four weeks. The measles, mumps, and rubella (MMR) vaccine is safe and effective. The MMRV vaccine also includes vaccine against varicella.
Rubella	At least one dose at nine months.
Human papillomavirus (HPV)	Two doses at least six months apart are given to females aged 9–14 years, before they become sexually active. After 14 years of age, three-dose schedule is followed.

DOI: 10.4324/9781032644257-71

VACCINE COVERAGE

Globally, coverage of the following vaccines ranges from 70% to 80%: BCG, OPV (three doses), DTP, Hib, HepB, IPV (one dose), and measles (two doses). Coverage of PCV and rotavirus vaccine is relatively low, hovering at about 50%.

COLD CHAIN

To preserve the efficacy of vaccines, they must be stored at a specific temperature right from the point of manufacture to the point of administration. This temperature-controlled supply chain network is called a cold chain.

Normally, vaccines are stored in a refrigerator at subnormal temperatures. In low-income settings, where power breakdowns are common, vaccines are stacked on ice packs in a special refrigerator called an ice-lined refrigerator (ILR). This keeps the vaccines safe during power outages. The ILR maintains a temperature range of +2 to +8 degrees Celsius. Sustaining this temperature requires a minimum of eight hours of power supply in a 24-hour period. The ice packs are prepared in a deep freezer that operates at –15 to –25 degrees Celsius.

Hospitals and health centers that provide vaccination services maintain an ILR for vaccine storage and a deep freezer for preparing ice packs.[3] For outreach, vaccines are transported in cold boxes lined with ice packs.

Although domestic refrigerators can also maintain temperatures of +2 to +8 degrees Celsius, their holdover time[4] is only four hours. Therefore, they are not recommended for vaccine storage in areas where power supply is unreliable. If consistent power supply is assured, they can be used for vaccine storage.

NEW VACCINES

In recent years, many countries have added new vaccines to their vaccination programs. These are:

Pentavalent Vaccine

The DPT vaccine has been replaced by a new pentavalent vaccine that provides protection against five diseases: Diphtheria, pertussis, tetanus, HepB, and Hib.

Tetanus and Adult Diphtheria (Td) Vaccine

To counter the waning immunity in adolescents and adults against diphtheria, the tetanus toxoid (TT) vaccine has been replaced by Td vaccine. This vaccine is now routinely administered to adolescents aged 10–16 years and pregnant women.

Tetanus, Diphtheria, and Pertussis (Tdap) Vaccine

Tdap is a safer version of DPT vaccine. It has lower concentrations of diphtheria and pertussis toxoids and is licensed for administration to people aged 10–64 years.

Measles-Rubella (MR) Vaccine

In 2017, the measles vaccine was combined with rubella vaccine. Target group for the new vaccine is children aged nine months to 15 years.

Rotavirus Vaccine (RVV)

This vaccine protects against rotavirus diarrhea.

Pneumococcal Conjugate Vaccine (PCV)

This is a vaccine for pneumococcal pneumonia.

Inactivated Polio Vaccine (IPV)

Historically, trivalent oral polio vaccine (tOPV) has been used to eradicate polio. This vaccine is effective against all three variants of wild poliovirus (types 1, 2, and 3).[5] Being an oral vaccine, tOPV is convenient for mass administration, but as it contains live attenuated virus, there is a small risk of vaccine-derived poliovirus (VDPV) infection. Over time, VDPV has become capable of spreading like wild poliovirus, causing paralysis in unvaccinated children.

IPV is an alternative to tOPV that is equally effective against all three poliovirus variants. IPV contains killed virus, so there is no risk of vaccine-derived viruses or diseases. However, since IPV is given by intramuscular injection, mass administration is a challenge in low-income settings.

In 2013, the WHO introduced the Polio Eradication and Endgame Strategic Plan. The initial phase aimed to eradicate vaccine-derived type 2 poliovirus by replacing tOPV with a bivalent vaccine (bOPV) targeting poliovirus types 1 and 3. By April 2016, all countries had successfully recalled and disposed of tOPV. However, there was a risk of resurgence of type 2 wild poliovirus during this transition. To mitigate this risk, at least one dose of IPV was recommended.

According to studies, two fractional doses of IPV (fIPV) are more effective against type 2 wild poliovirus than a full dose of IPV. A fractional dose is one-fifth of a full dose. It is given intradermally. In routine immunization, two fractional doses are administered at 6 and 14 weeks.

Once all three variants of wild poliovirus are eradicated, oral polio vaccine will no longer be included in routine immunization programs.

NEW VACCINES IN PIPELINE

In 2023, the RTS,S malaria vaccine was introduced in Ghana, Kenya, and Malawi for community implementation. The following vaccines are in various stages of development:

1. HIV
2. Tuberculosis
3. Respiratory Syncytial Virus (RSV)
4. Enterotoxigenic *E. coli*
5. Shigella
6. Norovirus

NOTES

1. BCG stands for Bacillus Calmette–Guérin vaccine, named after its inventors Albert Calmette and Camille Guérin. It protects against TB.
2. *Bordetella pertussis* is the bacterium that causes whooping cough.
3. Certain vaccines, such as MMRV vaccine and varicella vaccine, are stored in a deep freezer.
4. Holdover time is the time taken by a vaccine refrigerator to reach the maximum temperature threshold of +8 degrees Celsius during a power outage.
5. Wild poliovirus type 1 (WPV1) has been the most predominant poliovirus. It is also the most notorious variant due to its ability to cause paralysis in children.

64 Family Planning Programs

Family planning enables couples to plan their family size. They can have children by choice, not chance. They can avoid unwanted pregnancies.

In the past, people wanted to have many children as they thought children provided additional hands to work and protected the family from external threats. They also worried that some of their children might not survive, so they produced more children than they could afford to raise. As a result, populations kept increasing, more so in low-income countries.

Initially, the goal of family planning programs was to stabilize the population. Gradually, it was realized that, in addition to population control, family planning has an important role in reducing maternal and child mortality. High fertility is the root cause of numerous maternal and child deaths. In communities where child mortality is high, people continue to have more children, and a vicious cycle continues. Family planning can help break this cycle.

FOCUS AREAS OF FAMILY PLANNING PROGRAMS

Modern family planning programs focus on factors that significantly impact maternal and child health and contribute to population increase. These are:

Age at Marriage and Age at Birth of First Child

As we learned earlier, many girls in sub-Saharan Africa and South Asia are married before the age of 18 years, and many of them conceive soon after marriage. These underage pregnancies contribute to poor maternal health and high maternal mortality.

Spacing between Births

In low-income countries, in a bid to complete their families at the earliest, young couples end up having two or three children in quick succession before they consider contraception. In nearly half the cases in India (48%), birth interval is less than the recommended period of three years.

To encourage spacing between births, newlywed couples are advised to delay their first pregnancy and to maintain a minimum gap of three years between pregnancies. This requires the use of spacing methods. Condom, oral contraceptive pill (OCP), and intrauterine contraceptive device (IUCD) are good options. Even newly married women can opt for IUCD insertion.

Unmet Need for Family Planning

This refers to the proportion of couples who want to delay or stop childbearing but do not use any contraceptive methods. This is a low-hanging fruit, meaning that immediate results can be achieved by increasing these couples' access to contraceptives.

Additionally, increasing the proportion of institutional deliveries is an opportunity for service providers to promote family planning. It has been seen that people are more receptive to family planning when they are counseled immediately before or after delivery. In many cases, IUCD can be an ideal birth spacing method. The device can be inserted right after delivery and can be removed easily when the couple wants to have another child.

DOI: 10.4324/9781032644257-72

Increasing Male Participation

In conservative societies, male participation in family planning is very low, and this is mainly because family planning is considered women's responsibility. But considering that men constitute roughly half of a country's population, the full potential of family planning programs cannot be realized without their participation.

65 Methods of Contraception

Contraceptive methods are used to avoid pregnancy and to maintain spacing between births. Both natural and modern methods of contraception are available. Keeping in view the effectiveness and acceptance of modern methods, they are explained first.

Modern contraception can be broadly classified into two groups:

- Spacing methods
- Terminal methods

Spacing methods are reversible, which means fertility can be regained simply by discontinuing the method. Terminal methods are permanent. They are suited for couples who have completed their family and do not want more children. Figure 65.1 illustrates popular modern contraceptive methods.

As we can see, condom is the only spacing method available for men. For women, oral contraceptive pills and injectables are short-acting spacing methods, while IUCD and contraceptive implants are long-acting spacing methods. Among terminal methods, men can opt for no-scalpel vasectomy (NSV), and women can choose laparoscopic tubal ligation or mini-laparotomy tubectomy.

SPACING METHODS

Male Condom

A condom is made of latex or polyurethane. Known as a *barrier* method of contraception, it prevents entry of semen into vagina, thus preventing fertilization and pregnancy. It is also highly effective against STIs, including HIV/AIDS. Thus, it provides dual protection. Condom has been a popular contraceptive method in the West, but its acceptance in developing countries remained low until the HIV/AIDS surge in the 1980s.

Effectiveness

If used correctly, condom is an effective method of contraception. If 100 men correctly and consistently use condoms during every act of sexual intercourse in a year, only up to two pregnancies are expected. However, the actual failure rate is generally higher due to incorrect usage.

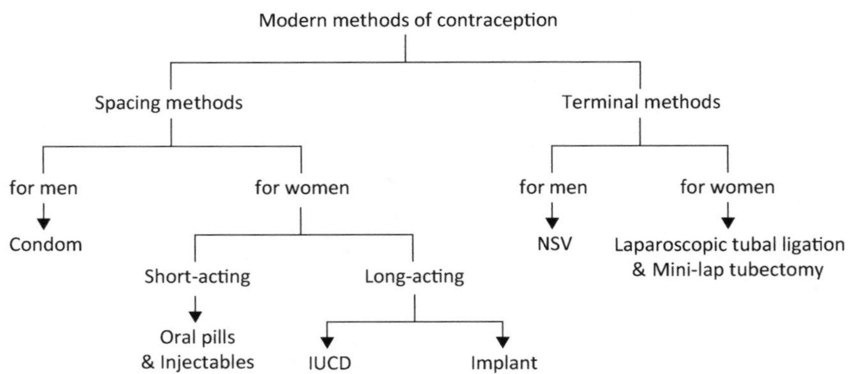

FIGURE 65.1 Modern contraceptive methods.

DOI: 10.4324/9781032644257-73

Advantages

Condoms are affordable and easily available. They can be used without consulting a healthcare provider, and there are no side effects of hormones or chemicals. Dual protection is a unique feature of this method.

Limitations

Some people experience reduced sexual pleasure when using a condom. In families where many people share a room, storing and using condoms may be a challenge for couples.

Method of Use

Condom is unrolled over erect penis before penetration. After ejaculation, penis is withdrawn from vagina while still erect, with the rim of the condom held at the base of the penis. The condom is then removed carefully, ensuring that seminal fluid does not spill over the vagina.

Oral Contraceptive Pills

Oral contraceptive pill (OCP) is a popular contraceptive method for women. Introduced in the 1950s, OCP was instrumental in reducing fertility rates in the West. Traditionally, OCPs contain female sex hormones, but now nonhormonal pills are also available. Hormonal OCPs are of two main types:

- Combined oral contraceptive pill
- Progestin-only pill

Combined Oral Contraceptive Pill

Combined oral contraceptive (COC) is the most commonly used contraceptive pill. It contains estrogen and progesterone. Over the years, the quantity of estrogen in the formulation has been reduced without compromising its efficacy.

Mode of action: COC primarily acts by preventing ovulation, that is, the release of eggs from ovaries. In addition, it causes thickening of cervical mucus.

Eligibility: Women of any age or parity can use COC, including adolescents and those with HIV.[1]

When to start: COC can be started on any day of the menstrual cycle, provided the woman is certain she is not pregnant.

Method of use: Many COC pills come in 28-day packs, each containing 21 hormonal pills and seven IFA pills. After a pack is finished, the next one should be started the very next day. The IFA pills should ideally coincide with the days of menstrual bleeding. Some brands come in packs of 21 pills, in which case the next pack should be started after a seven-day interval.

Effectiveness: COC is a highly effective contraceptive. Risk of failure is less than one pregnancy per 100 women consistently taking the pill over a year.

Advantages: COC is available over the counter and can be started without medical consultation, pelvic examination, or pregnancy test. It does not interfere with sexual pleasure. Fertility is restored immediately after the pill is discontinued.

Limitations: COC pill has to be taken every day, regardless of sexual activity. In public health programs, convincing women to adhere to this regimen can be a challenge.

Side effects: In the initial few months of COC usage, there may be changes in pattern of menstrual bleeding, such as irregular or lighter flow. There may be weight gain of a few kilograms. Blood pressure can increase by a few points, but it reverts to normal after COC is discontinued. According to some studies, COC use may increase the risk of deep vein thrombosis (clotting), a rare but serious complication. Other, minor side effects include nausea, headache, abdominal pain, breast tenderness, and mood changes.

Health benefits: COC can provide some protection against endometrial[2] and ovarian cancers. It may reduce ovulation pain and menstrual cramps.[3] Women experiencing heavy or irregular menstrual bleeding may also benefit from COC. Anemic women can benefit from COC as it generally reduces the amount of menstrual flow. It may reduce hirsutism (excess facial and body hair).

Contraindications: Following childbirth, COC should not be used for six weeks, as it may increase the risk of deep vein thrombosis. Women who are not breastfeeding or are partially breastfeeding can start taking COC six weeks after delivery. Women who are exclusively breastfeeding should avoid COC for six months after delivery as it may reduce milk production. They can take progestin-only pill (POP), discussed in the next section.

Other contraindications for COC include serious active liver disease, hypertension, and diabetes for more than 20 years. It is also not recommended for women with a history of coronary heart disease, stroke, deep vein thrombosis, breast cancer, seizures and taking antiepileptic medicines, tuberculosis and taking antitubercular medicines, or migraine with aura.[4]

Women above 35 years who smoke should avoid COC as it can increase their risk of hypertension. They can take POP.

Missed pill: If COC pill is missed for one or two days, one pill should be taken as soon as possible. If only one pill is missed, two pills can be taken together the next day. In this case, there will be little or no risk of pregnancy. If three or more pills are missed in a row, one pill should be taken at the earliest, and a backup method, such as condom, should be used for the next seven days. If unprotected sexual intercourse occurred during the missed days, an emergency contraceptive pill (explained later) can be taken to avert pregnancy.

Progestin-Only Pill

POP, also known as mini-pill, contains a low dose of progesterone. It does not contain estrogen. This pill acts by thickening cervical mucus and preventing ovulation.

A key benefit of POP is that it does not interfere with breast milk production, making it a suitable option for women who are exclusively breastfeeding. They can start taking POP six weeks after delivery. Women who are not breastfeeding can start taking it at any time after delivery. Women above 35 years who smoke can also take POP.

The effectiveness, side effects, and failure rate of POP are somewhat similar to those of COC.

Nonhormonal Pill

As the name implies, nonhormonal contraceptive pills do not contain any female sex hormones. They contain Centchroman, a drug that blocks estrogen receptors, thereby preventing implantation of fertilized ovum on uterine mucosa.

Recommended dosage of nonhormonal pill is twice a week for first three months and once a week thereafter. Breastfeeding women can start taking this pill shortly after childbirth.

Nonhormonal pills are slightly less effective than hormonal pills, with a risk of less than two pregnancies per 100 women who consistently use the pill over a year. Delay in menstrual periods is the only known side effect.

Emergency Contraceptive Pill

Emergency contraceptive pill (ECP) is a measure to prevent pregnancy after unprotected sexual intercourse. It contains levonorgestrel, a progestin,[5] and primarily works by preventing ovulation.

The ECP is effective if taken within five days of unprotected sex; the sooner, the better. It should be known that ECP is not a method of contraception, and it cannot terminate an existing pregnancy.

Efficacy: If 100 women engage in unprotected intercourse during their fertile period (typically the second or third week of their menstrual cycle), eight of them are likely to conceive. If all eight women take ECP within five days of intercourse, only one or two of them may become pregnant. This means ECP will avert pregnancy in nearly 85% of cases. There is no delay in return of fertility after taking an ECP.

Side effects: After taking an ECP, there can be irregular bleeding for one to two days. There can be nausea or vomiting. The menstrual cycle may get disrupted.

Injectables

Depot medroxyprogesterone acetate (DMPA) is the most commonly used injectable contraceptive. It contains progestin and works primarily by preventing ovulation. Any woman can use DMPA, including those who are breastfeeding, those above 35 years of age, and those who smoke.

DMPA is administered once every three months by intramuscular injection. Some formulations come in a prefilled syringe (Uniject™ system) for subcutaneous self-administration.

Effectiveness and side effects of DMPA are similar to those of POP, but it has some additional side effects. During the initial stages of DMPA usage, menstrual periods may become irregular. After a few doses, menstruation stops completely and does not resume as long as DMPA is continued. The cessation of periods may cause anxiety in some users, which can be addressed by counseling. Discontinuation of DMPA may be followed by heavy bleeding, which for some women lasts for a considerable period of time. Return of fertility takes four to ten months after DMPA is discontinued.

Intrauterine Contraceptive Device

Intrauterine contraceptive device (IUCD) is a widely accepted long-acting reversible method of contraception. There are two types of IUCD:

- Copper-bearing intrauterine device
- Hormonal intrauterine device

Some IUCD brands are effective for up to five years, and others for up to ten years. Two varieties of IUCD are presented in Figure 65.2. One has a flexible *T* shape and the other has an inverted *U* shape. A copper wire is coiled around the frame in both designs, with two nylon strings attached at the base to facilitate removal.

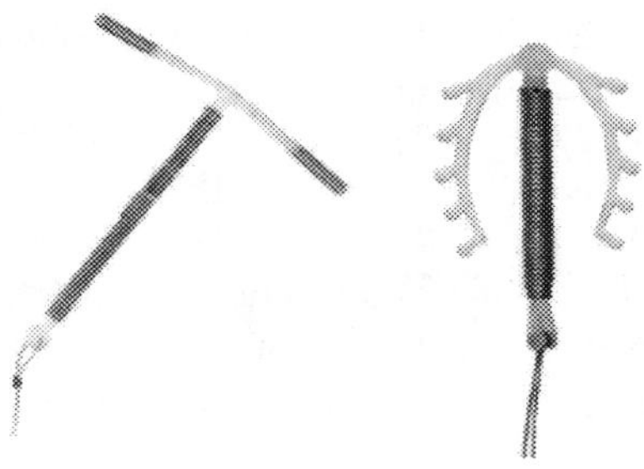

FIGURE 65.2 IUCD—Two varieties.

Effectiveness

IUCD is a highly effective method of contraception, with a failure rate of less than one pregnancy per 100 women during the first year of use. The risk of failure decreases further in subsequent years.

Contraindications

Before inserting an IUCD, the service provider must confirm the following:

- The woman is not pregnant.
- She does not have a reproductive tract infection.

Ruling out pregnancy: If IUCD is inserted in a pregnant uterus, it can harm the fetus or induce abortion, which would amount to medical negligence. Prior to insertion, pregnancy can be ruled out by taking history of last menstruation and recent sexual contact. In case of doubt, a urine pregnancy test should be done.

Ruling out infection: During IUCD insertion, any preexisting infection in vagina or cervix can be transmitted to the uterus through the IUCD device or the instruments used for insertion. An existing infection in the uterus may get potentiated. Therefore, ruling out infection is crucial. History of foul-smelling vaginal discharge, genital itching, or pain in lower abdomen indicates a reproductive tract infection. It can be confirmed by pelvic examination. Tenderness in cervix or fornix or a foul-smelling discharge confirms the suspicion.

Timing of insertion: Once pregnancy and infection are ruled out, IUCD can be inserted on any day of the menstrual cycle. The optimal period for IUCD insertion is the first week following menstruation (i.e., within 12 days of the first day of menstruation). This is because the cervix is relatively open after menstruation, which facilitates easier insertion. Additionally, the uterus is in a relaxed state, minimizing chances of expulsion.

After delivery, IUCD can be inserted immediately or within 48 hours. Insertion right after delivery of placenta has a higher risk of spontaneous expulsion. If insertion is not done within 48 hours, it is deferred for another six weeks to allow the uterus to revert to its prepregnancy size and position. In caesarean delivery, IUCD can be inserted during the surgical procedure.

Following an abortion or miscarriage, when the cervix is open, IUCD can be easily inserted immediately or within 12 days. However, chances of expulsion are high.

Advantages: IUCD is a highly effective long-acting method of contraception. There is no effect on sexual pleasure. The device can be easily removed when desired, and return of fertility is immediate. Copper-bearing IUCDs have no hormone-related side effects.

Limitations: IUCD must be inserted or removed by a trained service provider in a health facility.

Side effects: After IUCD insertion, the pattern of menstrual bleeding often changes. Some women experience heavy and prolonged bleeding that may be accompanied by cramps or pain. Some have irregular bleeding. These changes are temporary and generally subside within a few months; however, many clients who experience these side effects come back for removal. Experience is that if clients are counseled prior to insertion, continuation rates are high. Nevertheless, if a client complains of unbearable pain or discomfort, IUCD should be removed.

Second, carelessness in infection-prevention practices can result in infections.

Third, in rare cases, IUCD may get expelled spontaneously. If this happens, a new IUCD can be inserted. If the client does not want to continue with IUCD, other methods can be offered.

Fourth, an inexperienced service provider can inadvertently perforate the uterus while inserting IUCD. Minor perforations may go unnoticed and heal on their own.

Fifth, the risk of ectopic pregnancy[6] increases slightly after IUCD insertion.

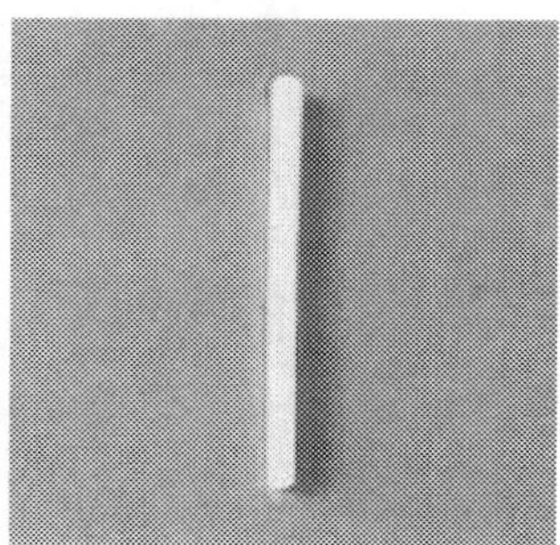

FIGURE 65.3 Contraceptive implant.

Contraceptive Implant

This is an effective long-acting reversible method popular across Europe, Africa, and East Asia. The implant consists of a small, flexible rod the size of a matchstick that releases levonorgestrel and works mainly by preventing ovulation. It is placed under the skin of the upper arm through a minor surgical procedure. One or two rods are implanted depending on the brand used. Figure 65.3 shows an image of a contraceptive implant.

A contraceptive implant is effective for three to seven years. It can be removed when desired, and fertility is restored shortly. Failure rate is less than one pregnancy per 100 women using the implant for a year.

TERMINAL METHODS

Male Sterilization

Earlier, vasectomies were done by a conventional method wherein two incisions were made on scrotal skin to expose and tie vas deferens on both sides. This method is rarely used nowadays.

No-Scalpel Vasectomy

This is a modern technique of conducting vasectomy. Instead of making two incisions, vas deferens on both sides are taken out through a single puncture in the middle of scrotum and tied as in conventional method.

Under local anesthesia, vas deferens is located through intact scrotal skin and clamped with forceps. A pointed and sharp forceps is then used to pierce the skin over the clamped vas, and the vas is pulled out and tied. This process is repeated for the other vas through the same puncture. The puncture is so small, suturing is not required. Since no incision is made on scrotal skin, this technique is known as no-scalpel vasectomy.

Advantages: NSV involves minimum trauma to tissues and takes around ten minutes to complete. The client can leave the facility walking after an hour of observation. Complications are rare. Hematoma[7] is a rare postoperative complication.

Disadvantages: Performing NSV requires a high level of expertise.

Female Sterilization

This is a surgical procedure that involves cutting or ligating the fallopian tubes. The following must be confirmed before accepting a client for sterilization:

- The client is not pregnant, which can be known by history-taking, pelvic examination, and urine pregnancy test.
- She does not have a reproductive tract infection, which can be excluded by pelvic examination.
- She is not anemic, which is confirmed by blood hemoglobin test.

There are two methods of female sterilization:

- Laparoscopic tubal ligation
- Mini-laparotomy tubectomy

Laparoscopic Tubal Ligation

Laparoscopic tubal ligation can be performed in a mini-operation theater of a hospital or health center. Under local anesthesia, a laparoscope is inserted into the pelvic cavity through a subumbilical incision measuring about 2 cm in length. The fallopian tube is located and gently pulled into a loop using the laparoscope's hook, and a plastic ring is slipped over the loop. The process is repeated on the other fallopian tube. A single suture is applied to close the abdominal incision.

Advantages: This procedure is less invasive and causes minimal trauma to tissues. The client can leave the hospital on the same day after two hours of observation. Recovery is fast.

Disadvantages: Failure rate of this method is relatively high due to many reasons. An inexperienced surgeon can make a mistake in identifying fallopian tubes. Second, in some cases, the tubes can become inflamed or swollen at a later stage, causing the plastic rings to slip out and the tubes to become patent (unblocked). Additionally, since the procedure is performed blindly, chances of complications, such as injury to bladder or intestines, are high. Lastly, the equipment is expensive and comes with a high maintenance cost, and its disinfection is cumbersome.

Mini-Laparotomy Tubectomy

Commonly known as mini-lap, this procedure can also be performed in a mini-operation theater of a hospital or health center. An incision, measuring 3–4 cm in length, is made above the pubic area under local anesthesia. The fallopian tubes are taken out one by one and a small section of each tube is cut off. The open end of the tube is closed with sutures. The client remains at the facility overnight for observation.

Advantages: Mini-lap is a relatively simple procedure that can be conducted by a general physician. Chances of failure or complications are remote. The surgical instruments used are inexpensive and can be sterilized by autoclaving, a simple and cost-effective method of disinfection.

A mini-lap should be performed within seven days of delivery, preferably right after delivery. If this timeframe is missed, the procedure should be deferred for six weeks to allow the uterus to revert to its prepregnancy state.

After an uncomplicated abortion, mini-lap can be performed within 48 hours.

OTHER MODERN METHODS

There are many other modern methods of contraception, but they are not very popular. Some of them are discussed here.

Female Condom

Introduced during the peak of the HIV epidemic, the female condom is a sheath of soft plastic film with flexible rings at both ends. It is coated with a silicon-based lubricant. One end of the condom is closed, and the other is open. Prior to sexual intercourse, the closed end is inserted into vagina. The open end remains outside through which tip of the penis is guided during intercourse.

Female condom offers similar advantages as the male condom, but it is not as popular due to its high cost and limited availability. It is also more difficult to use.

Combined Hormonal Patch

The patch is applied directly to the skin. It prevents pregnancy by releasing estrogen and progesterone, which are absorbed through the skin. A new patch is applied every week for three weeks, followed by a patch-free week. Effectiveness and side effects of hormonal patch are similar to those of COC pill.

Combined Vaginal Ring

It is a flexible plastic ring that is placed inside the vagina, where it continuously releases progesterone and estrogen into the bloodstream. Its mechanism is similar to that of COC pill.

Others

Some examples are diaphragm, cervical cap, and spermicidal jelly, but these methods are not popular due to their high failure rates.

NATURAL METHODS OF CONTRACEPTION

Natural contraceptive methods have been in use for centuries, but they are not very reliable. However, in places or situations where modern methods are not available, it might be worth educating people about natural methods. Some examples are given here.

Lactational Amenorrhea Method

Women who are exclusively breastfeeding are less likely to conceive. This is nature's protection—regular suckling of breasts suppresses ovulation. But for this method to be effective, three conditions must be met:

- The woman is exclusively breastfeeding. That means the child is not fed anything other than breast milk, not even water.
- The child is less than six months old.
- The mother's menstruation has not returned postdelivery.

Failure rate of this method is around five pregnancies per 100 women during the first six months after giving birth. In some societies, many women have a false notion that they will not conceive as long as they are breastfeeding. The need is to make them aware of the essential criteria for this method to be effective.

Withdrawal Method

During sexual intercourse, penis is withdrawn from vagina before ejaculation. The man ejaculates externally, ensuring that semen does not come in contact with his partner's genitalia. This can place undue pressure on the man, and despite good intentions, he may fail to withdraw at the right moment. Consequently, chances of failure are high.

Standard Days Method

An average menstrual cycle is of 28 days, and ovulation generally occurs around day 14. Five days before and five days after ovulation, or roughly the second and third weeks of the menstrual cycle, is the fertile period. Couples who want to avoid pregnancy but do not want to use any modern contraceptives should avoid sexual intercourse during this period. Miscalculation of safe period can lead to failure.

NOTES

1. HIV/AIDS patients on ritonavir, an antiretroviral drug, are not advised COC pill as ritonavir reduces the efficacy of COC.
2. Endometrium is the inner lining of uterine cavity. Endometrial cancer is a type of uterine cancer.
3. Some girls and women experience pain or cramps at the start of the menstrual period or at ovulation.
4. Women below 35 years who have migraine headaches without aura can use COC.
5. Some formulations contain both progestin and estrogen.
6. An ectopic pregnancy is when the fetus develops outside the uterus, typically in a fallopian tube.
7. Hematoma occurs when a blood vessel is injured during the procedure, leading to slow leakage of blood into surrounding tissues. Rarely, it may cause a serious problem.

66 What Is Demography?

The size and composition of a country's population have a strong bearing on the health, economic status, living standards, and quality of life of its citizens.

Demography is the study of human population in terms of its size, composition, and development.

Demographers study changes in population over time, analyze past trends, and make future projections.

HISTORICAL PERSPECTIVE

At the beginning of the twentieth century, the world's population was approximately 1.6 billion—about a fifth of today's figures. At that time, birth and death rates were high across countries, and maternal and child mortality were also high. In addition, infectious diseases, famines, and droughts took a heavy toll. Yet, with birth rates being slightly higher than death rates, the world's population continued to grow, albeit at a slow pace.

The discovery of penicillin by Alexander Fleming in 1928, along with other advancements in healthcare, helped to contain many infectious diseases. Vector-control measures increased agricultural yields, and improvements in famine and drought management reduced death rates worldwide. Collectively, these achievements accelerated population growth.

After the Second World War, economic progress in the West during the 1950s led to a substantial increase in women's literacy. This, along with the introduction of oral contraceptive pills, played an important role in lowering fertility rates and controlling maternal and child deaths, thus stabilizing the population in Western countries. Meanwhile, populations of low-income countries continued to swell.

Until recently, China was the world's most populous country.[1] In 1978, the Chinese government enacted the one-child policy to control the country's exploding population. Under this policy, couples were allowed to have only one child. This led to a steady decline in China's fertility rate. However, it also resulted in an entire generation being deprived of siblings, as well as widespread female feticide, infanticide, and abandonment of girl children. Amid rising criticism, the policy was repealed in 2015. Despite this, the decline in China's fertility did not halt.

In India, human rights violations and coercive measures in family planning during the National Emergency (1975–77) had long-lasting implications on population growth. People became averse to family planning. But the most significant fallout of the Emergency was that no subsequent government talked about family planning. As a result, India's population continued to grow unabated. In 2023, India became the most populous country in the world.

In the same year, the world's population reached eight billion, although the rate of this growth has been slowing over time. The rising cost of living, particularly that of healthcare and education, is now forcing people to have fewer children. High fertility is now mainly limited to 47 least-developed countries, most of which are in Africa.

Conversely, many high-income countries are grappling with the challenge of a shrinking population. With their birth rates falling consistently and death rates rising due to an aging population, at least 20 countries are facing this crisis.

DOI: 10.4324/9781032644257-74

MEASURES OF POPULATION

Size

India is the world's most populous country, followed by China, the USA, and Indonesia. India's population density is 423 people per square kilometer, eight times higher than the global average of 52. Common indicators for fertility and population growth are discussed below.

Total Fertility Rate (TFR)

The average number of children per woman is known as total fertility rate (TFR) of a country or region. TFR is an important indicator of population growth. Global TFR is 2.3 (2021). Other notable TFRs include the Democratic Republic of the Congo at 6.2, Ethiopia at 4.2, Iraq at 3.5, and India at 2.0. Developed countries have TFR below 2.

Crude Birth Rate (CBR)

It indicates the number of live births in a year per 1,000 population. Global CBR is 17 (2021). This means a population of 1,000 will grow to 1,017 in one year. Sub-Saharan Africa has a CBR of 35.

Crude Death Rate (CDR)

It is the number of deaths in a year per 1,000 population. Global CDR is 9 (2021). Japan's CDR is 12, and that of the USA is 10.

Annual Population Growth Rate

This rate represents the percentage increase in a country's population in a year relative to its total population for that year. The global population growth rate is 0.8. For sub-Saharan Africa, it is 2.5.

Population explosion: Exploding population has multiple disadvantages for a country. It places pressure on resources such as clean water, clean air, housing, food, electricity, and fuel. Land, educational institutions, healthcare, and transportation are stretched beyond capacity. Overpopulation also leads to large-scale unemployment, deprivation, and unhealthy competition. It fuels conflict, crime, and social unrest. Overall, quality of life deteriorates.

Composition

The composition of a population is as important as its size. It is examined from three perspectives:

- Age structure
- Sex ratio
- Literacy

Age Structure

Age structure pertains to the distribution of population across various age groups. People in the 15–64 age group constitute a country's productive, or working-age, population. This demographic group drives the country's economic growth and supports the dependent population—that is, children and the elderly. The ratio of productive population to dependent population has a strong bearing on a country's economic development.

Dependency ratio: It informs the number of dependents per 100 working-age individuals.

Demographic dividend: This is a phenomenon wherein a large portion of a country's population is in the productive age group. Many developing countries, including India, are presently in this category.

However, unless people are literate, they have the necessary skills, and there are income-generation opportunities, these countries will fail to capitalize on this unique opportunity. Further, with the growth of elderly population expected to accelerate in the coming decades, it is time for countries to make arrangements for social planning and healthcare needs of the elderly, failing which they will be facing an unmanageable crisis.

Age pyramid: Also known as a population pyramid, an age pyramid is a graphic representation of different age groups in a population. In low-income countries, this figure is a typical pyramid, with a broad base representing children and a tapering tip representing the elderly. As the number of young people in a population increases, the figure bulges in the middle. Conversely, an increasing proportion of older people widens the top of the pyramid. The shape of a country's age pyramid can provide some insight into its development.

Sex Ratio

Sex ratio, also called gender ratio, is the number of males per 100 females. Qatar has 266 males per 100 females, Pakistan has 101, and the United States has 98 males per 100 females (2022).

Ideally, populations should have a near-equal distribution of males and females. This balance is seen in most countries; however, countries in the Middle East, South Asia, and North Africa demonstrate a male-biased sex ratio.

Implications of skewed sex ratio: When there are more men than women in a society, social dynamics get disrupted. There is an increase in crimes against women, such as forced marriage, purchase of brides from poor families, polygamy, abduction and trafficking of women, and sexual violence. Fear of violence against girls leads to a preference for male children, contributing to practices such as female feticide and infanticide. Thus, a vicious cycle continues. It is worth noting that affluent families are more likely to resort to female feticide due to their ability to afford illegal prenatal sex-determination or sex-selective abortion.

It may be noted that sex ratio at birth and child sex ratio are better indicators than sex ratio, as they inform about current practices. Sex ratio at birth is the number of male births per female birth. Global sex ratio at birth is 1 (2021).

Literacy

As defined by the UN, literacy refers to a person's ability to read and write.

Literacy is the single most important factor in a country's social and economic development. Besides raising people's earning potential and living standards, literacy increases their awareness about health issues. Female literacy is particularly important. Educated women are more likely to delay marriage and exert control over their fertility. They are more likely to educate their children, provide them better nutrition, and ensure basic hygiene at home. They can take up a job or vocation and contribute to the family's income.

According to UNICEF, global literacy rates have been on a steady rise, with nearly 90% of youth aged 15–24 years now being literate. Note that school education is not a criterion for literacy.

NOTE

1. China's population is 1.45 billion, and its annual population growth rate is 0.29% (2022).

Section IX

Health Promotion

67 Health Promotion and Health Communication

To improve people's health, certain approaches are commonly used. These approaches and the challenges in their implementation are discussed here.

PROVISION OF MEDICAL SERVICES

When people are sick or injured, they seek treatment from a clinical practitioner, health center, or hospital. To improve access to healthcare, medical services should be provided close to where people live. But this is not always possible. Hospitals, in particular, have high capital and operating costs, and technical expertise is mostly concentrated in cities. With secondary and tertiary level hospitals located mainly in urban areas, large populations in rural and remote areas are deprived of quality medical care.

DISEASE-PREVENTION PROGRAMS

Immunization can help control vaccine-preventable diseases. Provision of safe drinking water and septic tank latrines can reduce waterborne diseases. Elimination of mosquito-breeding sites can control vector-borne diseases. Safe road conditions can reduce accidents. These are all useful interventions, but in low-income settings, cost is a constraint in large-scale implementation of such public health programs.

HEALTH LEGISLATION

Certain legislations safeguard people's health. For example, mandatory use of seat belt and helmet reduces fatalities in road accidents. Advertising of tobacco products and alcohol is prohibited in some countries. Marriage of girls before 18 years of age is unlawful in some countries. Harmful food additives are banned. Here again, there are limitations: Legislation is possible only for a limited number of issues, and compliance remains a challenge.

PROVIDING COMMODITIES

Some organizations provide commodities such as free or subsidized contraceptives, ORS, sanitary pads, spectacles, and medicines to specific communities. But this cannot sustain for long; financial and logistical constraints will eventually come in the way. Misuse of free supplies is another challenge.

HEALTH PROMOTION

Health promotion is the process of enabling people to increase control over, and to improve, their health (WHO).

Recognizing the need to promote public health, in 1986 the WHO organized the first Global Conference on Health Promotion (GCHP) in Ottawa, Canada. Proceedings of the conference, known as the Ottawa Charter for Health Promotion, emphasized the importance of food, shelter,

DOI: 10.4324/9781032644257-76

equity, social justice, and peace as prerequisites for good health. To date, ten GCHPs have been held. The ninth conference, held in Shanghai, China, in 2016, highlighted the importance of healthy cities and health promotion in schools. It also called on member countries to achieve SDGs by 2030. The latest conference was held virtually, in December 2021.

How can people have more control over their health? Increasing their knowledge about what is good for their health can help them make better food choices and adopt healthier practices. For example, people who are aware of the harmful effects of saturated fats are more likely to use unsaturated fats—a healthier option—to cook food.

How can we improve people's knowledge of health problems? Several terms have been used in this context, some of which are explained here.

Health Education

Informally, health education begins at home when children learn the basics of sanitation and nutrition from their parents, siblings, peers, and neighbors. School education also provides some knowledge on health and diseases.

In the context of public health, health education refers to planned interventions with groups of people to improve their knowledge of specific health issues. Both government bodies and NGOs carry out these interventions. It may be noted that health education is not limited to providing information; it goes a step further to develop people's ability to manage their health problems. For example, in a health promotion campaign to educate mothers of young children about the benefits of using ORS in diarrhea, a demonstration of ORS preparation may increase acceptance and encourage its use when necessary.

Information, Education, and Communication

According to some experts, the term *health education* conveys a one-way process akin to classroom teaching. They proposed a new term to highlight a three-step approach to health education: *Information, Education, and Communication (IEC).*

Information:	sensitize people about a health problem
Education:	provide them with detailed information, including how the health problem can be resolved and what are the available remedies
Communication:	organize one-on-one interactions with service providers where people can ask questions and clarify their doubts

For example, if a woman who wants to delay her pregnancy visits a health facility, the healthcare provider can tell her about the available contraceptive methods for both men and women. This is information. The provider can then educate her about the advantages and disadvantages of each available method. This is education. As a final step, the woman and her spouse can be counseled in privacy where they can ask questions and clear their doubts before making a choice. This is communication.

Behavior Change Communication

Some experts were not happy with the term IEC. They argued that the ultimate aim of health education is to induce a positive change in people's behavior in order to improve health outcomes. Thus, they proposed a new term: *Behavior Change Communication (BCC).*

It should be known that the aforementioned terms share the same meaning and are often used interchangeably. In the West, *health communication* has been the most widely used term, and this is the term we have used in this book.

HEALTH COMMUNICATION

Health communication refers to improving people's knowledge, skills, behaviors, and practices around a specific health issue with the ultimate aim of promoting their health.

The process of communication typically has four components: A source of information (sender), a target audience (receiver), a message, and a communication channel. Let us take an example.

To eliminate polio from a country, all children in the country should be immunized on the same day. How can we inform people about an upcoming pulse polio drive? We can make public announcements whereby a person can go around residential areas in a van and broadcast the message through a loudspeaker. In this scenario, the health department is the sender of information, the residents are the receiving audience, the message is about the upcoming pulse polio event, and the public address system (loudspeaker) is the channel of communication.

Approaches to Health Communication

A health communication campaign can be organized for the general public or it can be targeted to a specific group. A campaign to promote basic sanitation and nutrition, for example, would be relevant to the general population, whereas a campaign to improve menstrual hygiene would be better suited for adolescent girls.

Topics for Health Communication

What are some health issues for which communication can be useful? Topics can be selected based on the needs of the target community. The following health topics may be relevant for many communities:

Lifestyle Modification

In view of the increasing burden of noncommunicable diseases (NCDs), educating people about the benefits of physical activity, need for a balanced diet, and adverse effects of tobacco is becoming increasingly important.

Example 1

In the 1950s, public health authorities in the United States were alarmed by a rapid increase in the incidence of coronary heart disease (CHD). At that time, smoking was in trend and was considered a status symbol. In the 1960s, epidemiological studies identified smoking, hypertension, and a high-cholesterol diet as risk factors for CHD. Subsequently, the American Heart Association initiated efforts to control these risk factors and advocated with the government. A nationwide health communication campaign was implemented to educate people about the harms of smoking. This led to a significant decrease in smoking. In the 1970s and 1980s, the National High Blood Pressure Education Program and the National Cholesterol Education Program were introduced. Legislation against smoking in public places followed, with California becoming the first state to ban smoking in restaurants. Since then, there have been clear indications of a decline in mortality rates from CHD in the United States. Health communication played an important role in this achievement, although the contribution of other supportive interventions, such as treatment facilities for hypertension and CHD, cannot be underestimated.

Nutrition

Communities can be educated on the benefits of early and exclusive breastfeeding. To prevent iron-deficiency anemia, families can be encouraged to include fresh vegetables and eggs in their diet. An obesity epidemic is in the making. People, especially in affluent classes, should be educated on the harms of overeating and leading a sedentary lifestyle.

Utilization of Healthcare Services

Targeted campaigns can be organized within communities to increase the utilization of services such as institutional delivery, immunization, and family planning.

Sociocultural Practices

People can be sensitized to the harms of certain sociocultural practices. In 2015, the Government of India launched the "Save the girl child, educate her" program to address the country's distorted sex ratio and the rising incidence of female feticide and infanticide. The campaign raises awareness about gender discrimination and promotes girls' education. Some NGOs are working to discourage the practice of early marriage of girls.

Environment-Related Issues

The role of clean drinking water, food hygiene, basic sanitation, and vector-control measures in preserving health cannot be overemphasized. People need to be educated about these issues. However, a communication campaign will fail to serve its purpose if the targeted community lacks access to the required facilities. For example, it is no use educating people about the importance of clean drinking water if they do not have access to safe water supply or purification methods.

CHANNELS OF COMMUNICATION

Channels of communication refer to methods by which a message can be disseminated to the intended audience. Broadly, there are three channels of communication:

Mass Media

This includes radio, television, Internet, public address systems, banners, hoardings, and print media. Print media includes newspapers, books, posters, flyers, leaflets, and others. Mass media is useful when we want to reach a large audience in a short time. It has high credibility, which means people are more likely to trust the message. But the cost of mass media campaigns can be prohibitive.

Interpersonal Communication (IPC)

This refers to one-on-one communication between clients and healthcare providers. For example, a person with mental anxiety may visit a clinic to meet a counselor in privacy. This gives the client an opportunity to explain his problem, ask questions, and clear his doubts. The service provider can help the client understand the cause of the problem and suggest possible options to manage the problem. However, serving a large population requires a pool of trained service providers. This is often a constraint in low-income settings.

Mid Media

Mid media is used to reach out to smaller groups through activities such as street plays, puppet shows, and group talks. Many health organizations organize group talks in rural communities. In cities and towns, street plays or dramas are performed in university campuses, auditoriums, and open spaces such as markets and bus stops. Information is presented as a story relevant to the local context. For example, college students are educated about gender issues. In villages, mothers of young children can be educated on growth monitoring.

Demonstration

After a street play or group talk about the benefits of using ORS and zinc in diarrhea, the health worker can demonstrate the method to prepare ORS. Demonstration creates interest in the message and may increase its acceptance.

Group Discussion

After an entertaining session on a health topic, the health worker can initiate a discussion and invite the audience to ask questions and clear their doubts. Discussion and debate create interest and can help trigger behavior change.

BARRIERS IN HEALTH COMMUNICATION

Physical Barriers

If a street play attracts a large crowd, people may jostle with one another to watch the performance. This can weaken the message. If the speaker's voice is not audible or clear, the message may be lost. Noise of traffic can also interfere with communication. Campaign designers and planners should take such barriers into account.

Sociocultural and Economic Barriers

The message should be relevant to the local sociocultural and economic contexts. For example, advising extremely poor families to increase their intake of fruits and green vegetables may serve no purpose as they may not be able to afford these items. Instead, they should be informed about affordable local alternatives that can meet their nutritional needs.

In some situations, it may be helpful to involve a few local residents who are familiar with the language, sociocultural practices, and economic conditions of the area. These individuals can be educated on specific health topics and trained to educate others in the village.

SELECTING A COMMUNICATION CHANNEL

Which health communication channel is the most effective? In practice, a combination of different channels has greater impact.

Example 2

To increase men's participation in family planning, a combination of communication channels can be used. Mass media can be used to disseminate information about no-scalpel vasectomy, an effective contraceptive method available to men. Mid media can be used to sensitize men on gender equity and to encourage them to take responsibility for family planning. Health workers can have interpersonal communication with interested clients to provide them with detailed information about the procedure and clarify that the procedure will not affect their sexual performance. They can further inform the clients where and how the procedure can be availed.

Thus, mass media is useful for providing information to a large audience; mid media is useful for addressing sociocultural issues specific to a community; and interpersonal communication can be a powerful tool to induce behavior change.

In addition, word-of-mouth communication plays an important role in the success of a health communication campaign. Every community will have early adopters—people who are willing to try a new product, service, or practice. If they are satisfied, they can be encouraged to tell others about it. Communication by satisfied clients is especially valuable. Of course, care must be taken to protect the privacy and confidentiality of clients, particularly those availing of family planning services.

In traditional settings, personal decisions are often driven by sociocultural practices or family norms. When it comes to family planning, the family matriarch may be the final authority on whether a couple can opt for terminal contraception. She may not allow her son to undergo sterilization. Accordingly, the communication message can be designed to sensitize elders in the community.

In some situations, involving local community leaders can be helpful, as they may have some influence over the people. For example, religious leaders were instrumental in reducing sex-selective feticide in the state of Punjab in India. Muslim clergies helped to promote polio immunization in Nigeria. Similarly, support can be sought from traditional healers, traditional birth attendants, civil societies, and local NGOs.

Timing of a health communication campaign can also have some relevance. For example, people in rural areas are generally busy during the sowing and harvesting seasons. Communication campaigns can be timed accordingly.

EVALUATING THE EFFECTIVENESS OF A HEALTH COMMUNICATION CAMPAIGN

There are many ways to evaluate the effectiveness of a health communication campaign. After a street play, the organizer can pose questions to the audience to know whether they understood the key message or perceived the play only as entertainment. Similarly, people passing by a billboard in a hospital complex can be asked what they saw and whether they received any message.

If a campaign to promote men's participation in family planning leads to an increase in uptake of no-scalpel vasectomy, we can conclude that the campaign was effective. Similarly, a drive to promote the use of ORS and zinc in diarrhea can be considered successful if there is an increase in the sale of these products in the area. Often, a combination of methods is used to determine the effectiveness of a communication campaign.

Section X

Other Topics of Public Health

68 Health of the Elderly

Older people are at a higher risk of sickness or death. At what age should we consider a person old? Although some people experience reduced mobility in their sixties, many remain physically fit and self-sufficient well into their nineties. Retirement age is generally set at 60 or 65 years, and retired people are considered "senior citizens"; however, this may not be an accurate criterion for old age.

Geriatrics is a discipline that focuses on understanding the aging process and addressing health problems of the elderly.

MAGNITUDE OF THE PROBLEM

Currently, the elderly population accounts for 13%–14% of the global population, but it is growing at a faster rate than the general population. This is known as demographic aging. Increased life expectancy is one of the contributors to this phenomenon. Estimates show that by 2030, one in six people will be 60 years or older. Those aged 80 years or above are expected to triple by 2050. The process of demographic aging first started in high-income countries, such as Japan, where 30% of the population is now over 60 years old. In the coming years, low- and middle-income countries will see the greatest shifts in this regard. There is a concern that the additional years gained by humankind are generally spent in poor health.

The elderly population is often seen as a burden on society and the country, but the real problem is the lack of dedicated healthcare facilities and social support for this group. This creates challenges not only for the elderly but also for their families and the country's healthcare system.

THE AGING PROCESS

The following factors likely influence the aging process:

- Genetics: Characteristics with which one is born
- Nutrition: Quality of one's diet, particularly in the early stages of life
- Lifestyle: Level of physical activity and habits such as smoking or excessive alcohol consumption
- Environment: Whether one maintains basic hygiene, has access to clean water and food, and lives in clean air

The aging process eventually affects every organ of the body, but the order in which bodily functions or organs are impaired differs for people. Some people may develop cataract first, others may experience knee disability, yet others may get cardiac issues, and so on. It is sometimes challenging for clinicians to differentiate between the pathological changes caused by diseases and the physiological changes associated with aging.

HEALTH PROBLEMS ASSOCIATED WITH AGING

Common health problems of old age and ways to manage them are explained here.

DOI: 10.4324/9781032644257-78

Dentures

Tooth decay is a common issue of old age that may lead to removal of some or all teeth. When only a few teeth are removed and the jawbone is still strong, tooth implants are an option. If all teeth are removed, artificial dentures can be considered. However, our bones tend to shrink as we age, and the jawbone is no exception. This can cause artificial dentures to become loose and unstable. Some elderly people choose to eat without their dentures, but this limits the types of food they can eat. Maintaining good oral hygiene while one's teeth and gums are healthy can delay tooth decay in old age.

Vision

Deterioration of near vision, known as presbyopia, is common in old age. It can be corrected by spectacles. Cataract, another common problem, can be treated by a simple surgery where the eye's natural lens is replaced with an artificial lens called an intraocular lens. Presently, there is no known way to prevent or delay vision defects or cataract.

Hearing

Hearing loss associated with aging is called presbycusis. Nearly one-third of people over the age of 65 experience some hearing loss. Presbycusis is a slow process that affects both ears. It can be sensorineural or conductive. Sensorineural hearing loss is caused by damage to the inner ear or auditory nerve. It is permanent. Conductive hearing loss, caused by wax buildup or a damaged eardrum, is treatable. Prolonged exposure to loud noises is a common cause of hearing loss. Hearing aids or cochlear implants can be helpful in some cases.

Muscles

Age-related weakening and wasting of muscles affect a person's capacity to work. As the problem progresses, even walking or doing daily chores may become difficult. Reduced hand or foot grip increases the risk of falls and injuries. Regular physical exercise and a nutritious diet in younger years might help delay this process.

Skeletal System

Bone density reduces with advancing age. Some elderlies develop osteoporosis, which increases their risk of fractures. Spontaneous fractures can occur. Bone loss is more pronounced in women due to reduced levels of female sex hormones. A calcium-rich diet, regular physical activity, and exposure to sunlight can help maintain calcium levels in the body. Vitamin D and calcium supplements are known to reduce the risk of fractures in elderly.

Risk of arthritis also increases with age. Peripheral joints, knee joints, hip joints, and spine are more commonly affected. Physical exercise, regular joint movement, and weight control can be beneficial. In severe disability of knee or hip, joint replacement surgery may improve quality of life.

Endocrinal System

Risk of diabetes increases with age, but diabetes can usually be managed by a combination of exercise, weight control, dietary changes, and medicines.

Digestive System

Age-related changes decrease motility of intestines and their ability to digest and absorb food. This causes loss of appetite and constipation. Consuming more roughage can help reduce constipation. In persistent constipation, laxatives, anal suppository, or enema can be considered. Rarely, constipation can become severe and lead to fecal impaction, which may require digital removal.

Cardiovascular System

With aging, there is reduced tolerance to exercise. Postural hypotension can occur, leading to blackouts. Risk of atrial fibrillation, hypertension, cardiovascular accident, and heart failure increases with age. Regular physical activity can lower the risk of cardiovascular ailments. Blood pressure should be managed to reduce the risk of heart attack and stroke. This can be done by a combination of exercise, diet control, and medication.

Respiratory System

Aging leads to a reduction in vital capacity of lungs and peak expiratory flow. This increases the risk of pneumonia and other infections. Breathing exercises and physical activity can help maintain well-being of the respiratory system. Avoiding crowded places and maintaining distance from potentially infected people can help prevent respiratory infections. In Western countries, older adults receive vaccination against influenza virus once a year.

Nervous System

Alzheimer's disease, the most common form of dementia, is primarily an ailment of old age. Inability to remember new information is a key characteristic of this condition. Short-term memory loss is particularly obvious. Other symptoms include difficulty in performing purposeful actions (apraxia), difficulty in speaking or understanding language (aphasia), and denial of the disease (anosognosia). Depression is common. Some medicines are known to slow the progression of Alzheimer's disease.

Sleep disturbances, anxiety, and impaired balance and coordination are common in old age.

Genito-Urinary System

In older men, benign hypertrophy of prostate is common. It leads to difficulty in urination or inability to fully evacuate bladder. Medicines are helpful in initial stages. Intractable cases may need surgery to remove prostrate.

In some older women, weakening of sphincter muscles can lead to urinary incontinence. Effective medicines are available to treat this condition. Exercises to strengthen urinary sphincter and timed toileting can be helpful. Use of diapers may be necessary in some cases.

Filtration by kidneys reduces with age, increasing the risk of fluid and electrolyte imbalances. Erectile dysfunction and reduced libido are common in old age.

Cancer

Risk of some types of cancer increases with age. Prolonged breastfeeding, avoiding tobacco, and avoiding multiple sex partners may each reduce the risk of certain cancers.

Frailty

The body's capacity to withstand stress diminishes with age, and even a minor illness or a drug reaction can lead to a serious problem such as organ failure.

Multimorbidity

Presence of multiple diseases or disabilities is common in old age. The increased use of medicines raises the risk of drug interactions or drug reactions.

SOCIAL SECURITY ISSUES

In low-income countries, due to the absence of social security benefits such as pension or medical insurance, many elderlies face financial difficulties. Reduced mobility increases their dependence on others. Those with disabilities may need assistance with feeding or using the toilet. Some elderlies need constant medical care. Loneliness and isolation can affect their psychological health.

The need is to educate people about the importance of social security. They should be encouraged to save for old age, invest in pension plans, and purchase health insurance. The traditional culture of families caring for their elderly should be promoted. Care homes for elderly citizens who are destitute or lack family support are the need of the hour.

69 Mental Health
A Public Health Concern

Mental health is a state of positive mental well-being. People with good mental health can think, feel, act, learn, and work well. They can relate to others, make sound choices, realize their abilities, cope with life's stresses, and contribute to their community. Thus, mental health is much more than the mere absence of mental illness.

Mental health disorders include disturbances in mood, emotions, perception, cognition, or memory. Emotions are feelings, such as joy, sorrow, anxiety, fear, love, and hate. Perception is our ability to observe, listen, and be aware of our surroundings. Cognition pertains to mental processes that help us understand things through our senses and experiences. Learning is a cognitive process.

BURDEN OF MENTAL HEALTH DISORDERS

Mental illness is one of the most prevalent health problems globally, affecting over 10% of the world's population. According to the WHO, psychiatric, neurological, and substance abuse disorders cause the highest loss of productive years. The increasing prevalence of mental health disorders in developing countries is a cause of concern, where conditions like depression, anxiety disorders, adjustment disorders, and substance use disorders have become more common. Severe mental health disorders, although less common, can lead to premature death, reducing life expectancy by as much as 20 years in some cases. Suicide is the fourth leading cause of death in the 15–29 age group.

DETERMINANTS OF MENTAL HEALTH

Our mental health can be influenced by biological factors, such as genetics, or by individual factors such as emotional skills, interpersonal relationships, substance use, chronic physical illness, or poor education. Social or environmental factors, such as poverty, unemployment, stressful work conditions, violence, inequality, social exclusion, human rights violations, and rapid urbanization, also contribute to mental health disorders. In children, harsh parenting, punishment, and bullying are important risk factors. Mental illness in childhood can be particularly detrimental.

Nutritional deficiencies during early childhood can lead to physical or cognitive impairments that are mostly irreversible. Children born to iodine-deficient mothers may have intellectual disabilities. These conditions are preventable and should get priority attention in public health initiatives.

Personal development, family bonding, safe neighborhoods, community cohesion, and education about mental health can enhance people's resilience to mental illness.

PUBLIC HEALTH CONCERN

Although mental illness is one of the most prevalent health problems globally, most of the affected people suffer from less severe conditions, such as adjustment disorder or anxiety disorder. Effective treatments are available for these conditions. However, many people associate the term *mental illness* with a serious mental disorder or madness, which are relatively rare. The stigma and discrimination surrounding mental illness prevent people from seeking treatment. In underdeveloped countries, up to three-fourths of cases go untreated. The historical separation of mental health

DOI: 10.4324/9781032644257-79

hospitals from general hospitals adds to the problem. There is no doubt that some mental health disorders need specialized care in a psychiatric hospital, but many can be treated in a general hospital or clinic. The traditional distinction between mental and physical illness must fade.

A key public health challenge is to reduce the stigma around mental health. The need is to create a social environment where people with mental illness feel comfortable asking for help. Equally, healthcare providers should be trained to provide competent and empathetic care to patients. In view of the social stigma associated with mental health, the current practice is to use the term *psychiatric disorder* and avoid terms such as *mental disease.*

COMMON PSYCHIATRIC DISORDERS

Anxiety Disorders

Anxiety disorders are the most common type of psychiatric disorders. We experience anxiety as a physiological response to certain situations, such as before addressing an audience or making an important decision. While this is a natural response to difficult situations, exaggerated anxiety can interfere with our ability to function. It can cause fear, poor concentration, or uneasiness. It can trigger palpitations or breathlessness.

Anxiety can be transient or persistent, and it may be limited to specific situations. Women are more commonly affected than men. A combination of psychological support and medication is generally helpful in managing this condition.

Panic disorder is an anxiety disorder marked by recurrent episodes of severe anxiety, which can range from several attacks a day to a few attacks a year. Overbreathing, palpitations, chest pain, and blackout are common symptoms. Experiencing a panic attack in public can be embarrassing, and it may be risky during travel. Reassurance, psychological support, and medicines are helpful in managing this condition.

Phobia is an anxiety disorder marked by an excessive fear of a particular object or situation. For example, claustrophobia is a fear of confined spaces, such as a crowded bus or elevator, and aerophobia is fear of flying. Therapy and medicines are helpful in overcoming phobias and improving quality of life.

Obsessive Compulsive Disorder (OCD)

This condition involves recurring unwanted thoughts that may lead to repeated actions, such as washing one's hands even when they are clean or repeatedly checking the door to see if it is locked. These actions are done in an attempt to ease the anxiety induced by compulsive thoughts. Unlike anxiety disorders, OCD is equally common in men and women. Effective medicines are available to treat this condition.

Adjustment Disorders

A person with an adjustment disorder finds it difficult to adjust to a new life event, such as marriage, relocation, a new job, or loss of spouse. Symptoms include sadness, anger, tearfulness, a sense of futility, and sleep disturbances, but their manifestation is generally not severe and often goes unreported. Psychological support can help the affected person cope with life changes. Medication is not required in most cases.

Eating Disorders

An eating disorder is marked by abnormal eating behavior. Anorexia nervosa and bulimia nervosa are the most common eating disorders, with women accounting for 90% of cases.

Anorexia Nervosa

This condition is marked by significant weight loss due to food avoidance, which is often accompanied by excessive exercise, self-induced vomiting, or purging by use of laxatives. Despite losing weight, the patient feels overweight. Extreme starvation eventually affects all body organs. In women, menstruation may stop. Heart and skeletal system may show abnormalities.

Bulimia Nervosa

In this condition, the patient has normal body weight but has a morbid fear of fatness. Recurring episodes of binge eating are followed by compensatory behavior, such as self-induced vomiting. Bulimia is more common than anorexia.

Alcoholism

Some people may have a genetic predisposition to alcohol dependence. That means they have a natural tendency for alcohol addiction. Those with anxiety or depression are at a higher risk of alcohol dependence.

Excessive consumption of alcohol can lead to low mood, a known effect of alcoholism. Long-term effects include hypertension, peripheral neuropathy, fatty changes in liver, cirrhosis, cardiomyopathy, and depression. Alcoholism also leads to social problems, such as absenteeism from work, marital discord, financial difficulties, violence, traffic offenses, or child abuse.

Psychological support and medicines are helpful in overcoming alcohol dependence, although relapse is common. Stopping alcohol intake may lead to alcohol withdrawal syndrome, with symptoms such as tremors, sweating, agitation, and tachycardia (fast heartbeat). These symptoms need to be managed.

Depression

Depression is a common psychiatric disorder that affects nearly 5% of adults worldwide. It is a mood disorder marked by a persistent sense of sadness and a lack of interest or pleasure in activities that were previously considered rewarding or enjoyable. Anhedonia, the inability to experience pleasure, is common. Depression can cause low self-esteem, poor concentration, fatigue, sleep disturbances, loss of appetite, and a desire to cry. There can be both mental and physical afflictions, affecting one's ability to function and lead a productive life. Some people with depression may cause self-harm. Some may die by suicide. A significant proportion of global suicides occur in low- and middle-income countries.

Causes of depression are complex and include biological, psychological, and social factors. When depression starts early in life, genetic factors may have a greater role. Adversity in life, loss of a loved one, unemployment, or emotional deprivation can potentiate the condition. Psychological support and medicines are often helpful, but relapse occurs in nearly half the cases.

Bipolar disorder is a mood disorder that causes alternating periods of low and elevated mood. Post-treatment relapse rate is high.

Schizophrenia

Schizophrenia is a severe mental illness characterized by symptoms such as delusions, hallucinations, disordered thinking, and gradual social withdrawal. Delusion is a false belief, such as believing that one has special powers. Hallucination is false perception, such as hearing voices that do not exist. Hallucinations are mainly auditory, but they can be visual. The person may believe that someone else controls his thoughts and actions, or that he has an unusual ability to control the outside world. Speech is disorganized, with a lack of association between ideas and abrupt shifts between topics (flight of ideas). Attention is impaired, and there is insensitivity to the needs of others. There is risk of violence or suicide.

Schizophrenia generally begins before the age of 25 years and is more common in men. History of schizophrenia in a parent is a risk factor. Most people with schizophrenia are unable to live or work independently.

Brain imaging shows structural abnormalities, including a 3% reduction in brain size. Treatment may require hospitalization. Antipsychotic drugs are helpful, and one in three patients recover. Relapse occurs in one-third of patients, and in one-third the condition becomes chronic.

Psychiatric Disorders in Children and Adolescents

The human brain undergoes rapid development during childhood and adolescence. The cognitive and social-emotional skills we acquire during these phases of life shape our mental well-being as adults. Worldwide, 10% of children and adolescents experience psychiatric disorders. Early negative experiences, such as violence, poverty, or bullying at home or school, increase the risk of behavioral disorders, anxiety, and depression in children and young adults.

Psychiatric and Cognitive Conditions of Old Age

Neurocognitive disorders, phobias, and depression are common in old age.

Dementia

It is a neurocognitive disorder marked by a loss of previously acquired intellectual capabilities. People with dementia may struggle to do basic calculations or understand simple concepts. Cognitive functions, such as the ability to think and reach a conclusion, are impaired. Personality is distorted—the person may behave like a child. Memory loss is apparent—the person may not recognize family members or familiar places. Restlessness and depression may coexist.

Alzheimer's disease is a common form of dementia associated with old age.

Postpartum Blues

After giving birth, some women experience irritability, tearfulness, and labile mood. This likely happens due to the hormonal and physiological changes associated with childbirth and generally resolves on its own in a few weeks. However, severe postpartum depression requires medical treatment.

EPILEPSY

Epilepsy is the most common chronic disorder of the brain. It affects all age groups, with nearly 80% of cases seen in low- and middle-income countries. Risk of premature death is high. Besides affecting health and quality of life, epilepsy has high economic implications due to loss of productivity and high treatment expenses. People with epilepsy face social stigma, discrimination, and human rights violations.

With proper diagnosis and treatment, most epilepsy patients can remain seizure-free. However, shortage of trained health workers and medicines is a major bottleneck in epilepsy treatment in low-income countries. The need is to integrate epilepsy treatment with primary healthcare by training nonspecialist providers and ensuring availability of medicines at primary health facilities. Nearly one-fourth of epilepsy cases can be prevented by averting perinatal injuries, central nervous system infections, brain trauma, and stroke.

ROLE OF COMMUNITY AWARENESS

Increasing community awareness can reduce the stigma and misconceptions around mental illness. People need to be educated that, just like physical ailments, psychiatric disorders can be treated effectively with timely medical care.

70 Occupational Health Hazards

People in occupations such as mining, construction, manufacturing, and healthcare are exposed to certain health risks associated with their work environment.

Occupational health deals with occupation-related health hazards—how they can be prevented or minimized to ensure health and safety of workers.

Lung diseases are the most common occupational health hazards, and they have serious consequences. Some common occupational lung diseases are discussed here.

PNEUMOCONIOSIS

Pneumoconiosis is a group of diseases caused by inhalation of inorganic dust. Dust particles of coal, silica, and asbestos cause fibrosis of lung tissue. Particles of beryllium, a metal used in fluorescent lamps, electronics, and aerospace engineering, cause granulomatous changes in lungs. Interestingly, dust particles of iron, barium, and tin generally remain inert in the body.

In pneumoconiosis, it is the reaction of host tissues to dust particles that causes harm. Coal workers' pneumoconiosis, silicosis, and asbestosis are the three most common types of pneumoconiosis.

Coal Workers' Pneumoconiosis

China, India, Indonesia, and the USA are the world's major coal-producing countries. Extraction, transportation, and processing of coal release fine coal dust into the air, posing a serious health hazard for miners. When inhaled, these particles reach alveoli, where they are engulfed by macrophages. Macrophages aggregate to form macules. Fibroblasts are stimulated and they proliferate resulting in fibrosis of lung tissue. X-ray shows scattered discrete fibrotic nodules. Most patients are asymptomatic up to this stage. Terminating exposure to coal dust can stop further damage to lung tissue. However, if exposure continues, the condition can progress to progressive massive fibrosis (PMF). In PMF, the nodules enlarge and may cavitate. Symptoms such as cough, breathlessness, and black sputum start to appear. X-ray chest may resemble TB or lung cancer. PMF is irreversible. Even if exposure is stopped, lung pathology continues to progress. In extreme cases, it culminates in respiratory failure or right ventricular failure.

Coexistence of rheumatoid arthritis with pneumoconiosis is known as Caplan's syndrome.

Silicosis

Workers engaged in cutting, grinding, sanding, or polishing of stone and marble are exposed to crystalline silica. Inhaling silica dust over a long period causes silicosis, commonly known as grinder's disease. In most cases, the condition progresses insidiously, and symptoms can take 10–20 years to emerge. In others, it progresses rapidly and symptoms appear within a year. Like coal workers' pneumoconiosis, silicosis can progress to PMF.

Patients with silicosis are at a higher risk of contracting TB. Risk of chronic obstructive pulmonary disease (COPD) and lung cancer is also high.

DOI: 10.4324/9781032644257-80

Asbestosis

As stated in the chapter "Water Pollution and Treatment," asbestos is a naturally occurring mineral with thin fibers. Due to its resistance to heat, fire, water, and various chemicals, it is extensively used in industrial production. Exposure to asbestos fibers can cause pulmonary and pleural diseases. Long-term exposure causes fibrosis. Around 40% of asbestosis patients who smoke develop lung cancer.

HYPERSENSITIVITY PNEUMONITIS

Hypersensitivity pneumonitis, also known as extrinsic allergic alveolitis or interstitial lung disease, is caused by inhalation of organic dust. Recall that pneumoconiosis is caused by inhalation of inorganic dust.

Studies suggest that it is mainly the fungi present in organic dust particles that trigger an allergic reaction in host tissues. Repeated exposure leads to hypersensitivity pneumonitis, a condition characterized by a diffuse immune complex reaction in alveoli and bronchioles. IgG antibodies can be detected in serum. Flu-like symptoms—rhinitis, body ache, headache—are followed by attacks of acute asthma marked by shortness of breath and wheezing. Chronic cases end up in fibrosis, leading to reduced lung capacity. A notable feature of hypersensitivity pneumonitis is that it is more common in nonsmokers than smokers. The reason for this is not known.

Farmer's lung, byssinosis, bagassosis, bird fancier's lung, and saxophone lung are types of hypersensitivity pneumonitis.

Farmer's Lung

It is caused by inhalation of dust or fungi present in agricultural products such as moldy hay, straw, grain, animal feed, compost, and fertilizers. People with a history of allergy are commonly affected. In a small percentage of cases, prolonged exposure leads to fibrosis, known as chronic farmer's disease.

Byssinosis

This condition affects cotton mill workers who are exposed to dry leaves and debris of the cotton plant. It does not occur in industries that use processed forms of cotton, such as thread or fabric. Classically, asthma-like symptoms—cough, tightness in chest, breathlessness—appear on the first day of work. Due to this, byssinosis is also called Monday fever. The symptoms disappear or reduce in a few days, giving a false sense of assurance that the disease is regressing. In reality, the pathology continues to progress. Health can be regained at this stage by terminating exposure. If exposure continues, lung capacity declines, resulting in permanent damage similar to COPD.

Bagassosis

This is a rare disease caused by inhalation of bagasse contaminated by fungi or other microorganisms. Bagasse is the fibrous residue that remains after sugarcane is crushed to extract its juice. Inhaling contaminated bagasse causes inflammation of lung tissues, which may result in widespread bronchoconstriction similar to other types of extrinsic allergic alveolitis. Discontinuing exposure relieves symptoms. Complete resolution is also possible.

OTHER OCCUPATIONAL HAZARDS

Noise Pollution

Long-term exposure to the noise prevalent in some industries causes hearing loss in workers.

Vibration

Use of heavy drill machines and hammers exposes workers to vibrations, causing vasoconstriction that may lead to white finger syndrome. Nerves get damaged. Clinical picture is similar to Raynaud's phenomenon.

Accidents and Injuries

Some occupations carry a particularly high risk of accidents and injuries. Mine workers face a constant threat of roof collapse, buildup of toxic gases, fire, explosions, high temperatures, or flooding. In manufacturing operations, machine tools can cause injury or amputation. Construction workers are at risk of falling from height. Agriculture workers face dangers from farm machinery, snakebite, and insect stings. They are exposed to pesticides and chemical fertilizers. Transport workers are at risk of injury or death from road accidents. They are away from their families for long periods, which increases their risk of alcohol misuse, drug use, and unsafe sex. Sanitation workers are susceptible to infection or injury when handling waste. In low-income countries, manual scavengers who clean gutters or pipes are at risk of poisoning from toxic sewer gases. They can get trapped in a gutter.

Cancer

Exposure to certain industrial chemicals increases the risk of some forms of cancer. Lung cancer, skin cancer, bladder cancer, and leukemia are common cancers resulting from occupational exposure.

Dermatitis

Exposure to extreme temperatures, chemicals, or biological agents used in some industries can cause dermatitis.

Mental Health Afflictions

Long working hours, poor work-life balance, long commute times, workplace harassment, or lack of recognition can affect the mental well-being of workers.

PREVENTING OCCUPATIONAL HAZARDS

Workplace Safety

In mines, the use of technology can help maintain dust levels within prescribed limits. For example, water sprinkling and wet drilling reduce liberation of dust. In factories, an efficient exhaust system, proper ventilation, and regular housekeeping can minimize indoor dust. Relocating dust-producing activities to open spaces can further reduce exposure. Where exposure is unavoidable, miners and factory workers can use specialized respirators for protection.

Just as airbags in automobiles provide some safety in accidents, use of protective devices in factories can reduce the risk of injury from heavy machines and equipment.

Medical Examination

People with a history of allergy or asthma should avoid working in industries where they may be exposed to organic dust. Preplacement medical examination can help exclude such individuals.

Workers in high-risk industries should be provided regular medical checkups. In pneumoconiosis, for example, symptoms and X-ray chest can inform the stage of the disease. Early diagnosis and cessation of exposure can prevent the disease from advancing. Affected workers should be rehabilitated.

Notification

In many countries, employers are obligated by law to report certain occupational diseases and injuries to health authorities.

Surveillance

In some developed countries, a multidisciplinary team conducts inspections in mines, factories, and other commercial establishments to study work-related hazards. Employees are interviewed to identify factors that may be negatively affecting their health. Air samples are lifted to measure pollution levels, and dust or chemicals are tested for potential harm to workers' health. Equipment and infrastructure are inspected to assess the risk of accident or injury.

Information and Training

Employers, managers, and workers should be educated about the occupational hazards specific to their industry. They should be provided training on protective measures.

The International Labour Organization (ILO) formulates international labor standards to promote health and safety at work. According to ILO reports, several million people die from occupational hazards each year, and many more experience ill health. Besides causing suffering to workers and their families, occupational health hazards contribute to a loss of 4% in global GDP.

71 Occupational Safety of Healthcare Workers

Healthcare workers, particularly those employed in hospitals, face many occupational hazards. Common hazards in hospitals and related safety measures are explained here.

INFECTIOUS DISEASES

Nurses, doctors, and other hospital staff who work closely with patients are at high risk of contracting infections. To mitigate the transmission of contagious diseases like TB, COVID-19, chickenpox, and Ebola, patients are placed in isolation, preferably in a room with negative air pressure, as that helps to contain airborne pathogens. Healthcare providers use personal protective equipment (PPE) when tending to these patients. In some cases, providers may need respirators for additional protection. Washing hands is important both before and after examining a patient.

SHARPS INJURIES

Nurses and doctors can get needle-prick injuries when handling hypodermic needles. A study found that over 50% of nurses sustain a needle injury at some time in their career. Since needle injuries are treatable, they were not given much attention in the past. But after the HIV epidemic, they are taken seriously. As most needle-related injuries occur during the recapping process, recapping of needles should be avoided. Used needles should be disposed of in puncture-proof containers.

Sanitation workers who handle medical waste can sustain injuries from sharps. They should be provided puncture-resistant utility gloves as regular surgical gloves do not protect from sharps.

CONFLICTS

Hospitals in many settings are prone to conflicts. When a patient does not improve or dies, his family members may become agitated. Some may resort to violence against service providers. Such incidents are increasing in recent times. Healthcare providers can reduce chances of conflict by taking steps to improve patient satisfaction, such as attending to patients promptly, expressing genuine concern for their problems, and keeping family members informed about the patient's condition.

RADIATION

Radiographers, radiologists, and surgeons who use real-time X-ray imaging are exposed to harmful radiation. Lead shield provides protection against radiation.

FATIGUE

Emergency rooms frequently receive an influx of critically ill patients, increasing the pressure on healthcare providers. Long working hours with limited breaks for rest and meals lead to physical exhaustion. In most situations, the problem can be resolved by ensuring that a sufficient number of staff members are available for patient care.

DOI: 10.4324/9781032644257-81

Healthcare providers can suffer psychological setbacks when they are unable to save a patient's life. An open discussion about the incident, including the factors that led to it and whether it could have been prevented, can be helpful.

GUIDELINES FOR SAFETY OF HEALTHCARE WORKERS

The WHO and the ILO jointly framed guidelines for occupational safety of healthcare workers. Some of the recommendations are given below.

- Designate nodal persons at national and workplace levels to oversee health and safety of healthcare workers.
- Identify and address hazardous working conditions to eliminate or minimize risks.
- Promote hand hygiene and ensure proper management and safe disposal of hazardous hospital waste, disinfectants, and sterilants.
- Provide preservice and periodic immunization to healthcare workers against hepatitis B and other vaccine-preventable diseases.
- Encourage incident reporting and a blame-free environment.
- Facilitate healthcare workers' access to diagnosis, treatment, and care for TB, HIV, hepatitis B, and hepatitis C.
- Ensure compensation for job-related disabilities.
- Promote training and research on occupational safety of healthcare workers.

72 Disaster Management

A disaster is an event that disrupts the normal functioning of a community on a scale that is beyond the community's capacity to manage independently, necessitating external assistance.

A disaster can cause injuries, displacement, loss of life, and closure of schools and businesses. It can damage infrastructure, disrupt transport and communication, destroy crops, and sweep away livestock. Besides loss of life and economic damage, ecological imbalances occur due to uprooting of trees and displacement of land. Stagnant water, undisposed dead bodies, poor hygiene conditions, and scarcity of safe drinking water can lead to spread of diseases.

TYPES OF DISASTERS

Disasters can be natural or they can be caused by human activities. Natural disasters include:

- *Geological events:* Flood, cyclone, tornado, tsunami, drought, landslide, wildfire, earthquake, volcanic eruption, etc.
- *Biological events:* Outbreaks of COVID-19, SARS, H1N1, H5N1, Ebola, and cholera; pest infestations; etc.

Disasters caused by human activities include:

- *Technological events:* Air pollution, water or food contamination, traffic collision, fire, industrial accident, radiation accident, etc.
- *Societal events:* Mass shooting, bomb explosion, conflict, war

Some natural disasters, such as earthquakes, tsunamis, and landslides, occur without warning. Others, such as floods and cyclones, can be predicted hours or days in advance.

Natural Disasters

Earthquake

An earthquake is caused by continuous geological movements occurring inside the earth. There is no reliable method to predict an earthquake, except when premonitory shocks precede the main event. Sudden fluctuations in the water level of wells can be an indication. Impact of an earthquake depends on its intensity. High-intensity earthquakes cause greater mortality due to falling objects. Risk of harm is highest inside buildings, especially at night when people are sleeping. Fractures of pelvis, thorax, and spine are more common at night. Injuries of arms, legs, and skull are seen more in daytime.

Flood

Most floods can be predicted, but some floods occur suddenly due to intense rainfall (known as flash floods) or dam collapse. Generally, floods cause high mortality.

Tsunami

A tsunami is a series of extraordinarily large waves produced by a sudden displacement of the ocean floor due to an earthquake. A "wall" of water several meters high crashes down on the coast or several kilometers inland. Like earthquakes, tsunamis cannot be predicted. Most deaths are caused by drowning. Traumatic injuries can occur.

DOI: 10.4324/9781032644257-82

Tropical Cyclone (Also Called a Hurricane or Typhoon)

Cyclones tend to be seasonal, originating over tropical seas toward the end of summer. They have a calm center, measuring 20–150 km in diameter, within which high-speed winds move clockwise in the southern hemisphere and counterclockwise in the northern hemisphere. Cyclones move westward and die out upon reaching colder areas. There can be prolonged rainfall. Meteorologists can forecast a cyclone's intensity and path with precision. Destruction is usually caused by high-speed winds. Airborne debris can cause injuries and fractures. Mortality is usually not high unless tidal waves occur.

Drought and Famine

A drought is a long period of dry weather resulting from a combination of factors such as poor rainfall, soil erosion, and overuse of water resources due to an increase in human or animal population. A drought can lead to a famine, which can cause significant mortality. Protein-energy malnutrition, vitamin A deficiency leading to xerophthalmia, and child blindness can occur. Measles, respiratory infections, and diarrhea with dehydration can cause massive infant mortality.

Landslide

In hilly areas, heavy rainfall can dislodge large parts of land, causing a landslide. Landslides block roads and damage property. They may cause fatalities. Deforestation and unplanned construction in hilly areas have contributed to the increasing number of landslides in many countries.

PRECONCEIVED NOTIONS ABOUT DISASTERS

Certain preconceptions exist about human behavior during a disaster, such as: People panic or become numb or stupefied; most people flee, not caring about others; many resort to antisocial behavior and looting.

These notions are unfounded. Panic in the aftermath of a disaster is generally short-lived. Instead of fleeing, most people choose to remain in the affected area and take steps to protect themselves and their families. Some show exemplary courage and risk their lives to save others. Conflicts and class differences are replaced by a sense of solidarity that was missing earlier. Antisocial behavior is generally perpetrated by outsiders. The local community likes to participate in rescue operations, and with timely external assistance, they can act quickly and more efficiently.

DISASTER MANAGEMENT CYCLE

The disaster management cycle consists of five stages: prevention, preparedness, mitigation, response, and recovery. These are explained here.

Prevention

Not all disasters can be prevented—but some can, if we take timely preventive measures. Fire accidents in buildings are often caused by short circuits, which can be prevented by using high-quality electrical fittings and ensuring regular maintenance. People living in areas prone to monsoon flooding can be relocated to safer locations before the monsoon arrives. Constructing dams or reservoirs, strengthening river embankments, and planting trees along riverbanks can prevent some floods. Effective intelligence can foil some terror attacks.

Preparedness

When a disaster cannot be prevented, preparedness can reduce its impact. The provision of fire extinguishers in buildings, conducting regular fire drills, and locating fire stations at strategic sites are all part of fire safety preparedness. In hilly areas, heavy earthmovers and cranes are stationed at critical points to respond quickly to landslides. Deployment of security forces in vulnerable areas is part of the preparedness against potential terrorist attacks and other acts of violence. Mock drills are conducted in residential areas to train people on how to respond to a fire or an earthquake; this can save lives.

Hospitals, on their part, should be equipped to manage the sudden influx of patients during a disaster. They should have a comprehensive evacuation plan in place for emergencies like fires.

Mitigation

This includes measures to minimize loss of human life in the aftermath of a disaster. It may be noted that while preparedness comes before a disaster, mitigation comes after the disaster has occurred. The first few hours after a disaster are critical for saving lives. In a mass shooting, many lives can be saved if security personnel and civilians are trained to provide basic life support, control bleeding, and promptly shift casualties to an equipped hospital. In the early stages of a flood, when the water level is still negotiable, quick evacuation can save lives. During an earthquake, people in high-rise buildings can increase their chances of survival by taking cover under a beam or table.

Response

In most cases, local healthcare workers and community members are the first to start rescue work before external assistance arrives. Their key responsibilities are briefly discussed here.

Response of Local Community

Providing information: To alleviate fear and panic, people should be provided information on what they can do to stay safe; where they can find information about their missing family members; and where they can get food, water, blankets, shelter, and other assistance.

Assisting those who are trapped: In a disaster, many people come forward to help others. Volunteer teams work tirelessly to find and reach those who are trapped or isolated. For this, they need tools such as torches, ropes, ladders, and spades.

When people are believed to be trapped under the rubble, rescue workers should avoid walking over it. Rubble should be moved only if doing so will not cause further collapse of the structure. Before professional rescue teams arrive, people can try to reassure those who are trapped by talking to them or by shouting and tapping. If possible, their clothing or belts should be loosened. If airway obstruction is suspected, volunteers can try to clear the mouth and throat with their fingers. In cold weather, blankets should be provided to the survivors.

People with injuries should be moved as little as possible and carefully placed on a stretcher. If a stretcher is not available, one may be improvised. Several people should work together to lift the casualty in coordinated movements, ensuring that the head, neck, and trunk are in alignment. Once transfer to a stretcher is complete, the person should be fastened to the stretcher and moved headfirst.

When it is difficult to reach a trapped person, or if there is risk that the structure might collapse further, extrication is best left to experts such as firefighters or the military.

Setting up a reception area: This is to provide information and facilitate coordination between separated family members. In addition to providing food, water, and blankets, washing facilities may need to be set up.

Response of Local Health Workers

Local health workers should immediately report to their respective health facilities. If a facility has suffered damage, the first step is to assess whether it can still be used or if services should be relocated to a less affected building or a tent.

Receiving injured people: In the first few hours after a disaster, the injured are generally brought to the local health facility. A space should be set up to receive cases and evaluate them for the level of care needed.

Triage: If a health facility receives more cases than it can manage, they may be categorized as follows:

a. Emergency cases in need of intensive care or urgent surgery, such as those with severe external or internal hemorrhage, shock, acute cardiorespiratory insufficiency, or severe burns. These patients must be promptly sent to the nearest well-equipped hospital. Those handling transportation should know which hospitals have the capacity to take such cases.
b. Cases that can wait for a few hours for surgery, such as those with ligatured vascular injury or closed fracture-dislocation
c. Cases that can be managed at the facility. Very critical cases with no chances of survival are included in this category.

Providing first aid: Healthcare workers should be trained in the following first-aid procedures:

- Ligating tourniquet on crush injury and stopping external bleeding
- Providing cardiopulmonary resuscitation (CPR)
- Managing state of shock by administering intravenous fluids
- Safely transporting patients with fracture or dislocation

In addition, they should be able to estimate the additional requirement of medical experts, ambulances, and supplies. They should know from where medicines, equipment, blankets, linen, cleaning supplies, and other resources can be mobilized.

Post-disaster health problems: After the emergency treatment phase is over, new problems may arise. Poor sanitary and living conditions can cause disease outbreaks. Health workers should initiate preventive measures against diarrhea, malaria, malnutrition, and other conditions as necessary. They should educate people on responsible use of available water, safeguarding clean drinking water, proper waste disposal, maintaining cleanliness, proper use of latrines, and safe disposal of dead bodies. In the days following the disaster, some people may experience fatigue, sadness, loss of confidence, passivity, or depression. They need psychological support.

Recovery

Health workers should resume their routine services, including immunization, as soon as possible. To help the community recover from the disaster, arrangements should be made for tentage, potable water, food, toilets, and other essentials. Vector-control measures may be needed.

For long-term rehabilitation, livelihood opportunities and children's education need to be organized. Basic infrastructure, such as roads, electricity, mobile networks, schools, shops, and factories, needs to be restored. Sometimes, it can take years to stabilize a disaster-stricken area.

AGENCIES THAT SUPPORT DISASTER MANAGEMENT

Internationally, the WHO, UNICEF, World Food Program (WFP), the FAO, and Office for the Coordination of Humanitarian Affairs (OCHA) provide assistance to countries during disasters.

73 Emerging Diseases

EBOLA VIRUS DISEASE

Ebola Virus Disease (EVD) is a rare but severe illness that affects primates. It was first identified in 1976 near the Ebola River in the Democratic Republic of the Congo. Between 2014 and 2016, many African countries experienced EVD outbreaks.

The African bat is the natural reservoir for Ebola virus. Humans get the infection from contact with infected wild animals. Human-to-human transmission occurs through direct contact with the blood or body fluids of an infected person. The virus gains entry into the body through injuries or breakage in the skin or mucosa. Incubation period of EVD is 2–21 days, and case fatality rate is 25%–90% (average is 50%). It is believed that initial EVD outbreaks were caused by the reuse of infected needles in health facilities.

Ebola virus does not transmit by air.

Case Management

Presentation of EVD is similar to that of malaria, dengue, and typhoid. There is sudden onset of fever, headache, body ache, and sore throat. There can be vomiting, diarrhea, skin rash, and impairment of kidney and liver functions. Diagnosis of EVD is confirmed by a nucleic acid test (NAT). Rapid antigen detection test can be used where NAT is not available. Treatment of EVD involves maintaining hydration and providing symptomatic relief. In recent years, monoclonal antibodies have become available as a treatment option.

Among the six known strains of Ebola virus, vaccine is available for only one strain. Two vaccine doses are administered eight weeks apart.

Prevention and Control

Reducing animal-to-human transmission: Risk of transmission can be reduced by avoiding direct contact with wild animals, such as fruit bats, chimpanzees, antelopes, and porcupines; using gloves when handling animals; and avoiding consumption of undercooked animal products.

Reducing human-to-human transmission: Isolating infected individuals; using barriers, such as gloves, face masks, and gowns, when tending to the ill; and diligently practicing hand hygiene can significantly reduce the risk of transmission for healthcare providers.

Contact tracing: Contacts of the infected person are quarantined for 21 days.

Reducing transmission by sexual intercourse: Even after recovery from EVD, the virus can persist in the patient's semen for a long time. To reduce the risk of transmission, it is advisable to use condom for 12 months after symptoms have subsided or until a negative semen test report is received.

Reducing transmission through pregnancy-related fluids: If a pregnant woman gets EVD, the virus persists in the amniotic fluid. Therefore, service providers should use barriers when examining pregnant women and when conducting deliveries.

Safe burial practices: Using barriers during the burial process can reduce the risk of transmission through contact with blood or body fluids of the deceased.

DOI: 10.4324/9781032644257-83

In addition to the above measures, effective laboratory services, surveillance, and health education are crucial in controlling EVD.

SEVERE ACUTE RESPIRATORY SYNDROME (SARS)

SARS is a respiratory illness caused by SARS Coronavirus (SARS-CoV). It was first identified in China in 2003 and later spread to other countries. The disease spreads through saliva droplets and primarily affects adults in the 25–70 age group; rarely, children are affected.

Incubation period of SARS is two to seven days. High fever is generally the first symptom, which may be accompanied by malaise, body ache, and headache. Mild respiratory symptoms may also be present. In three to seven days, the lower respiratory phase begins, causing cough with dyspnea (labored breathing) that may progress to hypoxemia (deficiency of oxygen). Around 10%–20% of cases turn severe and need hospitalization for intubation and mechanical ventilation. Chest X-ray may be normal. White blood cell count decreases in early days; platelet count may also fall.

No specific treatment or vaccine is available for SARS. Treatment is supportive with preventive measures similar to other respiratory infections.

Case fatality rate of SARS is 3%. Since 2004, no SARS cases have been reported in any country.

MIDDLE EAST RESPIRATORY SYNDROME (MERS)

This disease is caused by the Middle East Respiratory Syndrome Coronavirus (MERS-CoV). First identified in Saudi Arabia in 2012, MERS-CoV is primarily a zoonotic virus associated with camels. Human-to-human transmission occurs through droplets during close-range contact.

MERS typically presents with fever, cough, and shortness of breath, with pneumonia being a common complication. Case fatality rate is around 35%, and no specific treatment or vaccine is available. Preventive measures include avoiding direct contact with sick animals, using barriers when handling animals, washing hands before and after touching animals, and avoiding undercooked animal products.

Transmission of MERS-CoV within healthcare facilities has been reported in many countries. As it may not be possible to identify MERS in early stages without testing, healthcare providers should take extra precautions.

CORONAVIRUS DISEASE

Coronavirus disease is an infectious viral disease that was first identified in China in 2019. Based on the history and examination of initial cases, it appeared that the virus came from animal meat sold at a local market. Laboratory tests identified a new virus similar to SARS-CoV. The new variant was named SARS-CoV-2, and the disease was named COVID-19.

SARS-CoV-2 is an enveloped, positive-stranded RNA virus. Its closest RNA sequence is similar to that of the bat coronavirus, so it appears that bats are the primary source of this virus. It is distantly related to MERS virus.

Transmission

Starting with a few cases in Wuhan, China, COVID-19 took the form of an epidemic and later turned pandemic by spreading across continents and infecting millions.

SARS-CoV-2 spreads by air. Transmission occurs mainly through droplets during close contact. There is possibility of long-distance transmission through aerosols, but this is not certain. Transmission through touch is also possible, but it should be rare. Attempts to isolate the virus from air or surface samples of hospitals have only rarely been successful.

Incubation period of COVID-19 is 2–14 days (median is five days). An infected person can start shedding the virus two to three days before onset of symptoms, but infectiousness peaks one day before symptoms appear. On average, people remain contagious for about eight days after the onset of symptoms. A person can be considered noninfectious after three days of being symptom-free, or after ten days from the onset of symptoms.

Spread of a pathogen from person to person in a community is known as community transmission.

Manifestation

COVID-19 can affect anyone. Manifestation can be mild to very severe, even fatal. Most people develop mild-to-moderate respiratory symptoms and recover without any specific treatment. Symptoms may include fever, chills, cough, sore throat, loss of taste or smell, congestion or runny nose, difficulty breathing, fatigue, body ache, headache, nausea, vomiting, and diarrhea.

Some people become seriously ill and need hospitalization. Older adults and those with underlying medical conditions such as obesity, diabetes, COPD, or CVD are at a higher risk of severe illness. Notably, proportion of COVID-19 deaths is higher in people above 65 years of age. Risk of severe illness is also high for people who are immunocompromised, such as cancer patients, those undergoing chemotherapy, organ transplant recipients, people on long-term corticosteroid therapy, or those living with HIV.

Danger signs of COVID-19 illness are as follows:

- Difficulty in breathing
- Blue-colored lips, skin, nails
- Inability to remain awake
- Persistent pain or pressure in chest
- Confusion

Since symptoms of COVID-19 are similar to those of the flu, this can make it difficult for healthcare providers to distinguish between the two. Yet, there are some notable differences. COVID-19 can take longer to produce symptoms, can cause more severe illness, and may be contagious for a longer duration. Specific tests are available to detect the presence of COVID-19 or flu or both.

Diagnosis

COVID-19 is a nationally notifiable disease. Case definition helps in counting the cases. The WHO's case definition for COVID-19 is any of the following:

• Clinical criterion:	acute onset of fever and cough
• Epidemiological criterion:	history of contact with a confirmed or probable case
• Laboratory criterion:	positive test for SARS-CoV-2

People displaying symptoms should be tested immediately. Those with a history of exposure or contact but no symptoms should be tested five days after the day of exposure.

Testing

Two types of tests are mainly used to diagnose COVID-19:

1. Nucleic acid test
2. Antigen test

Nucleic acid tests, such as RT-PCR, detect genetic material of the virus, and they are the most reliable. A positive NAT confirms infection even if the person is asymptomatic and has no history of contact.

After a person tests positive, the virus can remain in their body for up to 90 days. Therefore, repeating NAT during this period has no value. If reinfection is suspected, antigen test can be done.

Antigen tests are rapid tests that can give results in 15–30 minutes, but they are less reliable than NAT. Further, a single negative antigen test does not rule out infection; multiple tests may be required. Repeat testing should be done at least 48 hours apart. A positive antigen test confirms infection if the person has symptoms or history of contact. Self-tests, also called at-home tests, are antigen tests.

Antibody tests are also available, but they are not used for diagnosing active COVID-19 cases, as a positive antibody test means that the person was exposed to the virus in recent past but may have recovered from the infection. It does not tell of an active COVID-19 infection. However, antibody tests are frequently used at community level to assess the spread of infection. This can help public health authorities gauge the situation and plan further interventions.

Treatment

Depending on the patient's condition, acetaminophen, oxygen, and/or steroids may be required. Specific treatments for COVID-19 include the following:

- Antiviral medications, such as Remdesivir Injection. Oral medicines are now available to be taken at home.
- Monoclonal antibodies.

Specific treatment must be initiated within five to seven days of onset of symptoms.

Prevention

Risk of COVID-19 infection can be reduced by wearing a properly fitted mask, maintaining social distance of at least 1 meter, staying at home when feeling unwell, and following cough etiquette (e.g., coughing into flexed elbow).

COVID-19 vaccine can protect against severe illness, hospitalization, and death.

Mutation

Like other viruses, SARS-CoV-2 also undergoes mutations. These mutations impact the virus's transmissibility, as well as its capacity to escape humoral immunity, cause severe disease, or reinfect those previously infected with a different strain. Known variants of SARS-CoV-2 include alpha, beta, delta, gamma, and omicron.

Monitoring

Data is collected through epidemiological surveillance to calculate:

- Incidence rate
- Prevalence
- Hospitalizations
- Death rate

To make it easier to understand and use the collected data, an epidemic curve is prepared depicting number of cases, hospitalizations, and deaths over time. Normally, the complete shape of an epidemic curve becomes clear only after the outbreak has ended.

To predict the potential spread and duration of an outbreak, epidemiologists prepare mathematical models, known as epidemiological models.

Reducing Further Spread

People who test positive for COVID-19 are isolated and advised to take precautions to prevent transmission to others. Health workers talk to the infected persons to trace the chain of infection: When and where they may have contracted the disease and when they may have started spreading it to others. Recent contacts are notified, tested, and advised to self-quarantine to prevent further spread.

The list of people who have contracted a disease is called a line list.

ZIKA VIRUS DISEASE

Zika virus was first detected in 1947 in monkeys in Uganda. In 1952, it was found in humans in Uganda and Tanzania. Outbreaks have occurred in Africa, America, Asia, and the Pacific, with sporadic cases reported in Asia. Eighty-nine countries have reported cases of Zika virus globally (till 2022). Transmission of the disease seems to have declined since 2017.

Zika virus is transmitted by the *Aedes* mosquito, mainly *Aedes aegypti*, but it can also transmit through sexual contact or blood transfusion. Its incubation period is 3–14 days.

Most people infected with Zika virus remain asymptomatic. If symptoms appear, they are generally mild and may include fever, malaise, headache, conjunctivitis, or skin rash. Zika virus disease is especially dangerous in pregnancy as it can cause microcephaly (small fetal head with poorly developed brain) or other congenital malformations (known as Zika syndrome) or stillbirth. In adults and children, Zika virus can cause neurological complications. Treatment is mainly symptomatic.

Prevention

To prevent Zika infection, people should protect themselves from mosquito bites. *Aedes* mosquitoes are most active during daytime and early evenings. Even after symptoms have subsided, Zika virus can persist in semen and vaginal fluid. People who have had the disease or traveled to an area with an active Zika outbreak should use barrier methods during sex. Men should take precautions for six months and women for two months.

MONKEYPOX

Monkeypox is primarily a zoonotic disease found in the rainforests of Central and West Africa. Squirrels, rats, and other animals are natural hosts of monkeypox virus. The first monkeypox outbreak was identified in Congo in 1970. Most of the cases reported since then occurred in the forests or rural areas of Central and West Africa.

Human-to-human transmission of monkeypox occurs through close contact with skin lesions, body fluids, respiratory droplets, or contaminated bedding, among others. The incubation period is 6–13 days.

Monkeypox presents with fever, rashes, and swollen lymph nodes. Skin rash is more apparent on the face and extremities than on trunk. Manifestation of monkeypox resembles that of smallpox. Monkeypox is usually a self-limiting disease, and the person is cured in two to four weeks. Occasionally, it can be severe. Children are at a higher risk of developing severe disease. Its case fatality rate is 3%–6%.

The smallpox vaccine provides some protection from monkeypox. If a person immunized against smallpox does get monkeypox, the infection tends to be less severe. Discontinuation of the smallpox vaccine has led to declining immunity in humans and an increase in monkeypox transmission.

A positive PCR test confirms monkeypox. Material from skin lesions—fluid or crust of the vesicle—is collected for testing.

Treatment of monkeypox is mainly symptomatic. An antiviral agent is approved, but it is not yet widely available. A vaccine against monkeypox virus was developed in 2019. Active surveillance, early identification of cases, and effective contact tracing are key to containing a monkeypox outbreak.

NIPAH VIRUS INFECTION

Nipah virus infection is a zoonotic disease with its natural reservoir in fruit bats. It was first detected in Malaysia in 1999 among pig farmers, followed by Bangladesh in 2001 and then in several Southeast Asian countries.

Transmission

The first outbreak of the Nipah virus infection in Malaysia is believed to have resulted from direct contact with sick pigs or their contaminated tissues. Subsequent outbreaks in Bangladesh and India could have been caused by the consumption of raw date palm juice contaminated with saliva or urine of infected fruit bats. Human-to-human transmission occurs in caregivers through body fluids, secretions, and excretions of infected patients. Healthcare providers are at risk of getting the infection.

Manifestation

In humans, manifestation of a Nipah virus infection can range from mild to severe acute respiratory infection, sometimes leading to fatal encephalitis. The incubation period is around 4–14 days. Case fatality rate has been 40%–75%, which is reducing with improved epidemiological surveillance and clinical management capabilities.

Diagnosis

With nonspecific signs and symptoms, clinical diagnosis of Nipah virus infection is difficult at least in the initial stages. RT-PCR from body fluids and antibody detection with ELISA are the main diagnostic tests.

Treatment

There is no specific treatment for Nipah virus infection. Management is supportive against respiratory and neurological complications.

Prevention

No vaccine is currently available against Nipah virus. Preventive measures include the following:

Reducing risk of bat-to-human transmission: Fruits should be protected from bats and should be thoroughly washed and peeled before consumption. Those with signs of bat bite should be discarded. Fruit juice should be boiled before use.

Reducing risk of transmission from animals to humans: Contact with sick pigs and other animals should be avoided. Gloves should be used while handling animals and animal products.

Reducing risk of human-to-human transmission: Barrier precautions and frequent handwashing should be practiced while caring for sick people. Healthcare workers should particularly practice standard infection-control precautions at all times.

Reducing transmission in pigs: Pigs should be protected against bats. In pig farms, routine bathing of pigs with detergent can be helpful. If pigs develop abnormal behavior or diseases, and if an outbreak is suspected, the farm premises should be quarantined. Depending on the situation, culling of the animals and careful burial or incineration of carcasses might be required. Movement of animals should be banned.

74 International Health

In the fourteenth century, Europe was struck by one of the deadliest plague pandemics in human history. It is believed that the infection originated in China and spread to Europe by ship. In five years, it claimed 25–50 million lives. Back then, ships were the main mode of international transport, but since they were limited in number, many countries were spared from the outbreak. As trade and travel expanded, so did the potential for infectious diseases to spread across regions. HIV spread rapidly from the United States to other regions, devastating many African countries in just two decades. In other countries, large-scale funding and proactive efforts of civil societies helped contain the disease to some extent. More recently, the COVID-19 pandemic is a classic example of a disease that started with a few cases in Wuhan, China, and spread to the entire world in less than a year, infecting tens of millions of people.

In the late nineteenth and early twentieth centuries, London was known as the TB capital of the world. As of today, India bears the highest burden of TB. The causative pathogen continues to mutate, and a significant proportion of cases are now resistant to first-line antitubercular drugs. Under these circumstances, other countries cannot remain silent spectators—with movement between countries so high, the infection will eventually spread to other regions.

Yellow fever, a viral disease transmitted by mosquitos, originated in Africa and later spread to South America. An important strategy helped prevent its spread to other regions: People traveling to the affected countries are required to get vaccinated against yellow fever. This is a classic example where international cooperation led to the containment of an infectious disease. This is what international health is about.

Bioterrorism is another area that requires international cooperation.

INTERNATIONAL HEALTH REGULATIONS

International Health Regulations (IHR) is a legal treaty that defines the rights and obligations of countries in handling public health events or emergencies that could potentially cross international borders. The treaty is binding on 196 countries, which must report public health events that pose a risk at the international level. For this, countries should be able to promptly detect such events. The WHO provides support to countries in developing outbreak surveillance and response strategies.

Some diseases are always notifiable, regardless of when, where, or at what scale they occur. These are:

1. Smallpox
2. Poliomyelitis caused by wild virus
3. Human influenza caused by a new virus subtype
4. SARS

Some diseases become notifiable when they present an unusually high risk of transmission, constituting "a public health emergency of international concern." These are:

- H1N1 influenza
- Ebola
- Zika fever
- COVID
- Monkeypox
- Cholera

DOI: 10.4324/9781032644257-84

- Pneumonic plague
- Yellow fever
- Viral hemorrhagic fever
- West Nile fever
- Other biological, radiological, or chemical events that meet IHR criteria

When such an event is notified, the WHO helps countries coordinate an immediate response. Each country is asked to designate a focal person to communicate with the WHO.

IHR also safeguards the rights of travelers and other people with regard to their personal data, informed consent, and protection from discrimination. On their part, people should proactively check for any potential health risks at their travel destination and take preventive measures to minimize those risks.

INTERNATIONAL HEALTH ORGANIZATIONS

In the following section, we discuss some of the UN agencies that work on health issues and facilitate coordination between countries.

World Health Organization

The WHO is a specialized agency of the United Nations established after the Second World War, on April 7, 1948. The organization is headquartered in Geneva, Switzerland, and has six regional offices. It is headed by a director general and is funded through contributions from 194 member states. The WHO's main objective is the attainment of the highest possible level of health for all people. The World Health Assembly, composed of delegates from member countries, develops policies and programs for global health.

The WHO provides technical support to member states to combat communicable and non-communicable diseases and epidemics. It led the global eradication of smallpox and is presently coordinating efforts to eradicate poliomyelitis and contain the COVID-19 pandemic. Additionally, the WHO has played a key role in designing infectious-disease control programs in developing countries.

United Nations Children's Fund

UNICEF is another specialized agency of the UN that works in areas such as child nutrition, immunization, and education. It conducts surveys to assess nutritional deficiencies in children in different countries and publishes its findings. Additionally, UNICEF has been instrumental in promoting child immunization. It provided support to many countries in setting up their vaccine manufacturing units. In India, it helped to set up a plant for the production of iodized salt. In the early days of its immunization program, UNICEF provided deep freezers and ice-lined refrigerators to health facilities in low-income countries. It is playing an important role in polio eradication.

United Nations Population Fund

The UNFPA works in areas such as sexual and reproductive health, maternal health, family planning, HIV/AIDS, adolescent pregnancy, child marriage, gender equality, gender-based violence, engaging men and boys, and youth leadership.

United Nations Development Programme

The UNDP supports low-income countries in strengthening their human and natural resources. It extends assistance to improve governance at district and village levels.

Food and Agriculture Organization

The FAO assists countries to enhance their food production and agricultural efficiency.

International Labour Organization

The ILO works with countries to improve the working and living conditions of their labor force.

World Food Programme

The WFP provides food in deficient areas. It supports the production of corn soya blend (CSB), a precooked mixture of maize and soya fortified with iron, calcium, and vitamin A that is distributed to children in selected areas.

Section XI

Management of Health Projects

75 Health Project Management

The term *health project* generally refers to a time-bound intervention aimed at addressing a specific health problem in a community. On the other hand, *health program* refers to long-term interventions. Government interventions are generally called programs, for example, the tuberculosis control program. Donor-funded interventions, which run for a fixed duration of, say, three or five years, are called health projects. In practice, these terms are often used interchangeably.

The mechanisms and processes that enable a project to achieve its objectives with expense of minimum resources are collectively referred to as management.

The prime concern of management is that the project should achieve what was desired. In other words, the project should be *effective*. For example, if a public health project aims to promote the use of menstrual cups among female college students, it will be considered effective if a significant number of those students start using menstrual cups following the intervention.

The degree to which a project achieves its predefined objectives is termed its effectiveness.

Second, in the process of achieving the desired objectives, certain resources are utilized. In the above example, the project will deploy a few personnel to increase awareness among college students regarding menstrual cups. Additionally, it may use some communication materials. These resources should be used *efficiently*.

Efficiency of a project refers to achieving desired results by expending minimum resources.

FUNCTIONS OF MANAGEMENT

There are three cardinal functions of management:

- Planning
- Implementation
- Evaluation

To achieve our objectives, we start by preparing a plan. The next step is implementation, during which we monitor and supervise the activities to see if they are taking place as planned. Corrective actions are taken if any deviations are found. At some point during the implementation process, we can conduct an evaluation to see if the project is likely to achieve its objectives. Alternatively, an evaluation at the end of the project can tell us whether the desired objectives

DOI: 10.4324/9781032644257-86

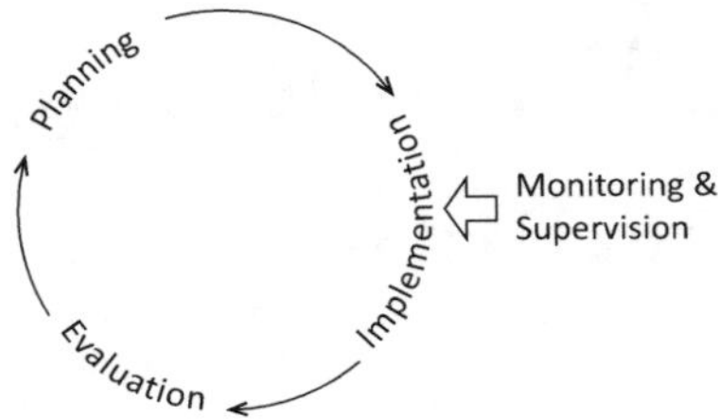

FIGURE 75.1 Management cycle.

were achieved. Based on the findings, we decide whether to continue the project in its current form or to redesign it before proceeding. Thus, a management cycle continues, as illustrated in Figure 75.1.

If the evaluation study finds that the project is unlikely to achieve its objectives, and if even redesigning the project will not help, the managers may decide to terminate the project.

76 Planning

Planning is the process of deciding what exactly we want to achieve and how. This involves outlining the steps to achieve the desired result and estimating the requirement of resources such as personnel, funds, expertise, and others.

STEPS OF PLANNING

Health project planning generally involves the following steps:

- Situational analysis
- Prioritization
- Strategizing
- Setting objectives
- Preparing an implementation plan and microplanning
- Budgeting
- Defining a mechanism for supervision and monitoring

SITUATIONAL ANALYSIS

The first step in planning a health project is to understand our potential clients and their needs. Here, *clients* are people who will utilize our services. We ascertain the size and composition of this population, their health problems, health-seeking behaviors, and paying capacity.

Community Diagnosis

Community diagnosis refers to assessing the health status and healthcare needs of a community. It involves understanding both quantitative and qualitative aspects.

In the same way that doctors first make a diagnosis before treating a patient, public health practitioners first make community diagnosis before making an intervention. To diagnose a patient's ailment, a clinical practitioner takes their medical history and conducts a physical examination. Similarly, to make community diagnosis, the public health professional collects information about the community—common health problems experienced by the people, the scale and distribution of these problems, and health-seeking behaviors. In low-income settings, the health status of a community can be gauged from the following information:

Basic sanitation

- Proportion of people not having access to safe drinking water
- Proportion of people not using septic tank latrines

Family planning

- Unmet need for contraception in eligible couples

Maternal health

- Proportion of home deliveries
- Number of maternal deaths

DOI: 10.4324/9781032644257-87

Child health

- Proportion of preterm births
- Number of neonatal and under-five deaths
- Incidence of pneumonia and diarrhea in under-five children
- Vaccination coverage

Nutrition

- Proportion of stunted under-five children
- Proportion of wasted under-five children
- Proportion of obese adults and children

NCDs

- Number of deaths from CVD, COPD
- Prevalence of diabetes in adult population
- Number of cancer cases
- Number of blind individuals

Infectious diseases

- Number of TB cases
- Number of malaria, dengue, chikungunya, or COVID-19 cases
- Any mosquito-breeding sites in the area

Socioeconomic status

- Literacy level
- Median income
- Proportion of underage marriages
- Proportion of people who regularly consume tobacco or alcohol

Interpreting Information

A few examples are given here to illustrate how health information is interpreted and interventions are conceptualized. If maternal deaths are high in a community, it points to a need to set up emergency obstetric services or make provisions to transfer cases to an equipped hospital at short notice. A high number of preterm births suggests the need to set up an NICU in a local hospital or make provisions to transfer such cases. If many children die before reaching age five, facilities to treat common childhood illnesses like fever, diarrhea, and pneumonia need to be strengthened. Low immunization coverage points to a need to increase awareness about the benefits of immunization and to improve the community's access to services. An increase in NCD cases calls for raising awareness about lifestyle modifications. A high incidence of vector-borne diseases necessitates the identification and elimination of mosquito-breeding sites. If underage marriage is prevalent in the community, families need to be educated about the risks of teenage pregnancy, and couples need to be counseled to delay childbearing until they reach an appropriate age. Access to contraceptives should be improved.

Assessing Existing Healthcare Facilities

We assess existing healthcare facilities in the area and the services they offer to determine whether some of these institutions can be utilized to address some health problems of the community. In some situations, it is more cost-effective to strengthen existing facilities than to establish a new one.

Health-Seeking Behavior

If a large number of people in the community prefer to seek treatment from traditional healers, we can consider training these practitioners in treating common health problems.

Assessing Resources

We review the resources at our disposal—available funds, expertise, technology, and supplies. Based on our strengths and the needs of our potential clients, we decide the type and level of services we will provide.

PRIORITIZATION

The community may have many health problems, but it may not be possible to address all of them at a time. A pragmatic approach is to prioritize problems that are manageable. Health problems that cause maximum mortality or affect a large number of people should be addressed first. Diseases that rapidly spread to others are also important. Availability of funds, expertise, and technology also influences our decisions.

STRATEGIZING

If there are many options to solve a health problem, the process of identifying the best course of action is known as strategizing. The selected approach is called a *strategy*.

For example, some projects make direct interventions by providing services directly to the people, while others provide technical support to local governments, grassroots NGOs, or civil societies serving communities. The latter option is preferable as it is more likely to be sustained.

Logframe

Logical Framework (logframe) is a project management tool used for designing and monitoring projects. It was promoted by the World Bank and USAID to improve the project design process. A logframe starts with defining the intended outcomes and then works backward to define activities and resources. In essence, it is a cause-and-effect model. Key steps of using a logframe are as follows:

1. Set project objectives
2. Define performance indicators
3. Distinguish between project deliverables and impact
4. Define critical assumptions and risks on which the project is based
5. Define systems for supervision, monitoring, and evaluation
6. List the activities necessary to get desired output
7. Define resources required for implementation

SETTING OBJECTIVES

After we have decided which services we will provide, the next step is to define exactly what we want to achieve. A broad goal can be broken down into several smaller objectives. For example, to reduce undernutrition in school children in a district, the specific objectives can be:

- Assess the nutritional status of school children in the specified district (baseline assessment)
- Provide midday meals to the children consistently for three years
- Provide deworming treatment twice a year for three years
- Ensure handwashing facilities in schools
- Educate the children and their parents on basic hygiene
- Reassess the children's nutritional status after three years (endline assessment)

Implementation Plan

An implementation plan lays down the required steps to achieve each objective. A tool known as a Gantt chart can be used to show activities against time and the people responsible for their execution. A sample Gantt chart is given in a later section, in Figure 76.1.

Microplanning

This entails defining the specific tasks within each activity. For example, if the activity is staff recruitment, we specify the categories and numbers of staff to be recruited. Eligibility criteria, job responsibilities, and salaries for each category are defined.

Budgeting

A budget is prepared to estimate the cost of implementing the plan. This includes:

- *Capital costs:* one-time expenses, such as purchasing a public address system or laptops
- *Recurring or operating costs:* expenses incurred regularly, such as staff salaries, office rent, and electricity bills

Plan for Supervision and Monitoring

Supervision and monitoring are critical parts of the implementation phase. We specify who will supervise whom, how they will determine whether the activities are being executed as planned, how they will evaluate the effectiveness, efficiency, and quality of services, and so on.

In addition, an evaluation can be planned midway through the implementation process to assess whether the desired results are likely to be achieved.

EXAMPLE OF A PUBLIC HEALTH PROJECT

Situational Analysis

Upon assessing the health problems of a community in a specified area, investigators found that child mortality was high, preterm births were common, many children were undernourished, and many others were suffering from scabies. Alcohol abuse and tobacco addiction were common in adults. Diarrhea was identified as the most common cause of child deaths. Additionally, the area had no piped water supply. People relied on water from a local tank for all their daily activities, including drinking, cooking, bathing, and washing clothes.

Prioritization

After carefully considering all the health issues prevalent in the community, the project manager decided to make an intervention that could help reduce child mortality from diarrhea: Provide safe drinking water to the community.

Strategizing

There were several options to make safe drinking water available to the community: (a) set up piped water supply, (b) dig a well or install a handpump, (c) arrange water tankers for regular delivery of clean water, or (d) distribute chlorine tablets to community members. In view of the limited resources, the project manager decided to go with the last option.

Activity	Weeks ⇨ Person responsible ⇩	1	2	3	4	5	6	7	8
Enumerate all households of the area	A	■	■						
Calculate requirement of chlorine tablets	A		■						
Procure chlorine tablets	B			■					
Determine staffing requirements	B		■						
Engage required staff and orient them	B			■	■				
Conduct health education sessions	B					■	■	■	
Distribute chlorine tablets	A						■	■	■
Supervise and monitor	B					■	■	■	■

FIGURE 76.1 Gantt chart for a public health project to provide safe drinking water.

Setting Objectives

Within the broader goal of providing safe drinking water, specific objectives were defined:

- Regular distribution of chlorine tablets to all households in the catchment area
- Educating people about the benefits of chlorination and the correct method to use chlorine tablets

Implementation Plan

Figure 76.1 shows a Gantt chart for implementing the intervention. As we can see in this Gantt chart, distribution of chlorine tablets is dependent on procurement of tablets and recruitment of staff. Timely completion of such critical activities is crucial.

Microplanning

Each activity in the Gantt chart was broken down into smaller tasks. To conduct health education sessions, for example, an estimate was drawn of the total number of people to be educated, the number of participants per session, and the total number of sessions required to educate all people in the area. A trainer was identified, and a suitable training method was selected. Training materials and demonstration equipment were arranged, a venue was selected, and proper seating arrangements were ensured. Participants were given prior information about the sessions.

Budgeting

The budget included monthly and annual expenses toward staff salaries, procurement of chlorine tablets, and educational sessions. No capital expenses were incurred in this project.

Supervision and Monitoring

Once the intervention was implemented, a supervisor was assigned to ensure regular supply of chlorine tablets to every household, monitor the distribution and usage of tablets, and assess the intervention's impact on the incidence of waterborne diseases in the community.

77 Implementation and Monitoring and Evaluation

IMPLEMENTATION

Implementation of a project involves developing a structure and then delineating relationships between staff members, as explained here.

Developing a Structure

A project team is raised to implement the project activities. A group of people who work toward achieving a common goal are called a team. A typical health project team has a band of outreach workers who work closely with community or service providers at grassroot. Above them, a level of supervisors is raised to supervise the outreach workers and monitor the project activities. Further, depending on the scale of the project, managers are deployed at various levels—district or province. A project director heads the project, supported by a human resources manager and a finance manager. Large projects, depending on their needs, engage technical specialists with expertise in specific domains, such as capacity building, demand generation, supply chain management, monitoring, learning and research, family planning, TB control, and so on.

Some projects prefer local, community-based workers who can work from home. Supervisors must be mobile. Some projects require supervisors to have their own bikes for field visits. Managers generally operate from office and need travel arrangements for field visits.

The project team requires an office to function. Depending on the scale of operations, they may set up several offices at different levels.

Delineating Staff Relationships

When several people work on a project or assignment, it is important to delineate their individual roles and the relationships between them. Ambiguity, if any, increases the risk of conflicts, and frequent conflicts are detrimental to the smooth functioning of an organization. Policies, standard operating procedures (SOPs), and job responsibilities are defined to outline relationships between staff members and state what is expected of each member. An organizational chart clearly displays who reports to whom.

KEY FUNCTIONS OF A PROJECT MANAGER

Motivation

The prime function of a manager is to maintain a lively and supportive work environment in the organization that encourages teamwork and keeps staff members motivated. But this is often challenging. When people need a job, they show a high level of enthusiasm, and many may be genuinely excited, but after some time of being in the job, many get demoralized. How can we motivate staff? Perks, benefits, and appreciation do motivate but for a very short time. One school of thought is that there is no way to motivate people as motivation comes from within. Despite this, the manager has a definite role to ensure that results are achieved. First and foremost, he must define a clear career path for each staff. They must have something exciting to look forward

DOI: 10.4324/9781032644257-88

to if they do well and produce results. He must then clearly explain to the staff what is expected of them—deliverables must be defined. An agreement should be reached with respect to deliverables and timelines. Additionally, the staff should be aware of the criteria based on which their performance would be evaluated. The manager should provide periodic feedback about their performance. It is said that supervisors who do not provide regular feedback to their staff commit an atrocity on them. Lastly, staff members should get opportunities to learn new skills. Learning new things keeps people active, motivated, and energized.

Division of Labor and Delegation

An important function of a manager is to divide the work among staff members. As staff members become competent and comfortable to perform certain tasks, they can be assigned higher-order tasks. This is a dynamic process.

Delegation reduces a manager's burden and allows him to take on higher-order responsibilities. At the same time, junior team members feel motivated when entrusted with important responsibilities. However, managers should know that delegation does not absolve them of their responsibilities. While junior employees are accountable for their assigned tasks, the ultimate responsibility lies with the manager. Therefore, managers should be mindful of what to delegate and to whom. Managers who delegate effectively get more respect from their staff.

Supervision and Monitoring

Supervision and monitoring are critical managerial functions throughout the process of implementation. Although the two terms are often used together or interchangeably, there is a small difference.

Supervision is directed toward staff members—for example, how they are performing, whether they come to work on time, and whether they perform their duties diligently. The manager ensures that:

- Team members know what is expected of them and the results they need to deliver.
- They have the necessary competence.
- They have access to the required facilities, equipment, and supplies to work.
- They are motivated to perform.
- They actually achieve the desired results.

In contrast, monitoring is focused on processes and activities—whether they are being carried out as planned. For instance, in a community-based awareness generation session conducted by outreach workers, their supervisor would monitor whether the expected number of community members have turned up to attend the session, whether they take interest in the topic, and whether they get the key message.

In both monitoring and supervision, if any deviations from the established plan are found, immediate corrective actions are taken. For example, if the supervisor finds that the staff are not comfortable conducting the awareness generation session, efforts would be made to strengthen the staff's capabilities. If very few community members participated in the session, arrangements would be made to give prior intimation to all community members. The sessions would be conducted at a time convenient to the community members.

Additionally, the manager prepares a periodic progress report of the project, providing a detailed overview of the completion of scheduled activities. Both quantitative and qualitative aspects are explained. The challenges faced as well as the future course of action are also explained. This report is submitted to higher authorities and donors.

Financial Management

Financial management entails proper documentation of funds received and expenses incurred. This is generally done by accounts or finance personnel, but the manager oversees this function and is eventually responsible. He ensures an adequate flow of funds in the system so that activities are not stalled for paucity of funds or delay in disbursement. To prevent such a situation, financial projections are made. The manager controls expenses, ensuring that resources are utilized judiciously and that expenses do not exceed income. For effective financial management, managers should have an understanding of the income-expenditure statement and balance sheet of the organization. After the end of a financial year, the manager arranges to get the accounts audited by an external auditor.

EVALUATION

Evaluation is different from monitoring in that it does not get down to the nitty-gritty of project activities. Further, unlike monitoring, it is a one-time activity that is generally carried out by an external expert, either at the end of the project or midway through implementation. While end-term evaluation aims to find out whether or not the project *achieved* the desired results, midterm evaluation examines whether the project is *likely to achieve* them. In the aforementioned example of the community-based awareness generation activity, an end-term evaluation would aim to find out whether people's awareness improved or not.

Evaluation may lead to wholesale changes in a project's design.

EXAMPLE OF A HEALTH PROJECT

In many developing countries in Asia, female sterilization is the mainstay of family planning programs. Male sterilization (vasectomy) is not popular. Considering the merits of no-scalpel vasectomy (NSV), a modern technique of male sterilization, the Government of Thailand decided to promote its utilization. An international NGO, with the support of a large donor, designed and implemented a project: Increasing men's participation in family planning. It is explained below.

Introduction

In Thailand, in 2010, female sterilization accounted for nearly one-fourth of all contraceptive methods, while male sterilization stood at around 3%. NSV is a safe and effective method of male sterilization. It can be completed in 30 minutes, and the beneficiary can leave the facility walking after an hour of observation after the procedure. There is lower risk of complications. Despite these advantages, NSV did not become popular in Thailand. What could be the reasons for this? The project management team decided to conduct formative research to answer this question and then design a project accordingly.

Formative Research

The study aimed to identify barriers to uptake of NSV services. Insights were gathered from eligible couples, healthcare providers, and other stakeholders. Three qualitative researchers conducted focus group discussions with young married couples in three provinces where NSV uptake was lowest, with each group comprising of four to five couples. Community workers and healthcare providers were interviewed to seek their opinions about the reasons for low uptake of NSV. Senior government officials were also consulted to know whether they would support the idea of promoting NSV. Additionally, existing NSV services in selected hospitals were reviewed. Key findings of the study are summarized here.

People desired to limit their family size. They wanted their children to be well-educated, but given the high cost of education, they realized that they could not afford to have many children. However, despite there being a need for permanent contraception, misconceptions about NSV prevented families from opting for it. Many men and women presumed that NSV impaired men's sexual performance—their erection and ejaculation. Due to this, many women opted for tubal ligation rather than allowing their husbands to undergo NSV. Also, it was believed that men being bread-earners of the family should not be bedridden even for a day.

The study also found that there was limited availability of NSV services in the targeted provinces. Only a few tertiary care hospitals offered NSV, one of which was a public-sector hospital with two doctors trained in NSV. Private hospitals providing NSV services were expensive. It was also realized that most senior officials in the health ministry were unaware of the benefits of NSV, and there was no existing program to promote it. However, all of them were positive about initiating a new project to promote NSV and assured their support.

Strategy

Based on the findings of the study, the project team developed a strategy to provide technical support to the state on three fronts: Supply, Demand, and Advocacy. Accordingly, three project objectives were defined:

- Increase availability of NSV services in three identified provinces
- Increase demand for NSV services in the intervention districts
- Create a supportive environment in hospitals and in the ministry

Project Area

Due to budget limitations, it was decided to implement the project in three selected provinces in the first phase. In each of these provinces, ten districts were identified for intervention, and their district hospitals were provided with support to offer NSV services.

Developing a Structure

A team headed by a project director was constituted to implement the project. A health communication specialist and an NSV surgeon assisted the project director. The health communication specialist led demand-generation interventions, and the NSV surgeon was to provide NSV training to doctors. The project director took up the responsibility of advocacy. Besides the health communication specialist and the NSV surgeon, a finance manager and an HR manager assisted the project director. An office was set up in Bangkok. For field activities, 30 program officers were recruited—one for each intervention district. These officers were required to stay in the intervention district and work from home. They were required to (a) identify doctors in their respective district hospitals who would be interested in undergoing NSV training and providing the service, (b) ensure preparedness of the facility to provide NSV services, and (c) generate demand for these services with the support of outreach workers.

Rather than employing a separate cadre of supervisors to manage the program officers, the project team thought of an innovative approach. Three senior program officers were selected and assigned the role of a supervisor—one for each intervention province. Each of these officers had prior experience of working in a family planning program. Thus, they now had a dual role: Perform the role of a program officer in their district, and supervise the other nine program officers in their province. With this arrangement, these officers gained an understanding of ground realities and the challenges faced by their fellow program officers.

A five-day orientation program was organized to familiarize the project team with the program's objectives, strategy, and activities, as well as their respective roles. The mechanism for supervision and monitoring was explained.

Improving Supply of NSV Services

It was decided to train at least two doctors as NSV providers in each of the 30 district hospitals selected for the intervention. A plan was drawn to organize training. The tertiary care public hospital where NSV surgeries were already being performed was designated as the training center. A master NSV trainer from China was invited to train and prepare three local NSV trainers, who would subsequently train resident doctors in NSV. The two existing NSV surgeons at the tertiary care hospital and the NSV surgeon from the project team received training from the master trainer. Subsequently, three doctors from three district hospitals were invited to be trained as NSV providers. The newly trained NSV trainers led this training, with the master trainer backstopping them.

Thereafter, the NSV trainers started training doctors from various district hospitals in small batches of two to three trainees. Initially, the duration of the training was five working days. To be qualified as an NSV surgeon, each trainee had to perform at least ten NSV procedures under the supervision of a trainer and then perform ten procedures independently. After some time, it was realized that the duration of training was not sufficient to transfer the required skills, and the training period was extended to two weeks.

Increasing Demand for NSV Services

The health communication expert designed a communication strategy to inform people about the benefits of NSV. The message emphasized that NSV did not interfere with men's sexual performance, particularly erection and ejaculation. Leaflets, pocket calendars, and a video film were produced.

Additionally, with the support of program officers, the health communication specialist trained two outreach workers at each facility, focusing on demand generation for NSV. The outreach workers, who were public health functionaries attached to the facility, were provided with leaflets and pocket calendars to educate community members. Program officers demonstrated to the outreach workers how to generate demand by organizing group educational activities and individual counseling. They made efforts to ensure a regular flow of clients to the facility.

Advocacy

The project director briefed senior government officials and hospital authorities about the merits of promoting NSV. Their permission was sought to train doctors at government facilities. They were invited to inaugurate newly established NSV centers.

Efforts were made to telecast the project's video film on a government TV channel, but that did not materialize.

Monitoring and Evaluation

The project team prepared a plan for monitoring and evaluation.

The senior program officers periodically visited the program officers in their respective provinces. During these visits, they observed the program officers and outreach workers interacting with potential clients. Support was provided to those who were finding it difficult to convert clients.

The NSV trainer from the project team found that when newly trained NSV providers returned to their respective facilities, they did not get ready NSV acceptors on whom they could practice their skills. And within a few weeks they lost their clinical skills. Later on, even if they had a client, they were not confident to perform the procedure independently. So it was decided to provide targeted support to the facility after a doctor was trained.

Both the health communication specialist and the NSV trainer camped at the district to provide support. Signboards informing the availability of NSV services were displayed in the facility. Other healthcare providers at the facility were encouraged to inform eligible couples to consider availing of NSV services.

When the newly trained NSV provider performed the procedure, the project NSV trainer backstopped him. That means, during the procedure, the project NSV trainer stood by his side and observed him. Only if the latter was stuck did the trainer intervene. Until the provider had completed at least 50 NSV procedures, the facility received continued support for demand generation and backstopping.

As part of the monitoring process, each senior program officer was required to provide monthly information about the number of educational campaigns organized by program officers and outreach workers in his province, as well as the number of clients who showed interest in NSV. The facilities provided monthly information about the NSV procedures performed by each trained NSV surgeon. The NSV training center provided data on training.

To assess the quality of services provided by the trained doctors, complications, if any, were recorded by their respective facilities.

The project lasted three years. During this time, a total of 67 doctors from 30 district hospitals were trained as NSV providers. Out of them, 43 NSV providers were able to complete a minimum of 50 procedures. However, at the end of three years, only 17 providers continued providing NSV services regularly. The others reported that they did not get the clients.

The evaluation study found that, at the conclusion of the project, the proportion of NSV relative to all contraceptive methods had increased from 3% to 6% across the three intervention provinces.

78 Quality Improvement

Quality improvement (QI) is a continuous and systematic approach aimed at improving services to provide better outcomes. In this context, several terms gained prominence at different points in time, but they all mean the same. Some of these terms are: Total quality management (TQM), quality assurance, six sigma, and lean six sigma.

To show improvement, we need to measure quality. But measuring quality in the health sector has been challenging. In 1966, Avedis Donabedian, a quality pioneer, proposed a systems framework that makes it easier to measure quality. To measure quality, we examine the following:

- Structure
- Process
- Output

Structure includes human resources, facilities, equipment, supplies, and technology. Processes are activities or procedures performed by service providers. Output is the result. Structure is needed to carry out processes, and processes produce output.

$$\text{Structure} \rightarrow \text{Process} \rightarrow \text{Output}$$

In a tuberculosis control program, structure comprises of a TB clinic, a TB specialist, a lab technician, a pharmacist, stock of anti-tuberculosis drugs, a functional laboratory, documents, and others.

Processes include registration of patients, their medical examination, laboratory tests, and providing prescriptions and medicines.

Output is the number of patients getting cured.

We can assess the quality of a TB clinic from the proportion of TB patients completing the treatment and the proportion of patients getting cured. Patients will be cured if the processes—that is, diagnosis and treatment—are correct. These processes are dependent on structure—that is, expertise of service providers, level of laboratory support, and regular supply of appropriate medicines. In other words, to get quality results, we need to perform the right activities, for which the right resources are needed. Deficiency in structure or processes will eventually affect the output. Therefore, all three components are important.

EXAMPLES

Example 1

Pneumonia is a leading cause of under-five deaths in low-income countries. In hospital settings, pneumonia is diagnosed by X-ray and blood test, but these facilities are generally not available in rural and remote areas of low-income countries. To fill this gap, community workers in public health programs are trained to diagnose pneumonia by measuring the child's breathing rate and fever. They can treat it locally by oral antibiotics.

How can we measure the quality of services to manage pneumonia cases in a specified population? We examine the situation from three perspectives:

Structure: We examine the availability of trained community workers, availability of appropriate antibiotics and antipyretic medicines, and availability of transport to shift a child to a hospital if needed.

DOI: 10.4324/9781032644257-89

Process: We check whether community workers are able to diagnose pneumonia by measuring breathing rate and body temperature, whether they administer the required medicines in right doses, and whether they can timely identify danger signs that warrant hospital referral.

Output: We examine whether the children with pneumonia were cured.

Taking Donabedian's model further, we can say that output leads to outcome, and outcome leads to impact. In the above example, children being cured of pneumonia is the output. This leads to reduced child mortality from pneumonia, which is the outcome. The impact is improved health status of children.

Structure → Process → Output → Outcome → Impact

Example 2

In low-income countries, maternal mortality is high. This is because many deliveries are assisted by traditional birth attendants, who are not able to identify complications, if any. To prevent this, most governments promote institutional deliveries. They subsidize maternity services or make them free. In India, the government provides financial incentives to women who deliver in public health institutions. This initiative has been a great success, and presently around 90% of deliveries are conducted in health institutions. However, the reduction in maternal mortality in India is not commensurate to the increase in institutional deliveries. This raises a question about the quality of obstetric services provided in these institutions.

Services that conform to standards are considered quality services. What are the quality standards for obstetric services? Obstetric services can be broadly divided into two categories:

- Essential obstetric care
- Emergency obstetric care

Some institutions are equipped for essential obstetric care. They can conduct only normal deliveries, and they refer complicated cases to institutions that provide emergency obstetric care.

Let us examine the standards of essential obstetric care in terms of structure, process, output, outcome, and impact.

Structure: The birth attendant is trained to conduct normal deliveries and to timely identify complications; delivery room is clean; sterile gloves, sterile pads, and gauze are available; there is provision for intravenous infusion, injection of oxytocin, and other emergency medicines; there is provision to transport the case to a higher facility should there be any complication.

Process: The birth attendant periodically measures the mother's vitals and fetal heart sound. She checks progress of labor by checking cervical dilation and position of fetal head. She is trained to perform episiotomy if required and assist labor. She is able to gauge the amount of vaginal bleeding. She can provide newborn care. She arranges to shift the case to a higher-level facility if complications arise.

Output: The baby is delivered uneventfully, and both mother and child are healthy. In case of complications, the woman is timely shifted to a higher-level center.

Outcome: Maternal mortality rate is reduced.

Impact: Maternal and child health are improved.

Example 3

To assess the quality of family planning services in a primary health center, the following standards can be used:

Structure: A trained counselor is available who has a basket of contraceptives to show to clients; a room is available where clients can be counseled in privacy.

Process: The counselor takes history of the client or couple to understand their requirement. She explains various options suited to their requirement along with the advantages and disadvantages of each option. She shows them the commodities if possible and leaves the final decision to the client. After the client has chosen a method, she explains where and how the service can be availed and also informs about follow-up. She maintains confidentiality of the client.

The client is provided with the contraceptive method. If a clinical procedure is required, such as insertion of IUCD or implant or sterilization, the procedure is carried out by a competent provider under aseptic conditions.

Output: The couple accepts a method of family planning.

Outcome: The couple is successful in preventing unintended pregnancies.

Impact: The mother's health is maintained.

79 Basic Communication Skills

We communicate with others for various reasons: To share information, feelings, or emotions; to seek help or give instructions; to negotiate or influence; to develop a relationship. Communication can be verbal (speaking and listening) or nonverbal (body language, facial expressions, written materials, visual aids). Generally, we use a combination of these methods to convey our message.

Communication is a two-way process. If a person is speaking and no one is listening, it does not qualify as communication.

Some people seem to be naturally talented at interpersonal communication. They make friends easily, they can influence others and get work done, they negotiate well, and they can resolve conflicts without causing offense. Some people create a pleasant environment wherever they go; people look forward to meeting them.

The ability to communicate effectively is an important life skill, but not everyone feels comfortable interacting with others. Understanding the fundamentals of effective communication can help us improve our communication skills. Some tips are given here.

FUNDAMENTALS OF EFFECTIVE COMMUNICATION

Rapport Building

The first step in communication is to build trust and rapport with the listener. Eye contact and a warm smile are powerful tools for this. When we make eye contact, it conveys our interest in the other person and encourages them to reciprocate. Conversely, avoiding eye contact conveys disinterest or lack of confidence. This can weaken communication. In unfamiliar situations, a sincere smile can be an effective icebreaker.

Active Listening

When interacting with others, we are often more interested in talking than listening. We mistakenly assume that we already know what the other person is going to say. This is not right. To be effective communicators, we should allow others to speak and express themselves, and we should listen patiently while they do so. People appreciate being heard, even if we cannot help them out.

Nonjudgmental Approach

We tend to believe that our own thoughts and opinions are always correct. If someone has a different perspective, we are quick to judge them. For effective communication, we must accept that everyone is unique and that we have no right to judge others based on their views or choices. By being mindful of these facts, we can learn to respect diverse opinions. Communication can then be productive.

Using Soft Skills

We generally give more importance to the spoken word. Interestingly, Albert Mehrabian, a communication expert, found through scientific studies that words play a limited role in communication. Instead, nonverbal cues, such as tone of voice, facial expressions, and body language, carry a more powerful message. As we know, even nice words can be counterproductive when spoken sarcastically. An agitated tone or facial expression can spoil a relationship, while a friendly demeanor encourages the other person to open up.

DOI: 10.4324/9781032644257-90

If someone uses offensive language with us, we should remind ourselves that words are not so important. We should try to understand the intent behind their behavior. Remaining calm and composed is the best response in such situations.

By being mindful of the nonverbal aspects of communication, we can make our interactions meaningful.

Clarity and Concision

To communicate effectively, we should keep our message concise, clear, and direct. Beating around the bush can put off some listeners. We should speak confidently and avoid discussing topics on which we lack clarity. If raising an issue or a problem, we should also try and propose a solution.

For important communications, we may practice by writing down key points in a logical sequence, providing reasons or rationale where needed. Repetition should be avoided in both writing and speaking.

Seeking Clarification

If we did not understand what someone said, we can politely ask for clarification: "I am sorry, I could not understand what you said; could you please give an example?" or "Could you explain it in different words?" Alternatively, we can rephrase what was said and request the speaker to confirm if we understood the message correctly.

Similarly, if we sense that our own words were not fully understood by the listener, we can ask specific questions to know what or how much they understood. Of course, we must be careful not to cause offense while doing so.

Providing Feedback

When someone expresses an opinion, we can offer them genuine feedback. We can convey whether we agree or disagree and share our own thoughts on the matter. If expressing disagreement, we should do it respectfully: "You have raised an important issue, but I am not sure it is the main reason for this problem." Similarly, we should be open to receiving feedback on our own views.

Respecting Others

If we treat people with respect, they are likely to reciprocate. As a principle, we should avoid blaming others. Mudslinging never helps.

Focusing on the Issue

During a discussion, it is common for people to deviate from the main point. A good communicator tactfully steers the conversation back to the original topic: "You have raised a valid concern, but let us first try to resolve the problem at hand."

Concluding a Discussion

When we are not sure whether all parties involved in a communication are aligned, or if there are actionable points involved, it is worthwhile to summarize the discussion before closing it.

To conclude, merely knowing the above concepts will not improve our communication skills; we need to put them into practice. We may also try and learn from others who are effective communicators—how they use their words, voice, tone, facial expressions, and body language to convey their message.

Index

C

D

E

I

J

K

L

M

N

O

P

T

U

V

Printed in the United States
by Baker & Taylor Publisher Services